Action and Interaction

Shaun Gallagher is the Lillian and Morrie Moss Professor of Excellence in Philosophy at the University of Memphis, and Professorial Fellow at the University of Wollongong. He has held visiting positions in Cambridge, Copenhagen, Paris, Lyon, Berlin, Oxford, and Rome. His research areas include phenomenology and philosophy of mind, embodied cognition, theories of self, intersubjectivity, and social cognition. Gallagher received the Humboldt Foundation's Anneliese Maier Research Award (2012-18) and was awarded the D.Phil (honoris causa) from the University of Copenhagen in 2021. He is a founding editor and co-editor-in-chief of the journal *Phenomenology and the Cognitive Sciences*. His previous publications include *How the Body Shapes the Mind* (Oxford 2005), *The Phenomenological Mind* (Routledge 2012), and *Enactivist Interventions: Rethinking the Mind* (Oxford 2017).

Action and Interaction

Shaun Gallagher

OXFORD
UNIVERSITY PRESS

OXFORD
UNIVERSITY PRESS

Great Clarendon Street, Oxford, OX2 6DP,
United Kingdom

Oxford University Press is a department of the University of Oxford.
It furthers the University's objective of excellence in research, scholarship,
and education by publishing worldwide. Oxford is a registered trade mark of
Oxford University Press in the UK and in certain other countries

Published in the United States of America by Oxford University Press
198 Madison Avenue, New York, NY 10016, United States of America

British Library Cataloguing in Publication Data
Data available

Library of Congress Cataloging in Publication Data
Data available

ISBN 978-0-19-884634-5 (Hbk.)
ISBN 978-0-19-286730-8 (Pbk.)

To Ida-Rose and Sandy,
and the future

Table of Contents

Part III. A Critical Turn

Acknowledgments

I started writing this book in 2009 while on sabbatical in Paris. In the ten years since, I authored three other books, but I continued to be engaged with this one, on and off. What this means is that it is truly difficult to count the number of people who have contributed to my thinking on the issues addressed here. Some of my colleagues and co-authors have played a significant role in shaping my thinking: especially Dan Hutto and Deborah Tollefsen on narrative; Somogy Varga on critical theory; and Dan Zahavi on time. I thank Anthony Chemero and Michael Wheeler for their comments on an earlier version of this manuscript. I've also benefitted from interacting with many people at different conferences and meetings where I presented some of the ideas in this book. I want to thank them all, but there are so many that once I started to draw up a list I knew it would be impossible to remember everyone, so I thought it better not to try to name everyone. Many of them, however, are authors of works included in my reference list. In addition I want to thank a number of people who have communicated with me about these issues, including Horacio Banega, Juan Botero, Anna Ciaunica, Jorge Davila, Juan González, Britt Normann, Gunn Øberg, Zdravko Radman, and Jean-Michel Roy.

I also thank my current and former PhD students who have participated in a number of seminars at the University of Memphis on topics covered in this book: Benjamin Aguda, Michael Ardoline, Nicolle Brancazio, Steph Butera, Benjamin Curtis, Morgan Elbot, Reese Faust, Christina Friedlaender, Christian Kronsted, Edward Lenzo, Zachariah Neemeh, Tailer Ransom, Corey Reed, Kevin Ryan, Jasper St. Bernard, Sarah Vincent, Stefano Vincini, Jonathan Wurtz, and James Zubko. In addition I must thank a number of visiting scholars to the Memphis Philosophy Department, many of whom contributed significantly to my seminars: Yochai Ataria, Mindaugas Briedis, Massimiliano Cappuccio, Marta Caravà, Mark-Oliver Casper, Anthony Chemero, Sabrina Coninx, Roy Dings, Ricardo Mejía Fernandez, Anika Fiebich, Bruce Janz, Michael Kirchhoff, Julian Kiverstein, Tetsuyo Kono, Dorothée Legrand, Kristian Martiny, Katsunori Miyahara, James Morley, David Morris, Albert Newen, Elisabeth Pacherie, Claudio Paolucci, Francesco (Cisco) Parisi, Marek Pokropski, Susana Ramiriz, Erik Rietveld, Matthew Ratcliffe, Ian Robertson, Zuzanna Rucinska, Allesandro Salice, Shannon Spaulding, Tobias Starzak, Helen Steward, Dylan Trigg, Bo Wang, and Anna Welpinghus.

Support for my research came from numerous sources, especially the Humboldt Foundation's Anneliese Maier Research Award (2012–18). I thank my Humboldt host and close collaborator, Albert Newen at the Center for Mind, Brain and Evolution, Ruhr Universität, Bochum for all of his support over these years. I also thank Lambros Malafouris who invited me as Senior Research Visiting Fellow, Keble College, University of Oxford (Trinity term, 2016); Dorothée Legrand who organized my several stays as a CNRS Visiting Researcher, first at the Centre de Recherche en Epistémologie Appliquée, Paris (2009–10), and then at the Husserl Archives, Ecole Normale Superior (2017); Francesco Parisi and Antonino Pennisi who hosted me as Visiting Professor of Cognitive Science, University of Messina, Sicily (2017); and Dan Hutto who arranged for my ongoing Professorial Fellowship at the University of Wollongong, Australia. Research on the first chapter, Actions and Abstractions, benefited from an Australian Research Council (ARC) grant (DP170102987), led by Hutto. I've followed a top-down (geographical rather than strictly philosophical) order in this paragraph of thanks, but I have to voice a really bottom-up and fundamental appreciation to the Lillian and Morrie Moss Chair of Excellence in Philosophy at the University of Memphis for significant research support, as well as to my colleagues at Memphis for their ongoing collegial support without which I would not have been able to pursue all of these research opportunities. As always, my greatest thanks and love go to my wife Elaine for the continuing adventure.

A number of sections in the following chapters include paragraphs and excerpts from some of my previously published papers. I thank the journals and publishers for permission to include this material. *Section 2.1* draws on my essay "Timing is not everything: The intrinsic temporality of action," in R. Altshuler (ed.), *Time and the Philosophy of Action* (203–21), London: Routledge, 2016. *Section 3.1* contains a number of excerpts (with revisions) from "Multiple aspects in the sense of agency," *New Ideas in Psychology*, Volume 30 (15–31), 2012. Likewise, *Section 3.3* draws a number of paragraphs (with revisions) from "Ambiguity in the sense of agency," in A. Clark, J. Kiverstein, and T. Vierkant (eds.), *Decomposing the Will* (118–135), Oxford: Oxford University Press, 2013. Several paragraphs in *Section 6.2* were revised from "The new hybrids: Continuing debates on social cognition," *Consciousness and Cognition*, Volume 36 (452–65), 2015. Some paragraphs in *Section 7.4* are taken from my essay "Narrative competency and the massive hermeneutical background," in P. Fairfield (ed.), *Education, Dialogue and Hermeneutics* (21–38), New York, NY: Continuum, 2011. *Section 8.1* was originally published as "The struggle for recognition and the return of primary intersubjectivity," in V. Fóti and P. Kontos (eds.), *Phenomenology and the Primacy of the Political: Essays in Honor of Jacques Taminiaux* (3–14), Berlin: Springer, 2017. *Sections 8.2* and *8.3* are based on "Social interaction, autonomy and recognition," in L. Dolezal and D. Petherbridge, *Body/Self/Other: The Phenomenology of Social Encounters* (133–60), Albany, NY: SUNY Press, 2017. Significant parts of *Section 9.1* were drawn from "The socially extended mind," *Cognitive Systems Research*, 25–6 (4–12), 2013.

In addition, *Sections 2.4, 6.3, 7.2, 7.3,* and *9.2* include paragraphs drawn from my work with several co-authors, including Dan Zahavi, Somogy Varga, Daniel Hutto, and Deborah Tollefsen, respectively. Thanks to the relevant publishers for permission to include excerpts from S. Gallagher and D. Zahavi, "Primal impression and enactive perception," in D. Lloyd and V. Arstila (eds.), *Subjective Time: The Philosophy, Psychology, and Neuroscience of Temporality* (83–99), Cambridge, MA: MIT Press, 2014; S. Gallagher and S. Varga, "Social constraints on the direct perception of emotions and intentions," *Topoi*, Volume 33, Issue 1 (185–99), 2014; S. Gallagher and D. Hutto, "Understanding others through primary interaction and narrative practice," in J. Zlatev, T. Racine, C. Sinha, and E. Itkonen (eds.), *The Shared Mind: Perspectives on Intersubjectivity* (17–38), Amsterdam: John Benjamins, 2008; and S. Gallagher and D. Tollefsen, "Advancing the 'we' through narrative," *Topoi: An International Review of Philosophy*, Volume 46, Issue 4 (724–6), 2017.

I also thank Ephraim Urevbu (https://www.artvillagegallery.com/artists/ephraim-urevbu) for the cover art, and the authors, journals, and publishers who provided permissions to include the following figures and table.

Figures

Table

Introduction

"To act is always to interact with others." (Paul Ricoeur 1984, 55)

"Action is never possible in isolation; to be isolated is to be deprived of the capacity to act." (Hannah Arendt 1958, 188)

Action is sometimes defined in a special way to mean a significant human engagement in the public world. Hannah Arendt (1958, 22–3), for example, defines action in this way. For her, as for Paul Ricoeur, action is, by definition, never intersubjectively isolated. In this sense, action is something different from merely moving, laboring, or working—phenomena that Arendt would define as falling short of truly intersubjective action. I accept that action is more than mere movement, but it can also be something less than the moral or political action that Arendt and Ricoeur have in mind. In agreement with Arendt and Ricoeur, however, I'll argue that the most significant kinds of action involve interaction with others, and indeed, that all action has roots in interaction.

This is certainly the order of things in developmental terms. From birth infants are in interactive relations with others, reflected in postural adjustments that are already more than mere movements as they are lifted and literally carried from here to there for purposes that are beyond anything that they, as infants, can comprehend. In some sense, our first actions emerge within and in response to the actions of others, as we are literally carried into action by others. At first, without knowing what we are doing, we move to find sustenance, we activate vocal cords to express needs, we move in reflex to grab onto others with hands and mouth. Those others move in response to us, and if on both sides some of these movements begin awkwardly, they soon smooth out into dynamically aligned responses to each other. Actions emerge on the infant side of these relations starting out as responses that may be perfected through learning from the actions of others. We don't learn to interact; but from interacting we learn to act, and *how* to interact. Such basic observations immediately raise questions about normativity and autonomy.

To work towards an understanding of how our encounters with others carry us into actions, and continue to shape our actions, and therefore our basic cognitive capacities, we need an account of social interaction. For my purposes this is best worked out in the context of the contemporary debates among different theories of social cognition. These debates involve questions that constantly border on action-related concepts, most importantly on the notion of intention. More than this, however, recent research has directed the discussion of social cognition to questions about action recognition as well as about the nature of interaction and joint action. Here also questions about agency and the sense of agency arise.

Although in some sense interaction is first and action second, in other ways we can think of action as more basic. Bodily movement, even if not yet action, is necessary for most animal existence. For most animals, it's everything; and for the human, it's almost everything. Breathing, for example, requires bodily movement. Heartbeat is a form of bodily movement. Finding your next meal requires movement. Complete paralysis approximates death; and if you are seriously paralyzed, as in quadriplegia, you will depend on another person's movement to stay alive.

Action, which is a certain type of movement, is, as most agree, more than just movement. For movement or behavior to be an action requires the agent to know in some way what he or she is doing. What does it mean for an agent engaged in action to have a sense of self-agency? Does the agent of an action have to be aware that he or she is acting (or has acted) for that action to count as an intentional action? Someone might say that actions are frequently on automatic pilot. When I get up to get a beer I may find myself at the fridge without having attended to what I did to get there. Or when I drive home I may do so without being able to remember long bits of the journey. Even if actions are on automatic pilot, however, I may still be (pre-reflectively) conscious of what I'm doing. I may not be thinking of what I'm doing—I may be doing it in an unthinking manner—but surely as I get up to get the beer, or when I'm driving my car, no matter how absorbed I am in something else—the football match, the music on the radio—I have a sense that I am getting a beer or driving my car, respectively, although I may be quickly forgetting the specifics (the motor details) of such actions simply because it serves no purpose to remember them. There's a difference between a philosophical zombie (a familiar philosophical character from discussions of consciousness) getting a beer and me getting a beer, and not just in terms of how the beer tastes, but in terms of the experience of movement as it comes to be structured into an action.

The first part of this book focuses on the nature of action, starting with questions about action individuation, context, the notion of "basic action," and the temporal structure of action (*Chapters 1 and 2*). These topics lead to questions about intention and the sense of agency. Action, understood as autonomous behavior that scales up to more than just a set of causal processes, involves meaning and agentive experience. The sense of agency turns out to be both complex and ambiguous, while the meaning of action generally goes beyond the agent's intention (*Chapter 3*). This is especially the case in social contexts.

In *Part II* I defend an approach to social cognition called "interaction theory," building on embodied and enactive accounts of cognition, and I contrast this theory to standard "theory of mind" (ToM) or mindreading approaches. The issues addressed here are contentious ones in ongoing interdisciplinary debates about intersubjectivity. At the edges of such debates, however, one starts to get a feel for the possible implications of the different approaches for some larger questions concerning autonomy, and the effects of norms and social institutions. This will lead, in the third part of the book, to more critical questions about the effects of social practices and institutions on our cognition, our actions, and our interactions.

In regard to action, interaction, and these related issues, one finds ongoing debates in every corner of the analyses necessary to work out a consistent theory, as well as in and across every discipline involved. In philosophy of mind, developmental psychology, cognitive neuroscience, and the cognitive sciences generally, anything that approaches consensus is short lived. Disagreements about whether processes are innate or learned, whether they are implicit or explicit, and whether they are internal or external cut across all of the disciplines. If one turns to empirical data to find resolution, disagreements again arise around different interpretations of the data. That is, even if there is agreement that the data are what they are, how one understands the data will depend on the set of suppositions one brings to the theoretical interpretation. In addition, however, a number of philosophers and scientists have started to realize that the empirical results that figure into their theories are themselves limited both by the technical limitations involved in the experiments and by basic assumptions about where one should look for the real action in situations of social cognition. It's not just the fact that experimental situations are limited and often non-ecological, but also that one of the driving methods in cognitive neuroscience, brain imaging, is significantly limited for the study of social cognition. In an fMRI experiment, for example, the experimental subject is necessarily alone in a large noisy machine, where bodily movement is extremely limited. If our primary form of social cognition depends at all on bodily, in-person interactions with other people, rather than passive observations, fMRI currently offers no way to study this (see Schilbach et al. 2013; Gallagher et al. 2013). At the same time, these limitations are reinforced by a philosophically informed methodological individualism, in the sense that for many theorists the goal is to identify mechanisms found within an individual, and specifically within an individual brain, to explain how that individual understands other people. This assumption closes off the possibility that what explains social cognition is something that involves more than cognitive processes in one individual (De Jaegher et al. 2010; Froese & Gallagher 2012).

Similar issues pertain to studies of intention formation, agency, autonomy, and responsibility (where scientific studies are now having an impact in ethics and law). Add to this the fact that most scientific investigations of causal mechanisms and neural underpinnings frame their conclusions without taking into account cross-cultural differences, or even intra-cultural factors that may limit their conclusions. Accordingly, the questions and debates just mentioned are set in philosophical frameworks that are rather shaky, and seemingly hanging in midair. They resemble an Escher drawing where one level is not clearly distinguished from another, and ambiguity undercuts any way to make sense of things.

It's not clear that we can rebuild or redesign the framework while still hanging in midair. Neither is it clear that there is one point of consensus that would act as a narrow ground from which to begin, or that if we began at that one point we would necessarily end up with the right framework. The controversies, debates, and disagreements nonetheless make this area of study an exciting one. My strategy is simply to jump into the middle of it with philosophical hammer, some sharp nails, and some other tools borrowed from developmental studies, phenomenology, and neuroscience.

In *Part III* I explore the implications of these analyses of action and interaction for thinking about how we, as human agents, are shaped by our social practices and institutions. I focus in this part on concepts such as recognition and autonomy. Here I find common ground with pragmatists, critical theorists, feminists, and a number of other contemporary theorists who have been developing the notion of relational autonomy (see, e.g., Honneth 2012; Mackenzie & Stoljar 2000; Christman 2009). I argue that socio-political conceptions of recognition, autonomy, and agency are best informed by an interaction theory of social cognition. That is, what we can learn from the interdisciplinary studies of intersubjectivity—including the significance of embodiment, interaction, and narrative—are important lessons for developing a critical understanding of the actual and potential effects of social relations and organizations. I argue that such lessons support the idea, nicely expressed by Annette Baier (1985, 84), that "Persons essentially are *second* persons." If autonomous agents are already limited in their autonomy by biological factors, they are also embedded in physical environments and social interaction contexts that can either further limit or expand their autonomy. Somewhere between biology and culture, a personal space opens up for morally responsible action.

If for feminist thinkers (like Baier), and pragmatists (from Dewey and Mead to Brandom) and critical theorists (like Habermas and Honneth) humans are social all the way down, precisely how that is the case—precisely what details about our intersubjective existence make it so—will be important for understanding basic socio-political concepts. Analyses that ignore such details will end up naively idealistic, or worse, philosophically solipsistic in a way that champions a detached individualism.

My point is not that the analyses of action and interaction provided here can solve all the problems that theorists of relational autonomy wrestle with, but rather that the details of how embodied interaction works will help to define the problems in the right way. Certain kinds of interactional and joint-action processes are precisely those that lead us into normative and institutional arrangements that support the kinds of practices that we may want to escape—practices where humans are robbed of autonomy, and where less than good dependencies and power structures are established.

PART I
Action

1

Actions and Abstractions

When one sets out to provide an analysis of actions, there are numerous ways to end up with abstractions. I'll argue that we can avoid some of these abstractions by keeping in mind that actions are defined and individuated by their circumstances; they are always situated or contextual. This idea raises some basic questions about the way to think of actions and circumstances, including the concept of basic action, which can also lead to abstractions. I'll argue that the concept of affordance and a pragmatic concept of situation as relational will help to address these questions.

1.1 Pump and Circumstance

There are no actions *simpliciter*. Actions carry along their full circumstances. One might think of this as a principle that would allow us to escape a lot of the debate about how to individuate actions. What an action *is*, is defined by its full circumstance. If we try out this idea we'll see that things are more complicated. It will help to consider an example contrived by Elizabeth Anscombe.

[A] single action can have many different descriptions.... Are we to say that the man who (intentionally) [A] moves his arm, [B] operates the pump, [C] replenishes the water supply, [D] poisons the inhabitants, is performing four actions? Or only one?... (1957, 11)

Anscombe opts for identity theory: the movement, operation, replenishing, and poisoning are really only one action.

In short, the only distinct action of his that is in question is this one, A. For moving his arm up and down with his fingers round the pump handle is, in these circumstances, operating the pump; and, in these circumstances, it is replenishing the house water-supply; and, in these circumstances, it is poisoning the household. So there is one action with four descriptions.

(1957, 45–6)

How we define the circumstances will necessarily vary from one description to another. What is the circumstance that would allow us to consider "moving one's arm up and down on a pump handle" to be a proper description of the action? It would surely be a circumstance different from the circumstance in which we consider "poisoning the household" to be the right answer. This is clearly signaled when I ask the person what he is doing. If he says, "I'm moving my arm up and down on this pump handle," and we accept this as an appropriate answer, then the relevant circumstance would have to be different from the circumstance in which his response is "I'm poisoning the household." Assuming he is giving an honest answer, then one can distinguish the circumstances by inquiring about, for example, how much the agent knows about what he is doing, and what precisely his intentions or motives are. The circumstance of his action of pumping the water is clearly different depending on whether he knows or doesn't know the well water is poisoned.

It might seem that the identity theorist who thinks that moving one's arm up and down is the same action as poisoning the household has a frame problem. The different descriptions would seem to be of the same action only if one were leaving out the different circumstances that frame the actions and make them different. Only at some level of abstraction, for example, looking at the action from a purely mechanical perspective, might one be able to see this as one action. If, however, an action carries its circumstances with it, that is, if there is an integral link between what the action is and its circumstance or context, then one could more definitively distinguish four different actions: moving an arm up and down, working the pump, replenishing the water supply, and poisoning the household. Given a certain collection of contextual factors, including the agent's state of knowledge and specific intention, but also, importantly, the physical relations among a set of factors in the environment, should we not say that these are four different actions? This would be a multiple actions theory.

A multiple actions type of analysis would lead us to say that this man, just by doing what he is doing, is performing four different actions. If action A, moving one's arm up and down with one's hand gripping the pump handle, and action D, poisoning the household, are identical, then A must have all and only the properties that D has (Goldman 1970). But they don't have the same properties. For example, A can be regarded as the cause of D, but D cannot be regarded as the cause of A. Likewise, the causal factors that define A, e.g., exercising one's muscles and bending one's joints, do not include the fact that the water is poisoned; but the causal factors that define D do include the fact that the water is poisoned. These causal properties are simply not the same for A and D, so A and D must be different actions. Under a slightly different description one could say that the agent performs action D by performing action A, but not vice versa. So one is tempted to say that there is a relationship here between two actions, "expressed by saying that the one act is a 'way' or 'method' by which the other act is performed" (Goldman 1970, 5).

Following this line of reasoning we seem to be led to the idea that the man at the pump is carrying out (at least) four different actions at once, but in a non-multi-tasking way. That is, if the man happens to be talking on his phone as he pumps the water, then there are relations between action A and action D that are not present between action A and the action of talking on his phone. The latter action may slow or disrupt action A, of course, but we would not say that he carries out action A by means of talking on his phone, or vice versa. But, as noted, he does carry out action D (poisoning the household) by means of doing A. Alvin Goldman, according to what he calls the "fine-grained method of act-individuation," takes this relation between A and D as an important factor in defining them as two different actions. We should hesitate to accept this conclusion, however.

Consider that on this view action A, moving one's arm up and down, would be one action, and B, pumping the water, would be a second action, instrumentally related to the first in some way. But now, in distinguishing two actions here, the multiple action theorist is the one excluding circumstances. Moving one's arm up and down is an action *simpliciter* only if we ignore that in this context one's arm is working a pump handle that is pumping water. And to identify the action as one of pumping water already has to include the pumping activity; i.e., moving one's arm up and down to work the handle. Separating A and B into two actions seems an abstraction. It seems more reasonable to say that A just is B; moving one's arm up and down with one's hand grasping the pump handle just is pumping the water. A and B are simultaneous events, and on standard synchronic or contemporaneous conceptions of constitution, we would say that A constitutes B—that is, A is at least part of what makes B what it is (see Pettit 2015, 145). On the one hand, one needs to add water to get B, but the addition of water flowing through the pump doesn't make A and B different actions. On the other hand one might think that if we introduce a bit of diachronicity—for example, a time lag between B, pumping the water, and D, poisoning the household—then, on the standard mechanist view, the relation between B and D is merely causal and not constitutive (Craver 2007; Gillett 2013). If we shift to a conception of *dynamical constitution* (see, e.g., Gallagher 2018a; Kirchhoff 2015), however, then B, even in its causal relation to D, partially constitutes D; D is constituted by A, B, and C plus a set of more extensive circumstantial factors—for example, that there is a household that draws its water supply from the well with the pump (concerning causality, see *Section 1.3*). Pumping the water just is, in some very real respects, poisoning the household. Should we return then to Anscombe and argue that rather than four actions, there is just one action under four descriptions that detail the relevant causal and constitutive relations?[1]

If we take circumstances or context (I'll use these terms interchangeably) to include both agent-related aspects (like intention, motivation, skill, knowledge) and world-related aspects (like the facts about objects and physical arrangements, and people in the action environment), then we should say that the four descriptions target four different sets of circumstances of the one action. If, for example, I happen to be making a study of the body-schematic processes involved in moving one's arm up and down, then a description in terms of muscles and joints and perhaps even neuronal activation, would be appropriate. That would be a perfectly good description relative to the kinds of questions a kinesiologist might ask because it picks out a set of aspects relevant to those questions. Likewise, relative to the kinds of questions that might be asked as part of a police investigation, the description of the action in terms of poisoning the household is the relevant description. Descriptions in terms of muscles, joints, and neurons are less relevant to the police investigation, but no one would deny that those muscular, joint, and neuronal processes are aspects of the same action that the police are investigating. For the police investigation, a larger (or different) set of circumstantial aspects will be important, including the agent's intention or motive, whether he knew there was poison in the water, what happened to the people in the house, etc.

The fact that these are aspects of one action, however, enters into defining what is relevant, both from the perspective of the agent and the perspective of an interested

---

[1] Issues that involve the notions of intention-in-action (see *Chapter 3*) and collective intentionality (see *Chapter 9*), as explicated in Searle (1983; 2002), mirror these discussions. For a complex, insightful analysis, see Salice (2015).

observer. The police detective will not (or should not) be satisfied just knowing that this man poisoned the household; she will want to know how he did it, what pump he used, whether he knew about the poison in the water, his intentions and motivations, etc. In some contexts, all of these aspects will be important. Moreover, all of these aspects are constitutionally related and make the action what it is (e.g., a case of homicide rather than an accident). In this respect, one still requires a fine-grained method of act-individuation, but one does not end up with an over-proliferation of actions or abstractions. After arresting and charging the man for poisoning the household, the police detective would not add additional charges for operating the pump, replenishing the water supply, and moving an arm up and down while holding onto the pump handle, respectively, not only because these are not charge-able offences, but because these aspects of the action are already included in the action of poisoning the household.[2]

The notion of "affordance," derived from James Gibson's (1979) ecological psych-ology, will be useful for defining the relation of action and circumstance. It's typical to think of affordances in terms of physical relations between the agent and objects in the world. A chair affords sitting for an agent who has bendable joints and a certain body shape. It affords sitting for a human but not for an alligator. This is, perhaps, the most basic way to think of affordances. Affordances are relational; they do not describe objective features of the environment unrelated to the particular agent involved. An affordance specifies a relation between an agent and some aspect of the environment. More specifically, affordances relate not just to body shape and function, but also to skill. The cliff affords climbing, but only for someone who has the training or skill to climb it. Things have multiple affordances; beyond the canonical affordance of sitting, I can stand on the chair; I can use it as firewood; likewise, I can climb the cliff or write a poem about it. Affordances can be defined more generally as relative to a form of life (Rietveld & Kiverstein 2014), and not just to an individual agent; they can be defined by social practices, they can be constrained by norms. The cliff affords climbing even if I, as an individual, don't have the skill right now to climb it, because it is nonetheless possible for a human who has acquired the requisite skill to climb the cliff, and this is a practice that humans sometimes engage in. Indeed, I could join a sports group, improve my skills, learn the proper way to do it, and climb the cliff. Without that skill or training, the affordance of such climbing remains somewhat removed, but it still exists. I just need to improve my skills.

As the last example shows, affordances can also be social and not just physical. A sports group affords the learning of a skill. More generally, other people afford a variety of interactions. In this regard, affordances can also be cultural (Ramstead, Veissière, & Kirmayer 2016). A certain cultural practice affords the possibility of learning a skill, or earning a wage. An institution, such as a court, affords the possibility of taking legal action. The notion of affordance, then, has wide and flexible

---

[2] But see Margolis (2012, 253) for some qualifications—the legal system doesn't necessarily follow psychology, folk psychology, or metaphysical theory. Also, consider, that in the light of various neuro-psychiatric discoveries, what neurons (or brain areas) were activated during the agent's pumping of the water may be relevant when the case goes to court. If the agent suffers from Anarchic Hand Syndrome, for example, that may constitute a mitigating circumstance.

application. Some philosophers would complain about this wide scope since it suggests that "affordance" can mean too many things. Others, like myself, however, think that the wide and flexible range of the affordance notion is one of its strengths. For my purposes here, however, let me explicitly narrow this concept down to mean only *action affordances*. It may be possible to think that certain objects afford an emotional experience, or an aesthetic or intellectual appreciation. In discussing action, however, I'll think of affordances as primarily affording possibilities for action (without denying that they may also afford these other things, and in some cases do so at the same time). Let me also note that some affordances solicit action. In a particular context, certain actions are more affordable than others. If I hear a knock on the door, the door handle suddenly becomes more salient, more solicitous than the moment before I heard the knock since it affords the means to open the door. In the literature, a solicitation is an affordance that is currently operative for an individual or group, given circumstances that include not only physical properties and positions of the objects, but also bodily conditions and skill levels, etc. of the agent or agents (see Dreyfus 2007; Rietveld 2012).

Returning to the question of how we should individuate actions, then, I'll argue that the best answer is to define an action relative to the context that reflects a complete ordering of its different aspects according to its highest realized affordance, where "complete ordering" means that all of its aspects—motoric, pragmatic, social, etc.—are organized to realize that affordance. I'll clarify this idea in the following sections, but for now let's reconsider Anscombe's example. We might start by saying that the pump affords a number of different things. It affords an exercise of one's muscles, and one could think of someone who is simply interested in building muscle strength using the pump to do so, and not caring about the water or what it might have to do with the household. In point of fact, however, the circumstance does afford pumping water and poisoning the household and if in fact the action does poison the household, then *ceteris paribus*, that would be the highest realized affordance because it incorporates all of the other (lower-level) aspects of the action. The man poisons the household by replenishing the water supply to the household, and does that by pumping the water, and does so by moving his arm up and down. Whether he does so intentionally or not, or whether he knows the water is poisoned are questions about further aspects of the action that may qualify the legal description of the action as a crime, or accident. Intention, motive, knowledge, skill level—these are aspects on the agent side of the affordance that contribute to the definition of the circumstance. There are other aspects on the worldly side of the affordance that also contribute to the context. Again, actions carry their circumstances, and different circumstances may change what we count as the highest realized affordance. Importantly, that we put this in terms of affordance links the agent side and the worldly side since an affordance is defined just in terms of such relations. If the household is the household of the head of state, then the highest realized affordance is political and, assuming poison in the water, and a specific intention on the part of the man who is pumping the water, the action is a political act of assassination, in which case the poisoning of the household becomes the means to a more complex goal, or may just be a more complex action. By moving his hand up and down on the pump handle, the man may be starting a revolution.

We can abstract away from the context of the highest realized affordance—focusing on only some incomplete set of aspects—and still describe the action by describing as many aspects as are relevant to the lower context; e.g., moving one's arm up and down. The further away from the highest realized affordance the more abstract the description.

To be clear, the circumstances or context can be quite complex on both sides of the affordance. (1) On the agent side, all the physical details of his movement in relation to the environment, his skills, his intentions, motivations, what he knows, what he thinks he is doing (e.g., just pumping water), his interactions with others, and (2) on the side of the world, the objects/artifacts and their arrangement in the environment, as well as aspects of the (physical, social, cultural) environment, the effects or consequences of the action. In addition, there is a third side—(3) the side of the interpreters of the action (observers, describers, detectives) who may frame the action according to their own interests; e.g., what they are asking or investigating, for example, as neuroscientists (e.g., what neurons were activated) or detectives (e.g., who poisoned the household and why). Even in cases where there seems to be only motoric aspects—for example, in physical exercise—this may still accomplish something; for example, improved health, or perhaps just the enjoyment of movement (see Cole & Montero 2007). This may be the case even when the agent does not intend such goals. Typically, however, intentions are important aspects of the action, and help to specify the context and increase the number of descriptions, but not the number of actions.[3]

To summarize, in these Anscombe cases, rather than thinking there are multiple actions when an agent intentionally engages in some action that is describable in terms of its highest realized affordance—e.g., poisoning a household—we should say that there is one action that can be described differently by specifying different circumstances. What the descriptions capture are more or less complete organizations of different affordance-related aspects of the same action. Goldman comes close to this point when he argues against theoretic reductionism, the idea that one can simply reduce more circumstantially complex acts into less circumstantially complex acts by translating from one description to another. The reductionist strategy would be to claim that for each statement describing an action D (e.g., poisoning the household), there is a set of logically equivalent statements describing the action or actions that generated D (e.g., moving one's arm up and down on the pump, or pumping the water). Goldman shows that logical equivalence does not obtain; but in fact the entailment fails in both directions. The reason it fails is that in order to get the logical entailment one needs to add extra facts or factors to the translation. "In general, statements describing lower-level acts alone do not entail statements

---

[3] Davidson writes: "Explaining an action by giving an intention with which it was done provides new descriptions of the action: I am writing my name on a piece of paper with the intention of writing a check with the intention of paying a gambling debt. List all the different descriptions of my action. Here are a few for a start: I am writing my name. I am writing my name on a piece of paper. I am writing my name on a piece of paper with the intention of writing a check. I am writing a check. I am paying my gambling debt. It is hard to imagine how we can have a coherent theory of action unless we are allowed to say here: each of these sentences describes the same action" (Davidson 1967, 85).

describing higher-level acts; some statements describing relevant conditions, such as causal effects, circumstances, rules, etc., must be added to get the entailment" (1970, 40; also see his discussion of causally relevant conditions, p. 75; also Vallacher & Wegner 2014, 40). I take this to mean (*contra* Goldman) not that the generated action (e.g., poisoning the household) is a different action from the generating action (e.g., pumping the water), but that the descriptions pick out different aspects that make up the circumstances of one action.

1.2 The Agentive Situation

To provide a better characterization of circumstances or context, and to emphasize the idea that for any action, context involves both an agent side and a worldly side connected in an affordance structure, I'll rely on John Dewey's (1938) notion of *situation*. For Dewey, situation is not equivalent to the environment—it also always includes the agent in such a way that agent and environment are co-defined. In this respect, a situation has the same structure as an affordance, although we may think of it as a broader concept, and we can say that a situation may contain a variety of affordances. As an agent, I cannot step outside the situation without changing it. If I am in what Dewey calls a problematic situation, I can point to a relevant part of the environment, but I cannot strictly point to the situation because my pointing is part of the situation. Reflectively trying to grasp the situation may be helpful, but it also changes the situation since it introduces a reflective element into it. My movement is a movement of the situation. The rearrangement of environmental objects is a rearrangement of the situation and it implies a rearrangement of oneself as well. A situation, then, is defined in relation to the performance of actions and, as we'll see, is characterized by varying degrees of and kinds of intentionality. I'll call this an *agentive situation* to emphasize the fact that the agent is part of it.

One way to study agentive situations is to look at cases in which the agent has been radically changed. We can do this by considering the variety of ways in which the effects of brain damage are mitigated by factors most easily described on the personal level, especially in terms of the intentionality of the behavior involved.

For example, in cases of aphasia the use of a therapeutic procedure called "de-blocking," which is a stimulation/priming technique, shows that for a particular subject, the employment of a word or syntactic structure in an unimpaired task (for example, reading) can make it temporarily available for use in an impaired task (for example, naming) (Laine & Martin 2013; Weigl 1961). Once gained in the context of the impaired function the word may remain available for that function for a significant time. It turns out that the most efficacious de-blockers are not defined objectively, but depend on the individual patient. That is, the word or phrase must have significance for that patient. Moreover, such techniques are less likely to work if the impaired function is confined to a relatively non-intentional process (for example, some instances of phonemic cueing). Their success depends on the involvement of a significant semantic component and a rich set of elicitation cues (gestures, synonyms) (Patterson, Purell, & Morton 1983). This type of therapy, then, appears to work best in situations that are richly contextualized in terms of semantic components. For the therapy to work, it must be taken up at a personal or agentive level, in a situation in which the agent can find meaning.

As another example, consider some research on the rehabilitation of impairments in hand use following stroke. Leontiev and Zaporozhets (1960) showed that in some cases hand movements can be more effectively rehabilitated by having the patient perform the impaired behavior in the context of meaningful activity than in the exercise of isolated movement or "meaningless orders," which tended to have "a chilling effect" on recovery (p. 149). In patients suffering from ideomotor apraxia, who are otherwise unimpaired in perception, comprehension, or motor performance, actions that cannot be produced on request or by imitation, can be produced or improved when they are performed in the course of normal activities that include such actions.

Anthony Marcel (1992) found this same phenomenon in experiments with motor-impaired neurological patients who showed characteristics of ideomotor apraxia in manual function but were not classified as ideomotor apraxics since their motor impairments were identified as relatively peripheral (rather than of central origin). These patients showed a significant improvement in various aspects of motor control, and increased fluency in impaired behaviors when these behaviors were performed as meaningful actions, compared with their performance when elicited as decontextualized behaviors. More significantly, in almost all of these cases even further improvement was found when nominally the same movements were performed in an agentive situation, usually a social situation, in which the movements constituted actions with personal and culturally derived signification. For example, one patient who had coordination, timing, and sequencing problems in finger control, found it difficult to copy letter-like figures, but improved when writing words to dictation, and performed best when writing her plans and achievements in her diary (Marcel 1992). Another female patient with whom Marcel worked, had difficulty in grasping, in lifting, and in motor fluency when asked in an experimental situation to lift a cylinder the weight and size of a glass of liquid and to move it toward or away from herself. She showed clear improvement in her performance when spontaneously drinking during a meal at home. This same woman was even more proficient, and indeed, close to her pre-stroke performance level, in the very same movements when serving cups of tea to guests in her home, although not when clearing up the cups.

Based on cases like these, Marcel (1992) distinguished three levels of action performance, the baseline level plus two levels of improvement. These levels were associated with two things: (1) the degree of semantic or pragmatic contextualization, where the situation allowed for the formation of a meaningful intention on the part of the agent, or where meaningful action was possible; and (2) social/self signification. In all but one of the subjects examined by Marcel, differences in the nature of intention strongly correlated with performance differences. Subjects performed poorly in situations in which they were instructed to carry out some meaningless or purely procedural action (usually in experimental or neurological examination contexts). Subjects performed measurably better in more semantically or pragmatically contextualized situations insofar as they were involved in some kind of (relatively) meaningful action or activity (e.g., eating or drinking at a meal, washing dishes, writing to dictation). Subjects performed best, however, in actions that were personally significant or that derived their signification from the social and cultural context (e.g., serving tea to friends, writing in a diary, dealing cards in a real game). This third level of action performance appeared to be associated with intentions that concerned the agent personally, and with those cases in which cultural practice usually assigns symbolic significance. For example, serving tea to guests involves the intention to engage in a cultural practice of offering hospitality, which contributes to the constitution of social competence and relates to the self-esteem of the agent. Changing from one type of context to the other, a specific motor performance can move from impossible, or near impossible, to possible or improved, to relatively fluent.[4]

Pursuant to these studies, Gallagher and Marcel (1999, 8–9) distinguished between three different kinds of situated intentions.

- Intentions formed in relatively *abstract* or decontextualized situations (e.g., test or experimental situations, or perhaps some exercise routines where I simply move my arm up and down).
- Intentions formed in *pragmatically* contextualized situations (e.g., those involving purposive behavior, or the exercise of an already known intention, or to return to our previous example, pumping water at the well).
- Intentions formed in *socially* contextualized situations, where the agent is socially embedded, or where actions reflect competence in an affectively rich social role (those involving self-reference or other persons, e.g., acting as an assassin by poisoning a household).

There is a close relationship between the action intention and the situation that gives rise to it. The abstract or decontextualized situation is one in which the agent is detached from what would ordinarily be considered a significant context—a situation where the agent has no normal or good reason for doing what is asked other than voluntary compliance; for example, a neurological examination in which the patient is asked to move her arm up and down. The pragmatically contextualized situation is one that is relatively more informed by a meaningful circumstance (relative to the individual subject). These two kinds of situations closely align with Kurt Goldstein's (1940) distinction between abstract and concrete behavior. Concrete behavior, corresponding to the pragmatically contextualized situation, is such that an agent performs and has a reason to perform in a situation that is closer to real life (e.g., pumping water at a well). The socially contextualized situation is clearly qualified by social and personal circumstances that involve cultural categorizations of activities and/or social interactions.

Importantly, no specific type of action per se can be exclusively assigned to any one kind of situation. The distinctions between these different kinds of agentive situations

---

[4] Actions do not need to be performed in the presence of others to have a social signification. However many of them were so performed. One might think that performance of such actions in the presence of others would lead to greater "self-consciousness," which would disrupt the fluency of action. In experiments, Marcel found that this did often occur. What is important is that in real social situations, after initiation of the activity, the opposite (greater fluency) occurred.

(and how they are defined) are relative to the subject's intentions, and to different reasons for acting or the relative absence of reason (as in the abstract, decontextualized situation). To move one's arm is not an intrinsically abstract or concrete behavior; its status in this regard depends on the situated intention and the circumstances.

This analysis can be extended to a further point. The notion of an abstract or decontextualized situation is one characterized not only by a lack of contextualization but also often by some degree of relatively high-level cognition or conscious attention directed to the bodily movement (e.g., understanding instructions and consciously translating them into motor actions that involve self-movement). When, for example, I'm told to walk a straight line as part of a neurological examination, I am more conscious of my movement than when I simply walk straight across the room to open a door for a friend. In a pragmatically or socially contextualized situation my attention is directed more toward the situation or task and less (if at all) towards my bodily movement (although this may differ in different circumstances). In walking to open the door for a friend, for example, I do not attend to (and possibly I am not even aware of) how I'm moving my legs; one might say that my walking is an unthinking (close-to-automatic) aspect of the larger intentional action. In a different circumstance, e.g., if I am in pain, I may attend more closely to the details of my movement. The same motor functions to which the agent attends in the abstract situation are, in a more contextualized setting, incorporated into and become an intrinsic part of a larger task that bestows meaning on the particular movement. The task itself may not be particularly meaningful (for example, washing dishes); but relative to the task a particular hand movement takes on meaning and is generated by that meaning. Of course, in many social situations what matters to the agent is indeed the manner or style of the action; e.g., not just walking, but walking elegantly or nonchalantly. The intended action can become disrupted when explicit attention is focused on the details of movement rather than on the intended goal. For example, it may be important for the actor, dancer, or athlete, once having learned such aspects of movement, to demote them from the focus of conscious intention in performance. Or more precisely, learning the movements often involves the diminution of attention to the movements, or at least the capability of focusing one's attention elsewhere.[5]

Action intentions, modulated in the agentive situation, have an effect on performance. Thus, in both optic ataxic patients and typical subjects perceptual-motor coordination is qualitatively different depending on whether the instruction is "to reach for and touch" (instrumental action) or "to indicate" (socially oriented action) an object (Brouchon et al. 1986). Movements performed under different descriptions or instructions involve differences in the agent's intention; the second instruction insofar as it requires deixis (pointing) implicates communicative reference to another person.

---

[5] A diminution of attention doesn't necessarily mean a complete unawareness; in specialized performance (e.g., in athletics or performing arts) one might have some form of enhanced pre-reflective awareness of one's movements (see, e.g., Gallagher and Ilundáin-Agurruza, 2020; Legrand 2007).

Changes in the contextual nature of the situation relative to the agent—which implicate changes in the organization of the agent's intentions—can result in changes in the performance level of action. In many of the cases cited, and even in typical subjects, actions tend to break down and become disintegrated in abstract situations. In pragmatically and socially contextualized situations actions tends to be more meaningfully coherent.

These generalizations do not hold in all cases, however. There are many pathologies (for example, some instances of aphasia and associative agnosia) where patients perform worse at the semantic level and better at the lower or more abstract level— some aphasic patients may be able to apprehend sensory and lexical characteristics of words, but not their meaning; many agnosic patients perceive sensory aspects of objects but fail to know what the object is or how to use it even when in context (Marcel 1983). Nonetheless it is difficult (although not impossible) to find corresponding instances in non-pathological populations. There are two reasons for this. First, action is normally attuned to the highest semantic or functionally useful level of behavior, or, building on our previous terminology, the highest realizable affordance. Second, most agents have the ability to engage in abstract actions; they are capable of finding meaning in such actions, even if with a lower level of performance. This does not rule out choking in high-performance athletics, or overly self-conscious behavior in highly contextualized social situations leading to a performance decline.

Here it makes sense to appeal to a gestalt principle I have appealed to in different contexts (e.g., Gallagher 2017a), summarized succinctly by Goldstein and Scheerer (1964, 8):

Although the normal person's behaviour is prevailingly concrete, this concreteness can be considered normal only as long as it is embedded in and codetermined by the abstract attitude. For instance, in the normal person both attitudes are always present in a definite figure-ground relation.

The disorders and recoveries mentioned above can be characterized as variances in this figure-ground relation—a relation that modulates the relationality of the agentive situation.

1.3 Basic Actions

I've been arguing, not simply that we need to understand action in context, but that context or circumstance is part of what constitutes an action. In this respect I'm in agreement with Vallacher and Wegner (2014, 43): "An act devoid of context, in sum, is an act devoid of meaning." They suggest that the identification (individuation) of an action is shorthand for "an entire complex of information – cause-effect relations, conventional social interpretations, configurations of circumstance, other comparable actions, and more" (43). Context is incorporated into the definition of action itself. Some theorists, however, suggest that to explain action, we can start at a non-contextualized bottom and work our way up.

For many philosophers it seems obvious that a complex action is composed of actions that are more basic. One might think that moving one's arm up is a basic action, where *basic action* means, following Danto's (1963) original formulation, an action not caused by another action performed by the same agent. When we add a second basic action—namely, moving one's arm down—to form a sequence of up and down, and add the circumstance of holding the pump handle (or one might consider this a third basic action of grasping the pump handle), these basic actions add up to the complex action of pumping the water. Notice that even in defining the action of pumping the water there is a bit of material circumstance that seems essential; i.e., holding the pump handle which is connected to a pump which is connected to a well with water in it. Also note that in this example we do not have strict simultaneity of basic actions, and the complex action is constituted in a diachronic way. It's the dynamic of movement (or the dynamic connection of the two or three basic actions) along with a coupling to the environment that constitutes the action of pumping the water. This type of analysis might be thought to be what Goldman (1970) has in mind as an instance of a "fine-grained method of act-individuation," or we might simply say "act analysis." A basic action, then, is simply an action that cannot be broken down by any further act analysis without explaining it in terms of non-actions. One can certainly analyze the basic action of moving one's arm in terms of what muscles, joints, and efferent neuronal activations are doing, but none of these component processes are actions.

The sequence of moving one's arm up and down, however, overly complicates the story. Goldman (1970, 20ff) provides a simpler example. (A) *John moves his hand.* By moving his hand, (B) *John moves his queen to king-knight-seven.* And by moving his queen, (C) *John checkmates his opponent.* According to Goldman's act analysis, we have identified three actions. The actions are simultaneous, but there is still a hierarchical (asymmetrical) generating relationship between them. *A* is a basic action by which John simultaneously performs *B*, and *B* is an action by which John simultaneously performs *C*. These are not simply three different levels of description; they are three different actions, according to Goldman, related in a "level-generational" way, signified by the locution "by"—e.g., John moves his queen *by* moving his hand; John checkmates his opponent *by* moving his queen.[6] Not all simultaneous actions performed by the same person are in a level-generating relationship; for example, one may be able to multi-task so as to chew gum and walk at the same time. Goldman, however, also rules out the example of the sequential movement of arm up and down as an example of a level-generating relationship. Although it seems legitimate to say that one pumps the water *by* moving one's arm up and down, it does not meet the following requirement that he imposes on the notion of level generation: "no member of a level-generational pair [can] be a temporal part, i.e. proper part, of its level-generational mate."

Consider, for example, S's act of playing the C-scale. This act is composed of a series of smaller acts ordered by the relation of subsequence—viz., S's playing note C, followed by S's playing note D, followed by S's playing note E, etc. Each of these shorter acts is a temporal part of S's

---

[6] The notion that there is a hierarchical arrangement among these actions—that there are lower and higher levels—is expressed precisely in the "by" relation (see Vallacher & Wegner 2014, 21ff). Empirical studies have shown that subjects do reason about actions according to these "by" relations (Vallacher et al 1981; cited in Vallacher & Wegner 2014, 44ff; and Kruskal & Wish 1978).

playing the C-scale. Because of this, none of these shorter acts is level-generationally related to the longer act of playing the C-scale.   (Goldman 1970, 22)

Goldman thus rules out diachronicity from level generation, so the sequence of two basic actions does not "level generate" a more complex action. Level-generation relations between acts are therefore not causal in the usual sense, where effect follows cause in time, although in some sense John's moving of his hand does cause him to move the queen and checkmate his opponent. Goldman calls this sense of causing "causal generation" and distinguishes it from causation more generally. The distinction is important for his account of basic action.

Before discussing basic action, let's note one more thing that Goldman rules out. After ruling out identity, and now diachronic and regular causal relations, as characterizing relations of level generation, he also rules out mereological reduction.[7] That is, action A is not a part or component of action B—John's moving of his hand is not part of moving his queen, and moving his hand and moving his queen are not parts that add up to checkmating his opponent. Thus, "in general the relation between a generated act and a generating act is not that of whole to part" (1970, 39). Once identity theory is denied and one thinks that in these kinds of Anscombe cases there are multiple actions rather than multiple descriptions of one action, then these various questions have to be answered. Is the relation between A and B diachronic, causal, or mereological? Goldman's answer is no to each question.

Danto (1963) originally defined basic action in terms of causal relations.[8] A is a basic action if it is an action not caused by another action performed by the same agent (S). But where does one start in defining a basic action? S moves his leg. That seemingly is a basic action. But it is caused by S's action of jumping into the pool. Goldman argues that we can still call the moving of the leg a basic action even if it is caused by the prior action, because it is not in a relation of causal generation with the prior action. So Goldman's refined definition of basic action (as distinct from Danto's) is that A is a basic action if it is an action not *causally generated* by another action performed by the same agent (1970, 72).[9]

For Goldman, basic action may be caused by mental states, specifically by intentions, desires, and beliefs, which are not themselves basic actions. "In order for S's raising his hand to be a basic act-token, his raising his hand must be intentional. And in order for it to be intentional, it must be caused by wants and beliefs of the agent,"

[7] I believe he would also reject the type of reductionism that would claim "Everything the agent does boils down to the performance of a set of temporally coordinated basic actions" (Allen et al. 2014, 144). Goldman's analysis pre-figures the "new mechanism" discussions of non-causal constitution. Goldman's notion of "level generation," however, is not equivalent to Carl Craver's (2007) notion of inter-level constitution relations (as distinguished from intra-level causal relations), since for Craver the relation is mereological. For more on this, see Gallagher (2018a).

[8] Danto suggested that everyone intuitively knows "which actions are basic ones" (1965, 145). Subsequent debates demonstrate that this is not true. Sandis' (2010) succinct review of the basic action literature suggests that no one knows which actions are basic ones.

[9] Goldman allows for one exception which is when a basic action is generated by another basic action via "augmentation generation." For example, the action of S raising his hand slowly (a basic act-token) is generated by S raising his hand, another basic act-token (1970, 46). Goldman treats these as two different actions. The generated action is augmented by an additional circumstance, but is nonetheless a basic action.

or by some integrated action plan composed of such mental states (71). There is a large debate, acknowledged by Goldman, about whether mental states are causes or reasons for action. Setting that debate aside for now, if one regards the basic action to be something integrated into the larger action, it's most likely that the wants and beliefs, and whatever plans might be in play, are about the goal of that larger action, not about the aspects of the basic action; e.g., the arm or hand movement.[10] It's not clear that one plans out (or even "acquires" [Mele & Moser 1997, 231] a plan for) a basic action, as it is standardly characterized. It's more likely that the basic action— e.g., of moving one's hand—is carried along by the larger dynamics of the more complex action.[11] Indeed, one could better describe the movements defined as basic actions in terms of sensory-motor contingencies and the kind of tacit skill or know-how such contingencies involve, rather than as caused by a set of mental states that, if they play any relevant role, are directed more towards the larger goals of the action. As Goldman admits, "an agent usually does a basic act A not because he wants to do A (per se) but because he wants to do A' [some non-basic action] and believes that A will generate A'" (72).

This is not to deny that we can explain actions in terms of beliefs, desires, motives, etc., even if these are somewhat oversimplified abstractions. Such explanations (by the agent or an observer) tend to be retrospective redescriptions, often given in response to the question "Why?" "I did this because I wanted X and I believed P and Q." Or "He did that because he believed this and desired that." One important question is whether such retrospective descriptions capture the actual action dynamics as they develop from the perspective of the agent in the action process, or simply introduce additional characterizations after the fact.[12] If, for example, there is a pre-action deliberation process where the agent explicitly forms a prior intention to do A, it may be the case that his beliefs and desires guide the process and on that basis contribute to the formation of his intention. In that case we might expect that a retrospective explanation in term of beliefs, desires, and intentions could match some of the processes that actually informed the action. Some theorists might also argue that whether the agent explicitly deliberates or not, his actions are going to reflect some set of beliefs and desires that can be made explicit by the retrospective

---

[10] In this respect I don't agree with Setiya (2007, 32) that "In the case of basic action, the crucial concept is that of guidance: when an agent A's intentionally, he wants to A, and this desire not only causes but continues to guide behavior towards its object." It's not clear that the agent wants or desires to move his hand thus and so in order to do B. It's much more likely that he wants to do B, and A is just the way he does it. Setiya (2004, 363–4) comes closer to the right formulation: "Suppose I am playing a particular piece of music. This is something I do by performing other actions, like playing a passage, or a movement of the piece, and finally by performing basic actions, like moving my hand in order to play a note.... What this comes to in the typical case is that I intend to be playing the piece, and that the further intentions that motivate the basic actions by which I have been doing so are motivated (in turn) by that original intention.... In this way, a complex motivational structure of basic actions (like moving one's hands) constitutes the performance of a non-basic action (like playing a piece of music)."

[11] On the limitations of planning theories of intention and action, and the role of improvisation, see Preston (2013, 48–58).

[12] It's also the case that in any retrospective narrative, and usually in standard relatively rigid scripts describing actions, normative ordering can distort what actually has occurred. People often use scripts to incorrectly reconstruct their complex actions (Lichtenstein & Brewer 1980) and find it easier to recall higher-order meanings than the lower-order movement details (Graesser 1978).

explanation.[13] It's also possible, and I tend to think this is usually the case, that such explanations are abstractions and that what is often driving action is a set of perceived affordances rather than a set of beliefs and desires.[14] Actions may be motivated more by ambiguous or problematic circumstances or other people's actions than by an agent's desires and beliefs.

It follows from the idea that in the Anscombe-style examples, if there is only one action under different descriptions, then there is no basic action amongst others, and that what is being called a basic action is simply the action itself as it is given in a basic description. Moreover, that basic action description is framed at a very abstract level—i.e., at a level that is abstracted away from the level of the highest realized affordance—and is inclusive of only the most basic motoric aspects of the action. What explains these motoric aspects? From below: body-schematic, motor-control details about muscles, joints, and kinematics as they are coupled to the physical environment. From above: the action described at the level of highest realized affordance, which involves the broader intentions and goals that generate a complete ordering or alignment of all of the motoric, pragmatic, and social aspects required to realize (i.e., take advantage of) that affordance. The ordering can still be explicated in an act analysis in terms of "by" relations without positing multiple actions where there is only one. Thus Vallacher and Wegner (2014, 47) suggest that this type of analysis provides an elemental form or "snapshot" of the identity structure of an action. "In its most elemental form, an identity structure involves the integration of low level identities under one superordinate identity that provides coherence and interpretation for the action as a whole." They point out, however, that this doesn't capture the full complexity of action structures, because they are more dynamic, and because different perspectives may lead to the identification of different structures as defining an action, and a single higher-order description will not necessarily incorporate all lower-level aspects as relevant. Agents also have multiple goals and may pursue means that are not unambiguous.

1.4 Basic Problems

The idea that we get a snapshot analysis of action—that is, a snapshot of something that is not reducible to a snapshot but which is clearly something temporal and more dynamic—points to an important problem involved in identifying an action as basic. Moreover, the idea that there is no basic action, but at best only a basic description of an action that can be described in multiple ways, points to a second problem, one that seemingly involves infinite regress. Fortunately, there is a way to solve both problems—or at least, a way to point to solutions. Let me start by stating the two problems.

---

[13] Goldman puts it this way: "Normally, when we say 'What are you doing?' we are not interested in being told what things the agent is actually doing; we want to know the desires or purposes out of which he is acting. Hence, an answer to such a question is normally taken as a specification of his desires or goals, not as a description of his actual act-tokens" (1970, 79).

[14] Dijksterhuis et al. (2006) do not present a positive thesis (about affordances or anything else) but do present evidence that we can make complex decisions (and make them better) without deliberation.

The first problem involves the dynamical, temporal structure of action. Although I'll address this issue in detail in the next chapter I'll refer to the problem here in terms outlined by Michael Thompson (2008), and following him, Douglas Lavin (2013). Thompson and Lavin suggest that there is a problem involving the temporal structure of basic actions. Most of the discussion in action theory conceives of action, whether basic or non-basic, as a complete or completed event rather than a process. Yet there is an important distinction to be made between a completed action (e.g., "I crossed the street") and an ongoing action in process ("I am crossing the street"). In the case of an ongoing or continuing action there is a progression towards completion so that as the action continues there is less and less to be done before completion, and more and more that has already been done. Some bits of the action have already happened, and other bits are yet to happen. "The action in progress (X is doing A) is at once an ever-increasing stack of have done's and ever shrinking list of still to do's. When all goes well, the accumulation of subordinate have done's constitutes the completed action (X did A): the subject's aim of A-ing is materialized in them" (Lavin 2013, 292). This same temporal structure, of course, applies to all actions; what are now completed action events were once in just such a process.

This way of conceiving of the temporality of action leads to problems when it is applied to basic action, premised on the idea that a complex action is composed of less complex actions, and at bottom, by basic actions. Thompson (2008) considers the following scenario. I am pushing a stone from point α to point ω. But to get to ω I have to pass through a midpoint β on the path. In this case, "as I began to push off from α" it would have been as much true for me to say "I am pushing it to β" as "I am pushing it to ω." That means that the initial segment of pushing the stone from α to ω is an intentional action of pushing the stone to β. I could say, "I was pushing and pushed the stone to β because I was pushing it to ω" (2008, 107–8). If this is right, then I could make the same analysis of pushing the stone from α to β. That is, there is a midpoint between α and β, and I would be engaged in an intentional action in pushing the stone to that point. In every intentional action of this sort there will be an initial segment so that one will never get to anything like a basic action at the start or bottom. Lavin provides a similar example of pointing to a map and tracing a line with his finger from one city to the next. In this process he traces the line first to a midpoint between the two cities. "And, now, what is to prevent us from applying this procedure again and again without end, each time isolating some initial segment of a movement and showing it to be something I did with a view to bringing off the whole?" (2013, 276). The Zenoesque challenge is to find the basic action in any of these intentional segments.

The general challenge here is to take some actual intentional action A, an action performed on a particular occasion, and to point to one of its basic parts. The difficulty is to find a describable part of A, A^*, which is something the agent did intentionally in order to do A, but which does not itself resolve into further subactions that the agent did intentionally in order to do A^*.

(2013, 276)

Following this logic, Lavin also suggests that in the case of the unfolding of a basic action, no part of it could be itself an intentional action, otherwise the basic action as a whole would depend on another action, and would not be basic, on the standard definition. Lavin takes the fact that the unfolding parts of the action are not intentional actions to mean that the agent is not aware of what he is doing, as he is performing a basic action. "It looks like performing a basic action is just being the subject of a mindless, automatic process which the subject has somehow initiated, triggered, or launched" (293). If this is the case in regard to the performing of the action, how is it possible to claim that the basic action itself, as completed, is in any sense intentional, or guided by the agent, or in fact, an action at all? If this is right, "then 'basic action' seems not to be action at all" (293).

The second problem follows from the idea that there is no basic action, whether for reasons just given, or because Anscombe is right that in any case there is only one action with multiple descriptions. It's the seeming infinite regress that the concept of basic action was meant to avoid. If, in order to perform an action C (e.g., turning on the light), I do so by performing action B (e.g., flipping the switch), and if in order to do B I do so by A (moving my hand on the switch), my action(s) have to bottom out someplace or lead to an infinite regress. That is, there has to be an action (a basic action) that initiates the process, and which is not performed by performing some other action. That's what a basic action is—an action the agent performs without performing it by performing another action (this is Frederick Stoutland's [1968, 467], terminology, adopted then by Danto [1969, 66]). If that basic action is missing or doesn't exist, then we are led to an infinite regress of doing an action by doing another action, which is done by doing another action, and so on.

I think the solution to both of these problems can be found in the concept of *basic activity* proposed by Jennifer Hornsby (2013). The notion of basic activity is clearly meant to address the issue of conceiving of action, not as a completed event, but as a process (Steward 2012). Hornsby is right, however, to point out that while starting with the notion that ongoing action has a temporal structure, Thompson and Lavin end up describing action as being made up of discrete, atomistic segments. I think this signals something about their conception of the temporality involved in the temporal structure of action. I'll address this issue in the next chapter. Here it is enough to say that activity, as Hornsby conceives of it, is not something that can be chopped up into discrete segments without leading to a falsifying abstraction. Being engaged in an action involves an indivisible process or activity. The problem with both critics and defenders of the concept of basic action is that they are taking that which is basic to be an action understood as a discrete event rather than as a dynamic process. As Lavin puts it, reflecting this standard view, "if basic action is to be anything at all it cannot be durative and telic" (2013, 300, n35). Hornsby argues that, from the perspective of starting to act, "One could never get started if one had always to do something *else* in order to do something. There must always be something that one can get to perform or to execute *just like that*" ([14]). For Hornsby, this is a matter of practical skilled activity where the person simply knows, "just like that" what to do. One knows how to walk, for example, without having to have theoretical knowledge of how one does it. Given suitable motivation, one just begins to walk and is immediately involved in an activity that eventuates in the complete action. Such action bottoms out, not in a basic action, but in a basic activity that one does "just like that," where the latter phrase doesn't signify something magical, but something as common as the activity of walking or moving in a certain way.

A point made by Goldman can help to clarify this notion of basic activity. Goldman would object to Thompson and Lavin's characterization of basic action since, "in general the relation between a generated act and a generating act is not that of whole to part" (1970, 39). In looking for a basic action in their examples, Thompson and Lavin mistakenly understand a basic action to be a part of a larger action whole. Again, they end up looking for basic actions in discrete, atomistic segments. Following Hornsby, we can say that Thompson and Lavin miss what is basic; namely, the continuing activity of pushing (in Thompson's example), and the continuing moving and guiding of the hand that is the activity of pointing to the map (in Lavin's example).

We can thus avoid any infinite regress, and still think of action in a dynamical, temporal fashion; something that bottoms out in basic activity. To get this right, however, we need to give a better account of the temporal structure of action, and to show that basic activity can be characterized as intentional activity rather than mindless movement.

To summarize, when one sets out to provide an analysis of actions, there are numerous ways to end up with abstractions. We can avoid some of these abstractions by keeping in mind that actions are defined and individuated by their circumstances; they are always situated or contextual. I've argued that the most appropriate way to think of actions and circumstances is to think of them as ordered according to the action's highest realized affordance within an agentive situation. The concepts of affordance and agentive situation are both relational; they reference both the agent (including the agent's intention) and the action environment (which is social and cultural). The concept of basic action, which can also lead to abstractions, is best understood in terms of basic activity. This allows us to escape problems tied to abstracting away from the temporality of action.

2

Time in Action

In her critique of Donald Davidson's causal theory of action Jennifer Hornsby demonstrates that when we fail to take temporality into account we end up with a set of relations between static objects (a subject's mental event in relation to an action event) rather than an ongoing process of action. She insists that, in contrast, "we live and think and act in time" (2017, 149). It's not clear, however, that this goes far enough. It is not just that action occurs as a process "in time"—rather, as I will suggest, action involves an *intrinsic* temporality. In this chapter I want to drill down into the micro-structure of action and the perceptual aspects that accompany action, in order to show how at a very basic level they self-organize into enactive processes that support the intentional lives of agents.

2.1 Timing Is not Everything

When we look at infants younger than 3 months of age our impression is that their movements lack proper coordination. When they move their arms and legs they seem to be flailing about, attempting, perhaps, to gain control over their movements as they adjust to the gravity (literally) of the situation (Hopkins & Prechtl 1984; Prechtl & Hopkins 1986). For this reason, in part, developmental studies have traditionally argued that body schemas (understood as mechanisms of motor control) are absent at birth and that their development depends on prolonged experience. Video studies, however, show that there is more organization in these movements than the casual glance reveals. Close to one-third of all arm movements resulting in contact with any part of the head lead to contact with the mouth, either directly (14 percent) or following contact with other parts of the face (18 percent) (Butterworth & Hopkins 1988; Lew & Butterworth 1995). A significant percentage of the arm movements that result in contact with the mouth are associated with an open or opening mouth posture, compared with those landing on other parts of the face (Lew & Butterworth 1997). In these movements the mouth *anticipates* arrival of the hand. This kind of coordination can be traced to even earlier points in development. Ultrasonic scanning on fetuses shows that similar hand–mouth movements occur 50–100 times per hour from 12 to 15 weeks gestational age (De Vries, Visser, & Prechtl 1984; Hadders-Algra 2018),[1] and that fetuses also anticipate their hand

---

[1] The ultrasonic scans were sufficiently fine-grained to show jaw openings, yawns, and even movements of the tongue. De Vries et al. (1984) state: "There was a striking similarity between prenatal and postnatal movements, although the latter sometimes appeared abrupt because of the effect of gravity" (p. 48).

arrival by opening the mouth (Fagard et al. 2018; Myowa-Yamakoshi & Takeshita 2006; Reissland et al. 2014).

Accordingly, even prior to birth, a basic hand–mouth coordination is an aspect of early, motor-organizing processes in humans. This should not be a surprise. We've known for a long time that just such temporal organization characterizes animal movement generally. And for the human, as John Gibbon and Chariklia Malapani put it, "Timing is everything: in making shots, in making love, in making dinner" (Gibbon & Malapani 2001, 305).

Timing is not everything, however. Timing is something that we can see and measure. Yet timing can be accidental or merely coincidental. The fact of a more consistent timing, the fact that the mouth almost always anticipates the hand, for example, suggests deeper temporal processes involved in bodily systems capable of such timing. In other words, it is not just a matter of the system carrying or processing temporal information; rather, the important thing is that the system is capable of organizing itself, its processes, and its behavior in a temporal fashion. For the system to have this anticipatory aspect in its movement, it needs to have a practical orientation towards what is just about to happen. Throughout its movement the system also needs to keep track of how previous movement has brought it to its current state, and this is especially true if the movement is intentional, and if a conscious sense of movement or sense of agency is generated. The anticipation involved in hand–mouth coordination, then, suggests that at the very least from early post-natal life onwards, human (and animal) movement involves an apparent timing that reflects an intrinsic or inherent temporality. I note then, the distinction between timing and temporality of this intrinsic type.

This intrinsic temporality is not objective time that can be measured by a clock, although action certainly does take place in time, and it may be important in various scientific contexts that its duration can be measured. This more basic intrinsic temporality, however, can be found in bodily movement and action, and manifests itself at both the subpersonal and the personal levels of analysis. In regard to the personal level, phenomenologists distinguish objective time from lived time (e.g., Husserl 1991; Merleau-Ponty 2012; Strauss 1966). The latter is time as we experience it passing, sometimes seeming to pass slowly and sometimes rapidly. Intrinsic temporality, however, includes more than lived or phenomenological time; it includes temporal structures that shape action and experience, but might not be experienced as such.

2.2 The Intrinsic Temporality of Movement

This intrinsic temporality is expressed in Henry Head's definition of the body schema. Head noted that the body schema dynamically organizes sensory-motor feedback such that the final sensation of position is "charged with a relation to something that has happened before" (Head 1920, 606). He uses the metaphor of a taximeter, which computes and registers movement as it goes. Merleau-Ponty borrows this metaphor from Head and suggests that movement is organized according to the "time of the body, taximeter time of the corporeal schema" (1968, 173). Being "charged with a relation" to what has happened before means that the body schema incorporates past moments into the present:

At each moment in a movement, the preceding instant is not forgotten, but rather is somehow fit into the present, and, in short, the present perception consists in taking up the series of previous positions that envelop each other by relying upon the current position.

(Merleau-Ponty 2012, 141)

This kind of effect of the past on the present is a rule that applies more generally on the level of neural systems: a given neural event is normally encoded in the context of preceding events (Karmarkar & Buonomano 2007), but, as we'll see below (*Section 2.3*), not necessarily on a neat linear model.

Such retentional aspects of movement are integrated into a process that includes the ubiquitous anticipatory or prospective aspects already noted in hand–mouth coordination in infants. Empirical research has shown that anticipatory or prospective processes are pervasive in low-level sensorimotor actions. Visual tracking, for example, involves moment-to-moment anticipations concerning the trajectory of the target. Our gaze anticipates the rotation of our body when we turn a corner (Berthoz 2000, 126). Similar to the mouth's anticipation of the hand, when I reach down to the floor to grab something, my body angles in a backward direction in order to adjust its center of gravity so I don't go off balance and fall over when I bend forward (Babinski 1899). Reaching for an object involves feed-forward processes that allow last-minute adjustments if the object is moved. On standard models of motor control, for example, a copy of the efferent motor command (efference copy) is said to create anticipation for the consequences of action prior to sensory feedback, allowing for fast corrections of movement (Georgieff & Jeannerod 1998). Likewise it is said that forward control models involve an anticipatory character so that, for example, the grasp of my reaching hand tacitly anticipates the shape of the object to be grasped, and does so according to the specific intentional action involved (Jeannerod 2001; MacKay 1966; Wolpert, Ghahramani & Jordan 1995). My grasp moves in a teleological fashion, anticipating its target in specific spatial detail. In this sense, anticipation is "an essential characteristic" of motor functioning, and it serves our capacity to reorganize our actions in line with events that are yet to happen (Berthoz 2000, 25). Similar anticipations characterize the sensory aspects of perception (see Wilson & Knoblich 2005 for review). Since these prospective processes are present pervasively, even in infants, the "conclusion that [anticipatory processes] are immanent in virtually everything we think or do seems inescapable" (Haith 1993, 237).

What is inescapable, ubiquitous, and pervasive for human experience and action is not just the anticipatory aspect, but the full intrinsic temporality of the processes involved. A good model for this, as Alain Berthoz has suggested, is the Husserlian analysis of the intrinsic retentional-protentional structure of experience (Berthoz 2000, 16; Husserl 1991; Gallagher 1998). Husserl, who was influenced by William James' analysis of the specious present (which Husserl called the "living present") finds phenomenological evidence for the "retention" of the just past, and the "protention" or anticipation of that which is just about to occur, and considers these to be structural features of consciousness. That is, attending to one's own experience, one

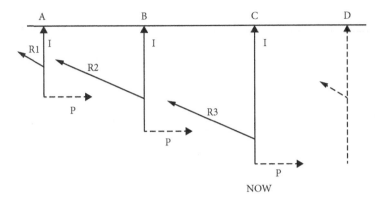

Figure 2.1 Husserl's model of time-consciousness.

always finds both an anticipatory sense of what is just about to happen, however indeterminate, and a continuing sense of the experience that one has just lived through. The general structure of this temporality, however, can also be applied to movement and to motor processes that are not conscious.

Here is a brief summary and diagram (*Figure 2.1*) of Husserl's model. Husserl's favorite example is the perception of a melody. The horizontal line ABCD represents a temporal object such as a melody of several notes. The vertical lines represent abstract momentary phases of an enduring act of consciousness. Each phase is structured by three functions:

- *primal impression* (I), which allows for the consciousness of an object (a musical note, for example) that is simultaneous with the current phase of consciousness;
- *retention* (R), which retains previous phases of consciousness and their intentional content; and
- *protention* (P), which anticipates experience which is just about to happen.

In the current "now" phase of the living present there is a retentioning (R3) of the previous phase, and this just-past phase includes its own retentioning of the prior phase. This means that there is a retentional continuum—R3(R2[R1]), and so forth—stretching back over recent (on the order of seconds) prior experience. The protentional aspect provides consciousness with an intentional sense that something more will happen. If I am listening to a favorite melody, there is some sense of what is to come, an anticipation of the notes to follow, and the best indication of this is that if someone hits the wrong note, I am surprised or disappointed. If a person fails to complete a sentence, I experience a sense of incompleteness. This kind of perceptual disappointment is based on a lack of fulfillment of protention; what happens fails to match my anticipation. A similar protentional feature is found in the phenomenon of "representational momentum" where movement or implied movement results in the extrapolation of a trajectory that goes beyond what was actually perceived (Wilson & Knoblich 2005). We end up looking at where we expect the trajectory to end, even when it stops short of that point. The content of protention is never completely determinate, however. Indeed, to the extent that the future itself is indeterminate, the content of protention may approach the most general sense of "something (without specification) has to happen next."

This model, or its broad structural features, can be extended to non-conscious motor processes as well, and is reflected in Head's description of the retentional aspect of the body schema and the anticipatory aspects of motor control. The same retentional-protentional structure can act as the organizing principle for proprioceptive and efferent processes that give rise to a phenomenal sense of movement and agency—specifically a very basic pre-reflective sense of agency.

2.3 Dynamical Timescales and the Sense of Agency

A number of theorists have characterized the subpersonal processes that would instantiate this Husserlian model by using a dynamical systems approach (Thompson 2007; van Gelder 1996; Varela 1999). On this view, action and our consciousness of action arise in a way that involves the concurrent participation of distributed regions of the brain and their sensorimotor embodiment (Varela et al. 2001). The integration of the different neuronal contributories involves a process that is understood as an integration of different scales of duration directly relevant to the protentional-retentional processes of intrinsic temporality. Francisco Varela (1999) distinguishes three relevant timescales:

(1) The elementary timescale (measured in milliseconds).
(2) The integration timescale (measured in seconds, approximating the living present).
(3) The narrative timescale (measured in durations greater than the living present).

Within the elementary timescale (of 10–100 msec), corresponding to neurophysiological processing, two successive stimuli, falling within a 30–100-msec window, for example, are perceived as simultaneous.[2] This facilitates intersensory integration across sense modalities where visual, auditory, tactile, etc. have different processing times. For example, particular token events of audition activate early sensory areas quicker than vision. Activation of primary visual cortex (V1) is usually assumed to occur 45–55 msec after stimulus; auditory input reaches the cortex in less than half the time (9–15 msec) (Clark, Fan & Hillyard 1995; Foxx & Simpson 2002; Vaughan, Ritter & Simson 1980; Vaughan & Arezzo 1988).[3] This discrepancy of timing

---

[2] E.g., two light flashes presented within a span of less than 50 msec are experienced as simultaneous; beyond a 100-msec threshold they are experienced as sequential; and between 50–100 msec "appear to move" from one spot to another. "These thresholds can be grounded in the intrinsic cellular rhythms of neuronal discharges, and in the temporal summation capacities of synaptic integration. These events fall within a range of 10 msec (e.g., the rhythms of bursting interneurons) to 100 msec (e.g., the duration of an EPSP [excitatory postsynaptic potential]/IPSP [inhibitory postsynaptic potential] sequence in a cortical pyramidal neuron) (Varela 1999, 273).

[3] Adding some complexity, Semir Zeki (2003, 215) points out that, in the visual cortex color is processed "before motion by ~80 ms [milliseconds]" and spatial location is processed before colors, "which are processed before orientations." I've suppressed what I take to be Zeki's controversial claim that, despite his not allowing for non-conscious perception, we "perceive" and are ("micro") conscious of these differences—i.e., that we are conscious of color before we are conscious of motion because of this temporal

(measured in objective time) on the elementary timescale is not experienced as such on the integrative scale. Although auditory and visual stimuli are not processed simultaneously, we experience the sound and the seen object as simultaneous due to temporal binding on the elementary scale (Pöppel 1994; Varela 1999). Accordingly, at the ballet my visual perception of the ballerina's movement is not out of sync with the music because this syncing between different temporally processed modalities happens within a window where there is no experienced succession.

At the integration scale these subpersonal processes are integrated *via* phase locking of "long-range" reciprocal connections or cell assemblies distributed across "vast [relatively speaking] and geographically separated regions of the brain" organized in dynamical networks (Varela 1999, 274; see Varela 1995; Varela et al. 2001).[4] Phenomenologically, the integration scale corresponds to the experienced living present, the level of a fully constituted cognitive operation; motorically it corresponds to a basic action; e.g., reaching, grasping, or what we called in the previous chapter, following Hornsby, basic activity.

An experiential event arises, flourishes, and subsides in the flow of consciousness in a structure that integrates experiential phases into and across cognitive acts and basic action activity. This is precisely where the retention/primal-impression/protention process does its work and forms an incompressible living present. This intrinsic temporality arises in these dynamical processes, not in the order of objective time tied to an external or internally ticking clock or a fixed integration period, but in a nonlinear manner, contingent on the integration of variable numbers of dispersed cell assemblies. Consistent with Husserl's contention that the coherence of this integrative temporal experience does not depend on a separate recollection or act of expectation, with regard to retentional-protentional processes we need not consider the narrative timescale, which starts to involve (semantic or episodic) memory, etc.

Elementary and integration scales can be plotted on linear objective clock time, as indicated by the temporal variations in milliseconds and seconds. Yet objective time doesn't capture the significance of the relations among these scales, and it does not govern consistently across them. For example, the integrative timescale of conscious experience is not equivalent to the simple composition of intervals on the elementary scale. As we saw with intersensory integration, an inter-scale (elemental to integrative) temporal compression occurs such that from the perspective of the integrative scale there is no experiential difference between an interval of 10 and 20 msec as measured on the elemental scale. Successive elemental processes falling within a 30–50-msec time frame, for example, may be experienced as simultaneous

difference in neural processing. See my discussion of "naked intentions" (*Section 3.3*) for a similar confusion.

[4] Thompson (2007, 332) summarizes: "integration happens through some form of temporal coding, in which the precise time at which individual neurons fire determines whether they participate in a given assembly. The most well-studied candidate for this kind of temporal coding is *phase synchrony*. Populations of neurons exhibit oscillatory discharges over a wide range of frequencies and can enter into precise synchrony or phase-locking over a limited period of time (a fraction of a second). A growing body of evidence suggests that phase synchrony is an indicator (perhaps a mechanism) of large-scale integration.... Animal and human studies demonstrate that specific changes in synchrony occur during arousal, sensorimotor integration, attentional selection, perception, and working memory."

(Milton & Pleydell-Pearce 2016; Ronconi & Melcher 2017; Varela et al. 1981; Wutz et al. 2014). Accordingly, between the elementary and the integrative timescale, relations are not straightforwardly linear or additive such that one can simply sum up a number of elementary time periods or put them in a specific order to get to an integrative second or an experience of that same order. Because temporal integration is dynamically dependent on activation in a number of dispersed neural assemblies, it doesn't necessarily preserve an objective linear sequence that would reflect the neural events. For example, when a stimulus of 50 msec is followed by a stimulus of 100 msec the integrated event (i.e., the combined event experienced on the integrative level) is not necessarily an additive sum of 150 msec. "Instead, the earlier stimulus interacts with the processing of the 100 msec. interval, resulting in the encoding of a distinct temporal object. Thus, temporal information is encoded in the context of the entire pattern, not as conjunctions of the component intervals" (Karmarkar & Buonomano 2007, 432). The integration occurs according to dynamical, non-linear principles.

Temporal masking is another example of non-linear processing determining the experienced temporal order of things. For example, the tonal arrangement of sounds presented in a sequence can affect the perception of that sequence. If in the sequence of sounds ABCDBA, the tones A and B are of a particular low frequency, the order of C and D will be masked. That is, you will not be able to distinguish the order of C and D. You can also vary the tones A and B, so that C will appear to come before D, or so that D will appear to come before C (Bregman & Rudnicky 1975). But it's not simply that the conscious retention of A and B determines the phenomenal order of C and D, since the later sounds of B and A are also required to get these effects. That is, the sounds that follow C and D in the objective sequential order will also determine the way C and D play out on the conscious level.[5] The subpersonal processing of these sounds will result in one experience rather than another, but the temporal experience of the tonal sequence will not necessarily match the sequence of the processing on the neuronal level (also see Dennett & Kinsbourne 1992; Gallagher 1998).

The processes that define the integration scale correspond to the experienced or living present, a temporal window of experience describable in terms of the protentional-retentional structure explicated by Husserl (Varela 1999; Thompson 2007). Whatever falls within this window counts as happening "now" for the system, and this "now," much like James' (1890) notion of the specious present, integrates

---

[5] The effect here is similar to the color *phi* phenomenon, where the color of a dot that appears later has an effect on my experience of the apparent color of the apparently moving dot. Consider, as another example, that in many cases the meaning of a word in a sentence is deferred until a phrase or the sentence is complete, so that the word itself, as it is read or sounded, motivates a certain anticipation towards the fulfillment of its meaning. The word "cases" in the previous sentence is an example. It doesn't refer to a container (e.g., cases of wine), or to grammatical cases (cases of a noun or pronoun); but it's meaning is already anticipated before that ambiguity gets resolved, and the remainder of the sentence fulfills that anticipation. If the content of the paragraph that preceded this paragraph had been about a grammatical point, then it could have biased my anticipation of the meaning of the word "cases," and clearly my subsequent primal impressions would have been different since they would not have fulfilled the prior protention. Depending on the clarity of writing (or lack thereof), such things often slow down our reading and make us go back over text to get clarification. Other examples of effects of content on experienced temporal sequence are discussed in Gallagher (1998).

some indeterminate elemental processes that are ongoing or have just happened. Varela recognized in Husserl's account a "dynamical bent" that he took as opening towards a neural dynamics that applies to the intrinsic temporality of action as well as consciousness, and which connects with enactivism by means of this emphasis on action and a dynamical coupling between brain, body, and environment. "It is this active side of perception that gives temporality its roots in living itself" (Varela 1999, 272). From the enactivist view, experience and action are

[. . .] characterized by the concurrent participation of several functionally distinct and topographically distributed regions of the brain *and their sensorimotor embodiment.* From the point of view of the neuroscientist, it is the complex task of relating and integrating these different components that is at the root of temporality. A central idea pursued here is that these various components require a frame or window of [integration] that corresponds to the duration of lived present.   (Varela 1999, 271; emphasis added)

The system dynamically parses its own activity according to this intrinsic temporal structure. Each emerging present bifurcates from the previous one determined by its initial and boundary conditions, in such a way that the preceding emergence is still present in (still has an effect on) the succeeding one as the trace of the dynamical trajectory (corresponding to, or causally constituting *retention* on the phenomenological level). The initial conditions and boundary conditions are defined by embodied constraints, including affect, and the experiential context of the action, behavior, or cognitive act. They shape the action at the global level and include the contextual circumstance of the task performed, as well as the independent modulations (i.e., new stimuli or endogenous changes in motivation) arising from the contextual setting in which the action occurs (Gallagher & Varela 2003, 123; see also Varela 1999, 283).

The point is that modulations across these different timescales are dynamically non-linear. This also shows up in cases of intentional binding that occur when subjects are asked to judge the timing of their voluntary movements and the effects of those movements (see Engbert et al. 2007; Haggard et al. 2002). Intentional binding refers to the compression in time estimation that occurs when one's intentional action is involved in movement. If A and B are two perceived events separated by one second and you are asked to estimate the temporal interval between them, you are likely to estimate about one second. If, however, A is your action and B is the worldly effect of that action, you are likely to estimate something significantly less than a second. This intentional binding effect, where we experience two events as temporally closer than they actually are, correlates to, and has been proposed as a measure of the pre-reflective sense of agency that is tied to efferent motor-control processes.

Farrer et al. (2013) have shown that the sense of agency for a particular action depends on its effect falling within a specific time window and that this varies by degree. Thus subjects have a full sense of agency where delays between action and effect are less than 334 msec; but once the delay approaches a window that overlaps with the integration scale, subjects experience lesser degrees of the sense of agency (for delays between 334 and 707 msec) or a loss of the sense of agency (for delays beyond 707 msec). In their experiments Farrer et al. (2013) varied either internal (pre-motor) cues or external environmental cues and concluded that "the sense of agency . . . depends [in part] on a time window within which internal and external agency cues are integrated, and that only external agency cues that are time-locked to action onset are integrated with internal agency cues" (2013, 1439). Because of such embodied and environmental factors, the integrating neural synchronization is dynamically unstable; it constantly and successively gives rise to new assemblies, such transformations defining the trajectories of the system.

That there is some ambiguity attached to the sense of agency is consistent with the idea that the temporal window of the integration scale is flexible (0.5–3 seconds) and that the integration process depends on these embodied and environmental factors which include *context* (which may involve physical environmental aspects, but also meaning—the environment as the agent perceives it), as well as factors of bodily affect that may include hunger, fatigue, general physical condition, age of subject, and so on (see *Chapter 1*; Gallagher and Bower 2014). Protention, in this respect, is closely connected with affect and action. If the experiencing subject is always characterized by some affective disposition, that disposition will modulate anticipatory processes of perception and action. This idea finds application when considering certain pathologies that may involve the loss of one's sense of agency. Thus, in the case of schizophrenia, where there are modulations in affect, there is also in some cases a disruption in the sense of agency that may be tied to a problem involving anticipatory experience (Gallagher 2000a & b; 2005a; Gallagher & Varela 2003). One might also think of anomalies related to the experience of time in subjects with major depression (Gallagher 2012a).

2.4 Why Action and Experience Are Enactive all the Way Down

The enactivist view holds that perception and cognition are action oriented; that is, they are characterized in most cases by a structural coupling between the agentive body and the environment, which generates action-oriented meaning (e.g., Varela, Thompson, & Rosch 1991; Noë 2004; Di Paolo 2009). When, for example, I perceive something, I perceive it as actionable. That is, I perceive it as something *I can* reach, or not; something *I can* pick up, or not; something *I can* hammer with, or not, and so forth. If I perceive an event rather than an artifact, I perceive it as something I can intervene in, or not. Such affordances (Gibson 1977; 1979) for potential actions (even if I am not planning to take action) shape the way that I actually perceive the world. One can find the roots of this kind of approach not only in the pragmatists,[6] but also in phenomenologists like Husserl, Heidegger, and Merleau-Ponty.[7]

---

[6] John Dewey, for example, holds that in perception "we find that we begin not with a sensory stimulus, but with a sensori-motor coordination, the optical-ocular, and that in a certain sense it is the movement which is primary, and the sensation which is secondary, the movement of body, head and eye muscles determining the quality of what is experienced" (1896, 358). Likewise, George Herbert Mead suggested that what is present in perception is not a copy of the perceived, but "the readiness to grasp" what is seen (1938, 103)—"the readiness of the organism to act toward [objects].... We see the objects as we will handle them.... We are only 'conscious of' that in the perceptual world which suggests confirmation, direct or indirect, in fulfilled manipulation" (ibid. 104–5).

[7] Merleau-Ponty (2012) is most often cited in this regard, but Merleau-Ponty himself points us back to Husserl's analysis of the "I can" in *Ideen II* (Husserl 1989), and to his analysis of the correlation between

Consistent with this enactivist view evidence presented in *Section 2.2* supports the idea that action shares the same intrinsic temporal structure as consciousness and perception, and more generally, cognition. Moreover, as I now want to argue, if perception and cognition are enactive, then at a minimum, their intrinsic temporal structure should be such that it allows for that enactive character. We can start to see this by considering an important revision that Husserl himself introduced into his analysis of the temporal structure of consciousness.

In Husserl's *Bernau Manuscripts*, written around 1917–18, we find a revision of his original account of the temporal structure of experience. In these texts he starts to think of the primal impression (or what he calls here the "primal presentation" or "primal perception"), not as the origin and "unmodifiable" point of departure, as he did in earlier lectures (Husserl 1991, 67), but as the result of the interplay between, or as the "boundary" between retention and protention (Husserl 2001, 4). In short, whereas retention and protention in the early texts were defined by taking primal impression as a starting point, Husserl argues in his later texts that the primal impression must be considered the point of intersection between the retentional and protentional tendencies that make up living present. More precisely, the point of departure for his analysis, rather than being the primal impression (or primal presentation), is the current, yet-to-be fulfilled protentional anticipation:

First there is an empty expectation, and then there is the point of the primary perception, itself an intentional experience. But the primary presentation comes to be in the flow only by occurring as the fulfillment of contents relative to the preceding empty intentions, thereby changing itself into primal presenting perception.   (Husserl 2001, 4)[8]

In short, the primal impression is conceived as the fulfillment of a previous protention; the now is constituted by way of a protentional fulfillment (Husserl 2001, 4, 14). Occasionally Husserl even describes the matter in a way that doesn't mention the primal impression at all:

Each constituting full phase is the retention of a fulfilled protention, which is the horizon boundary of an unfulfilled and for its part continuously mediated protention.   (Husserl 2001, 8)

The notion of an isolated primal impression seems to be an abstraction and not something that exists in itself. As Klaus Held (1966, 19) puts it, "from a phenomenological perspective, there is no such thing as an infinitely short momentary perception"—that is, experientially there is no such thing as an isolated primal impression. On the other hand, however, one could argue that there must be something like a limit or division between retention and protention—aspects which do characterize our experience, but which need to be differentiated.

Here I want to exploit the license that Husserl himself seems to give us for shifting around some terminology. It will be helpful to have a terminology that is relatively neutral between discussions of consciousness and action. The terms "retention" and "protention" already work well in this regard. Instead of the term "primal

---

kinesthetic activation and perception (1973; see Gallagher 2017a; Gallagher & Zahavi 2012; Zahavi 1994 for further discussion).

[8] Translations from the *Bernau Manuscripts* are by Dan Zahavi. See Gallagher and Zahavi (2014).

impression" (or "primal presentation") I'll use the term *"primal enaction."* As will become apparent, this is consistent with (and perhaps anticipating) what I want to say—namely, that intrinsic temporality is enactive even in its most basic aspects. "Primal enaction" captures the idea that even in what is seemingly its most basic aspect, consciousness is not merely a passive impression. In the case of action, "primal enaction" is meant to signify a process that begins as the very basic activity involved in the initial moment of any particular action, and continues as the ongoing point of action actuality. Primal enaction, however, is something of an abstraction, and really nothing on its own.

Husserl is consistent in conceiving of the experienced now as more than a mere point. He doesn't equate the experiencing or the experienced now with primal enaction. Any momentary phase of consciousness, which itself is an abstraction, is composed of protention-primal enaction-retention. Primal enaction is not itself a momentary phase of consciousness—it's part of the structure of any momentary phase. In that sense it is something like an abstraction within an abstraction—it's an abstract piece of the structure of an abstract piece (momentary phase) of consciousness that has been lifted out of its flow. It is a part of the structure centered on the knife-edge now point of the temporal object.

As we saw in the previous section, the protention-primal enaction-retention model applies to action and non-conscious motor processes, as well as it does to consciousness. Both human experience and human action are characterized by a ubiquitous intrinsic temporality. In this regard, when we look at action we can say that at any one moment the body is in some precise posture—as it might be captured by a snapshot, for example. That momentary posture, however, is a complete abstraction from the movement since in each case the body is not posturing from moment to moment, but is constantly on the way, in the flow of the movement such that the abstract postural moment only has meaning as part of that process. One could argue that *objectively speaking*, at any moment the body actually is in a specific posture. But if that postural moment (that snapshot of primary enaction) is anything, it is already the movement beginning or underway, shaped by the anticipated trajectory of where the action is heading. Furthermore, we can define that abstract postural moment only when it is already accomplished—but that means, only in retention, and as an end point of what had been a movement characterized primarily by anticipation.

Action is like consciousness in that it has a flow structure and an intentional direction. Consciousness is intentionally directed in such a way that when I am hearing the current note of a melody I'm already moving beyond it, and such protentional/anticipatory moving beyond is already a leaving behind in retention. What we have as the basic datum of experience is a process, through which the primal enaction is already collapsing into the retentional stream even as it is directed forward in protention. Hearing a melody (or even a single note in some context—and there is always a context) never involves hearing a currently sounded note (or part of a note), *and then* moving beyond it; rather, the "and then" is already effected, already implicit in the experience.

One way to express this, for action or for consciousness, is to say that talk of any one of the three aspects of retention, primal enaction, or protention in isolation runs into an abstraction. Our experience of the present is always dynamic and it is so because it is always structured by protention-primal enaction-retention. Pre-reflectively, consciousness and action have this structure. There is no primary enaction that can be taken as a knife-edge or snapshot phenomenon *simpliciter*; rather, as Husserl suggests, primal enaction is already fulfilling (or failing to fulfill) protentions that have already been retained, and in doing so is already informing the current protentional process. The living present is already a structured, dynamically organized present.

The proposal is not that we should eliminate the concept of primal enaction. The point is rather that we should abandon the idea that primal enaction is a direct, straight, and simple apprehension of some now-point of a stimulus, or simple beginning point of some action, unaffected by retention and protention. To talk of primal enaction as intuiting the current moment without accounting for the effects of retention and protention that are already at work, shaping primal enaction, is to talk of an abstraction. If we say that primal enaction is part of the structure of the living present—that's true, but it's not enough. We also have to say that the primal enaction is itself structured by its very dynamic participation in its relations to retention and protention (and vice versa). This is consistent with Husserl's indication that "it pertains to the essence of conscious life to contain an intentional intertwining, motivation and mutual implication by meaning..." (1977, 26).[9]

The processes of protention, primal enaction, and retention form an *enactive* structure in the sense that a certain anticipatory aspect (already shaped by what has just gone before) is already complicating the immediacy of the present. Action is never without a trajectory. Likewise, consciousness, as a self-organizing or self-constituting flow, is never a mere passive reception of the present. Action and consciousness constitute meaning in the shadow of what has just been experienced, and in the light of what they anticipate.

To be even more explicit on this point, what primal enaction is, and how it relates to retention and protention, are not independent of the intentional nature of consciousness or action. As in the case of action, the intrinsic temporality of experience is pragmatically directed towards the meaningful possibilities the agent sees in the world. This accommodates Husserl's conception of embodied experience as an anticipatory "I can" – action is oriented towards possibilities, drawing on prior experience and current state. As Husserl suggests, "every living is living towards (*Entgegenleben*)" (1991, 313). This anticipatory intentionality is not an apprehension of an absence (*Entgegenwärtigung*), although it is directed toward the not yet; it is rather an apprehension of the possibilities or the affordances in the present, of what some object, artifact, or event *can be* for my experience, possibilities that will be fulfilled or not fulfilled as perception trails off in retention.

The important question is not whether any one element of this temporal structure has priority. Primal enaction, retention, and protention are not elements that simply add themselves to each other. They are rather in a genetic relation; they have a self-constituting effect on each other. Moreover, together they constitute the possibility of

---

[9] Husserl goes on to say that it does so "in a way which in its form and principle has no analogue at all in the physical" (1977, p. 26). This is not something we need to adopt here; for further discussion see Thompson (2007, 356).

an enactive engagement with the experienced world. Just as I perceive the hammer as affording the possibility of grasping it, or in a different circumstance, as affording the possibility of propping open my window, I likewise perceive the melody as affording the possibility of dancing or of sitting in peaceful enjoyment, etc. Such action-oriented perceptions reflect the temporality of affordances and enactive engagements. Nothing is an affordance for my enactive engagement if it is presented to me passively in a knife-edge present; that is, nothing would be afforded if there were only a series of primal enactions, one after the other, without protentional anticipation, since I cannot enactively engage with the world if the world is not experienced as a set of possibilities, which, by definition, involves the not-yet. Likewise, if there were only retentions, everything I experience would already have just happened; we would be pure witnesses without the potential to engage. If there were only protentions, there would only be unfulfilled promises of engagement. Meaning itself would dissipate under any of these conditions.

Thus, the enactive character goes all the way down, into the very structure of the intrinsic temporality of experience and action. Action and experience have an enactive character, not only in regard to intention or intentionality, but also in their most basic self-constituting, self-organizing aspects, in their temporal micro-structure.

2.5 Intentional Action and the Narrative Scale

If action processes are enactive all the way down, they are also enactive all the way up, into the narrative timescale. Narratives are typically about actions; they reflect meaning tied to action goals and the significance of such goals to the agent. Actions take time to unfold, and narratives typically map out this unfolding in a temporal structure of beginning-middle-end.

Narratives frame this temporality of action within a twofold temporal structure. First, there is an "external" temporality that defines the narrator's temporal relation to the events portrayed in the narrative. We can think of this external temporality in terms of what John McTaggart Ellis McTaggart (1908) called the A-series, which is a perspectival or relative time frame. That is, from the narrator's current perspective (the present), the narrated events happen either in the past, the present, or the future. Even if this relation is left unspecified ("Once upon a time . . . ") it is usually open to specification that these events happened in the past, or will happen in the future, relative to the narrator's present. In the case of fictional events, of course, the events may never have happened and never will happen, yet they are still specified as having a place in time relative to the narrator.

Second, there is a temporality that is "internal" to the narrative itself, a serial order in which one event follows another. This internal time frame contributes to the composition of narrative structure. Paul Ricoeur (1992) notes the dialectic of "discordance" and "concordance" in the process of narrative. In some way each event in the narrative is something new and different (discordance); yet in another way each event is part of a series (concordance), determined by what came before and constraining what is to come. Configurations of concordance and discordance compose the basic structure of plot in stories. Even if there is no plot, however, there is always a serial order in the narrative.[10] One can think of this internal order of narrative as what McTaggart (1908) defines as the B-series, in which one event follows another. This serial order does not depend on when (in the A-series) these events happened or will happen (past or future).

Clearly, however, the meaning of an action involves more than its location in a narratival A-series or B-series, and is not determined by objective measures of how long it takes, as measured by the clock. For example, person A is 5 feet away from a door; person B is 15 feet away. There comes a knock on the door. Person A strolls over to the door to answer it; person B dashes to the door arriving at the same time as A. In one respect A and B's actions are equivalent actions; both of them answered the knock. Both actions took exactly the same amount of time. I can see, however, that B's action was hurried in a way that A's was not. The kinematic properties of this movement convey meaning (see Berthoz 2000, 137); they define the intentional nature of the action at very basic levels of motor control, but in a way that scales up to intentions and motivations (if, for example, B is already enthusiastic to greet an expected friend). But the hurriedness, and its meaning (e.g., enthusiasm) are not simply a matter of covering more ground in less time. What the meaning is depends on many other circumstances to which I, as an observer, may or may not have access: not only how motivated B is by what she already knows, but also by what has just been happening, by her specific expectation of who is knocking, by the present circumstances that either enable her or hinder her from reaching the door, including her own physical position and motor capacity, and by her intention to reach the door as fast as possible. These factors are ordered in the intrinsic temporality of the action, and they manifest themselves in that action as meaningful.

An occurrent action is, *per se*, ongoing towards the future, specifically towards its future end, and this feature is not reducible to the fact that this action requires more time to be complete. If we treat action merely as a physical event stretched out and confined to objective time, we are naturally led to questions about causality (rather than motivation or intention). Causality is typically defined in the framework of objective time. A cause always precedes its effect; an effect always follows its cause. Billiard ball *A* hits billiard ball *B* and causes it to move. One can try to push this kind of causal account into the psychological domain. What causes me to perform this particular action? To answer this question we naturally look to something that precedes the action. Perhaps my physical (brain) states or some social circumstances cause me to act the way I do (accordingly we can easily arrive at some version of physical or social determinism). Alternatively, on a mental causation view, I have a certain belief and a desire that "cause" me to act the way I do. These are often the terms of the traditional discussion. Such accounts fall short, however, if we think of them in terms of billiard-ball causality. Corris and Chemero, citing the work of van Orden, Hollis, and Wallot (2012), point out that there is something of a physics problem involved in thinking that the brain causes a bodily action: "the amount of energy in the firing of neurons is simply insufficient to lift a 10 kilogram leg off the

---

[10] This does not rule out such things as temporal "anachronies" (flash-forwards and flash-backs) (Genette 1980, 36) but actually makes them possible.

ground" (Corris & Chemero 2019, fn.7). van Orden et al. argue for a more dynamical set of reciprocal relations between body and brain in an account involving complex variables in timescale, constraint, synergy, and criticality. Likewise, a belief doesn't have causal power in the same way a moving ball does. My belief that it will rain today doesn't cause me to carry an umbrella. To get an account that actually works we need to reframe the question in dynamical terms that include the intrinsic temporality of action. It is not something in the past that causes or determines my action; rather, it is some possibility of the future, some affordance or goal that draws me out of my past and present circumstances and allows me to transcend, and perhaps to change, all such determinations.

Narratives map out what Jerome Bruner (1986) calls the "landscape of action." It's clear that actions do have a structure that gets reflected in narrative. Action structure includes "initiation toward the goal, progression with fast rhythmic timing of corrective maneuvers keeping the movement on track, and final climactic contact with its object, as a unit of meaning-making that tests and confirms a knowledge of expectations" (Delafield-Butt & Trevarthen 2015, 3). Although Delafield-Butt and Trevarthen suggest that this is already a narrative structure, there are good reasons to think that the structure of narrative derives from the structure of action, and not vice versa.[11] As Ricoeur puts it, "temporal structures [of action] evoke narration.... [T]here is no structural analysis of narrative that does not borrow from an explicit or implicit phenomenology of 'doing something'" (1984, 47, 56). On this view, embodied actions reflect a pre-narrative, albeit narrative-ready, structure (Kerby 1993; Hutto 2006).

Richard Menary captures this precisely: "[o]ur embodied experiences are ready to be exploited in a narrative of those experiences. Narrative arises from a sequence of bodily experiences, perceptions and actions in a quite natural manner" (2008, 75). At the same time, narratives do not simply report sequences of events or actions. Catriona Mackenzie suggests, that by "explaining the causal connections between the events or actions they recount, they give shape and coherence to our lives, or at least to the various sequences that make up our lives..." (2007, 268–9). This does not mean that in every case our intentional significant actions are reflectively guided by our narrative conception of who we are, or are implicitly structured by narrative (see, e.g., Schechtman 1996; 2011). Menary (2008) cautions us about taking this too far. He wants to safeguard the idea that most of our actions remain pre-reflective skillful accomplishments that do not require reflective guidance. We should resist reading narrative structure back into pre-narrative action. The extreme version of this view would hold that narratives implicitly impose structure on actions, and bestow coherency and meaning where there was none. Pre-narrative actions are neither incoherent nor meaningless to begin with, and do not require the imposition of narrative structure to make them coherent and meaningful. At the same time narratives do add meaning. What gives shape and coherence to our lives are not

---

[11] I note here that there is a broad debate in narrative theory about the issue of whether action already has an intrinsic narrative structure with defenders of this view (e.g., Bruner 1990; Halliday 1978; MacIntyre 1984) lining up on one side, and opponents (e.g., Mink 1970; Ricoeur 1984; Gallagher and Hutto 2019) lining up on the other.

only the causal connections in the landscape of action, but also motivational, normative, and intentional connections in the "space of reasons" (Sellars 1956).

We know, at least from the time Socrates explained it (in Plato's *Phaedo*), that it is not enough, or even relevant, to provide an account of one's actions in terms of strictly causal motor control mechanisms if one is asked "Why" one acted thus and so. "Why did you poison the people in that house?" The answer is not "Because I moved my arm up and down on the water pump." The question calls for an answer, not in terms of motor control or internal mechanisms, but in terms of a narrative. "I didn't know the water was poisoned. I was walking past the well and was asked to help pump by someone who said this was a way to help the people who lived there." Each part of the account could be fleshed out further to extend the narrative. Such an account is framed in terms of intentions and motivations that are not reducible to objective temporal determinates. Kant's antinomy concerning freedom and determinism is deflated once we adopt the perspective of intrinsic temporality. The practical analysis of possibilities as they are outlined in the intrinsic temporality of action opens the door to the possibility of understanding autonomy as measurable in relational terms involving the number, range, and temporal proximity, and the quality (i.e., salience and affective allure) of affordances (see *Section 8.4*).

Most of our actions are pre-reflective skillful accomplishments that do not require reflective guidance and are not necessarily or primarily transcribed by narratives. Yet intentional action often does involve the formation of prior intentions that may involve conscious and thoughtful deliberations and planning about what to do and what goals to aim at. In these prospective respects intentional action also involves narrative practices through which we can make sense of possible actions in terms of reasons (Velleman 2006). In deciding to purchase a new car next spring, I may imagine myself driving around in a certain model; I may imagine what my wife will say about my plan; I may have to think about the effect of my driving behavior on the environment, etc. Intentions are future-directed; they are about goals and possibilities. I can talk or write about my future goals, or about the affordances I encounter; and I can also put into narrative form what I remember about the goals that I have attained or failed to attain. Such reflective and narrative practices can lead to what Ian Hacking (1995a) calls "looping effects," or what one could think of as an intertwining of living and telling. Narratives, our own or more general cultural narratives reflecting norms and customs, may infect our actions through more implicit means.[12]

My action is always and already situated in a particular set of circumstances, and these circumstances are shaped by what has gone before, which includes my own action up to this point, and in addition, in the many cases of looping effects, my own or a set of cultural narratives. My actions, what I *can* do, what my possibilities are, are shaped by those circumstances and the effects of my own narrative and normative understanding of what is possible. Accordingly, at the same stroke, my action incorporates the situation that has been shaped by *past* actions, and by the projected

---

[12] This may start very early. I'll come back to this developmental issue in *Chapter 7*.

future toward which it is moving, in the *present* circumstances that can both limit and enable it. This is the intrinsic temporal structure of action that is not captured by objective time, but is shaped in part by the fact that action is dynamically embodied and situated. Initial and boundary conditions are determined not simply by anatomical and neural parameters but also by what, in *Chapter 1*, I called context or circumstance, which includes agent-related aspects (like intention, motivation, skill, knowledge—but also things like fatigue, physical condition, processes associated with age, emotional experience, starting posture, etc.) and world-related aspects (like facts about objects and physical arrangements, and people in the action environment). This intrinsic temporality is reflected at the macro or narrative scale where actions are always existentially situated in a world of meaning, and intentions are always future-oriented towards possibilities that transcend present circumstances.

This chapter and the previous one have been preliminary in regard to action and preparatory in regard to a continued investigation of action of a special sort—interaction. In this chapter we've looked at issues pertaining to the temporality of action. The intrinsic temporality of action can be captured in the dynamic model of the retentional-protentional structure developed by Husserl, which characterizes not only the enactive nature of experience, but also the integration of body schematic activity in actions, expressed (on the integrative scale) in our first-order (pre-reflective) conscious experience of action and the sense of agency. Action is characterized by an intrinsic temporal structure on the micro scale of motor control (on elemental and integrative timescales), and this intrinsic temporality is reflected and re-framed on the narrative timescale, which includes the realm of prior intention formation and retrospective evaluations, and maps out both the landscape of actions and the space of reasons. To develop this into a conception of autonomy, however, we will need to navigate through a wide-ranging set of considerations concerning social interaction.

3

Action, Intention, and the Sense of Agency

Whatever our first action might be, it almost certainly emerges out of our early interactions with others. Moreover, to the extent that we learn to act in specific ways, and that our actions aim at some goal, we learn to act in contexts of interaction, and we learn from others what counts as possible and preferred goals. We don't act or learn to act first, and only then enter into interactions. Rather, social dimensions are built into action from the very start. Accordingly, interaction has a primacy both when it comes to understanding others and in regard to our own actions. I'll present evidence in support of this idea in this chapter.

Philosophical accounts of action often ignore the interactional or social aspects of action. Such accounts are characterized by methodological individualism. That is, the focus tends to be on processes within the individual that lead to or follow from action: intention formation, the sense of agency, motor-control mechanisms, or free will understood as characteristic of the individual person. It is undeniable that some conception of an individual self has to enter into the analysis of action, but I will argue that the self in the "landscape of action" (Bruner 1986) always needs to be understood as located as well in what we might call the landscape of interaction. This is reflected not only in narratives and communicative practices, but also in the actual doings that we call actions.

Both reflective introspection and neuroscientific accounts of the self abstract from or ignore the situated agent as she is normally embedded in contextualized social situations, and this can lead to surprising and seemingly counter-intuitive results. Famously, when David Hume (1739) looks closely and introspectively within his own individual theater of experience, without regard for action or how we engage with others, he finds nothing that could count as a self. And more recently, when Thomas Metzinger (2004) explores the workings of the individual brain, substituting the tools of neuroscience for introspection, he concludes that "no such things as selves exist in the world: Nobody ever *was* or *had* a self" (p. 1). At best we find a "self-model"—a phenomenal experience constituted in neural representations. In this model, action is treated in terms of motor control, and the social is reducible to certain brain processes—notably, simulation processes that, in principle, could be instantiated in a disembodied brain in a vat (2004, 363). Likewise, when Galen Strawson (1997; 2009) sets agency and social relations aside in his account of the self, he ends up equating the self with a momentary abstract existence, seemingly without memory or possibilities.

In the first part of this chapter I focus on the sense of self-agency. I show two things: first, that the phenomenology of the sense of agency is both complex and ambiguous. By looking at some recent studies on the experience of self-agency we can see that this experience is complex. I'll argue that although there surely is some degree of ambiguity in the conceptual analysis of this experience, perhaps because many of the theoretical and empirical studies cut across disciplinary lines, there is also a genuine ambiguity in the experience of self-agency itself. Second, most studies of the sense of agency fail to take into consideration the social dimension. This social dimension accounts for some of the ambiguity.

3.1 Initial Complexities in the Sense of Agency

I start with the following question: What is action if it is something more than bodily movement? My answer is that action, which is more than bodily movement and which scales up to more than a set of causal processes, is characterized by three elements or aspects beyond the movement itself: intention, a sense of agency, and meaning which generally goes beyond the agent's intention. Action, in this sense, cannot be unintentional, although there can be unintentional consequences to actions. I'll argue that these aspects are involved in most (although not all) actions, and are, despite their close relation to one another, irreducible to one another, and irreducible to purely causal or mechanical or neural processes.

Ordinarily, in everyday experience, when I engage in action I have a sense of agency for that action. How is that sense or experience of agency generated? It turns out that there are a number of things that can contribute to this experience. In every case, some, but not necessarily all of these things, are integrated into the experience of agency. I'll start with what seems most basic.

3.1.1 Motor-control processes

We can start with the idea that action, whether relatively direct and simple (as when I reach and pick up a glass to take a drink), or indirect and complex (as when I author a book, or lead an army to war), whether locomotive, instrumental, or communicative, usually involves intentional bodily movement of some sort. Not always, since, arguably, there are exceptions. If we consider thinking to be an action, I can sit very still and, without moving, multiply four times seven "in my head." I may be able to do this quicker, however, if I'm allowed to gesture with my hands (see Goldin-Meadow et al. 2001). A person with Locked In Syndrome, incapable of bodily movement, may, with the help of a brain–computer interface, control a cursor on a computer screen just by thinking. Usually, however, even thinking, as a form of action, involves movement—sometimes speech and gesture, sometimes assuming a specific bodily posture, sometimes wrinkling one's brow, making facial expressions, or nodding one's head. Such movements may contribute to the accomplishment of thought, as has been shown with gesture (Goldin-Meadow 1999; Gallagher 2005a).

If we think of the sense of agency as the experience that I am the one who is generating and/or controlling my action, then we can distinguish the sense of agency from the sense of ownership. The sense of ownership, or what phenomenologists call the sense of mineness, applies to the most basic and pre-intentional aspects of action (aspects such as movement and experience), and then scales up to apply immediately to action itself. Accordingly, I can say that this is *my* movement ("I am the one moving"), or this is *my* experience, just as well as I can say that this is *my* action or *my* thinking, and so forth. When my body moves, for example, I have a proprioceptive/ kinesthetic experience of that movement, and I can easily sense that it is my body moving; this is the case with either voluntary or involuntary movement (Gallagher 2000a). In the case of voluntary movement or intentional action the sense of agency and the sense of ownership cannot be easily distinguished, and in fact they tend to reinforce each other. In the case of involuntary movement, however, they can be dissociated since for involuntary movement a sense of agency is missing, but the sense of ownership is still involved. If somebody pushes me, for example, I still have the sense that I am the one moving, even if I did not cause the initial movement or have immediate control of it. Sense of agency and sense of ownership also depend on distinguishable neural systems and can be manipulated independently of each other (Tsakiris, Haggard, & Longo 2010).

In terms of phenomenology, sense of agency and sense of ownership, as we are defining them here, are pre-reflective, which means that they neither are equivalent to nor depend on the agent taking an introspective reflective attitude. Nor do they require that the agent engage in an explicit perceptual monitoring of bodily movements. Just as I do not usually attend to the motor details of my own bodily movements as I am engaged in action, my sense of agency, which may involve an experience of control over my movement, is not normally something that I attend to or something of which I am explicitly aware. In this respect sense of agency and sense of ownership, as pre-reflective, are phenomenologically recessive.

Action as self-generated physical movement involves motor-control processes. These include efferent brain processes involved in issuing a motor command. Let's think again about involuntary movement. In the case of involuntary movement there is a sense of ownership for the initial movement but no sense of agency. I feel it to be *my* movement, in the sense that my body is moving; but I do not feel that I am causing the movement. Awareness of my voluntary or involuntary movement comes from reafferent sensory feedback (visual and proprioceptive/kinesthetic information that tells me that I'm moving). The "proprio" in proprioception is just that self-specific aspect of the process. Thus, in both involuntary and voluntary movement the sense of ownership is generated by these sensory-feedback processes. In the case of involuntary movement, however, there are no initial motor commands (no efferent signals) issued to generate the initial movement. Accordingly, one hypothesis is that in the case of voluntary movement a basic, pre-reflective sense of agency is generated by efferent signals. Tsakiris and Haggard (2005) review empirical evidence to support this division of labor. Sensory-suppression experiments suggest that the sense of agency arises at an early efferent stage in the initiation of action and that awareness of the initiation of my own action depends on pre-motor processes which precede actual bodily movement (Tsakiris & Haggard 2003). Experiments with subjects who lack proprioception but still experience a sense of effort reinforce this conclusion (Lafargue, Paillard, Lamarre, & Sirigu 2003; see Marcel 2003). As Tsakiris and Haggard put it,

[. . .] the sense of agency involves a strong *efferent* component, because actions are centrally generated. The sense of ownership involves a strong *afferent* component, because the content of body awareness originates mostly by the plurality of multisensory peripheral signals. We do not normally experience the efferent and afferent components separately. Instead, we have a general awareness of our body that involves both components.

(Tsakiris and Haggard 2005, 387)

Indeed, to this last point, they also suggest that efferent processes underlying the sense of agency modulate sensory feedback resulting from movement, supporting the idea that the sense of agency and sense of ownership are closely integrated in voluntary action. The pre-reflective sense of agency arises not simply when I initiate an action; rather, as I continue to control my action, continuing efferent signals, and the afferent feedback that I get from my movement, contribute to an ongoing sense of agency, which may include a sense of effort.

Also note that to the extent that I am aware of my action I tend to be aware of *what* I am doing rather than the details of *how* I am doing it; e.g., what muscles I am using. Even my awareness of what I am doing is struck at the most pragmatic level of description, or at the level of what we called, in *Chapter 1*, the highest realized affordance (e.g., "I'm getting a drink") rather than at a level of motor-control mechanisms. That is, the motor-control aspects of the sense of agency (and the sense of ownership) tend to be phenomenologically recessive because the phenomenal experience of my action already involves an intentional aspect, and that's what occupies my attention. Indeed, whatever I am trying to accomplish in the way of basic movements (e.g., moving out of the way, walking to open the door, reaching for a drink)—that is, my intention—informs my body-schematic (motor-control) processes, which are intentional just because they are constrained by what I am trying to do. We'll return to this idea of motor intentionality shortly.

3.1.2 *Intentional aspects in the sense of agency*

Both phenomenological reflection and brain-imaging experiments suggest that the whole story about the sense of agency cannot be told in terms of efferent processes, even reinforced by reafferent signals. The intentional aspects, and the meaning of what I am trying to do (my aim, goal, or intention), and what I actually accomplish in the world, enter into my sense of agency. Several experiments (e.g., Chaminade & Decety 2002; Farrer & Frith 2002) help to distinguish between the purely motor-control contributories to the sense that I am moving my body, and the most immediate and perceptually based intentional aspects of action; i.e., the sense that I am having an effect on my immediate environment. These experiments, however, already introduce a certain theoretical ambiguity, since they fail to make explicit the difference between motor-control aspects and intentional aspects.

For example, in Farrer and Frith (2002), an fMRI experiment designed to find the neural correlates of the sense of agency, subjects are asked to manipulate a joystick to drive a colored circle moving on a computer screen to specific locations on the screen. In some instances the subject causes this movement and in others the experimenter or computer does. The subject is asked to discriminate self-agency and other-agency. Farrer and Frith begin with the distinction between sense of agency and sense of ownership in motor-control terms of efferent and afferent processes, but in the experimental design they associate sense of agency with the intentional aspect of action; i.e., whether the agent is having some kind of effect with respect to the goal or intentional task—in this case, whether the agent is controlling something on the computer screen. Accordingly, their claim is that the sense of ownership (the sense that it is "my hand moving the joystick") remains constant while the sense of agency ("I'm manipulating the circle on the computer screen") changes. When subjects feel that they are not controlling the events on the screen, there is activation in the right inferior parietal cortex and supposedly no sense of agency for the intentional aspect of the action. When the subject does have a sense of agency for what happens on the screen, the anterior insula is activated bilaterally.

Although Farrer and Frith clearly think of the sense of agency as something tied to the intentional aspect of action and not to mere bodily movement or motor control, when it comes to *explaining why* the anterior insula should be involved in generating the sense of agency, they switch back to their original characterization and frame the explanation in terms of motor control and bodily movement.

Why should the parietal lobe have a special role in attributing actions to others while the anterior insula is concerned with attributing actions to the self? The sense of agency (i.e., being aware of causing an action) occurs in the context of a body moving in time and space...[and] critically depends upon the experience of such a body. There is evidence that...the anterior insula, in interaction with limbic structures, is also involved in the representation of body schema [important for motor control]. (Farrer and Frith 2002, 601–2)

More specifically they point to integrative processes in the anterior insula that involve aspects of both efference and afference.

In particular there will be a correspondence between three kinds of signal: somatosensory signals directly consequent upon our movements, visual and auditory signals that may result indirectly from our movements, and last, the corollary discharge [efferent signal] associated with motor commands that generated the movements. A close correspondence between all these signals helps to give us a sense of agency. (Farrer and Frith 2002, 602)

Likewise, in a separate study, Farrer et al. (2003) have the same goal of discovering the neural correlates of the sense of agency. In this experiment subjects provide a report on their experience; however, all questions about agency are focused on bodily movement rather than intentional aspect. In fact, subjects were not given an intentional task to carry out other than making random movements using a joystick, and the focus of their attention was directed towards a virtual (computer image) hand that either did or did not represent their own hand movements, although at varying degrees of rotation relative to true position of the subject's hand. That is, they moved their own hand, but saw a virtual hand projected on screen at veridical or non-veridical angles to their own hand; the virtual hand was either under their control, or not. Subjects were asked about their experience of agency for control of the virtual hand movements. The less the subject felt in control, the higher the level of activation in the right inferior parietal cortex, consistent with Farrer and Frith (2002). The more the subject felt in control, the higher the level of activation in the right *posterior* insula. This result is in contrast with the previous study where sense of agency was associated with activation of the right *anterior* insula. Referencing this difference, Farrer et al. state: "We have no explanation as to why the localization of the activated areas differ in these studies, except that we know that these two regions are densely and reciprocally connected" (2003, 331). One clear explanation, however, is that the shift of focus from the intentional aspect (accomplishing a task in Farrer and Frith) to simple control of bodily movement (in Farrer et al.) changes the aspect of the sense of agency that is being studied. Accordingly, to make sense of these experiments it would help to clearly distinguish between the intentional aspect and the motor aspect of agency, and to say that there are at least these two contributories to the sense of agency (Farrer et al. 2013 do make a clear distinction in this regard).

What we learn from these experiments supports a significant phenomenological point; namely, that even the pre-reflective sense of agency is complex, deriving in part from motor-control processes and in part from a perception of what I am accomplishing by my action (the intentional aspect). Normally these two aspects are tightly integrated. If, for some reason, I lose motor control over my movements, however, I would likely lose my sense of agency (specifically, my sense of control). In a slightly different way, if I start to feel that my actions are not having the intended effect in the world, my sense of agency (specifically, my sense of efficacy) would be diminished.[1] As we'll see, however, this still does not give us the full picture of the sense of agency.

3.2 Intention Formation and Attribution

3.2.1 Intentions

Over and above the sensory-motor processes that involve motor control, and the perceptual processes that allow us to monitor the intentional aspects of our actions, there are higher-order cognitive components involving intention formation that also contribute to the sense of agency.[2] Pacherie (2007), and others like Bratman (1987) and Searle (1983), distinguish between *distal* intentions (sometimes referred to as future or prior intentions) and *proximate* (or present) intentions. Distal- or D-intentions relate to prior deliberation processes that allow us to formulate our relatively long-term (future) goals. For example, I may decide to purchase a car tomorrow (or next week, or next month, or at some undetermined time in the future), and form the intention to go out and engage in that action when the appropriate time comes. When the time comes, I put my D-intention into action in a very specific way; for example, when I actually go to shop for a car. In this regard, my action reflects a proximate or P-intention. The P-intention specifies the action in terms of the particular requirements of the action situation, including the

---

[1] See Farrer et al. (2013) for the importance of temporality in this regard; also see Braun et al. (2018) for a review of the experimental literature, and Deans (2019) for how these complexities can affect experimental studies of the sense of agency.

[2] I note that the term "intention" as it is used in the following discussion most often signifies action intention. On my understanding the concept of action intention is not unrelated to the more general concept of intentionality understood in the sense of "aboutness," as found, for example, in Brentano and the phenomenological tradition. Action intention is one kind of intentionality in this sense; my action intends (is about or is directed towards) something (e.g., a goal).

circumstances tied to particular environments. I decide to go to a particular car dealership; I walk around looking at different cars; I kick tires; I discuss financing; I decide to purchase a specific car. The P-intention is what Searle calls the "intention-in-action," and I form it as I go, or in an ongoing way, sometimes out of habit or custom, and often in an *ad hoc* way depending on circumstance.

Not all actions involve prior D-intention formation. For example, I may decide right now to get a drink from the kitchen and find myself already moving in that direction. In that case I have not formed a D-intention, although my action is certainly intentional. Rather I may simply form a proximate or P-intention. My intention to get a drink from the kitchen may involve acting on an inclination to get up from my desk and move around and for contingent reasons having to do with the layout of my abode, that means I move in the direction of the kitchen. In doing so I may be monitoring what I am doing in a more or less general way, if, for example, it turns out to be a rather complex action, stepping over children, or around a pile of books. At my university office the kitchen is located down the hall and is locked in the evening. If I want to get a drink I have to walk up the hall, retrieve the key for the kitchen from a common room, and then proceed back down to the kitchen, unlock the door, retrieve the drink, relock the door, return the key, and then return to my office. Although I may be thinking of other things as I do this, I am also monitoring a set of tasks that are not automatic. The ongoing formation of the P-intention keeps the action on track.

In other cases I may be so immersed in my work that I don't even notice that I'm reaching for the glass of water on the table next to me. Here my intentional action may be closer to habitual action, with no P- or D-intention involved. In such cases, my action is still intentional, and I would still have a pre-reflective sense of agency, connected with what Pacherie (2007) calls a motor or M-intention, and consisting of the above-discussed pre-reflective sense generated in motor-control processes and a rather recessive intentional aspect (which I may only notice if I knock over the glass or spill the drink).

Following Pacherie, then, we can distinguish between three kinds of intention.

- **D(istal) intention:** I deliberate about what I will do at a later point and prospectively form my intention (e.g., considering certain facts, I decide to buy a car next week).
- **P(roximate or Present) intention:** Searle's concept of intention-in-action (e.g., I reflectively or perceptually monitor/guide my actions in terms of specific means-ends relations as I carry them out to meet a particular goal).
- **M(otor) intention:** involves the control processes that keep an action on track; in relation to a P-intention it's involved in selecting the movement appropriate for carrying out the intended action (e.g., without conscious perceptual monitoring, I move my arm thus and so in order to pick up the cup and take a drink).

It seems feasible that when there is a D- and/or P-intention involved, such intentions generate a stronger sense of agency. Certainly, if I form a D-intention to buy a new car tomorrow, and tomorrow I go to the car dealership and purchase a car, I will feel more in charge of my life than if, without prior intention I simply find myself lured into a car dealership, and purchasing a car without prior planning. In the latter case, even if I do not deny that I am the agent of my action, I might feel a bit out of control. So it seems clear that part of the phenomenology of agency may be tied, in some cases, to the prospective formation of a prior intention. It's important here to distinguish between the second-order reflective, prospective type of cognitive process involved in D-intention formation—which may be framed in terms of a narrative, and which may involve making judgments and decisions based on beliefs, desires, or evaluations (see, e.g., Frankfurt 1978; Velleman 2006)—and a first-order (pre-reflective) level of experience where we find the sense of agency as an experience of agency. The sense of agency is not itself a judgment, although I may judge that I am the agent of a certain action based on my sense of agency for it. But what is clear is that intention formation may generate a stronger sense of agency than would exist without the formation of D- or P-intentions.

3.2.2 Retrospective attribution

The effect of the formation of a prior intention is clearly prospective. But there are post-action processes that can have a retrospective effect on the sense of agency. Graham and Stephens (1994; Stephens & Graham 2000) provide an account of two kinds of introspective self-attribution.

- *Attributions of subjectivity or ownership*: the subject reflectively realizes and is able to report that he is (or was) moving.
- *Attributions of agency*: the subject reflectively realizes and is able to report that he is the cause or author of his movement. For example, he can say "I caused this action."

Distinguishing between agency and ownership, and between reflective attribution and pre-reflective experience, we can map out differences between sense of agency, sense of ownership, attribution of agency, and attribution of ownership (*Table 3.1*).

In contrast to the idea that the sense of agency is pre-reflective and generated in motor-control processes and intentional aspects, according to Graham and Stephens the sense of agency originates at the higher-order level of attribution. In other words, for them, the sense of agency is equivalent to the attribution of agency. They propose an explanation of the sense of agency in terms of "our proclivity for constructing self-referential narratives" which allow us to explain our behavior retrospectively: "such explanations amount to a sort of theory of the person's agency or intentional psychology" (1994, 101; Stephens & Graham 2000, 161). If we take thinking itself to be a kind of action on our part, then, on this account, our sense of agency for that thinking action, as for any action, derives from a reflective attitude toward it.

[W]hether I take myself to be the agent of a mental episode [or bodily action] depends upon whether I take the occurrence of this episode to be explicable in terms of my underlying intentional states. (1994, 93)

On this view our sense of agency for a particular action depends on whether we can reflectively explain our action in terms of our beliefs, desires, and D-intentions. Accordingly, if a subject does or thinks something for which she has formed no intention, and her action fails to accord with her beliefs and desires—mental states

Table 3.1 Terminology varies from one theorist to another; sometimes a distinction is made between agency and authorship, and sometimes that distinction is denied. Likewise with respect to the sense of ownership it is sometimes equated with a sense of subjectivity (a sense that I am living through an experience), and sometimes with a feeling of mineness (this is *my* experience), or both, where these two experiences are either distinguished or collapsed.

Experience	Pre-reflective	Reflective
Agency (Authorship)	*Sense of agency*—as I act or think, the pre-reflective *experience* that I am the cause/initiator of my action or thinking, and have some control over it.	*Attribution of agency*—the reflective (retrospective) attribution or *judgment* that an action or a thought was caused by me.
Ownership (Subjectivity, Mineness)	*Sense of ownership*—the pre-reflective *experience* that I am moving (or keeping still) or thinking—that the movement, action, or thinking is mine.	*Attribution of ownership*—the reflective (retrospective) realization or *judgment* that I am the one who moved or had a specific thought.

Source: Adapted from S. Gallagher, "Deflationary accounts of the sense of ownership" in: F. de Vignemont and A. Alsmith (eds.), *The Subject's Matter: Self-Consciousness and the Body*, pp. 145–62, Cambridge, MA, Copyright © 2017 Massachusetts Institute of Technology, published by The MIT Press, Table 7.1, p. 146, doi: 10.7551/mitpress/10462.003.0010.

that would normally explain or rationalize the action—then the action or thought may not appear for her as something she intentionally does or thinks. Whether I count something as my action thus

depends upon whether I take myself to have beliefs and desires of the sort that would rationalize its occurrence in me. If my theory of myself ascribes to me the relevant intentional states, I unproblematically regard this episode as my action. If not, then I must either revise my picture of my intentional states or refuse to acknowledge the episode as my doing. (1994, 102)

I think this is an overly intellectualized view. One seemingly has a sense of agency because one has a properly ordered set of second-order retrospective interpretations concerning a particular action (see Graham & Stephens 1994, 102; Stephens & Graham 2000, 162ff).

Pacherie indicates that D-intentions are subject to normative pressures for consistency and coherence relative to the agent's beliefs and other intentions. This would also seem to be the case with Graham and Stephens' retrospective attributions. The fact that retrospectively I may fail to justify my actions, or that I may think that my actions fail to fit with my theory or my self-narrative, does not necessarily remove my pre-reflective sense of agency for the action. Indeed, on the one hand, one could think that for me to be able to pick out any particular action as one that I would attribute to myself, it would have to be one that I have actually lived through and experienced in an agentive fashion, with a pre-reflective sense of agency. In this respect, my attribution of agency may just be a report of that pre-reflective sense of agency that I experienced as I acted. On the other hand, if the action seems to be inconsistent with my self-narrative (e.g., about what sort of person I am and what sort of action

I typically engage in), this modification of failure of attribution may diminish my sense of agency.

My own view is that retrospective attribution (or judgment) of self-agency may have an effect on a continued (temporally extended) pre-reflective sense of agency for my action, either strengthening it or weakening it, but not that my attribution actually constitutes the sense of agency. In this respect Synofzik et al. (2008) rightly distinguish between an experience of agency and a judgment of agency, where the latter is something over and above the pre-reflective sense of agency.

Given these different contributories it seems possible to speak of different (stronger or weaker) degrees of the sense of agency. In regard to some aspects of my life I may generally feel that I am in control of my life because I usually follow through and act on my intentions. I think and deliberate about an action, and form a D-intention to do it. When the time comes I remember my D-intention and I see that it is the appropriate time and situation to begin acting to fulfill that intention. My P-intentions coincide with the successful guidance of the action; my motor control is good and all of the intentional factors line up. There is a good alignment of my D-, P-, and M- intentions. Subsequently, as I reflect on my action, it seems to me to be a good fit with how I think of myself and I can fully attribute responsibility for that action to myself. It seems that in this case I would feel a very strong sense of agency for the action, all contributing aspects—prospective intention formation, contemporary control, and intentional factors, as well as reinforcing retrospective attributions—giving me a coherent experience of that action (see *Figure 3.1*), although this may not always be the case (see Deans 2019). Alternatively, however, I may have a minimal sense of agency because there is no D- or P-intention and no retrospective attribution or evaluation. My sense of agency for the action may just be my thin experience of having motor control over something I am doing. Likewise, I may experience a diminished sense of agency if I am depressed or in cases of anxiety or depersonalization (Gallagher & Trigg 2016; Gentsch & Synofzik 2014).

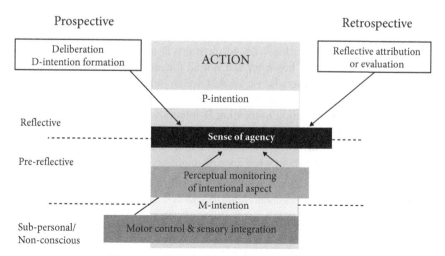

Figure 3.1 Complexities in the sense of agency.

3.3 Ambiguities

According to some neuropsychologists, the sense of agency and the sense of owner-ship may be generated by subpersonal comparator mechanisms.[3] According to this comparator hypothesis, motor-control mechanisms associated with M-intentions involve inverse and forward models. An inverse model derives the motor commands required for a particular movement or body position by comparing current body position with desired body position. When the inverse model generates a motor command the efference copy of that command is sent to a forward model, which compares the intended body position with the predicted sensory feedback (from the anticipated body position) that will result from an issued motor command. If there is a mismatch (or prediction error) in the system, the forward model allows for quick, online correction as the action is in process, without waiting for sensory feedback from the movement. Pacherie suggests that D- and P-intention formation can also be analogized to these kinds of forward and inverse motor-control mech-anisms (2007, 4).

That our deliberation about future actions involves thinking about the means and ends of our actions seems uncontroversial, although it is not necessarily the case that when I form a D-intention I consciously employ an inverse model to determine the means or the strategy I will follow to achieve it. Pacherie's proposal does raise an important question, however. If we regard thinking, such as the deliberative process that may be involved in intention formation, as itself a kind of action, then do we also have a sense of agency for the thinking or deliberation involved in the formation of D-intentions? It seems right to suggest that if I engage in a reflectively conscious process of deliberating about my future actions and make some decisions on this basis, I would have a sense of agency for this deliberation. You could interrupt me during this process and ask what I am doing, and I could say: "I'm sitting here deliberating about buying a car." The sense of agency that I feel for my ongoing deliberation process may be based on my sense of control over it; my response to your question is a retrospective attribution that may confirm this sense of agency. It's also possible that my sense of agency for my deliberation derives in part from a previous deliberation process; for example, I may have formed the D-intention yesterday to do my deliberations (i.e., to form my D-intentions) about car buying today. It is clearly the case, however, that not all forming of D-intentions require a prior intention to do so, otherwise we would have an infinite regress. We would have to deliberate about deliberating about deliberating, etc. Furthermore, it is possible to have P-intentions for the action of forming D-intentions, where P-intentions in this case may be a form of metacognition where we consciously control our cognitive strategies as we form our D-intentions (e.g., I first better consider reasons for and against, and I won't worry about what my wife might say about purchasing a car until

---

[3] When I use terminology associated with comparators, forward models, efference copy, emulator, etc. in the context of motor-control processes, it is for purposes of discussion. I don't mean to endorse such models. These are standard concepts used by many theorists, but there are alternative ways of explaining such processes; e.g., dynamical systems theory or notions of synergy, more consistent with my enactivist inclinations. See, e.g., Chemero & Turvey (2007); Kelso (1995); Turvey (2007). Thanks to one of OUP's reviewers for a caution in this regard.

later). Certainly, however, it is not always the case that we engage in this kind of metacognition as we formulate our D-intentions. It seems, then, that we can still have a minimal first-order sense of agency for our deliberations without prior deliberation or occurrent metacognitive monitoring.

On the one hand, my sense of agency for actually carrying out a particular action (X) is different from my sense of agency for the process of forming the D-intention to do X. They are obviously not equivalent since there are two different actions involved, X and the act of deliberation about X. On the other hand, it seems likely that the sense of agency for my deliberation may contribute to my reflective sense (including my retrospective attribution) that I am the agent of my own actions. This relates to what Pacherie refers to as the long-term sense of agency:

a sense of oneself as an agent apart from any particular action, i.e. a sense of one's capacity for action over time, and a form of self-narrative where one's past actions and projected future actions are given a general coherence and unified through a set of overarching goals, motivations, projects and general lines of conduct.   (2007, 6)

As such this long-term sense of agency may enter into and reinforce the occurrent sense of agency for any particular action. Furthermore, if I lacked a sense of agency for my deliberation process, that process might feel more like an intuition or unbidden thought, or indeed, if I were schizophrenic, it might feel like an inserted thought. In any case, it might feel less than integrated with what Graham and Stephens call the "theory or story of [my] own underlying intentional states," something that itself contributes to the sense of agency for the action. So it seems that the sense of agency for the deliberation process itself may contribute to the sense of agency for the action X in two indirect ways. First, by contributing to my long-term sense of agency, and second, by contributing to the effect of any retrospective attribution I may engage in. Still, as I indicated, there need not be (and, under threat of infinite regress, there can not be) a deliberation process for every action that I engage in.

The case is similar for P-intentions. If action monitoring, at the level of P-intentions, is itself a kind of action (if, for example, it involves making judgments about or actively directing my attention to certain environmental factors), there may be a sense of agency for that action monitoring. The processes that make up a P-intention, however, are much closer to the intended action itself and may not feel like an additional or separate action. Yet there could be a very explicit kind of P-intention in the form of a conscious monitoring of what I am doing. For example, I may be putting together a piece of furniture by following a set of instructions. In that case I could have a sense of agency for following the instructions and closely monitoring my actions in terms of means-ends. Certainly doing it that way would feel very different from doing it without following the set of instructions. But the sense of agency for following the instructions would really go hand in glove with the sense of agency for the action of assembling the furniture. How we distinguish such things would really depend on how fine-grained we get in defining the action.

In the process of assembling the furniture, I may start by reading instruction #1; I then turn to the pieces of wood in front of me and join two of them together. I can distinguish the act of reading from the act of joining, and I can delineate a sense of agency for each of them. In that case, however, one can ask whether my sense of agency for the act of reading doesn't contribute to my sense of agency for the act of joining. I might, however, think of the reading and the joining as one larger action of assembling the furniture, and my sense of agency might be defined broadly in a way that pertains to all aspects of that assembling. It might also be the case that when I put together a second piece of furniture I remember rather than read the instructions, and when I put together the nth piece of furniture I don't follow instructions at all, in which case the sense of agency is more concentrated in the joining. In most practiced actions a P-intention is really unnecessary because motor-control processes and a minimal perceptual monitoring of the intentional aspect (especially based on specific environmental or artifactual features) can do the job; i.e., can keep my action on track. I might simply make up my mind to do this habitual task, and I go and immediately start to do the task without further monitoring in terms of means-ends. All of this suggests that how we experience agency is relative to the way we individuate specific actions, and how practiced those actions are.

This means that there is some serious ambiguity, not simply in the way we define the sense of agency, but in the sense—in the experience—of agency itself. This phenomenological ambiguity—the very ambiguity of our experience of agency—should be included in any considerations about the sense of agency. Clear-cut and unambiguous definitions may create a neat conceptual map; but the landscape itself may not be so neat. It is not always the case that P-intentions serve to implement action plans inherited from D-intentions, since there are not always D-intentions. It is not always the case that "the final stage in action specification involves the transformation of the perceptual-actional contents of P-intentions into sensorimotor representations (M-intentions) through a precise specification of the spatial and temporal characteristics of the constituent elements of the selected motor program" (Pacherie 2007, 3), since there are not always P-intentions associated with actions. Pacherie also suggests that a sense of action initiation and a sense of control are "crucial" components in the sense of agency (2007, 17–18) and that in both components the P-intention plays a large role. But the fact that some actions for which we have a sense of agency take place without P-intentions puts this idea in question.

The *sense of action initiation*, Pacherie suggests, is based on the efference binding of the awareness of P-intention and awareness of movement onset in the very small time frame of 80–200 msec prior to actual movement onset. This corresponds to the time of the lateralized readiness potential, a neuronal signal that seemingly corresponds to selection of a specific motor program (Libet 1985; Haggard 2003) or to motor execution (Schurger, Sitt, & Dehaene 2012; but see Schlegel et al. 2013). Pacherie associates the P-intention with what Patrick Haggard distinguishes as the urge to move and a reference forward to the goal of the action. These aspects of action experience, however, generated by pre-motor processes, more likely correlate with the M-intention (see Desmurget et al. 2009 for relevant data). In this regard it is important to distinguish P-intention from more basic motoric processes that can occur without a formed P-intention, as in practiced action. Even in practiced, habitual, or skilled action I can have a sense of action initiation without involving a conscious monitoring or P-intention. Since intentional control of action can contribute to the sense of agency whether we have a conscious monitoring in terms of specific means to goals or not (Aarts, Custers, & Wegner 2005), engaging a well-formed P-intention does not seem crucial for the sense of agency.

Pacherie (2007) further suggests that the *sense of control*, as a component of the sense of agency, has three dimensions corresponding to the rational control aspects of D-intentions, the situational control aspects of P-intentions, and the purely motor-control aspects of M-intentions. Again, however, a number of qualifications can be made given that D- and P-intentions are not involved in all cases of action, and the sense of control associated with the M-intention may be very recessive as long as the action is going well; e.g., as long as I don't stumble over or knock into something. In some cases, the engagement of a P-intention—i.e., the monitoring of specific means to goal, or the conscious navigation through a complex environment, and a more explicit conscious sense of control (or loss of control) are absent until motivated at that point when something starts to go wrong at the motor-control level. The same might be said about what Terry Horgan (2017, 157) calls the feeling of "optional-ity"—the feeling that you could veto the action or that you could have done otherwise. This may be an intrinsic dimension of the phenomenology of agentive control, but not one that necessarily stands out in our experience.

More generally, what seem to be legitimate conceptual distinctions on the theor-etical level—"awareness of a goal, awareness of an intention to act, awareness of initiation of action, awareness of movements, sense of activity, sense of mental effort, sense of physical effort, sense of control, experience of authorship, experience of intentionality, experience of purposiveness, experience of freedom, and experience of mental causation"—all of which Pacherie (2007, 6) suggests are distinctions that can be found in the phenomenology of the sense of agency—may not in fact show up as such in the actual first-order phenomenology. Indeed, in any particular case, some of these aspects may be the product of theoretical reflection on the first-order phenom-enology rather than actual aspects of the experience. As I engage in action, for example, I may not experience a difference between my sense of effort and my sense of control, although I can certainly make that distinction in my reflective consideration of my action. That distinction may show up clearly at the level of my retrospective attribution, but may be entirely absent in my current, situated pre-reflective sense of agency. As previously indicated, my awareness of what I am doing and that I am doing it is usually struck at the most pragmatic level of description ("I'm getting a drink") rather than at a level that distinguishes between the action and my agency, or within the action between the goal and the means, or within agency between intentional causation, initiation, effort, purposiveness, control, and so forth. The sense of agency is complex, but it may not be *that* complex.

At another extreme, we should resist an overly simplified phenomenology of agency. Phenomenologically, for example, there is no such thing as a "naked inten-tion"—that is, the idea that, in the case of our own action, we can be aware of the action without being aware of *who* the agent is (Jeannerod & Pacherie 2004)—or what Pacherie (2007, 16) calls "agent-neutral" action experience. This concept confuses neurological and phenomenological levels of analysis. It is possible to identify neurons that are activated both in the case of one's own action and in the case of another person's action. Mirror neurons (MNs) are an example. In this regard, it's often claimed that MNs, by themselves, are neutral with respect to who the agent is—they do not distinguish whether oneself or the other is acting (Vignemont 2004; Gallese 2005; Hurley 2005; Jeannerod & Pacherie 2004).[4] This idea motivated Georgieff and Jeannerod (1998) to posit a mechanism called the "Who system" to account for the determination of agency. On this model, if some set of neurons (e.g., mirror neurons) fire in both cases of self- and other-agency (that is, if there is an overlap of neuronal activation that registers intentional action), there must be, in addition, other neurons activated in the non-overlapping areas that signal that the action is mine rather than yours, or vice versa. This mechanism, according to Georgieff and Jeannerod, answers the question: "Whose action is it?" Although there is no claim that these processes are not simultaneous, one might conceive of such processes as involving two logically distinct steps: activation for intentional action (without agent specification—thereby neutral or naked) plus activation for agent identification.

Jeannerod and Pacherie assume that an articulation at the level of neural activations, specifically between (1) those activations responsible for registering the "naked" intention of an action (e.g., this is an action of opening the door), and (2) those activations responsible for registering the agent for the action, means that there is an articulation *in experience* between awareness of intention and the experience of agency. They suggest: "We can be aware of an intention, without by the same token being aware of whose intention it is.... [S]omething more than the sole awareness of a naked intention is needed to determine its author" (Jeannerod & Pacherie 2004, 140). Even if it were possible for the brain to process information about intentions distinct from assigning an agent to the intentions, is it legitimate to say that our experience is similarly articulated? Jeannerod and Pacherie suggest that it is.

When the naked intention one is aware of yields an overt action, the extra information needed to establish authorship may be found in the outside world. The question "Is this intention mine?" would then be answered by answering the question: "Is this my body performing the corresponding action?".   (140)[5]

Phenomenologically, however, intentions in every case come already clothed in agency.[6] The "who" question, which is rightly posed at the neurological level, doesn't

---

[4] There are good reasons to doubt that this is the case. See *Section 4.3.6.*

[5] This extremely articulated process, diagrammed in the form of answering separate questions, is set out in an explanation that resembles Brentano's theory of intentionality and self-awareness. On this view, perception of a tree involves primary and secondary objects. The primary perceptual object is the tree; the secondary object is myself as perceiver. "We claim that it is like this with the perception of intention: when Mary watches John open the door, she is primarily aware of an intention to open the door, rather than being primarily aware that John intends to open the door. Similarly, when Mary herself intends to open the door, she is primarily aware of an intention to open the door, rather than being primarily aware that she herself intends to open the door. Let us call this awareness of an unattributed or 'naked' intention" (Jeannerod & Pacherie 2004, 116). For a critique of Brentano's theory of intentionality, see Gallagher and Zahavi (2012). Even if Brentano were right about self-awareness, the idea that we perceive naked intentions in another's action, and secondarily attribute agency, seems to be based on a supposed isomorphism between subpersonal and personal-phenomenological levels.

[6] Even in schizophrenic delusions of control, the subject does not experience naked intentions; he attributes agency to someone else, even as he experiences the movement as his own, in the sense that it is his own body moving. Indeed, in such a case, the question "Is this intention mine?" is not asked as a separate question, or answered by answering the question: "Is this my body performing the corresponding action?"

come up at the level of experience, because the neural system has already decided the issue—one way or the other. That is, even if I'm wrong about who the agent of an action is (something that may happen even in regard to one's own action in schizophrenic symptoms of delusions of control), I still experience or perceive the intended action as already determined with respect to who the agent is.

A similar problem arises with claims that the phenomenology of the sense of agency and the sense of ownership are inflationary (see, e.g., Bermúdez 2011; Grünbaum 2015); i.e., that a positive sense of agency or sense of ownership does not arise until something goes wrong with action, or that it is generated as the result of reflection. Thor Grünbaum (2015), for example, suggests that there is no separate and distinct pre-reflective sense of agency that acts as the basis for a judgment about agency. He specifically challenges the idea that comparator processes generate a distinct experience of agency, and he takes the claim that the sense of agency is generated by such mechanisms to mean that the sense of agency is intention-free. That is, on the comparator model, the sense of agency is generated even if the agent has not formulated a prior, personal-level D-intention to act in a certain way. As we've seen, however, a D-intention is not the only kind of intention, and is not always involved in action. Reaching for my cup of tea as I work on my computer does not require that I have a prior intention to do so, or that I consciously deliberate and form a plan to do so. Yet it still counts as an intentional action and may involve a present intention-in-action, and motor intentions (Pacherie 2006; 2007). Moreover, at least some comparator models include the idea that there is some functional element in the system that counts as an intention, and that this intention is compared to efference copy or sensory input from the movement to facilitate motor control (e.g., Frith 1992; Wolpert & Flanagan 2001). In this respect it's not clear that even on the comparator model, the sense of agency can be characterized as intention-free.

Grünbaum may be right about comparator mechanisms not generating the sense of agency; indeed, there are other models, and good reasons to question whether comparator models of motor control offer the best explanation (see, e.g., Friston 2011; Synofzik, Vosgerau & Newen 2008). That issue aside, however, the pre-reflective sense of agency may be constituted by a number of contributories, including not only motor-control aspects, but also the pre-reflective intentional aspect discussed above; that is, one's perceptual monitoring of what one's actions are accomplishing in the world.

If actions were intention-free, or agent-anonymous (i.e., characterized by naked intentions), or if we did not have an intrinsic sense of agency and sense of ownership for our actions,[7] we would be constantly puzzled by our actions, or asking: did I just

---

[7] Bermúdez (2011), for example, denies that there is a positive first-order phenomenology of ownership or non-observational (or pre-reflective) feeling of "mineness." He takes the sense of "mineness" to be inferential or a result of introspective attribution. It's not clear, however, that Bermúdez would deny the idea that we have a proprioceptive and kinesthetic awareness of our bodily (and limb) posture and movement. By definition, proprioceptive/kinesthetic awareness is experience of my own body—an intrinsic experience that it is *my own* body that is positioned such and such, or moving so and so. That's the *proprio* in proprioception. A recessive/attenuated (uninflated) sense of ownership or feeling of mineness, however, does not include anything more than that; rather it is an intrinsic structure of experience itself. See the notion of a "perspectival" sense of ownership (Albahari 2016); i.e., a minimal sense of ownership

do that, or was that you? The fact that such puzzles are rare, and sometimes considered pathological when they do occur (as in schizophrenic delusions of control), supports the phenomenological view that these aspects of pre-reflective self-awareness typically are intrinsic aspects of experience (see Gallagher, 2017b; Gallagher & Trigg 2016; Gallagher & Zahavi 2012). In this respect, although Peter Langland-Hassan (2008) raises similar worries as Grünbaum about the positive phenomenology of the sense of agency, he concludes that the phenomenology of agency is "one that is embedded in all first order sensory and proprioceptive phenomenology as diachronic, action-sensitive patterns of information; it does not stand apart from them as an inscrutable emotion" (392).

In *Chapter 2* I focused on the intrinsic temporal structure of action at the elementary and integrative timescales and I explored the micro-structures that characterize subpersonal processes and the pre-reflective level of experience. I argued for a dynamical enactive account of these phenomena. At this point it should be clear that the threefold distinction among elementary, integration, and narrative timescales usefully maps onto the three kinds of intention or intention formation discussed in this chapter (see *Figure 3.2*). The elementary scale correlates to the motor-control processes (including forward and inverse models) that define M-intentions. The integration scale corresponds roughly to P-intentions, which involve quick decisions and ongoing monitoring of actions in the detailed parameters of the current environment. The narrative scale involving longer-term memory, deliberation, and planning corresponds to D-intentions.

Pacherie is right to note that a conceptual analysis cannot "preempt the question whether these various aspects are dissociable or not, for instance whether we can be aware of what we are doing independently of an awareness of how we're doing it or whether we can be aware of what we are doing without at the same time experiencing this action as ours" (2007, 7). What can decide the issue, however, is agreement on where to draw the lines between *phenomenological* analysis (i.e., of what we actually

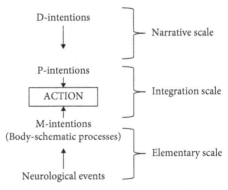

Figure 3.2 Intentions and timescales.

experience), *neuroscientific* analysis (which, as we've seen in the non-linear relations between elementary and integrative time scales [*Chapter 2*], may find a much finer grain of articulations at the neuronal level than what shows up in phenomenology), and *conceptual* analysis (which may introduce distinctions that are in neither the phenomenology nor the neurology, but may have a productive role to play in constructing cognitive models or, in regard to the individual, explaining psychological motivations, or forming personal narratives, etc.).

I suggest that when we integrate these analyses in the right way, we find that the sense of agency and processes of intention formation are complex and ambiguous. Some aspects of action can involve cognitive and conscious reflection and deliberation; many other aspects of action are non-conscious. Likewise, as suggested in previous sections, the sense of agency has multiple contributories, some of which are reflectively (prospectively or retrospectively) conscious, some of which are pre-reflectively conscious, and some of which are non-conscious. Consistent with the phenomenology of embodied experience, in everyday engaged action reafferent or sensory-feedback signals are attenuated, implying a recessive consciousness of the body in action (see, e.g., Gallagher 2005a; Tsakiris & Haggard 2005). We do not attend to the details of our bodily movements in most actions. We do not stare at our own hands as we decide to use them; we do not need to look at our feet as we walk, we do not attend to our arm movements as we engage the joystick.[8] Although efferent, motor-control, and body-schematic processes are non-conscious, just such processes nonetheless contribute to a conscious sense of agency by generating a pre-reflective embodied awareness of our actions.

For most of our everyday actions, then, the sense of agency runs along with and is experientially indistinguishable from a basic sense of ownership, consistent with the integration of efferent and reafferent signals in the insula and other brain areas. The sense of agency involves, in part, a basic feeling of embodiment without which actions would feel very different. In addition, we also experience, pre-reflectively, a form of *intentional feedback*, which is not afferent feedback about our bodily movements, but a perceptual sense that my action is having an effect in the world. This effect is not something that we need to reflectively dwell on, or even retain in memory, especially if there is a consistency between the action intention and what the action actually accomplishes.

The sense of agency for most of our actions may amount to nothing more than these embodied and pre-reflective processes. In some cases, however, we may be reflectively conscious of and concerned about what we are doing and why we are doing what we're doing. We may feel good or bad about our actions. For such actions the sense of agency may become more reflective, tied more directly to a D-intention, involving attention directed toward the project or task that we are engaged in, or toward the means and/or end that we aim for.

---

[8] Deafferentation, as in the case of IW, counts as an exception to this kind of lack of conscious monitoring. See Cole (1995); Gallagher (2005a); Gallagher and Cole (1995). Also, in some cases of expert performance there may be different kinds of self-awareness involved (Gallagher and Ilundáin-Agurruza, 2020).

Conceptually, then, we can identify at least five different contributories to the sense of agency that may be connected with a particular action.

- Formation of D-intentions, often involving a prospective reflective deliberation or planning that precedes some actions
- Formation of P-intentions; that is, the conscious monitoring of action in terms of specific means-ends relations in specific situations
- Basic efferent motor-control processes that generate a first-order experience linked to bodily movement in and towards an environment
- Pre-reflective perceptual monitoring of the effect of my action in the world
- The retrospective attribution of agency that follows action

We can add to this the long-term sense of one's capacity for action over time, related to self-narrative, where past and projected actions provide a general coherence "unified through a set of overarching goals, motivations, projects and general lines of conduct" (Pacherie 2007, 6).

Although conceptually we may distinguish between different cognitive levels (first-order, second-, or higher-order), or aspects (reflective, pre-reflective, non-conscious), and neuroscientifically we may be able to identify different brain processes correlated with these different contributories, in action and in our everyday phenomenology we tend to experience agency in a more holistic, qualitative, and ambiguous way which may be open to a description in terms of degree. The conceptual articulation of the different aspects of the sense of agency, however, suggests that the loss or disruption of the sense of agency in different pathologies may be varied. In schizophrenic delusions of control, for example, the motor-control aspects may be disrupted. In other cases the attribution of self-agency may be disrupted by problems with retrospective higher-order cognition or the prospective formation of D-intentions. A good example of this is the case of narcotic addiction, as discussed by Frankfurt (1988). If a drug addict invests himself in reflectively resisting drugs he may feel that something other than himself is compelling him to drug use. If he withdraws from taking the drug, when he starts using again he may not experience himself as the agent.

It is in virtue of this identification and withdrawal, accomplished through the formation of second-order volition, that the unwilling addict may meaningfully make the analytically puzzling statements that the force moving him to take the drug is a force other than his own, and that it is not of his own free will but rather against his will that this force moves him to take it.   (Frankfurt 1988, 18; see Grünbaum 2010, for discussion)

In effect, the sense of agency may be present or absent, diminished or increased depending on processes, or disruptions of processes, at different levels and across different timescales. The degree of presence/absence, and the experiential feel of agency in any case (pathological or non-pathological) may depend on a range of factors, from very specific neurological processes to the type of action in which we are engaged. As I'll suggest in the next section, however, the kinds of ambiguities that we can discover in considering the details of actions and the sense of agency may be either intensified or smoothed over by the circumstances of larger social arrangements.

3.4 Pushing this Analysis into the World

So far, although we have acknowledged a role for the body and the environment in action, including many of the pre-reflective aspects being generated in motor control and the intentional aspects of what we are accomplishing in the world, one might argue that almost all of the processes described in previous sections remain "in the head," insofar as they are considered either mental processes, such as deliberation, intention formation, judgment, evaluation, perceptual monitoring, or brain processes, such as efferent commands, integration of afferent signals, premotor processes, and motor control. On such analyses it seems as if all of the action, all of the important processes concerning intention and action, take place in the narrow confines of the mind or brain, even though we know that action takes place in the world, and most often in social interactions. I want to challenge this kind of narrow internalism or methodological individualism; i.e., the idea that actions, or indeed social processes, are best explained by identifying some mechanism or set of mechanisms within the individual agent. To be clear, the argument depends on a conception of *dynamical constitution* in which many elements come into relations of reciprocal causal couplings (Gallagher 2018a; see *Section 1.1*). This does not eliminate a role for brain processes, but it takes them to work only in dynamical relations with bodily processes and factors best described as elements of the physical and social environment.

How do other people and social forces enter into intention formation, meaning generation, and the sense of agency? This turns out to be a very large question that pushes the analysis towards a host of other issues. To some extent, the remainder of this book is concerned with those issues. For now, and as an initial indication, we can point to some basic ideas.

On the very basic pre-reflective level, the presence of others has an effect on what my possibilities for action are, and the way that I perceive the world in terms of action affordances. Jean-Paul Sartre points in this direction. In his example he is sitting alone in a park. Someone else then enters the scene.

Suddenly an object has appeared which has stolen the world from me. Everything [remains] in place; everything still exists for me; but everything is traversed by an invisible flight and fixed in the direction of a new object. The appearance of the Other in the world corresponds therefore to a fixed sliding of the whole universe, to a decentralization of the world which undermines the centralization which I am simultaneously effecting. (1956, 255)

This somewhat dramatic philosophical description is supported by some interesting science. Consider the Social Simon Effect. The Simon Effect is found in a traditional stimulus-response task. Participants are asked to respond to different color stimuli, pressing a button to their left with their left hand when blue appears and a button to their right with their right hand for red. They are asked to ignore the location of the color (which may be displayed either in their right or left visual field). An incongruence (mismatch) of right *versus* left between the color location and hand used to respond results in increased reaction times (Simon 1969). That is, my response is slower when, for example, red appears on the left rather than on the right and I have to indicate this by pushing the right button with my right hand. When a subject is asked to respond to just one color with one hand, as you might expect there is no conflict and no effect on reaction time. The surprising thing is that when the subject has exactly the same task (pushing one button for one color) but is seated next to another person who is responding to a different color—each person responding to one color—each acting like one of the hands in the original experiment—reaction times increase for the incongruent trials (Sebanz, Knoblich, & Prinz 2003; Sebanz et al. 2006; Takahama, Kumada, & Saiki 2005). The presence of the other agent seemingly has an effect on my action even in this very simple task.

The Social Simon Effect is controversially the subject of ongoing debates (see Dolk et al. 2014 for a good review). On the one hand, some evidence suggests that the effect is really the result of the sensory-motor contingencies involved with the spatial arrangements of the experiment, and is not really a social effect (Dolk et al. 2011; 2013). On the other hand, there is also evidence that the effects are even more complex and that the specific nature of the interpersonal relationship can affect the results. A cooperative relationship with the co-actor can strengthen the effect, whereas competitive co-actors can abolish or significantly decrease the effect (Hommel et al. 2009; Iani et al. 2011). The effect is also strengthened if the co-actors are romantic (indeed, passionate love) partners, compared with non-romantic partners (Quintard et al. 2018). Even cultural factors may modulate the effect since it is increased among members of a collectivistic religion (Colzato, de Bruijn, et al. 2012 & Colzato, Zech, et al. 2012). It is also increased when there is perceived similarity (*versus* dissimilarity) between co-agents (Müller et al. 2011) and when the subject takes the other to be acting intentionally or as an intentional agent (*versus* non-intentional robot) (Stenzel et al. 2014).

Slowing of reaction times are not necessarily conscious for the agent, and they may have only a minimal effect on one's pre-reflective sense of agency. In some circumstances, however, they may become much more explicitly self-conscious. Consider instances where you are quite capable of and perhaps even proficient at doing action A; for example, successfully free throwing a basketball through the hoop. Your performance may be detrimentally affected, however, simply by the fact of having an audience of very tall basketball superstars. You might in fact feel a degree of inadequacy in such a circumstance, simply because certain people are present.

More generally, the prospective and retrospective dimensions of intention formation and action interpretation, which can have an effect on one's sense of agency, are often shaped by others, and by the situations in which one encounters others. My deliberations to buy a certain kind of car (or any other commodity) may be influenced by what my friends consider to be an appropriate choice. In contrast to internalist views—for example, where simply having a belief about action A encompasses the motivation to A (e.g., Nagel 1970)—and in contrast to many analyses of agency in philosophy of mind and action theory, deliberations, intentions, and motivations to act are not simply mental states (propositional attitudes), or causal brain states—they are often co-constituted with others, and extend beyond any one individual. My decision to buy a new car might be a decision that I've made in conversation with my family. Phenomena such as peer pressure, social referencing, which may be implicit or explicit, or our normatively shaped habitual behavior when in the presence of others, as well as the formation of shared or collective intentions—these phenomena may detract from or increase one's feeling of agency.

In this regard, there are extreme cases, like compulsive or addictive situations. In addictive behavior, for example, there is a loss of the sense of agency for one's actions—but this is not just the result of chemically induced dependency. Compulsive drug-related behaviors correlate neither with the degree of pleasure reported by users nor with reductions in withdrawal symptoms as measured in placebo studies and the subjective reports of users. Robinson and Berridge (1993; 2000) propose the "incentive-sensitization" model: pathological addiction correlates highly with the *salience* of *socially situated* drug-related behaviors and stimuli. For example, specific situations (including the agent's perception of his social world) are altered, and become increasingly hedonically significant to the agent.

To be clear, to challenge internalism and methodological individualism is not to deny that there are some internal (brain) processes involved in such phenomena, or that the individual agent is not playing some role in the action. Rather, it's simply to deny that the only thing of importance is the brain's or the individual's processes, and to affirm that in some cases a conception of *dynamical constitution* is at stake, such that the reciprocal-causal couplings of body and environmental features contribute in a constitutive (and not just an enabling) way to such phenomena (Gallagher 2017a, 2018a). The fact that the brain regions mediating incentive-sensitization are the same areas that process action specification, motor control, and social cognition—thus, regions of the brain thought to be involved in action-oriented intention formation, social navigation, and action—suggests that the explanatory unit is brain-body-environment rather than just brain (see Miller, Kiverstein & Rietveld 2020). This reinforces the idea that situational saliency—including perceptual saliency of the social situation—contributes to intention formation and the sense of agency—sometimes enhancing, but also (as in extreme addictive behavior) sometimes subverting the sense of agency. Intentions can be dynamically shaped by culturally defined situations, by how others are behaving, and by what may be deemed acceptable behavior within specific subcultures.

The importance of both the meaning context of actions (related to environmental saliencies) and their social dimension can be seen even in some of the simplest actions that we perform. This takes us back to some of the studies discussed in *Chapter 1*, showing the importance of meaningful action and socially contextualized action in the context of rehabilitation (e.g., Brouchon et al. 1986; Leontiev & Zaporozhets 1960; Marcel 1992). In many of these cases rehabilitation improved when nominally the same movements were performed in a social situation, in which the movements constituted actions with personal and culturally derived signification. The *socially contextualized* situation is clearly marked by social and personal dimensions that involve norms and cultural categorizations of activities in terms of self–other relations (Gallagher & Marcel 1999).

Another example is both clear and dramatic. It involves congenitally deaf users of American Sign Language (ASL) who suffer from hemispatial neglect following stroke. In cases of left-hemispatial neglect subjects entirely ignore their left perceptual and/or motor field, or the left side of their body. Such patients fail to refer to things in their left hemispace and have a tendency to fail to perceive or attend to what is to their left. They obviously experience difficulty with spatial tasks that are in their left hemispace or that refer to it; so, for example, they may be unable to map out a room or properly describe the layout of objects in place (Jeannerod 1987). It is important to note that some of the syntactical and discursive aspects of ASL make use of peripersonal space. For example, when entities are introduced in discourse they may be assigned a spatial location around the signer to which the signer returns for anaphoric (especially pronominal) reference. The same ASL users with acquired hemispatial neglect who ignore their left side and have profound difficulties with tasks in their left perceptual field have little to no problem in discursive or syntactical use of left hemispace when involved in socially contextualized communicative acts of signing (Poizner, Klima, & Bellugi 1987). Peripersonal space in this case does register in perceptual or instrumental terms (for recognition or for reaching or grasping, for example), but only as relevant to the agent's intention to represent the reference of discourse in a culturally determined sign system in the conversational situation where it affords communicative possibilities. Such communicative practices are clearly related to social cognition, but the social aspect may be even clearer in the fact that hemispatial neglect patients unable to register objects in their left hemispace are able to identify those very same objects when they are asked to say what another person sees in that space (Becchio et al. 2012).

Importantly, it's not simply that an action intention is shaped by a specific kind of behavioral or social environment. It also goes the other way: action intentions can define or redefine the meaning of the agent's circumstances and how they perceive the environment. It's also the case that the availability and execution of an action is influenced by the description or the intention under which the action is generated. On the one hand, personal goals and motives, as well as the social pragmatics of the situation, can clearly provide the energizing dynamics that smoothly transform intentions into actions; on the other hand, social and personal dynamics can easily be disrupted by any number of factors.

Let me conclude with one further example to indicate how such factors can scale up to affect the long-term sense of agency. Several years ago my daughter Laura worked in the Peace Corps in South Africa, focusing her efforts on HIV education. She recounts that her attempts to motivate residents in a small village outside Pretoria to help themselves by engaging in certain activities in organizing their local communities were met by a sardonic attitude and even polite laughter. They explained to her that such ideas were impossible for them; they were unable to help themselves simply because, as everyone already knew, they were lazy. That's just the way they were, they explained, and they knew this because all their life, under the apartheid regime, they had been told so by various educational and governmental institutions. In effect, because of certain long-standing racist social arrangements, arrangements with prolonged effects even after the dismantlement of apartheid, they had no long-term sense of agency. Social-political-institutional arrangements thus robbed them of possibilities for action, reduced their social and cultural affordances, as well as their sense of agency.

If, to understand action, agency, and intention formation we need to consider the most relevant pragmatic (or highest affordance) level from the perspective of the agent, there is strong evidence that the most relevant pragmatic level is not the level of internal mental or brain states. We shouldn't be looking exclusively inside the head. Rather, embodied action happens in a world that is physical and social and cultural and political; a world that reflects not only perceptual and affective valiances, but also the effects of forces and affordances that are normative and social. Notions of agency and intention, as well as notions of autonomy and responsibility, as I'll try to make clear later, are best conceived in terms that include social-cultural effects. Intentions often get co-constituted in interactions with others—indeed, some kinds of intentions are simply not reducible to processes that are contained exclusively within one individual. In such cases, the sense of self-agency will be a matter of degree; it can be enhanced or reduced by physical, social, economic, and cultural factors that work their way into and through our own practices, but also, in pathological cases, for example, by loss of motor control or disruptions in pre-reflective action-consciousness.

To return to the question I started with: What is action if it is something more than bodily movement? I began by suggesting that action, in the sense of autonomous behavior which scales up to more than a set of causal processes, is characterized by intention, a sense of agency, and meaning, all of which go beyond simple bodily movement. At the same time, intention (specifically M-intention) and the sense of agency (specifically, the pre-reflective sense of agency that is generated in motor-control processes) are not detached from bodily movement. Action carries movement into the realm of meaning and reason; it imbues movement with meaning and intentionality. In this section I've pushed further to provide evidence that intention formation, the sense of agency, and the meaning of action are significantly affected by factors that involve social contextualization; that is, by dynamical arrangements that are intersubjective, normative, cultural, and/or political.

PART II
Interaction

4

The Case Against Theory of Mind

Considerations in the previous chapters led to an acknowledgment of the important role played by social context and intersubjective relations for understanding action. In this and subsequent chapters I want to explore in more detail, not only how action is related to social interaction, but also the nature of social interaction itself. How we understand others, how we interact with them, how we engage with them in joint actions, and how our social institutions shape these aspects of our lives—these are the issues I will address in order to flesh out an analysis of our everyday life of action and interaction.

In this chapter I start with the critical task of showing how contemporary standard approaches to questions about social cognition and theory of mind (ToM) go wrong and fail to explain how we understand others, and more generally how they cover up the importance of embodied interaction in social contexts. The standard approaches discussed here include *theory theory* (TT) and *simulation theory* (ST), as well as hybrid versions of these theories. In *Chapter 5* I'll develop the alternative, "interaction theory" (IT), that emphasizes the central role of interaction. I think it is important to start with TT and ST, however, since IT has benefited from multiple refinements over the past dozen years, especially in response to theorists that continue to defend TT and ST.

4.1 Two Theories of Theory of Mind

In psychology, philosophy of mind, and more recently in the neurosciences, studies of how one person understands and interrelates with another person have been dominated by two main approaches: theory theory and simulation theory. The major tenets of TT are based on some classic scientific experiments that suggested that children develop an understanding of (or theory of) other minds around the age of 4 years. One version of TT claims that this understanding is based on an innately specified, domain-specific mechanism designed for "reading" other minds (e.g., Baron-Cohen 1995; Leslie 1991). An alternative version claims that the child attains this ability through a course of development in which the child tests hypotheses about the behavior of others and learns from the social environment (e.g., Gopnik and Meltzoff 1997). Common to both versions is the idea that children attain their understanding of other minds by using folk or common-sense psychology to make theoretical inferences about certain entities to which they have no access; namely, the mental states of other people. Taking this theoretical stance involves postulating the existence of mental states in others and using such postulations to explain and predict another person's behavior. When we make such inferences and attribute specific mental states to others, we are said to be *mentalizing* or *mindreading*. According to TT, the 4–5-year-old child's mentalizing ability involves "first-order belief attribution" in which she distinguishes her own belief from someone else's belief. Later in development mindreading involves "second-order belief attribution"—the ability to "think about another person's thoughts about a third person's thoughts about an objective event" (Baron-Cohen 1989, 288). Typically children aged 6–7 are able to achieve this more sophisticated level of mindreading. The very few autistic children who attain first-order belief attribution do so late in development, and they fail to attain the more sophisticated level.

The second approach, simulation theory, argues that rather than theorizing or making inferences about the other person's mind, we use our own mental experience as an internal model for the other's mind (e.g., Gordon 1986; 1995; Heal 1986; 1998). To understand others, I simulate the thoughts or feelings that I would experience *if I were in their situation*, exploiting my own motivational and emotional resources. I imagine what must be going on in the other person's mind; or I create in my own mind pretend beliefs, desires, or strategies that I use to understand the other's behavior. My source for these simulations is not a theory that I have. Rather, I have a real model of the mind at my immediate disposal; that is, I have *my own mind*, and I can use it to generate and run simulations. I simply run through the sequence or pattern of behavior or the decision-making process that I would engage in if I were faced with the situation in question. I do it "off line," however. That is, my imaginary rehearsal does not lead to actualizing the behavior on my part. Rather, I simply attribute this simulation to the other person who is actually in that situation. According to some versions of ST, this simulating process may remain non-conscious; the simulator may only have an awareness of the resulting understanding or prediction. The non-conscious process itself, however, is structured as an internal, representational simulation (Gordon 1986). On other versions of ST, the simulation is explicit or conscious, perhaps even a matter of introspection. This was Alvin Goldman's original "introspectionist ST" view (1995, 216), for example, and is now what he calls high-level mindreading (2006, 245ff).[1]

Despite the clear distinction between the TT and ST accounts of mindreading, and despite the fact that for the last thirty years the dominant debate in the field of social cognition has been between proponents of TT and the proponents of ST, any neat division between these theories is an oversimplification. Not only because of the existence of several hybrid theories that combine TT and ST, but also because neither of the main positions are theoretical monoliths. Both camps are split on the issue of whether the social-cognition processes in question are innate and modularized, or whether they are acquired through experience. There are also debates in both camps concerning to what degree these processes are conscious or non-conscious, deliberate

---

[1] Thus, for example, Goldman writes: "'High-level' mindreading is mindreading with one or more of the following features: (a) it targets mental states of a relatively complex nature, such as propositional attitudes; (b) some components of the mindreading process are subject to voluntary control; and (c) the process has some degree of accessibility to consciousness" (Goldman 2006, 147).

or automatic. And yet despite both external debates and internal squabbles, classic statements of TT and ST share three basic suppositions.

(1) The unobservability principle (see, e.g., Krueger 2012): social cognition is a problem due to the lack of access that we have to the other person's mental states. Since we cannot directly perceive the other's thoughts, feelings, or intentions, we need some extra-perceptual cognitive process (mindreading or metalizing) that will allow us to infer or simulate what those mental states are.

(2) The observational stance: our normal everyday stance toward others is an observational one. We observe their behaviors, and based on what we observe we mindread their mental states. We do this in order to *explain* their behaviors, or predict what they will do next.

(3) The supposition of universality: our primary and pervasive way of understanding others is by way of one of these processes, either theoretical inference or simulation.

Let me note, however, that all three of these assumptions are the subject of ongoing revisions and continuing debates. As stated, for example, the third supposition is challenged by a possible pluralism about social cognition according to which we use many different resources for understanding others, and we may do it differently in different situations. On at least some pluralist views, the use of theoretical inferences or simulation routines is, at best, a specialized ability that allows us to attribute mental states to others in specific circumstances when we are puzzled by their behavior, or when we try to explain or give reasons for their behavior. Pluralist approaches have recently come to prominence (see, e.g., Andrews 2008; Fiebich & Coltheart 2015; Fiebich, Gallagher, & Hutto 2017; Gallagher and Fiebich 2019; Wiltshire et al. 2015), even among theorists who continue to champion mindreading (e.g., Butterfill and Apperly 2013; Michael, Christensen, & Overgaard 2014; Spaulding 2018), and they have put pressure on the supposition of universality. Statements in support of that supposition, however, deny the idea that mindreading is a specialized capacity. Here are several examples.

[M]ind-reading and the capacity to negotiate the social world are not the same thing, but the former seems to be necessary for the latter.... [O]ur basic grip on the social world depends on our being able to see our fellows as motivated by beliefs and desires we sometimes share and sometimes do not.   (Currie & Sterelny 2000, 145)

[I]t is hard for us to make sense of behavior in any other way than via the mentalistic (or "intentional") framework. [Here a quote from Dan Sperber]—"attribution of mental states is to humans as echolocation is to the bat. It is our natural way of understanding the social environment."   (Baron-Cohen 1995, 3–4)

The strongest form of ST would say that all cases of (third-person) mentalization employ simulation. A moderate version would say, for example, that simulation is the *default* method of mentalization...I am attracted to the moderate version.... Simulation is the primitive, root form of interpersonal mentalization.   (Goldman 2002, 7–8)[2]

---

[2] There are abundant examples that could be cited here. See, e.g., Frith and Happé (1999, 2); Jeannerod and Pacherie (2004, 128); Karmiloff-Smith (1992, 117); Leslie (2000, 1236); Wellman (1993, 31–2). As psychologist Helen Tager-Flusberg (2005, 276) puts it: "Social situations and events cannot be interpreted

Goldman's notion of a moderate version of ST not only expresses this supposition of universality, but also clearly signals a difference between a hybrid theory and a pluralist theory. Goldman (2006) embraces a hybrid theory where simulation is the default method that is used in every case of mindreading, and where any use of theoretical inference may work simply in support of the simulation process. A hybrid theory is precisely one where a default (either simulation or theoretical inference) is identified, and the non-default strategy serves, not as an alternative strategy, but in support of the default strategy. In this regard, the supposition of universality holds even for hybrid theories. In contrast, in a pluralist approach, it may be that in some circumstances simulation works best; in other circumstances theoretical inference, or some other alternative works best. For the pluralist, there is no default (Fiebich et al. 2017); rather, the process that works best, or more efficiently (Fiebich & Coltheart 2015)—for example, given differences in circumstance or context—is the one that takes the lead.[3]

The second supposition about the observational stance is reflected in statements that indicate that the task of mindreading is just this: "to provide fine-grained intentionalistic predictions and explanations" based on "inferences from *observation*" (Carruthers 1996, 26, emphasis added). This is an issue of contention. Despite the fact that Peter Carruthers frequently characterizes mindreading as something done by "a third-party observer" (2009, 134), "when processing a *description* of someone's state of mind as well as when *observing* their behavior" (2002, 666, emphasis added), he has recently suggested that this emphasis on third-person observation is not essential to mindreading.

In particular, it is simply false that theory-theorists must (or do) assume that mentalizing usually involves the adoption of a third-person, detached and observational, perspective on other people. On the contrary, theory theorists have always emphasized that the primary use of mindreading is in interaction with others... (2009, 167; also see Overgaard & Michael 2015)

I note, however, that interactions do not figure prominently in most descriptions of theory theory, and that, rather, the standard phrasing about mindreading— namely, that it involves an *explanation* of the other's mental states based on a theory or a science-like method (Gopnik & Meltzoff 1997) (rather than *understanding* or *affectively responding* to the other)—reemphasizes the idea that this process is a reflective, third-person, observation-based process in which we "hypothesize" about the other's mind (Baron-Cohen 1995, 27). As we'll see (*Section 4.2*), this observational stance is clearly reinforced by its institution in *the* scientific paradigm that is

on the basis of overt behavior without representing the mental states underlying people's actions. Understanding people as intentional, mental beings is at the core of social cognition, within which the ability to interpret people's behavior in a mentalistic explanatory framework using a coherent, causally related set of mental constructs is central to a theory of mind [or folk psychology]." Goldman is more liberal or pluralist when he suggests that "there are many varied forms of social cognition, not all of which involve understanding mental states" (2006, p. 210).

[3] There is another, perhaps even more obvious issue connected with the universality claim; namely, the idea that mindreading processes are the same across cultures. There is empirical evidence against this (see Gut & Mirski 2016; Strijbos & De Bruin 2013). I return to this issue later.

designed to best support the notion that we mindread the other's mental states—namely, the false-belief test.

To be clear, when one is in the observational stance, what one observes is the other's behavior, but not the other's mental states. From within this stance, to get to the other's mental states one requires something more than perception. This leads us back to the first supposition, the unobservability principle. In one of the earliest statements of theory of mind, for example, Premack and Woodruff wrote:

In saying that an individual has a theory of mind, we mean that the individual imputes mental states to himself and to others (either to conspecifics or to other species as well). A system of inferences of this kind is properly viewed as a theory, first, because *such states are not directly observable*, and second, because the system can be used to make predictions, specifically about the behavior of other organisms. (1978, 515; emphasis added)

Likewise, Alan Leslie (1987, 139) explains why theoretical inference is necessary:

One of the most important powers of the human mind is to conceive of and think about itself and other minds. Because the mental states of others (and indeed of ourselves) are completely hidden from the senses, they can only ever be inferred.

Prominent proponents of TT and ST have argued that it is because of the lack of any direct access to the mental states of others—which are frequently described as "inherently unobservable constructs" (Mitchell 2008)—that we need to employ either theoretical inferences or internal simulations. Indeed, as Epley and Waytz repeatedly write in their frequently cited survey chapter on "Mind perception" in *The Handbook of Social Psychology* (2010):

Others' mental states are unobservable and inherently invisible and it is precisely because people lack direct information about others' mental states that they must base their inferences on whatever information about others that they do, in fact, have access to. They must make a leap from the observable behavior to the unobservable mental states, a leap employing either simulation or theoretical inference. (499; also see 505, 518)

Despite this long-standing tradition of describing mental states as inaccessible to perception, some theory theorists have recently rejected the unobservability principle in the context of discussing the possibility of directly perceiving intentions and emotions in others (see, e.g., Bohl & Gangopadhyay 2013; Carruthers 2015; Lavelle 2012). Still, the role of perception and what one actually perceives remains under debate. I return to this issue in *Chapter 6*.

4.2 The Science Behind ToM

That ToM approaches are most often framed in terms of understanding others from a third-person observational stance can be clearly seen in the paradigm experiments of false-belief tests typically cited to support TT. In such experiments a subject (usually a child) is asked to observe the behavior of two other children (or sometimes dolls or puppets). For example, Sally puts a marble in a basket and leaves the room; another child Anne moves the marble from the basket to a box. Sally comes back into the room and the subject is asked where he thinks Sally will look for the marble. On average, 4-year-olds tend to answer correctly that Sally will look in the basket, where she still believes (falsely) the marble to be located. This is successful mindreading. However, 3-year-olds on average tend to answer incorrectly that Sally will look in the box, where the marble actually is. This is taken as evidence that 3-year-old subjects (and some autistic subjects) are unable to appreciate that having a different perspective could lead to Sally's false belief; 4-year-old children apparently have developed a theory of mind that can deal with false beliefs (Wimmer & Perner 1983; Leslie & Frith 1988). They can either make the proper inference, or they can adopt the other's perspective and perhaps simulate what she is thinking.

Notice however, that such experiments are designed to test the subject's third-person observation of events; the subject never participates in the events (moving or looking for the marble) nor does he interact with Sally or Anne. The child is in an observational relation to the person (or puppet) he is asked about—that is, he is observing, but not interacting with that person. As Wellman et al. (2001, 666) point out, in these experiments "often children are essentially passive onlookers; for example, they watch as someone transfers Maxi's chocolate from one place to another." Indeed, in the Maxi version of the false-belief test (which is very similar to the Sally-Anne test), the scenario is typically presented as a story featuring Maxi as a character;[4] in some cases it is acted out using dolls and other props. That is, the subject's observations are not even observations of real people, and the test is primarily an intellectual one.

Although it is rarely noted by those who appeal to these experiments in support of ToM accounts, the child is also in a *second-person* relation; namely, with the experimenter to whom he is responding when asked the questions. He is *interacting* with the experimenter (and seemingly even 3-year-olds have no problems with this), but he is not interacting with the third person (character or puppet, Sally or Anne or Maxi). Clearly the test is not about the second-person interaction the child is having with the experimenter. So one question is whether false-belief experiments are actually testing our everyday interactions with others, rather than a set of more specialized observational mindreading abilities we might have.

Theory theorists have traditionally appealed to the false-belief experiments and have taken such experiments to demonstrate that at around the age of 4 years the non-autistic child comes to have a theory of mind; that is, starts to employ folk psychology at a level sophisticated enough to be able to recognize that the other person has a false belief. Children younger than 4 years, on average, and autistic children, lack this ability. This view has been challenged, however, by experiments showing that much younger children, indeed, around the age of 13 months, are capable of passing false-belief tests (Onishi & Baillargeon 2005; Surian, Caldi, & Sperber 2007). There are, of course, various interpretations of these experiments. Carruthers (2009), for example, from a TT perspective, takes it to be evidence that children have ToM abilities much younger than was first thought. The experiments suggest to him that 13-month-olds already have metarepresentational ability (that is,

---

[4] As Gordon and Barker (1994, 176) put it, such experiments "offer the subject only a narrative rather than a live, expressive protagonist."

an ability to have a mental representation about some other representational state), so he sees this as completely consistent with TT. Others, however, doubt that infants of that age have metarepresentational ability or a concept of belief, and they suggest that ST can best explain the experimental results (e.g., Herschbach 2008). Still others offer a behavioristic interpretation where the infant's performance can be explained by a disappointment of expected contextualized behavior (Perner & Ruffman 2005). It's also possible to formulate an enactivist interpretation that emphasizes context and the potential for interaction (Gallagher 2015b; Gallagher & Povinelli 2012).

At the very least one might think that the appeal to ST in this regard may seem more reasonable than an appeal to metarepresentational ability, especially if we consider what Goldman calls low-level simulation—a form of simulation that is fast and automatic and does not require the use of conscious imagination or introspection. This view of simulation has received important support from the neuroscience of mirror neurons. Recall that mirror neurons are neurons that are activated in two conditions: (1) when we engage in intentional actions, and (2) when we see others engage in intentional actions. It is claimed that mirror neurons in the pre-motor cortex, in Broca's area, and in the parietal cortex of the human brain, for example, are activated both when the subject engages in specific instrumental actions, and when the subject observes someone else engage in those actions (Rizzolatti et al. 1996). In effect, on observing another's action, one's motor system reverberates or resonates in a way that seems to mimic one's own possible action. One claim that has been made by simulation theorists is that these processes underpin (or are the neural correlates) of low-level simulation, or that they in some way support high-level (explicit) acts of simulation (Goldman 2006; 2009a; Ruby & Decety 2001). Alternatively, other simulation theorists claim these subpersonal processes themselves just are (i.e., constitute) a simulation of the other's intentions. Gallese summarizes this position clearly in his claim that activation of mirror neurons involves "automatic, implicit, and nonreflexive simulation mechanisms..." (Gallese 2005, 117; also Gallese 2007; see Goldman 2009a for the relevant causal versus constitution distinction). Gallese refers to his model as the "shared manifold hypothesis" and importantly distinguishes between three levels (2001, 45):

(1) The *phenomenological level* is the one responsible for the sense of similarity...that we experience anytime we confront ourselves with other human beings. It could be defined also as the *empathic* level....

(2) The *functional level* can be characterized in terms of simulation routines, *as if* processes enabling models of others to be created.

(3) The *subpersonal level* is instantiated as the result of the activity of a series of mirror-matching neural circuits.

On this hypothesis, at the phenomenological level, one is not explicitly (or introspectively) simulating; rather one is experiencing an empathic sense of the other person, and this is the result of a simulation process that happens on the subpersonal level.

Neural ST understood in these or in similar terms has been a growing consensus. Indeed, use of the term "simulation" is the standard way of referring to mirror system activation. Thus, for example, Marc Jeannerod and Elizabeth Pacherie write:

As far as the understanding of action is concerned, we regard simulation as the default procedure.... We also believe that simulation is the root form of interpersonal mentalization and that it is best conceived as a hybrid of explicit and implicit processes, with subpersonal neural simulation serving as a basis for explicit mental simulation.

(Jeannerod & Pacherie 2004, 129; see Jeannerod 2001,
2003; also see Decety & Grèzes 2006)

Goldman (2006, 113), as we saw, distinguishes between simulation as a high-level (explicit) mindreading and simulation as a low-level (implicit) mindreading where the latter is "simple, primitive, automatic, and largely below the level of consciousness." This mirroring process, he suggests, is the prototype of simulation (147). The idea that mirror neuron activation is a simulation not only of the goal of the observed action but also of that agent's intention, and is therefore a form of mindreading, is suggested by research that shows mirror neurons discriminate relatively identical movements according to the intentional action and the contexts in which these movements are embedded (Fogassi et al. 2005; Iacoboni et al. 2005; Kaplan & Iacoboni 2007). Neural simulation has also been proposed as an explanation of how we grasp emotions and pain in others (Avenanti & Aglioti 2007; Ferrari & Coudé 2018; Gallese, Eagle, & Migone 2007; Minio-Paluello, Avenanti & Aglioti 2006). In addition, evidence of dysfunction in "simulator neurons" has suggested an explanation for the social problems found in autism (Oberman & Ramachandran 2007; also Cole, Barraclough, & Enticott 2018).

4.3 Eight Problems for ToM

Having sketched some of the ideas behind TT and ST, I now want to outline a number of problems that can be found in one or both of these approaches. Some of these problems are logical-conceptual, others are phenomenological, and still others concern the interpretation of the science.[5]

4.3.1 *The starting problem*

The starting problem is a version of what cognitive scientists call the frame problem, which concerns the determination of what is relevant and what is not in any situation (Shanahan 2016). For TT and ST it comes at the very beginning of the mindreading process. Neither theory has a good explanation of how the process gets off the ground—or more precisely, what ground we stand on as we engage in the process of mindreading.

For example, some theory theorists claim that we simply use our folk-psychological theory by applying some specific rule (platitude, principle, or general proposition) that

---

[5] This is not an exhaustive list of problems. I leave aside, for example, a more contentious debate about representationalism, the so-called "problem of foundationalism" (Mirski & Gut 2018). Although some of the problems I outline here apply to TT, most apply to ST. I note that there may be other problems that relate more directly to the neurophysiological theory of MN function, which underpins some versions of ST. Hickok (2009), for example, lists eight problems in this regard. The eight problems that I list, however, do not overlap with those identified by Hickok. One can accept the scientific data on MNs and still challenge the theoretical interpretation of that data in a number of ways.

will explain the other person's behavior. But that seems to assume that we already know what the appropriate rule is for the specific situation; that is, that we are able to recognize a particular situation as one that calls for the application of a particular rule. For example, as I drive down the road I see my neighbor, who happens to be a police officer, raise her hand as I approach. Since I don't have access to her intention, I have to infer from her behavior what she wants. Should I interpret her wave as a wave of hello from someone I know. My neighbor *wants* to say hello. Or, should I interpret this as a police officer ordering me to stop. How do I know which rule to apply to interpret this signal? When someone I know waves to me, that usually means that she wants to say hello. But when someone with police authority waves to me, that usually means she wants me to stop. The rules of folk psychology are rather abstract—they supposedly apply to human behavior in general, and, in part, that's what makes them theoretical. The application of such rules may be especially troublesome in ambiguous situations. The issue is this: faced with a particular situation, how do we know which rule to apply? Clearly I have to depend on more than just a rule of folk psychology—contextual details and social roles are seemingly relevant (see Heal 1996).

To solve this problem, some theory theorists would define folk psychology in a wider (connectionist) fashion to include knowledge of contextual details and social roles (e.g., Stich & Nichols 1992). It's not clear, however, that the wide background knowledge endorsed by this "liberal" TT is a genuinely theoretical knowledge rather than a particularistic knowledge about the type of person the other person is, or about relevant situational details (knowledge that is more narrative-based than theory-like), or a form of know-how involving embodied skillful or cultural practices (knowledge that is more practical than theory-like). I will return to these issues later.

The situation is no easier for the simulationist. One can see this, for example, in Goldman's description of the steps involved in running a simulation routine.

First, the attributor creates in herself pretend states intended to match those of the target. In other words, the attributor attempts to put herself in the target's "mental shoes". The second step is to feed these initial pretend states [e.g., beliefs] into some mechanism of the attributor's own psychology...and allow that mechanism to operate on the pretend states so as to generate one or more new states [e.g., decisions]. Third, the attributor assigns the output state to the target...[e.g., we infer or project the decision to the other's mind].   (Goldman 2005, 80–1)

The first step seems tricky. How do I know which pretend state matches what the other person has in mind. Indeed, isn't this what simulation is supposed to give me? If I already know what state matches the target, then the problem, as defined by ST, would already be solved.[6] ST also claims that, in contrast to TT, it does not need to be knowledge- or information-rich (Nichols & Stich 2003), so it seems that it cannot make a start by being well anchored in rich background knowledge.

---

[6] The same problem is clear in the description provided by Nichols and Stich (2003, 39–40): "The basic idea of what we call the 'off-line simulation theory' is that in predicting and explaining people's behavior we take our own decision making system 'off-line,' *supply it with 'pretend' inputs that have the same content as the beliefs and desires of the person whose behavior we're concerned with,* and let it make a decision on what to do" (emphasis added). Again, it's not clear where I get inputs with the same content, if I have not completed the simulation process.

Starting the process seems to be a problem for both TT and ST. To address this problem some theorists have pursued hybrid versions that combine TT and ST. For example, I'm in a position to take the first step in the simulation process precisely because I already have a folk psychology that allows me to make a supposition about what the other person is thinking. Hybrid theorists thus suggest that folk psychology provides, not a sense of what is going on with the other person, but some general rules about how people think and behave in certain situations, and that this is what the simulationist can use to generate the pretend mental states needed for the simulation process (e.g., Currie & Ravenscroft 2002). Some theorists would push this further. The unobservability principle implies a certain conception of the mind— namely, a Cartesian conception of a hidden space where mental states reside. On a strong version of TT the problem is not only the problem of accessing other minds, or coming up with an appropriate inference, but also the problem of accessing my own mind (e.g., Carruthers 2009)—something that is essential for the simulationist. On this view, I don't have privileged access to my own mental states and the only way to know them is by means of theoretical inference. If this is true, ST would be forced into a hybrid position, since I would first have to employ theoretical inference to gain access to my own mental model. Theory is necessary to get my simulation off the ground.

But how does theoretical inference itself get off the ground in any particular case? Perhaps it can go the other hybrid route. The only reason I know what rule of folk psychology to apply is because I begin by simulating the other person's situation (see Heal 1996). But then, again, how do I start the simulation? It seems to me that these hybrid approaches simply push the problem back a step; one ends up in a circle of starting problems which turns from abstract rules to unsure suppositions and then returns to abstract rules. What seems to be lacking is an account of how we get the right kind of particularistic or contextual knowledge that would be the ground for getting things off the ground.

To be clear, I am not suggesting that theorists of TT and ST would deny that both folk psychology and simulation depend on what I will call, following terminology suggested by Bruner and Kalmar (1998), a *massive hermeneutical background*. But neither TT nor ST says much about it; they don't explain how we get this background, what sort of thing it is, or how precisely it comes into play when we attempt to use folk psychology or simulation. A liberal version of TT, for example, may want to build this background knowledge into the system, or make it part of folk psychology, but it's not clear that the kind of knowledge at stake is theoretical in nature. I'll argue (*Section 7.4*) that the massive hermeneutical background knowledge one requires to get theoretical inference or simulation off the ground already incorporates a non-theoretical, non-simulative understanding of others based on embodied, communicative, and narrative practices.

4.3.2 *The diversity problem*

What I call the diversity problem pertains primarily to some of the various versions of simulation theory. It's reflected in the starting problem for simulation, but it is directly tied to the supposed nature of simulation. Simulation depends specifically on one's own first-person experience as the basis for what goes into the simulation.

Thus, one possible response to the starting problem for ST is that we depend on our own prior experience to have a sense of what the other person may be thinking in a particular situation. We start with our own experience and project some tentative empathic conception of what must be going on in the other's mind. Even at the level of neural simulation there is evidence that our MNs activate only if we have previously engaged in the sort of action that we see being done by the other (see, e.g., Calvo-Merino et al. 2006). The question is this: when we project ourselves imaginatively into the other's mind, are we not merely reiterating ourselves? Goldman, for example, describes simulation in the following way: "In all these cases, observing what other people do or feel is therefore transformed into an inner representation of what we would do or feel in a similar situation—as if we would be in the skin of the person we observe" (Keysers & Gazzola 2008, 390; see Goldman 2008, 27). But how does knowing what *we* would do help us know what someone else would do?[7] Indeed, many times we are in a situation where we see what someone is doing, and know that we would do it differently, or perhaps, not do it at all.

The diversity problem is actually an old objection raised against ST's older cousin, the argument of inference from analogy. Both the phenomenologist Max Scheler (1954), and the original philosopher of mind, Gilbert Ryle (1949), took issue with that argument suggesting that the logic of simulation isn't correct. If by simulation I impute to a variety of others what is true of my own experienced action, this ignores the diversity of possible actions that we can encounter. Thus, as Ryle indicates, "the observed appearances and actions of people differ very markedly, so the imputation to them of inner processes closely matching [one's own or] one another would be actually contrary to the evidence" (1949, 54). Goldman, even in defending ST, acknowledges that the agent is presumed to be psychologically similar to us; we ascribe beliefs that are "natural for us" (Goldman 1989, 178) and, thus, it seems, reject or fail to consider beliefs that we consider to be less like our own. Given the vast variety of actions, beliefs, experiences, and feelings that people experience, it seems presumptuous to suggest that one's own limited first-person experience is capable of capturing that diversity. If I project the results of my own simulation onto the other, I understand only myself in that other situation, but I don't necessarily understand the other. The question then, is whether simulation so conceived will ever allow for a true understanding of the *other*, or merely let me attain an understanding of myself in a different situation.

---

[7] Gordon (1986; Gordon & Barker 1994) recognizes this problem and proposes that in the simulation process we imagine what the other experiences in the particular situation. "Rather than simulate ourselves in Smith's situation, we must simulate Smith in Smith's situation (as it appears to Smith)" (Gordon & Barker 1994, 172). As they suggest, however, this involves "a more complex use of pretense." First, it requires some kind of knowledge, either about Smith or about what others generally do in such cases (in which case theory theorists may suggest that this is a case of theoretical inference based on folk psychology). Second, it requires discounting the similarity between self and other on which simulation is supposedly based and which most simulation theorists (including Gordon) typically emphasize. Third, to imagine what Smith will do in that situation, "one tries to become [Smith] in imagination" (Gordon & Barker 1994, 173). Rather than assimilating Smith to my perspective, I accommodate my perspective to Smith's (based on some kind of knowledge), and at the same time I "become" Smith not in my situation but in Smith's situation. This kind of complexity seemingly suggests a conscious reasoning process involving knowledge resources that most simulation theorists eschew.

There is much more to say about the diversity problem. Here I can only point to some of the further complexity involved in this issue. Research in social psychology, for example, suggests that an adequate account of social cognition requires going beyond the relatively narrow realm of mindreading. Specifically, insights concerning in-group and out-group distinctions can manifest themselves in different ways in social cognition—as ideological constructs, cultural narratives about otherness, gender, race, and class relations in societies, and so on. A study by Gutsell and Inzlicht (2010), for example, shows that negative beliefs about out-group members can interfere with one's ability to recognize emotions. Although there is no shortage of this kind of research on in-group and out-group relations (see especially Haslam et al. 2005, Haslam & Bain 2007; Bain et al. 2009; Bastian & Haslam 2010; Fiske 1991; 2004; Likowski et al. 2008), the results of this research have rarely been taken into account in the philosophy of social cognition.[8]

Furthermore, the kind of diversity connected to cultural differences can certainly complicate accounts of social cognition. ToM accounts, however, often assume that we are hardwired to intuitively grasp others as "fellow human beings" by means of innate, modular ToM mechanisms or preprogrammed mirror systems operating in an automatic and context-independent fashion, yielding a uniformity of the sort described by Scholl and Leslie (1999, 136–7).

One hallmark of the development of a modular cognitive capacity is that the end-state of the capacity is often strikingly uniform across individuals. Although the particulars of environmental interaction may affect the precise time-table with which the modular capacity manifests itself, what is eventually manifested is largely identical for all individuals. As the modular account thus predicts, the acquisition of ToM is largely uniform across both individuals and cultures. The essential character of ToM a person develops does not seem to depend on the character of their environment at all. It is at least plausible, *prima facie*, that we all have the same basic ToM!...The point is that the development of beliefs about beliefs seems remarkably uniform and stable.

Others like Segal (1996) maintain that the pattern of ToM development is identical across species, which is in marked contrast to the uneven and culturally dependent development of many other capacities. Such culture-independent views are inconsistent with research in social psychology, which shows that mechanisms of social cognition are constitutively dependent upon historical-cultural situatedness and group membership. This suggests that understanding others as persons is essentially context dependent—an aspect that any theory of social cognition must account for (see *Section 6.3* and Gallagher & Varga 2014 for further discussion).

4.3.3 *The simple phenomenological objection*

This is an objection directed only at versions of TT and ST that maintain that theoretical inference or simulation is (1) explicit or conscious and (2) pervasive and characteristic of our everyday understandings of others. Goldman's conception

---

[8] Spaulding (2018) is a very recent exception. Also see Gallagher and Varga (2014). This question relates to cultural constraints on understanding others, and phenomena connected with in-group/out-group dynamics. I'll return to these issues in *Chapter 6*.

of a conscious introspectionist ST may be a good example of this, if we combine it with his contention that simulation is the default mechanism for social cognition.

The simulation idea has obvious initial attractions. Introspectively, it seems as if we often try to predict others' behavior – or predict their (mental) choices – by imagining ourselves in their shoes and determining what we would choose to do. (Goldman 1989, 169)

Gregory Currie's description of simulation theory also makes it an explicit, conscious process: "I imagine myself to be in the other person's position [...] I simply note that I formed, in imagination, a certain belief, desire or decision, then attribute it to the other" (1995, 144–5). Imagining, noting, and attributing all seem to be conscious processes in this description. Since the claim is that these processes are both explicit and pervasive, then we should have some awareness of the different steps that we go through as we simulate or theoretically infer the other's mental states. But there is no phenomenological evidence that we do this in most of our everyday encounters with others. When I interact with or come to understand another person, there is no experiential evidence that I use such conscious (imaginative, introspective) simulation routines, or explicit theoretical inferences. That is, when we consult our own common experience of how we understand others, we don't find such processes. Goldman himself admits this:

[T]here is a straightforward challenge to the psychological plausibility of the simulation approach. It is far from obvious, introspectively, that we regularly place ourselves in another person's shoes, and vividly envision what we would do in his circumstances.
(Goldman 1989, 176)

Of course, this is not to say that we never use conscious simulations or theoretical inferences. It may be the case that confronted with some strange or unaccountable behavior I do try to understand the other person by running a simulation routine or by consciously making a folk-psychological inference. This type of process may also occur in specialized situations; for example, when we are playing poker, or practicing psychotherapy, or, as Overgaard and Michael (2015) suggest, on a first date. Just such instances are telling, however, since they are in fact special circumstances or specialized cases. Moreover, such cases tend to stand out in their rarity. I can easily become aware that I am in fact taking this approach, and it is all the more apparent when I do this simply because it tends to be the exception. In most of my encounters I do not find myself resorting to mindreading, because most of my encounters are not third-person puzzles solved by first-person introspective procedures, or third-person inferences.

To be clear, it is no longer common to find theory theorists or simulation theorists who think that these processes are explicit or conscious. Most proponents of TT and ST have come to consider these processes as implicit and non-conscious. Perhaps simulation or inference making can become so habitual that it becomes implicit, so that we do it without being aware that we do it, in the same way that we drive a car without being explicitly aware of all of our driving habits, or in the same way that an expert may employ cognitive strategies that become so habitual that the expert is no longer aware of how she does what she does (see Stich & Nichols 1992). The slightly more complex phenomenological objection in response to the claim that these processes become habitual would be that if such implicit processes stay at the personal level, they would remain accessible to conscious reflection, or at least they would become apparent, as unworkable habits, in problematic situations when our habitual strategies break down. We can become aware of a habit that we are not usually aware of in such circumstances. This simply does not seem to be the case for the sort of processes described by TT or ST. Again, it seems to go the other way: we may find ourselves initiating simulation processes or appealing to folk psychology precisely in the odd cases where our habitual practices for understanding others break down.

Such phenomenological objections, however, are not able to say anything directly about processes that may be subpersonal. Phenomenology cannot decide the nature of the cognitive mechanisms that underpin a psychological process—whether, for example, they involve mirror neurons or a ToM module that correlates with specific brain processes (Stich & Nichols 1992; Jacob 2011). This does not mean, however, that phenomenology is completely irrelevant to questions about social cognition. First, it's not clear that all aspects relevant to an explanation of social cognition are in fact subpersonal. Indeed, just as it would be a fantastical claim to say that all aspects of social cognition are phenomenologically accessible, it would be a fantastical claim to say that social cognition is entirely subpersonal and lacking in any relevant or efficacious experiential elements. Second, even those who limit explanation to subpersonal processes need an account of how such processes relate to what happens on the experiential level, assuming that we do experience something as we interact with others. Addressing these issues, however, goes beyond what I am calling the *simple* phenomenological objection, which, again, has a very limited target.

4.3.4 The integration problem

Another problem for some versions of TT and ST, especially explicit/conscious or introspectionist versions, involves the temporal aspects of what might be regarded as metarepresentational or high-order cognitive processes. In this regard, it's indicative that high-functioning individuals with Autism Spectrum Disorder who have difficulty understanding others often report that they use explicit theoretical inference or intellectual mentalizing to figure out what others mean by their behaviors (Sacks 1995, 258; Zahavi & Parnas 2003). In this regard, however, they complain that this is a slow process and that frequently they only figure things out after relatively long delays when the social interaction is already completed. If the processes described by TT and ST are conscious and involve multi-step routines, as in Goldman's description of introspectionist or high-level simulation, it would be difficult to see how they integrate into the typical flow of our everyday experiences of intersubjective interactions with others, where things often seem to flow smoothly in quick back and forth responses that depend on anticipatory processes (in elemental and integrative timescales).

Carruthers (2015) recognizes this issue and stipulates that the processes involved have to be very fast to avoid problems. This means, for him, that they have to involve very fast subpersonal binding processes. In the context of integrating mindreading with perceptual processes, he suggests: "The only limit will be whether mindreading inferences can be drawn fast enough for binding to take place. Since many forms of mental-state awareness are seemingly simultaneous with awareness of the behavior and/or circumstances that cause them, we can presume that ordinary mindreaders *can* draw the requisite inferences fast enough" (2015, 13). We revisit this issue in *Chapter 7*. Here we can say simply that such questions about temporal integration count against conscious or introspectionist versions of TT and ST.

4.3.5 *The developmental problem*

Another objection mentioned by Scheler (1954) can be raised against both TT and the more explicit versions of ST. The kind of inferential or simulation processes found in explicit versions of TT and ST are too cognitively complex to account for the ability to understand the intentions of others found in infancy. Robert Gordon, from a simulationist perspective, has made the same argument against TT. He suggests that children as young as two-and-a-half "already see behavior as dependent on belief and desire" but that it is unlikely that children so young could acquire and use "a theory as complex and sophisticated" as the one that TT requires (cited in Stich & Nichols 1992; also see Goldman 1989, 167–8).

We already mentioned, however, that there is now evidence to support the idea that even younger infants are able to grasp intentions (or purportedly, false beliefs) in others. In experiments with 13- and 15-month-old infants the infant observes an agent who looks for a toy where she (the agent) shouldn't be looking, since the information she has should lead her to look in a location where she falsely believes the toy to be. The infant looks longer at such behavior, indicating a violation of expectations (Onishi & Baillargeon 2005; Song et al. 2008; Surian et al. 2007; Yott & Poulin-Dubois 2012). In other experiments infants show anticipated looking at targets where they expect the agent to look for the toy (Southgate et al. 2007; Neumann et al. 2009). The experiments are consistently presented as experiments that test false-belief comprehension, where the young infants seemingly recognize that the agent has a false belief, predict how she will act, and are surprised at the unexpected action. The experimental results are themselves surprising precisely because the consensus had been that infants this young did not have a concept of belief, and certainly would not be capable of representing (or engaging in the kind of metarepresentational process necessary for attributing) false belief.

Here the debate on how to interpret such results raises the developmental problem. It's almost standard to simply assume a ToM framework for interpreting the results of these experiments (Carruthers 2009; Onishi & Baillargeon 2005). Is the infant actually capable of metarepresentational processes that would involve having a conception of belief, as Carruthers suggests? Stich and Nichols (1992) would see no problem in this since infants are already picking up sophisticated theoretical knowledge (folk physics) that allows them to understand how middle-sized physical objects work; and they are already in a process of mastering language, which, according to Stich and Nichols, depends on an internally represented theory. Seemingly, these are all cognitively complicated accomplishments. Why, however, should we think of language acquisition or the infant's ability to grasp how things work, or to grasp the intentions of others, as involving theoretical knowledge rather than a very practical kind of know-how? The infant learns about objects by grabbing them, putting them in its mouth, playing with them, etc. She learns language by pragmatic engagement with others; it seems possible that she learns about others in the same kind of pragmatic engagements rather than through processes that require sophisticated (i.e., overly intellectualized) cognitive abilities.

It might be easier to think that the infant understands the intentions of others by running a simulation routine. On this score perhaps a neural simulation theory would have an advantage over TT. Assuming that mirror neurons are already functioning in the young infant, then, ST could argue that simulation would be automatic and the infant would be capable of something like an intuitive mind-reading.[9] But this interpretation motivates a number of other questions that are not fully resolved. Does the mirror neuron system register mental states, per se—that is, can we say that neural simulation is a form of mindreading (as suggested by Goldman), or is it primarily a form of action recognition, which requires further cognitive processing to reach the level of mindreading or belief attribution? If it doesn't reach the level of mindreading, then the neural simulation account indicates nothing about the concept of false belief. Furthermore, there are questions about how mirror neurons would function if the infant did not first engage in, or have prior experience of the type of action that is observed (Calvo-Merino et al. 2005; Campbell & Cunnington 2017; Gerson, Bekkering & Hunnius 2015). A strict version of ST might say that the infant cannot understand anyone's actions until she engages in such actions herself so as to properly attune her mirror neuron system to such action. Whether or not ST can respond to these developmental worries, it's not clear that it can respond to some other, more fundamental doubts about the nature of simulation.

4.3.6 Problems of pretense and instrumental control

Consider, for example, a problem that concerns the very definition of simulation. Simulation, as initially defined was said to involve two aspects: (1) pretense and (2) instrumental control. That is, simulation was originally characterized in terms of a mechanism or model or process employing pretend beliefs that we manipulate or control in order to understand something to which we do not have direct access. We find both aspects discussed across the ST literature; indeed, they are ubiquitous and have been considered essential to the concept of simulation. Dokic and Proust (2002, viii) provide a good example of the instrumental aspect: simulation means "*using* one's own evaluation and reasoning mechanisms as a model for theirs." Gordon (2004, 1) extends this instrumentalism to the neuronal level by suggesting that on the "cognitive-scientific" model, "one's own behavior control system is employed as a *manipulable model* of other such systems. (This is not to say that the 'person' who is simulating is the model; rather, only that *one's brain can be manipulated to model other persons*)."[10]

---

[9] One ongoing debate concerns whether our motor systems are hard-wired with mirror neurons, so they operate at (or shortly after) birth (see Gallese et al. 2009), or whether mirror neurons develop via sensorimotor associative learning after birth (Cook et al. 2014). This is an issue we don't need to decide if we assume that by the time of the early false-belief experiments the infant has already been intensely exposed to others' behavior for a sufficient number of months so that sensorimotor learning will have attuned their mirror neurons to the behavior of others.

[10] Note that this quote from the *Stanford Encyclopedia of Philosophy* was retrieved 12 January 2007 (from: http://plato.stanford.edu/archives/fall2004/entries/folkpsych-simulation/). The entry has since been

Both instrumental control and pretense are reflected in Goldman's (2002, 7) explanation: simulation involves "pretend states" where, "by pretend state I mean some sort of surrogate state, which is *deliberately adopted* for the sake of the attributor's task.... In simulating practical reasoning, the attributor *feeds* pretend desires and beliefs into her own practical reasoning system." Adams (2001, 384) likewise indicates that "it is a central feature of ST that one takes perceptual inputs off-line"—that is, that simulation involves pretense (also see Bernier 2002).

The aspect of pretense seems essential for simulation if it is to be distinguished from a theoretical model or a simple practice of reasoning (see Fisher 2006). Simulation involves the use of a model "*as if*" I were in the other person's situation. As Gallese puts it, "our motor system becomes active *as if* we were executing that very same action that we are observing" (2001, 37). Likewise for Gordon (2005, 96) the neurons that respond when I see your intentional action respond "*as if* I were carrying out the behavior ....'

According to some of the major simulation theorists, then, it seems that for some process to be considered a simulation, it clearly needs to meet these two conditions: it is a process that I control in an instrumental way (in the explicit version it is "deliberately adopted"), and it involves pretense (I stand "as if" in the other person's shoes). It seems clear, however, that neither of these conditions is met by mirror neurons. First, in regard to the instrumental aspect, if simulation is characterized as a process that I (or my brain) instrumentally use(s), manipulate(s), or control(s), then it seems clear that what is happening in the implicit processes of motor resonance is not simulation. We, at the personal level, do not manipulate or control the activated brain areas—in fact, we have no instrumental access to neuronal activation, and it is not clear how we could use our brain processes as a model. Neither, arguably, does it make sense to say, that at the neurological level the brain itself is *using* a model or methodology, or that one set of neurons instrumentally uses another set of neurons as a model in order to generate an understanding of something else.[11] Indeed, in precisely the intersubjective circumstances that we are considering, these neuronal systems do not take the initiative; they do not activate themselves. Rather, they are automatically activated by the other person's action. The other person's action *has an effect on my brain* and *elicits* this activation. It is not me (or my brain) *initiating* a simulation; rather, my brain responds, primed by the perception of the other's action.

Second, in regard to pretense, there is no pretense in subpersonal mirror processes. Obviously, as vehicles or mechanisms, neurons either fire or don't fire. They don't pretend to fire. More to the point, to put it in standard representational terms, what these neurons represent or register cannot involve pretense in the way required by ST. At least on some readings, because mirror neurons are understood to be activated both when I engage in intentional action and when I see you engage in intentional

---

revised by Luca Barlassina and Robert Gordon and no longer contains this statement. The revised version does respond to some of the concerns raised here, as found in some of my previous publications (e.g., Gallagher 2007a).

[11] In the predictive coding literature the concept of a generative model is important, but at best it is metaphorical to say that the brain uses such a model. Friston (2013) avoids the idea of instrumental use by suggesting that, rather than *having* a model, the system *is* the model.

action, the mirror system is thought to be neutral with respect to the agent; no first-
or third-person specification is involved (Gallese 2004, 2005; Hurley 2005;
Vignemont 2004; Jeannerod & Pacherie 2004; also see the discussion of naked
intentions in *Section 3.3*). If that were the case, it would not be possible for them to
register *my* intentions as pretending to be *your* intentions; there would be no "as if"
in mirror neuron activation of the sort required by ST because there would be no "I"
or "you" represented.

There are several responses that can be made to this last point, and specifically
against the idea that mirror neuron activation is neutral with regard to agency. First,
as Georgieff and Jeannerod (1998) point out, even if there is no self *versus* other
distinction involved in the mirror neurons themselves, there needs to be some
accompanying neuronal process involved that discriminates between my action
and yours. They refer to this as the "Who system" and note that there is not a
complete overlap in the activation pattern of mirror neurons or "shared representations" for action *versus* observation of action. In that case, the non-overlapping
aspects of the activation pattern can act as the discriminatory mechanism, sorting
out my action from my observation of your action. "I" and "you" get represented in
that way. More generally, since MNs are never activated in isolation from other
ongoing processes in the rest of the system, some other factors in the system may
code for agent differentiation—e.g., the presence (in the case of action) or absence (in
the case of observation of action) of specific efferent signals. A second possibility is
that there may be differential timing involved in mirror neuron activation for action
versus observation of action. Activation of mirror neurons in the premotor cortex
may be prior to action for (my) action since such activation is usually regarded as
involved in motor planning; in contrast activation would be subsequent to action in the
case of observation of (your) action, the result of me seeing an action which obviously
has already begun. This temporal differentiation may be what codes for differentiation
in agency. A third possibility is that intrinsic differences in firing rates (spikes) of
mirror neurons between self-action and other-perception could provide differentiation
between self and other (Legrand 2007; see Gallese 2014) (see *Figure 4.1*).

All of these possibilities, in contrast to the claim of mirror neuron neutrality (or
the concept of naked intentions), suggest viable explanations for self-other differentiation. Still, self-other differentiation, although necessary for pretense, is not sufficient for pretense. Perhaps one could argue that despite the fact that pretense is a
complicated affair involving self-other differentiation plus some kind of "as-if"
process (I *as if* you), we do at times engage in pretense at the conscious or personal
level, and this possibility must have some kind of complicated neural correlates,
which may or may not involve mirror neurons. So whatever those neural correlates
are, minus those aspects that make it a conscious process, could be counted as a
neural (and non-conscious) simulation. As far as I know, no one has suggested this,
and perhaps for good reason. Since pretense at the conscious level, at least as it is
described by simulation theory, is not only complex, but, a significantly temporally
extended process compared to the fast and automatic firing of neurons, it's not clear
that such a process, whatever it might be, could meet the time constraints called for
by what is supposedly the quick pretense required for the neural simulation story.
Going "off-line" into a pretense routine costs time.

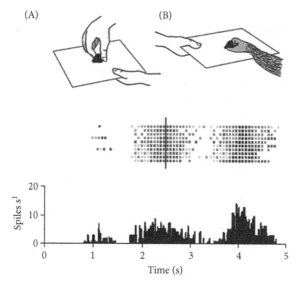

Figure 4.1 Mirror neuron activation in the macaque monkey, (A) for observation of action and (B) for self-action. Note the difference in firing patterns.

Source: Reprinted from *Cognitive Brain Research*, Volume 3, Issue 2, G. Rizzolatti, L. Fadiga, V. Gallese, and L. Fogassi, "Premotor cortex and the recognition of motor actions," pp. 113–41, Copyright © 1996 Published by Elsevier B.V., Figure 2, p. 133, with permission from Elsevier: https://www.sciencedirect.com/science/article/pii/0926641095000380

4.3.7 *The matching problem*

In response to just these kinds of worries simulation theorists have shifted away from pretense and instrumental use as definitional for simulation; they now argue that the instrumental and pretense conditions are not necessary conditions for simulation, and that simulation involves something more minimal. Goldman (2006; Goldman & Sripada 2005), for example, with respect to the concept of neural simulation, acknowledges a discrepancy between the ST definition of simulation (in terms of pretense and instrumental control) and the working of subpersonal mirror processes. "Does [the neural simulation] model really fit the pattern of ST? Since the model posits unmediated resonance, it does not fit the usual examples of simulation in which pretend states are created and then operated upon by the attributor's own cognitive equipment (e.g. a decision-making mechanism), yielding an output that gets attributed to the target..." (Goldman & Sripada 2005, 208). To address this discrepancy Goldman and Sripada propose a generic definition of simulation in terms of what has been called the "matching hypothesis":

[W]e do not regard the creation of pretend states, or the deployment of cognitive equipment to process such states, as essential to the generic idea of simulation. The general idea of simulation is that the simulating process should be similar, in relevant respects, to the simulated process. Applied to mindreading, a minimally necessary condition is that the state ascribed to the target is ascribed as a result of the attributor's instantiating, undergoing, or experiencing, that very state. In the case of successful simulation, the experienced state matches that of the target. This minimal condition for simulation is satisfied [in the neural model]. (2005, 208)

Goldman (2006, 131ff.) realizes, however, that if matching is a necessary condition for simulation, it is not a sufficient one, since without something further it is not clear why I would treat this state as something other than simply my own state, or why I would treat it as representative of someone else's state. One could argue that what one needs to add to this minimal condition of matching in order to make it a simulation of the other's action, intention, or mental state are precisely the pretense and instrumental conditions that Goldman sets aside. Another way to say this is that the very notion of simulation implies that it is a personal-level process. Indeed, in part, this is what motivates Goldman to adopt a hybrid simulation model. If implicit mirroring, in the sense of being in a matching state, may be considered a minimal condition for simulation, for the full-fledged simulation that constitutes mindreading (the attribution of mental states to others) one requires higher-level processes of "classification" (which he characterizes as introspective), as well as "projection" (2006, 245ff.). Although pretense is not required for low-level mirroring, it, or something like it, seems necessary to realize high-level simulation and mindreading (49).

Mirror neuron researchers, who defend the idea that mirror neurons instantiate a subpersonal simulation, also embrace the matching hypothesis (e.g., Rizzolatti et al. 2001). The "direct matching hypothesis" involves an automatic neural resonance of the mirror system when observing the actions of others. Matching means "mapping the visual representation of the observed action onto the motor representation of the same action" (2001, 661).[12] Matching of some sort, therefore, is an essential characteristic of simulation.

Let me suggest, however, against any version of ST that makes matching the primary requirement, that the minimal condition of matching, or any simulation that one can build on this, cannot be the pervasive or default way of attaining an understanding of others. There are many cases of encountering others in which we simply do not adopt, or find ourselves in, a matching state. Furthermore, with respect to neural ST, if simulation were as automatic as mirror neuron firing, then it would seem that we would not be able to attribute a state different from our own to someone else. But we do this all the time. Consider the example of the snake woman. At the

---

[12] Based on these descriptions, one can note here a difference between Rizzolatti and Goldman concerning the concept of matching. For Rizzolatti, the matching is "*intra*-cranial matching"—the match is between the activation in the observational state and activation in the action state in the same neuron or neuronal system; in contrast Goldman, although he cites Rizzolatti, describes in the quotation above, and elsewhere (e.g., Goldman 2006 and Jacob [2011, 527] seems to agree), a match between the observer's brain and the target's brain—an *inter*-cranial matching. Rizzolatti's *intra*-cranial matching is closely tied to the mechanics of mirror neuron activation and involves a specific claim about what constitutes a match; namely, my observation of your action activates the same neuronal patterns that would effect my own motor performance of that action. For Goldman's *inter*-cranial matching, seemingly, the neural processes in my brain that correlate to observing your action match the neural processes in your brain that correlate to your action. Such inter-cranial matching, however, seems a wider concept complicated by the fact that your action (the meaning of which involves intentions and circumstances beyond mere motoric aspects) likely involves neuronal components beyond mirror neurons. Nonetheless, given the nature of mirror neurons, it's likely that inter-cranial matching logically depends upon intra-cranial matching.

zoo I see a woman in front of me enthusiastically and gleefully reaching to pick up a snake; at the same time I am experiencing revulsion and disgust (or maybe just fear) about that very possibility. Her action, which I fully *sense* and *understand* from her enthusiastic and gleeful expression to be something that she likes to do, triggers in me precisely the opposite feelings. In this case, neither my neural states, nor my motor actions (I may be retreating with gestures of disgust just as she is advancing with gestures of enthusiasm), nor my feelings/cognitions match hers. Yet I understand her actions and emotions (which are completely different from mine), and I do this without even meeting the minimal necessary condition for simulation; that is, matching my state to hers.

If most social cognition takes place in interactive settings rather than observational ones (something that neuroscience has recently started to realize; e.g., Schilbach et al. 2013), the idea that my motor system goes into a state that matches or mirrors the other person's motor system may work for instances where imitation is called for, but is problematic when I have to respond in a non-imitative way to the other. The motor system, of course, is quite complex, so it may be possible that other-directed processes (mirror neurons go into a matching state in reference to observed action) and self-directed processes (action preparation for my own immediate response) can happen simultaneously. Yet, as Hurley points out, "movement priming predicts interference if you watch me doing X while you are doing Y" (2008, 15). This suggests that a constant automatic replication of your action in my motor system would slow down or interfere with my own action, since it is not often that I am doing precisely the same thing as you.

Furthermore, even in the case of observation (i.e., even when I am not interacting with another person), my motor system is often activated for what I would *like* to see happen, rather than what I actually see. For example, when I am watching a football game and see a player make just the wrong move I may find myself emulating (even physically performing or gesturing) the right (i.e., different) move, or what I think should have happened. Likewise, if I see an angry face of a stranger coming towards me, it is not clear that I have to match or simulate his facial expression in order to understand it as anger, and it is quite likely that I will not be replicating anger in myself or that I will start moving aggressively toward the stranger. Indeed, my motoric-affective systems will likely be in very different states—involving fear and cautionary retreat—and precisely because I understand what I see. The angry face registers and elicits a response, but not a mirroring match or simulation.

Even if there were some matching going on in my motor system (and clearly different parts of the motor system can instantiate different patterns simultaneously), the matching (or the matching alone) is not going to explain my response. Rather, there is a sense in which we can say that my motor system responds to the other not by matching the other's state, but by generating a compensating or opposing or supporting action. These considerations motivate an enactive interpretation rather than a simulation interpretation of mirror neuron activation (see *Section 5.4*).

In this regard, also consider the difficulties involved if we were interacting with more than one other person, or trying to understand others who are interacting with each other. Do we enter into a set of matching states and thereby simulate the neural/motor/mental/emotional states of more than one person at the same time? Or do we alternate quickly, going back and forth from one person to the other, instantiating, undergoing, or experiencing the states in question? How complicated does it get, however, if there is a small crowd in the room? Would there not be an impossible amount of cognitive work or subpersonal matching required to predict or to understand the interactions of several people if the task involves simulating their mental states, especially if in such interpersonal interactions (as in team work) the actions and intentions of each person are affected by the actions and intentions of the others (Morton 1996 makes a similar point).[13]

Over and above (or perhaps under and below) such behavioral complications with matching, neuroscientific studies have put the matching hypothesis into question. Dinstein et al. (2008) have shown that in fact, in certain areas of the brain where mirror neurons are thought to exist—specifically the anterior intraparietal sulcus (aIPS)—areas activated for *producing* a particular hand action are not activated for *perceiving* that hand action in another person. The experimenters use the paper-scissors-rock game, asking subjects to alternate executing a specific hand gesture and viewing a specific hand gesture. They show that for matching gestures, "distinctly different fMRI response patterns were generated by executed and observed movements in aIPS ... aIPS exhibits movement-selective responses during both observation and execution of movement, but ... the representations of observed and executed movements are fundamentally different from one another" (Dinstein et al. 2008, 11237). That is, even for matching gestures, there are no neuronal matching patterns found across action *versus* observation of action conditions in this mirror neuron area.

Also consider a study by Catmur, Walsh, and Heyes (2007). They demonstrate that learning can work against matching. The experimenters trained subjects to move their fingers in a manner incongruent with an observed hand; for example, moving the little finger when they observed movement of the index finger. After training, motor-evoked potentials (MEPs) were greater in the little finger when index finger movement was observed. "The important implication of this result is that study participants who exhibited incongruent MEP responses presumably did not mistake the perception of index finger movement for little finger movement ..." (Hickok 2009, 1236). That is, the lack of matching in the motor system does not preempt some kind of recognition of what the other person is doing.

Further empirical research on mirror neurons suggests good reasons to think mirror neuron activation does not always, or even usually, involve a precise match between motor system execution and observed action. Csibra (2005) points out that conservatively, 21–45 percent of neurons identified as mirror neurons are sensitive to multiple types of action; of those activated by a single type of observed action, that action is not necessarily the same action defined by the motor properties of the

---

[13] The requirement that the simulation has to be concretely similar also raises the starting problem again in relation to the instrumental and pretense conditions even for the explicit version of ST. If our simulation has to be concretely similar to the simulated state for it to be considered a simulation, assuming explicit instrumental control of our simulation process, how will we know how to run or control our simulation unless we already know in some detail what the other's state is like. And how do we come by that knowledge? If the answer is through simulation, then we have an infinite regress.

neuron; approximately 60 percent of mirror neurons are "broadly congruent," which means there may be some relation between the observed action(s) and their associated executed action, but not an exact match. Only about one-third of mirror neurons show a one-to-one congruence. Newman-Norlund et al. (2007, 55) suggest that activation of the broadly congruent mirror neurons may represent a complementary action rather than a similar action. In that case they could not instantiate simulations defined on the matching hypothesis.

Finally, I note that depending on how strictly one defines matching, there is an extensive empirical literature that counts against the matching hypothesis. Consider, for example, claims made about neural matching for experiencing and recognizing emotion. Goldman (2009a) argues that the most important and extensive evidence for mindreading based on mirror or matching processes is to be found in the case of emotion simulation. The evidence for this is found in neuropsychology where one can show that neuronal processes that are activated for the experience of a particular emotion are also activated for emotion recognition. Goldman cites a study by Calder et al. (2000) showing that a patient who suffered damage to the insula and basal ganglia was selectively impaired in experiencing disgust, and was also selectively impaired in disgust recognition. Goldman also cites evidence from Wicker et al. (2003) suggesting that when normal subjects experience or recognize disgust, the left anterior insula and the right anterior cingulate cortex are activated in a matching pattern. In citing this type of evidence, it's not clear how much weight to put on the term "selective," since that term suggests that damage to a particular brain area—e.g., the insula—disrupts the mirroring process specifically for instances of disgust in contrast to other emotions (Goldman 2009b cites Adolphs, Tranel, & Damasio 2003 in this respect). It's not clear, however, that we can find anything like a consistent one-to-one selective correlation of matching in a particular brain area for a particular emotion. Heris (2017a & b), for example, in a critical review of the experimental literature on disgust, found multiple studies that showed activations correlated to the experience and recognition of disgust in brain areas other than the insula (e.g., Gorno-Tempini et al. 2001; Schienle et al. 2002; Stark et al. 2003; Winston et al. 2003), and studies that showed no activation of the insula for processing disgust experience or recognition (Schienle et al. 2005, 2006). Other studies show that similar damage to the insula as documented in the Calder study resulted in no impairments in the experience or recognition of disgust (Couto et al. 2013; Straube et al. 2010). Heris (2017b) showed similar results for claims about matching type simulation of fear and pain. At the very least, this collection of studies shows that it is not easy to demonstrate the matching hypothesis.

4.3.8 Problems with the reuse hypothesis

ST is something of a moving target insofar as the definition of simulation keeps shifting. Not only has there been a move away from the standard definition of simulation as involving instrumental control and pretense towards a more minimal definition found in the matching hypothesis, but Vittorio Gallese, who at one point joined Goldman in defining the mirror system as a "matching system" (Gallese and Goldman 1998), has now shifted his understanding of simulation toward a more predictive action-control model.

When a given action is planned, its expected motor consequences are forecast. This means that when we are going to execute a given action we can also predict its consequences. The action model enables this prediction. Given the shared sub-personal neural mapping between what is acted and what is perceived – constituted by mirror neurons – the action model can also be used to predict the consequences of actions performed by others. Both predictions (of our actions and of others' actions) are instantiations of embodied simulation, that is, modeling processes.   (Gallese 2004, 1)

Gallese comes to this understanding of simulation *via* the *neural reuse hypothesis* which holds that specific neuro-mechanisms that originally served sensory-motor functions involving action planning are reused in the service of social cognition. Robert Gordon (2021) also makes a similar shift towards reuse and what he calls an agent-neutral action-planning process. The idea derives, in part, from the late Susan Hurley (1998) and is taken up in her posthumously published BBS paper, "The shared circuits model (SCM): How control, mirroring, and simulation can enable imitation, deliberation, and mindreading" (2008). Michael Anderson (2010) develops it further, drawing on Hurley, Gallese, and others. Although Hurley used the term "simulation" in developing her shared-circuits model, her concept of simulation has an ambiguous relation to the mindreading concept as used by ST. Originally she ties her concept of simulation to the use of that term in explanations of dynamic, subpersonal, online motor-control mechanisms, and it is this conception rather than any of the ones established in ST that comes into play in the idea of reuse. In the context of ST, however, the main question posed by the reuse idea is whether we can use the motor-control concept of simulation to give a subpersonal explanation of mindreading, without running into the same kind of trouble involved in the other definitions of simulation. Gallese thinks we can.

This perspective on simulation holds that the same neural structures involved in our own bodily self-experiences are also reused when facing others, enabling the pre-reflective under-standing of their behaviours and of some of their mental states, thus introducing a novel conceptualization of simulation with respect to its standard account in the philosophy of mind.
(Gallese 2014, 4)

The central thesis of Hurley's shared-circuits model is that "associations under-writing predictive simulation of effects of an agent's own movement, for instrumental control functions, can also yield mirroring and 'reverse' simulation of similar per-ceived movements by others" (Hurley 2008, 3). Here, "instrumental control" means subpersonal motor control of action. When we engage in intentional action our motor systems simulate the anticipated consequences of our movement in a quick forward model for purposes of controlling and correcting the movement so as to achieve our intention. This same online model, according to Hurley, can be reused to run offline and inversely in cases where we perceive another person's action. That is, when we see someone else act we can use the same model and neural mechanism in our system to simulate her action and in principle generate a prediction about her intention. This helps to explain our capacity for imitation, but also for social cognition.

Hurley's shared-circuits model distinguishes between five different layers of sub-personal processes.

Layer 1:   Basic adaptive feedback control: this is a comparator feedback control system found in many models of motor control.[14] Reafferent (sensory feedback) signals from the visual and proprioceptive systems are compared to the efferent motor commands issued by the system.

Layer 2:   Simulative prediction of effects for improved control: this is a feed-forward model that offers quicker motor corrections by comparing efferent signals (or efferent copy) with predicted sensory feedback even before sensory feedback is generated. The prediction involves a simulation of the anticipated sensory feedback.

Layer 3:   Mirroring for priming, emulation, and imitation: while the first two layers describe a now standard conception of how motor control works within an individual motor system, layer 3 opens up the system to the actions of others. It allows for running layer 2 inversely: "not only does efference copy produce simulated reafferent input in forward models [in the case of my own action], but [in the case of another's action] input signals can evoke mirroring efference or motor output [in my system]. Mirroring in effect runs the predictive simulations of forward models in reverse" (Hurley 2008, 13). Observed actions are thereby mirrored in the observer. In Hurley's terms, the control of my own action *shares the same circuits* as perception of the other's action.

Layer 4:   Monitored output inhibition combined with simulative prediction and/or simulative mirroring: inhibitory processes prevent us from automatically imitating the actions that we see others perform. This makes the mirroring offline, providing resources for understanding the other's action (introducing a self *versus* other distinction when combined with layer 3), or planning our own action (when combined with layer 2).

Layer 5:   Counterfactual input simulation: here "counterfactual inputs can simulate different possible acts by others and their results" (2008, 18). Hurley proposes that the theoretical inferences found in TT might come into play at this point, supplementing the basic understanding of others' actions with deliberations or inferences about possible actions.

Although Hurley does not rule out explicit forms of simulation, for the most part her use of the term refers to implicit, subpersonal simulation (in layers 2 and 3), which she associates with low-level resonance and mirror neurons. Simulation, she writes, "has a generic sense... including but broader than that in simulationist theories of mindreading." She cites Gallese and Goldman, and continues: "Simulation can be subpersonal or personal; in [the shared-circuits model] it is subpersonal" (2008, 3). Mirroring—i.e., running an inverse model of the other's actions—is initiated only in layer 3. The inverse model takes sensory input (e.g., the observed action of others) and generates the motor commands that would be necessary to construct that input. "Observed actions are thus mirrored in the observer" (2008, 13).

What is important for Hurley is that this is a direct resonance rather than an indirect inference. If there were any claim about pretense involved in this version of ST, there would be a problem since in layer 3 there is no differentiation between self

---

[14] The comparator model is discussed above in regard to the sense of agency, in *Section 3.3*.

and other. This differentiation does not emerge until the fourth layer where the system begins to monitor its simulations. Layer-4 monitoring processes thus generate a capacity for action understanding where self/non-self distinctions are in place. Hurley thus realizes that layer-3 matching resonance is not going to do the full job of action understanding, and she acknowledges some important limitations on the notion of mirroring. She points to the actual data about mirror neurons that limits the notion of matching (see above, and Csibra 2005)—some mirror neurons being only broadly congruent. Hurley rightly takes this kind of evidence to indicate flexibility in the system. But it also places some limitations on layer-3 processes. Mirror neuron activation (or Hurley's mirroring at layer 3) would not necessarily be sufficient for the kind of simulation that ST wants. That is, mirroring would not be sufficient for mindreading, and more complex aspects of layers 4 and 5 are required for the full story. With the introduction of layer 5, supposedly to explain how simulation can scale up to full-fledged mindreading, however, Hurley feels the need to go beyond simulation and to appropriate elements of theoretical (folk-psychological) inference.

Although Hurley shares common ground with more embodied and enactivist approaches to cognition, she also holds onto the idea that these approaches can be reconciled to the more standard ToMistic approaches. Indeed, while she clearly acknowledges the complexity of the problem of social cognition and recognizes that our relations with others are not reducible to one form of activity—either simple simulation or simple employment of folk psychology—she argues that the shared-circuits model can reconcile TT (mindreading by theoretical inference) and ST. Accordingly she adopts some aspects of the established ToM framework within which those theories have been developed. As Goldman makes clear in his commentary on Hurley's article, her "major theses apply equally across all applicable types of [social] cognition" (2008, 27). It is also clear from her article that Hurley's intention was to provide a "unified framework" (2008, 11) that would integrate TT and ST, and thus provide an account of mindreading as our primary and pervasive way of understanding others. Furthermore, Hurley seemingly provides a way to make sense of the different definitions of simulation. Simulation starts out as a very basic motor-control mechanism that then gets reused in layer 3 where it becomes capable of subpersonally mirroring or matching the actions of others. Layer 4 registers the difference between self and other, which is essential for the possibility of pretense, which then seems possible with a more instrumentally controlled process (involving the use of counterfactual reasoning to interpret the possible actions of others) in layer 5.

What specific role does the concept of reuse play in these explanations? What precisely does reuse tell us about simulation? Although Gallese suggests that the concept of reuse provides a "novel conceptualization" of simulation, this new concept doesn't tell us anything new about how the simulation mechanism works; it is rather part of an evolutionary account of how we get the mechanism in question—that is, how the mirror system comes to function the way it functions. Gallese also cites Dehaene's (2005; Dehaene et al. 2002) "neuronal recycling" hypothesis, which explains ontogenetic changes in the visual system (specifically in the "visual word form area") when a person learns to read. Through plastic changes the brain reuses or recycles an area that would otherwise be limited to one specialized function. This is a theory of brain plasticity. Gallese, however, favors a more phylogenetic story, and he endorses Anderson's (2010) more systematic account of "neural reuse." On this view, brain areas can adapt to different functions via their dynamical connections with different brain circuits, "the newer in evolutionary term[s] a cognitive function is, the wider is the brain circuit underpinning it" (Gallese 2014, 6). The more specialized term here is "exaptation." "Exaptation refers to the shift in the course of evolution of a given trait or mechanism, which is later on reused to serve new purposes and functions" (2014, 6). What precisely is the wider circuit to which motor neurons connected so that they were transformed into mirror neurons? This is not clear, and as Gallese admits, we have a lot more to learn about these mechanisms (2014, 7).

Accordingly, if we ask what the notion of reuse adds to ST, we can say that it provides the beginning of a phylogenetic account of how certain neural areas originally used only for motor control of one's own actions came to have an additional purpose; i.e., mirroring the actions of others. On Hurley's model, it's the story of how we get from layer 2 to layer 3. The important point is that the reuse hypothesis doesn't actually introduce any new or alternative understanding of the simulation mechanism into the account of subpersonal simulation; to the extent that we understand how the mechanisms—mirror neurons and/or forward-inverse models—work, we understand them independently of the reuse hypothesis. Whether we stay with the matching hypothesis, or add to it processes of inverse modeling or other processes found in Hurley's layers 4 and 5, these remain the candidates for explaining how simulation works at the subpersonal level. In that case, the notion of reuse does not solve any problems associated with such understandings of simulation. Specifically, reuse doesn't resolve problems that are associated with concepts of matching, or the limitations that Hurley herself saw with respect to layer-3 processing. Furthermore, even if the reuse hypothesis is consistent with the mirror neuron story, it does not support the simulationist interpretation over any other interpretation of what mirror neurons are doing.

If the reuse hypothesis doesn't solve any of ST's problems, it also doesn't avoid other problematic complications. I'll mention just three issues that arise if we take the reuse story to be closely linked to the notion of simulation in forward models. First, I suggest that Hurley was motivated to conceive of social cognition as involving something more than just simulation because simulation based on matching or forward models cannot give an adequate account of another person's intention. Hurley suggests that when the self-other distinction is introduced (in layer 4) simulation would target the intentional, means/end structure of action. Forward models, however, are very basic motor-control mechanisms. When it is said that the forward model compares efference copy with the intention, it is never clear precisely how much specification is included in the intention, or indeed, what kind of status the intention has (see above, *Section 3.2*). Let's assume that intention is specified as an M-intention, which seems appropriate for this type of motor-control system. In that case, the intention could be described as very basic. That is, in these models, the basic M-intention at stake may be summarized, for example, as "I will move my hand to target X in order to pick it up and throw it." The specifications of how to do this are reflected in the efferent signals sent to the muscles specifying things like direction, trajectory, speed, angular adjustment, etc. This process also integrates dorsal visual pathway information about where the target is, its estimated weight, the shape of the grasp needed to pick it up for one or other purpose, etc. It's not at all clear what further information might be in the system at this level. That is, we should not expect it to specify high-level information, such as, that you are going to throw the ball to first base.[15] That insight will have to come from elsewhere (e.g., context).

Accordingly, it is not clear how much work the inverse model or simulation can do with regard to understanding the intention of the other person, even if, as claimed, it can reconstruct an M-intention from the other person's actual movements. M-intentions, on their own, are often ambiguous. I see Jane picking up a book. Even if I can tell from the kinematics of her movements that she intends to hold onto it rather than throw it at me, it's not clear from this basic motoric simulation why she is doing what she is doing, or where precisely that action is heading. Perceived actions are often specified by situational factors, so that I may know her intention because I have some background sense of her circumstances or the situation in which Jane is acting. It's not clear, however, that I would be able to know that *via* the processing of a layer-3 emulator. Indeed, one may ask, what does the layer-3 emulator add to what I already know by means of vision, if I see her pick up the book. Perhaps some sense of the effort or the lack of effort it took to pick it up? I am not discounting the importance of motor-control mechanisms or M-intentions in regard to their role in what we can perceive; but whatever these things do for us, and even if we agree to call this a simulation process (without pretense, without matching) it's not clear that it is a form of simulation that would satisfy ST claims about mindreading.

Second, Hurley suggests that these emulation or mirroring processes can prime the observer's motor system to do the same action observed, and can prepare the observer for imitation. This, of course, may be very useful for learning certain skills. It's not clear how useful it is in other contexts. One result, according to Hurley, is that watching you eat your sushi with chopsticks will prime my system to facilitate my finger movement in a similar way. And one prediction from this is that there would be some degree of interference if I watch you do X while I am doing Y. Watching you eat your sushi should therefore, if indeed I am running a simulation of your action, make it more difficult for me to take a sip of my wine. I suspect, however, this may depend on my proficiency in wine drinking.

Priming effects may not seem far removed from the concept of matching, but they may be quite different. If, as we walk along together I see you starting to fall, I do not find myself matching your fall; rather, I find myself quickly responding in an attempt to catch you. If there is some matching process in my motor system, the more important processes are not the matching ones. Rather, the important thing is that

---

[15] Hurley suggests that more is included. Her example makes this clear. "I can move my hand to operate chopsticks to pick up sushi to dip it in soy sauce and then move it to my mouth to eat it, *in order to impress my boss; given associated simulative mirroring functions, I may start to resent you for eating the last piece of sushi as soon as you reach for your chopsticks*" (2008, p. 15, emphasis added). I've italicized the part that seems questionable to me. That is, I don't know precisely how motor-control emulators can include information about impressing my boss, etc., and my resentment may only be motivated *via* processes in layer 5.

my motor system comes into a process that is quite different from yours. If anything, it seems primed to respond in a way that does not match your movement. Rather, my subpersonal motor processes are quite busy controlling my attempt to catch you. Likewise, as noted above, if I see an angry face of a stranger coming towards me, it is not clear that I have to match or simulate that facial expression in order to understand it as anger—my motor and emotion systems seem to be in very different states—and yet I still understand what I see.

Third, as Goldman (2008) points out, Hurley's action-control model may apply to action, but will not apply to understanding another person's emotion or pain. These aspects of the other's behavior will not correspond to any of the forward/inverse control processes that pertain to action. For Goldman this prevents Hurley's model from being a general theory of social cognition, and puts certain limitations on what it can explain.

There are a number of questions that I must leave open at this point. I note, however, that this discussion of social cognition has brought us back to issues that concern action. I am in agreement with much of Hurley's enactivist view of action and perception, as well as many aspects of Gallese's embodied view of intersubjectivity.[16] I think, however, that such views lead to a better story than the simulation or theory theory story. It seems to me quite possible that in these subpersonal processes something other than matching or priming is going on; something other than attempting to replicate or reconstruct the action of the other. In the following chapters I try to give a more positive account of what that is.

---

[16] I have been engaged in an ongoing debate with Gallese on these issues. Our disagreements are quite focused on questions about simulation, but both Gallese and I acknowledge that we agree on most other issues (see Gallese 2010 especially pp. 85–6; Gallese 2014, 2017; Gallese & Sinigaglia 2011).

5

Interaction

It's not enough to criticize TT and ST without offering something in their place. The alternative that I will propose is interaction theory (IT). IT contends that understanding other people is primarily based on neither theoretical inference nor internal simulation, but rather on forms of embodied practices. In explicating this idea I do not want to deny that we do develop capacities for both theoretical interpretation and simulation, and that in some cases we do understand others by explicitly (i.e., consciously) enacting just such theoretical attitudes or simulations. The broader picture of social cognition, however, involves a pluralism of different practices, within which, as I suggested in the previous chapter, instances of theoretical inference or simulation that target mental states per se are rare relative to the majority of our interactions. Interacting with others, especially in circumstances that involve established cultural practices, is often governed in large part by social norms (Ratcliffe 2007, 86ff); our understanding of someone's action is frequently shaped in terms of the social roles they play (Bermúdez 2003). Sitting in my local café I typically do not have to worry about the mental states of the waiter as he approaches my table. I understand the people I'm sitting with, not by puzzling about their mental states, but, for example, by catching their glance, noticing their expressions, seeing what they are doing, listening to what they are saying, and how they are saying it. On this view TT and ST, at best, explain a very narrow and specialized set of cognitive processes that we sometimes use to relate to others. Neither theoretical nor simulation strategies constitute the primary way in which we relate to, interact with, or understand others.

5.1 This Is IT

Let me try to head off some misunderstandings before providing the details of interaction theory. There has been some confusion about the precise claims of IT with respect to mindreading and the conception of mental states. I take mindreading to be the process that is defined precisely and narrowly by TT and ST—that is, as the process (whether explicit or implicit) of inferring or simulating mental states that are purportedly hidden away and inaccessible to perception. In this regard, mindreading is defined in close connection to a very orthodox conception of mental state as some kind of *purely internal* mental phenomenon unavailable to anyone other than the person having that mental state (although in some cases TT suggests that even one's own mental states may not be available in any first-person way to the cognizing subject). Mindreading, so defined, is the attempt to get to such hidden states.

If the concept of mindreading is tied to this orthodox notion of mental state, then the claim made by IT is that in most of our everyday encounters with others, mindreading is not necessary. That's not simply because in many cases embodied interactions, in relatively well-defined social and cultural contexts, are sufficient to give us an understanding of the other person, but also because a different, non-orthodox conception of the mind, understood as embodied, action-oriented, and enactively contextualized, is at stake.[1]

The concept of interaction is central to this chapter, and to the rest of the book. For the sake of clarity, then, it is important to offer a precise definition of interaction.

Interaction: a mutually engaged co-regulated coupling between at least two autonomous agents, where (a) the co-regulation and the coupling mutually affect each other, and constitute a self-sustaining organization in the domain of relational dynamics, and (b) the autonomy of the agents involved is not destroyed, although its scope may be augmented or reduced.

(Based on De Jaegher, Di Paolo, & Gallagher 2010)

Specifically, IT comes along with the claim that if we think of social cognition in terms of embodied and enactive processes of interaction, rather than in terms of mindreading, this has significant implications for how we think of the mind and mental states. Specifically we should start thinking of the mind as embodied, environmentally embedded, and extended, and not simply as something hidden away inside the head, or something generated exclusively by brain states. Accordingly, we should also think of the mental more in terms of dynamical embodied *processes* than in terms of static states. Mental processes (like intentions and emotions) are not states hidden from view in an inaccessible mind. In *Chapter 3* I discussed different concepts of action intention, where M- and P- intentions are said to be in the movement or in the action. In that sense, as I will argue (in this chapter and the next), intentions are not unobservable. I'll also suggest a way to think about emotion so that it is not reducible to a covert mental state.

The standard and dominant approaches to social cognition rarely emphasize intersubjective interaction per se, and even when they do mention interaction they frame the problem in terms of two minds that have to communicate across the seemingly thin air of an unbridgeable gap. On this view, interaction is not a solution but simply another way to state the problem of other minds. Consider, for example, the following formulation.

[. . . T]he study of social interaction . . . is concerned with the question of how two minds shape each other mutually through reciprocal interactions. To understand interactive minds we have to understand how thoughts, feelings, intentions, and beliefs can be transmitted from one mind to the other.   (Singer, Wolpert, and Frith 2004, xvii)

On the standard ToM accounts, to bridge this gap some kind of cognitive process in one individual's mind will have to provide the means to infer or simulate, and

---

[1] This is what some critics miss or misunderstand. For example, Michael, Christensen, & Overgaard (2014) who consider "low-level" embodied and perceptual processes to be inadequate to get to mental states such as intentions and emotions, and therefore require "higher-order" mindreading to do the full job, operate with an orthodox view of mental states. IT is working with a different concept of mind, where intentions and emotions are themselves embodied processes (see Gallagher 2017a).

thereby mindread, the hidden mental states of the other. As we've seen, ToM appeals to standard false-belief tests to show how children under 4 years are unable to read minds. In contrast, IT draws on evidence from developmental psychology to show that significant intersubjective interaction and understanding begins long before a child reaches the age of 4. IT also offers an alternative (i.e., non-simulationist), enactivist interpretation of the neuroscience of mirror neurons. It further draws on phenomenological evidence and theories of embodied cognition to argue that the various embodied processes that characterize interaction from the earliest age do not disappear, to be replaced by ToM mechanisms or simulationist talents; they rather mature and continue to characterize our adult interactions. Moreover, with respect to the more sophisticated and nuanced understandings found in those interactions, IT emphasizes the importance of context and circumstance, and the role of communicative and narrative practices.

Developmentally, one can think of IT as building on three sets of processes or abilities, taking as its point of departure the notion of primary intersubjectivity (Trevarthen 1979).

- **Primary intersubjectivity** (starting from birth)—sensory-motor abilities and enactive perceptual capacities in processes of interaction
- **Secondary intersubjectivity** (starting around 1 year of age)—abilities to jointly attend, share contexts, engage pragmatically, and act *with* others
- **Communicative and narrative competencies** (starting from 2 to 4 years)— communicative and narrative practices that enhance intersubjective interactions, make motives and reasons for acting more explicit, and provide a more nuanced and sophisticated social understanding

Appealing to these capacities IT challenges the three suppositions associated with ToM approaches (outlined in *Chapter 4*). In their place IT argues for the following propositions.

(1*) Other minds are not hidden away and inaccessible.[2] The intentions, emotions, and dispositions of others are at least partially instantiated in their actions and embodied practices in situ. In most cases of everyday interaction no inference or projection to mental states beyond those actions or practices is necessary.

(2*) Our normal everyday stance toward the other person is not third-person, observational; it is second-person interaction. We are not *primarily* spectators or observers of other people's actions; for the most part we are interacting with them in some communicative action, on some project, in some pre-defined relation; or we are treating them as having the potential to interact with us.

(3*) Our primary and pervasive way of understanding others does not involve mentalizing or mindreading; in fact, these are rare and specialized abilities that we develop only on the basis of a more embodied engagement with others.

---

[2] For a Wittgensteinian version of this idea, see Carpendale and Lewis (2004).

In this chapter I'll summarize the scientific evidence that supports these statements, and I'll argue that IT is able to address or avoid all of the problems found in
the ToM approaches.

5.2 Primary Intersubjectivity

Primary intersubjectivity consists of the innate or early developing sensory-motor
capacities that bring us into relation with others and allow us to interact with them.
These capacities are manifested at the level of action and perceptual experience—as
we engage with others we *see* or more generally *perceive* in their bodily postures,
movements, gestures, facial expressions, gaze direction, vocal intonation, etc. what
they intend and what they feel, and we respond with our own bodily movements,
gestures, facial expressions, gaze, etc. On this view, in second-person interactions, the
"mind" of the other is given and manifest in the other person's embodied comportment.[3] The basis for human interaction and for understanding others can be found
already at work in early infancy in certain embodied practices that are emotional,
sensory-motor, perceptual, and nonconceptual.

The developmental evidence for primary intersubjectivity suggests that pre-
theoretical (nonconceptual) sensory-motor capabilities for understanding others
already exist in very young children. Infants already have a sense, from their own
self-movement and proprioception, of what it means to be an experiencing agent.
They respond, in the interactive mode, to certain kinds of entities (but not to all
entities) in the environment—that is, they respond to other agents. Infants are able to
distinguish between inanimate objects and agents. They can respond in a distinctive
way to human faces; that is, in a way that they do not respond to other objects
(Legerstee 1991; Johnson 2000; Johnson, Slaughter, & Carey 1998). Infants from
birth are capable of perceiving and responding to facial gestures presented by another
(Meltzoff & Moore 1977; 1994). This interaction depends on a distinction between
self and non-self, and a proprioceptive sense of one's own body (Bermúdez 1996;
Gallagher & Meltzoff 1996).

Primary intersubjectivity includes infant imitation—a phenomenon that is open to
many different theoretical interpretations. Strong claims by some researchers who
interpret this behavior in neonates as a form of imitation (e.g., the infant responding
to a facial gesture such as tongue protrusion with a matching tongue protrusion—
e.g., Meltzoff & Moore 1994) remain controversial. In contrast to those who argue
that the infant's response involves differential imitation (see Vincini et al. 2017a & b;
Vincini & Jhang 2018; and recent experimental studies by Nagy et al. 2013, 2014),
others argue that this phenomenon is a case of perceptual priming, contagion, or a
simple arousal response (Anisfeld 2005; Keven & Akins 2017; Jones 2006; 2009; Ray
& Heyes 2011). From the perspective of IT, however, even if this behavior is mere
arousal, perceptual priming, or a form of contagion, and not a case of differential
imitation, it nonetheless can lead directly to intersubjective interaction. For example,

---

[3] This is not to deny that there is some private aspect to mental experience. The possibility of deception
attests to the fact that we do not always have complete access to the other person's mind. The argument
here is simply that we do not appeal to a hidden mind when we interact with others in this primary way.

an initial adult facial gesture may motivate the infant's arousal and response; in turn the infant's response has an effect on the adult who is encouraged to continue with facial games, etc. In this way, a mere arousal response could facilitate early social interaction and could be easily integrated into theories of the indispensability of affective interaction for the development of social cognition (Gallagher 2001; 2005a; Reddy 2008; Trevarthen & Aitken 2001). Thus, "an alert newborn can draw a sympathetic adult into synchronized negotiations of arbitrary action, which can develop in coming weeks and months into a mastery of the rituals and symbols of a germinal culture, long before any words are learned" (Trevarthen 2011, 121).

Regardless of how we interpret the data (imitation *versus* arousal *versus* perceptual priming or contagion), the developmental evidence is fully consistent with the phenomenological idea of an emerging shared affective intentionality—what Merleau-Ponty (2012) calls "intercorporeity"—which comes to be established between or across the perceiving subject and the perceived other. As Husserl (1973) suggested as early as 1907, and as recent research on the neuronal mirror system confirms, our perception of the other person induces a sensory-motor process that reverberates kinetically and kinesthetically. Neuroscientific experiments indicate that this occurs even in infants as young as 7 months (Meltzoff et al. 2018; Meltzoff, Saby, & Marshall 2019). As Gopnik and Meltzoff put it, in a way that undermines their own theory-theoretical perspective, "we innately map the visually perceived motions of others onto our own kinesthetic sensations" (1997, 129).

Primary intersubjectivity can be specified in much more detail. Let me begin by noting, however, that although these aspects of infant behavior are sometimes considered to be "precursors" of ToM (see Baron-Cohen 1995, 55; Gopnik & Meltzoff 1997, 131), they support a more immediate, less theoretical (non-mentalizing) mode of interaction. One such ability involves what Baron-Cohen (1995) calls the "intentionality detector." He considers this to be an innate capability that allows the infant to perceive "mental states in behavior" (1995, 32)—to perceptually interpret the bodily movement of others as goal-directed intentional movement. In effect, the infant is capable of perceiving other persons as intentional agents. This perceptual ability is, as Scholl and Tremoulet suggest, "fast, automatic, irresistible and highly stimulus-driven" (2000, 299). This suggests that for an agent involved in interaction, the other person's intention is in the first place accomplished in their action or the dynamic comportment of their body.

The neonate's ability to respond to perceived gestures, and intentionality detection, however, are not the only things that characterize primary intersubjectivity during the first year. Here is an incomplete list of processes that should be included.

- At 2 months, infants are already attuned to the other person's attention; they follow the other's head movements and gaze (Baron-Cohen 1995; Maurer & Barrera 1981). The infant is able to follow the gaze of the other person, to see that the other person is looking in a certain direction, and to sense what the other person sees (which is oftentimes the infant herself), in a way that throws the intention of the other person into relief.
- Also at 2 months, second-person *interaction* is evidenced by the timing and emotional response of infants' behavior. Infants "vocalize and gesture in a way

that seems [affectively and temporally] 'tuned' to the vocalizations and gestures of the other person" (Gopnik & Meltzoff 1997, 131). This "attunement" is part of a mutual alignment that characterizes interactions and that can be specified in detail in their dynamical relations and the integration of the intrinsic temporalities of the agents' movements (Trevarthen 1999; Trevarthen et al. 2006).

- At 5–7 months infants are able to detect correspondences between visual and auditory information that specify the expression of emotions (Walker 1982; Hobson 1993; 2002).

- At 6 months infants start to perceive grasping as goal directed, and at 10–11 months infants are able to parse some kinds of continuous action according to intentional boundaries (Baldwin & Baird 2001; Baird & Baldwin 2001; Woodward & Sommerville 2000). They start to perceive various movements of the head, the mouth, the hands, and more general body movements as meaningful, goal-directed movements (Senju, Johnson, & Csibra 2006).

Buckner et al. (2009, 140) have referred to these different capacities as a "weakly integrated swarm of first-order mechanisms." But we should not think of these as mechanisms or capacities that belong strictly to the individual. It's important to highlight the *interactive* nature of the infant's relations with others in precisely these primary sensory-motor processes. First, the kinds of interactions that constitute primary intersubjectivity are not automatic or mechanical procedures; Csibra and Gergely (2009) have shown, for example, that the infant is more likely to respond to another person's actions only if that person is attending to the infant. The methodological individualism that defines the quest for underlying mechanisms or individual capacities, and which motivates much of the developmental ToM literature, is misguided insofar as it overlooks the essential contribution of the other agent and the interaction process to social cognition. Second, we should discount the idea that the infant is simply a passive spectator trying to figure out what is going on. The analyses of infant–caregiver interactions (as well as of social interactions in shared activities, in working together, in communicative practices, and so on) show that agents unconsciously coordinate or align their movements, gestures, and speech acts (Issartel, Marin, & Cadopi 2007; Kendon 1990; Lindblom 2015), entering into synchronized resonance with others, with slight temporal modulations (Gergely 2001), in either in-phase or phase-delayed rhythmic co-variation (Fuchs & De Jaegher 2009). The key idea is that *in some cases* interaction itself plays an essential role in constituting social cognition (De Jaegher et al. 2010).[4] In pre-linguistic proto-communication, as much as in later verbal communication, as we listen to or engage with another person, we coordinate our perception-action sequences; our movements are coupled with changes in velocity, direction, and intonation of the movements and utterances of the speaker (see *Section 7.1* for more detail).

---

[4] I add emphasis to *"in some cases"* because critical commentators on the De Jaegher et al. (2010) paper sometimes ignore this qualification (e.g., Spaulding 2012). Although this still remains a strong claim, there is no extreme claim here that *in every case* interaction constitutes social cognition. See, e.g., Herschbach (2012); Michael and Overgaard (2012).

Developmental studies show the very early appearance of, and the importance of, timing and coordination in the intersubjective context where what matters is the interaction dynamics.[5] In still-face experiments, for example, infants are engaged in a typical face-to-face interaction with an adult for 1 to 2 minutes, followed by the adult assuming a neutral facial expression. This is followed by reengagement in another typical face-to-face interaction. Infants between 3 and 6 months become visibly discouraged and upset during the still-face period (Tronick et al. 1978; see Muir 2002 for an extension of this to interactive touch). Murray and Trevarthen (1985) have also shown the importance of the mother's live interaction with 2-month-old infants in their double TV monitor experiment where mother and infant interact by means of a live television link. The infants engage in lively interaction in this situation. When presented with a recorded replay of their mother's previous actions—that is, precisely the same actions that they saw before, but without the dynamical timing that would characterize true interaction—they quickly disengage and become distracted and upset. These results have been replicated, eliminating alternative explanations such as infants' fatigue or memory problems (Nadel et al. 1999; Stormark & Braarud 2004).

The way that such interaction can constitute social cognition can best be explained from the enactivist perspective. On the enactivist view, as embodied agents, we do not passively receive information from our environment and then create internal representations of the world in our heads; rather, we actively participate in the generation of the shared meaning we experience, the result of pragmatic and dynamical interchanges between agent and environment (Gallagher 2017a; Varela et al. 1991). In the intersubjective context, interaction has an autonomy that goes beyond what the participating individuals bring to the process (De Jaegher et al. 2010). Indeed, much like dancing the tango, the interaction is not reducible to a set of mechanisms contained within the individual; it takes (at least) two embodied individuals who are dynamically coupled in the right way. Continuous dynamical movements between synchronized, desynchronized, and the states in-between, drive the process of social interaction (De Jaegher 2009). Attunement, loss of attunement, and re-established attunement maintain both differentiation and connection between individual agents. These processes result in the creation of meaning that goes beyond what each individual qua individual can bring to the process.

In this regard, it is the interaction itself that contributes something that is not reducible to the actions of the individuals involved (Gibbs 2001). Infants perceive others as agents and are able to see and respond to bodily movement as goal-directed intentional movement. These kinds of interactive engagements, without the intervention of theory or simulation, give the infant a non-mentalizing (pre-theoretical) understanding of the intentions and dispositions of other persons (Allison, Puce, & McCarthy 2000), and such understandings are operative by the end of the first year (Baldwin 1993; Johnson, 2000; Johnson et al. 1998), if not before. Understanding in this context does not mean an intellectual or ideational form of knowledge that could

---

[5] Indeed, interaction likely predates strictly intersubjective relations and can be traced to prenatal motor experience and the non-conscious motor coupling between mother and fetus (Della-Butt & Trevarthen 2013; Lymer 2010).

count as a proto-theory. Rather, the concept of understanding at stake here is both *pragmatic* and *affective*. Pragmatic means that it is a form of "know-how," which on the enactivist view means that I understand others in terms of my actual or potential interactions with them. I know how to respond to them. This idea broadens into the notion of social affordance. Affectivity refers to what Hobson (2011) calls our affective engagements with the attitudes of others, a feature of typically developing infants' social relations, at least from the age of about 2 months. This is not a theory-based mentalizing engagement with *propositional* attitudes, but engaged interactions with motoric, emotional, and hedonic aspects (see Cole & Montero 2007). In some cases our interactions can take on an autonomy that multiplies or magnifies the affective aspects of our experience. In other cases, affective aspects remain subtle and nuanced, yet still capable of affecting our intersubjective life. In still other cases the emotional dimension seems to be embedded in social practices, rituals, and contexts and can have a contagious character; e.g., sing-song movements and intonations between infant and caregiver or, at the crowded athletic event or at concerts when the music starts to play.

In these pragmatic, affective, and hedonic embodied dimensions, saliency and meaning emerge. Grasping, pointing, moving towards, moving away, staying close, nodding, gazing in a certain direction, etc.—all of these things occurring in specific styles (Hobson 2011)—register, often non-consciously, as inherently meaningful aspects of the interaction (Goodwin 2000; see *Section 7.1*). The point here is that in the context of engaging with others, in seeing or participating in the actions and expressive movements of the other person, one already grasps their meaning; no inference to a hidden set of mental states (beliefs, desires, etc.) is necessary.

Importantly, primary intersubjectivity is not something that disappears after the first year of life. It is not a stage that we leave behind, and it is not, as Greg Currie suggests, a set of precursor states "that underpin early intersubjective understanding, and *make way* for the development of later theorizing or simulation" (2008, 212; emphasis added; cf. Baron-Cohen 1991, 1995). Rather, citing both behavioral and phenomenological evidence, IT argues that we don't leave primary intersubjectivity behind; the processes involved here don't "make way" for the purportedly more sophisticated mindreading processes—these embodied interactive processes continue to characterize our everyday encounters even as adults. That is, we continue to understand others in strong interactional terms, facilitated by our grasp of facial expressions, gestures, postures, and actions as meaningful.

Scientific experiments bear this out. Point-light experiments (involving actors in the dark wearing point lights on their joints, presenting abstract outlines of emotional and action postures), for example, show that not only children (although not autistic children) but also adults perceive emotion even in movement that offers minimal information (Hobson & Lee 1999; Dittrich et al. 1996). Close analysis of facial expression, gesture, and action in everyday contexts shows that as adults we continue to rely on embodied interactive abilities to understand the intentions and actions of others and to accomplish interactive tasks (Lindblom 2015; Lindblom & Ziemke 2008). In this regard, the capabilities of primary intersubjectivity continue into secondary intersubjective contexts. Neither do the secondary intersubjective aspects of joint attention and social referencing disappear from our repertoire of adult social-cognitive capacities. In effect, the various processes that ToM approaches call "precursors" arc not precursors; they are part of a permanent repertoire that, short of pathology, continue to characterize adult social cognitive processes.

IT contends that these embodied practices of primary intersubjectivity constitute a significant part of our ability to understand others, and continue to do so through adulthood. In much of our ordinary and everyday intersubjective situations we have an action-oriented perception-based understanding of another person's intentions because their intentions are explicitly instantiated in their embodied actions. This kind of primary understanding does not require us to postulate some belief or desire that is hidden behind the other's actions. This is not a return to behaviorism, however, or a denial of phenomenal consciousness or inner experiential life—indeed, primary intersubjectivity depends significantly on affective processes that are experienced by the interacting participants. Such conscious and affective phenomena are continuous with, and indeed, are often accomplished in embodied, intersubjective interaction processes and practices. Bodily expressions are not externalizations of something hidden in the mind; they rather continue or, in some cases, accomplish what we, in reflective and often abstract considerations, come to call mental states.[6]

5.3 Secondary Intersubjectivity in Joint Attention and Joint Action

Sometime during the first year of life infants build on the person-to-person immediacy of primary intersubjectivity, and enter into *contexts* of shared attention—shared situations—in which they begin to learn how people engage with things, and what those things mean (see Trevarthen & Hubley 1978). Peter Hobson nicely summarizes this notion of secondary intersubjectivity.

The defining feature of secondary intersubjectivity is that an object or event can become a focus *between* people. Objects and events can be communicated about.... [T]he infant's interactions with another person begin to have reference to the things that surround them.

(Hobson 2002, 62)

If children start, not simply as passive spectators or observers of others, and in their interactions they cope by responding to and seeing others in terms of the possibilities of joint actions, they then develop further capabilities in the contexts of those interactions. Eighteen-month-old children, for example, can comprehend what another person intends to do with an artifact. They are able to re-enact to completion the goal-directed behavior that the other agent fails to complete. Seeing an adult who tries to manipulate a toy in the right way and who appears frustrated about being unable to do so, the child, given the opportunity for interaction, quite readily picks up

[6] As Carpendale and Lewis (2004) suggest, this is consistent with a Wittgensteinian view. They quote Racine (from personal communication, November 2002), "when people in the field speak of beliefs as mental contents, they reify belief into a new form of mental content that is independent of activity but yet causes activity. There are no such contents. Belief exists and is created in action, not in the head. We should not take the development of an ability to re-present activities off line to be the development of an ability to experience inner states of belief" (10).

the toy and shows the adult how to do it (Meltzoff 1995; Meltzoff & Brooks 2001). The understanding demonstrated in such a situation depends on shared attention and the pragmatic context. Just as we tend to understand our own actions, as I suggested in *Chapter 1*, relative to the context that reflects an ordering of its different aspects according to its highest realizable affordance, we tend to understand the actions of others in the same way. We understand the actions of others in terms of the affordances that they, and the situation, offer. This means that we understand actions at the most relevant pragmatic (intentional, goal-oriented) level, ignoring possible subpersonal or lower-level descriptions (Gallagher & Marcel 1999; Jeannerod 1987), but also, importantly, ignoring ideational or mentalistic interpretations. Just as when we are asked "What are you doing?" we tend to say things like "I'm getting a drink," rather than "I'm activating my neurons" or "I'm flexing my muscles," so also we don't say "I'm acting on a belief that I am thirsty." Likewise as we engage with others in pragmatic circumstances, we do not typically look beyond their actions in order to identify the beliefs that motivate them. If I see you reach for a glass and a bottle of water, I know what your intentions are as much from the glass and bottle of water as from your reach, and I don't need to worry about what your belief is, if indeed it is anything beyond what you are doing. We interpret the actions of others in terms of their goals and intentions set in contextualized situations, rather than abstractly in terms of either their muscular performance or their beliefs.

Both phenomenology and science offer some guidance in understanding secondary intersubjectivity. For example, Aron Gurwitsch (1978) offers a non-cognitivist, phenomenological account of intersubjectivity. He argues that our everyday engagements with others do not involve special cognitive acts or some "magical psychical mechanism." For Gurwitsch, pragmatic involvement rather than cognitive observation is the primary basis for intersubjective understanding. In this respect, however, he tends to ignore the contribution of primary intersubjectivity contending that our access to the meaning of the other person is due more to pragmatic contexts than to the expressive movements of others (Gallagher 2005b). Gurwitsch's account is not inconsistent with Josef Perner's (1991) emphasis on the situation. Perner attributes to young children what he calls "situation theory," meaning that 3-year-olds employ contextual aspects of the environment to understand others. Gurwitsch, likewise, would emphasize that the environment, the situation, or the pragmatic context is not something that the child, or the adult, brandishing a theory, objectively confronts as an outside observer. This is the same notion of *agentive situation* that we found in Dewey (1938; see *Section 1.2*), and it should be understood to include the experiencing subject who is at the same time an agent of intentional actions within that situation. Even as an observer one is pragmatically situated as an agent of potential action and interaction.

5.3.1 *Joint attention*

Developmentally, joint attention is located at the intersection of a complex set of capacities that serve our cognitive, emotional, and action-oriented relations with others. It forms a bridge between primary intersubjectivity and secondary intersubjectivity. "In joint attention the child coordinates her attention to the object and the adult at the same time as the adult coordinates her attention to the same object and the child" (Tomasello 1995, 107). In joint attention, the child alternates between monitoring the gaze of the other and what the other is gazing at, checking to verify that they are continuing to look at the same thing. Infants around this time learn to point and between 9 and 18 months look to the eyes of the other person to help interpret the meaning of an ambiguous event (Phillips, Baron-Cohen, & Rutter 1992; Reddy 2008). Joint attention has tremendous importance for social interaction and for our ability to generate meaning through such interaction. In regard to the nature of joint attention I want to emphasize two things. First, the kind of coordination needed for joint attention is the kind of movement found in embodied interaction rather than a psychological coordination of mental states. Second, emotion plays an important role in shaping the meaning outcome of joint attention.

What exactly does it mean to coordinate attention? One view, consistent with the suppositions of TT and ST, is that since attention is a psychological state, then the coordination must be a psychological coordination. The notion of psychological coordination is often framed in terms of propositional attitudes, or being in certain mental states, here having to do with attention—i.e., we recognize or know that the other person is attending, and the other person knows that we are attending. John Campbell summarizes this view.

There are various ways in which propositional states could be involved in coordination. Propositional states might enter into the control of attention itself and they might enter into my recognition of how my attention, or your attention, is being controlled. First, it might be that I know what you are attending to, and that this knowledge is a factor in sustaining my attention on the thing. Secondly, I might intend to attend to whatever you are attending to. And thirdly, it might be that I know that the reason I am attending to the thing is, in part, that you are attending to it. And finally, it might be that I know that the reason you are attending to the thing is, in part, that I am attending to it.   (Campbell 2005, 245)

Such accounts suggest that joint attention involves mindreading (of the TT or ST variety) rather than embodied interaction. I not only have to know that you are attending, but also I have to know that you are capable of having such a mental state as attending to something, and that is something I have to infer or simulate. Such mindreading, as Campbell points out, "is 'off-line' in that its upshot is not permanent and it is decoupled from action" (242). *Decoupled from action* because TT and ST, as already noted, have traditionally been cast in terms of third-person observation rather than second-person interaction. Just this by itself should tell us that TT and ST are going to have a difficult time explaining the interactional nature of joint attention.

The fact that joint attention capability develops during the first year is already problematic for TT and explicit versions of ST; that is, for any account of social cognition that depends on some kind of complex cognition or some additional step of interpretation beyond what is available perceptually and contextually. Johannes Roessler makes this point clearly.

The problem is that while there is compelling intuition to the effect that 1-year-olds have some grasp of others' attention, there is also prima facie grounds for doubting that they have the conceptual abilities for interpretation (such as the ability to give causal explanations).

(Roessler 2005, 236)

What is the nature of the perceptual and contextual factors that seemingly give us access to the other person's mental state of attention? This, however, is just the wrong way to frame the question, because once we admit that what is required for joint attention is the discernment of mental states that are not accessible and that must be inferred or simulated, then joint attention in young infants is problematic, and anything so simple as perception and context seem insufficient to the job.

IT suggests that the task is not to access interior propositional attitudes (even if there is an undeniable dimension of experience and affect associated with the other person), but to perceive intentions, emotions, and dispositions in the embodied behaviors, movements, facial expressions, gestures, and actions of others. This approach makes sense if we do not rig the problem in such a way that only theory or simulation could solve it. On this view, the coordination required for joint attention is the intercorporeal coordination of interaction rather than a psychological coordination of propositional attitudes. Joint attention decoupled from action is the rare case (perhaps the case in which my connection or coordination with the other person breaks down). Instead, the kind of coordination at stake in joint attention is in some respects motoric. In this regard, joint attention is itself a kind of *basic joint action* (Fiebich & Gallagher 2013). The idea of a basic joint action is akin to the notion of a basic action or activity (see *Chapter 1*). Intentionally engaging in joint attention, at least, can be considered a basic joint action, which enables a transition from a dyadic interaction (in primary intersubjectivity) to joint action (in secondary intersubjectivity).[7]

Campbell (2005) suggests two relevant examples. In the first one I find myself in a pasture looking at some cattle that start to move toward me. As the individual animal moves, Campbell suggests, it seems to be checking that its fellow animals are coming along. Whether the cattle are themselves engaged in a kind of social referencing, however, is not the issue. Standing in the pasture, my own response is the issue, and my response is not to try to get into their minds, or to work out some set of propositional attitudes that I attribute to them. Rather, my understanding of their attention on a particular object (namely, me) and my own coordinated attention on

---

[7] That joint attention can be considered a *basic* joint action means that (1) it fulfills the minimal conditions to be a joint action, (2) it can be part of a more complex joint action, and (3) it is not itself composed of other joint actions. The minimal conditions of a joint action are (a) having a shared intention; (b) having shared awareness of aiming for the same goal; and (c) participating in cooperative behavior patterns in order to achieve the goal (Fiebich & Gallagher 2013; see *Section 5.3* for the concept of joint action and shared intention). It's interesting to note that the kind of problems involved in the notion of basic action (which in *Chapter 1* led us to Hornsby's idea of basic activity in order to avoid ending up with an abstraction or an infinite regress) don't apply to the notion of a basic joint action. For example, the suggestion that basic actions are just abstractions and therefore not real (Sneddon 2006) does not apply to the concept of a basic joint action since there is no claim that we perform a basic joint action without performing some other action, and, unlike the concept of basic action, there is a clear motivational history that can be defined for a basic joint action such as engaging in intentional joint attention. The components of a basic joint action are not more *basic joint* actions, since they are not joint actions at all, even if they are interactional. The components of basic *joint* actions are very real non-joint actions (e.g., bodily movements of coordination) and interactions without shared intentions. This would then be an *instrumental account of basic joint action*: a joint action is a basic joint action if two (or more) agents perform the joint action without performing it by performing some other joint action.

the same object (i.e., me as I try to figure out what to do) translates immediately into movement on my part.

I might put this in terms of trying to figure out their intentions. But if I try to discern whether they are going to change direction before they reach me, I don't do this by trying to mindread their mental states (I'm not even sure what this would mean); I try to see it in their movements—or in the movement of the herd as a whole—and this in reference to the shape of the field and the possibilities for their moving this way or that. I can *see* that they have me as a target, and I can *see* that there is nothing else in this pasture that would capture their attention. My attention to what and where they are attending sets my feet in motion.

In some cases the joint attention that I share with other humans involves nothing more than something like this. If, for example, my friend John and I happen to be in the pasture looking at a stampede coming towards us, if we catch each other's eye, as they say, if he grabs my arm and yells and we start to run, is there anything more to the coordination that we have to explain? Is there any reason to engage in mind-reading? Do I have to consider John's beliefs and desires? Do I need folk psychology or do I need to employ a theory to understand why someone grabs another person's arm? Do I need to simulate my friend's situation or what he might be thinking? No, the kind of knowledge I need is a very practical kind that is based on occurrent perception, along with his yell and his grabbing my arm.

To get a better sense of what perception and context can do for us in this respect, let's look at the other example suggested by Campbell. This is the kind of joint attention coordination required when playing team sports like football. Campbell puts it this way: "a team playing football are continuously monitoring one another's attention. But this does not require them to be engaged in conceptual thought, or to have even iterated knowledge of the direction of each other's attention" (2005, 245). I think we can put this more positively by extending what Merleau-Ponty had already said about playing football. He emphasizes the role of the environment.

For the player in action the football field is not an "object" [that would] remain equivalent under its apparent transformations. It is pervaded with lines of force (the "yard line"; those lines that demarcate the "penalty area") and is articulated in sectors (for example, the "openings" between the adversaries) which call for a certain mode of action and which initiate and guide the action as if the player were unaware of it. The field is ... present as the immanent term of his practical intentions; the player becomes one with it and feels the direction of the "goal", for example, just as immediately as the vertical and the horizontal planes of his own body. (Merleau-Ponty 1983, 168–9)

The player's intentions and actions are shaped by the physical environment and by the nature of the game he is playing. Controlling the ball on this field, and strategizing on how to get to the goal are not things accomplished in the player's head, but necessarily are processes that are laid out on this field from the perspective of the player as he is positioned and as he moves across the grid. As Merleau-Ponty acknowledges, this field is not empty of others. And many of these others are clearly in relations of joint attention with the one who controls the ball. Everyone is attending to the ball (among other things), and the player knows that everyone is attending; and everyone knows that he is attending, and so forth.

More than this, everyone's intentions are quite transparent and are specified by the context and rules of the game. No need for ToM (TT or ST) here; I don't have to infer anything about your propositional attitudes if you wear a different colored uniform. I don't have to put myself in your place and work up some pretend beliefs in order to know your intentions. Your specific intentions are quite apparent in the way you are moving towards me or positioning yourself between me and the goal.

My football-field-understanding of particular others is pragmatic and enactive in the sense of being a knowing-how to deal with them, rather than a knowing-that. It's geared to action and interaction with them, in the context of the game. Theory-theorists might argue that all of this presupposes a theory of or a set of rules about how players will act on the field (see Monty Python's sardonic critique of such a position in their "Philosophy Football" [https://www.youtube.com/watch?v=7E_8EjoxY7Q]). But it's not clear that any such theory is what enters into the pragmatic understanding that helps to constitute the meaning of the others' behavior. One learns football by *practice*; and one comes to understand the precise actions of others on the field in terms of that practice, rather than in terms of some general theory.

One might object that practices on the football field are rather limited in terms of what we need to understand in more everyday contexts. One's intentions on the football field are, as we said, relatively transparent; movements have well-defined goals even if they are sometimes fabulously complex.[8] So on the football field there is not much of a challenge when it comes to working out patterns of coordination in joint attention. But again I think this applies to many human situations, circum-scribed by time, place, and custom.

We know, for example, that things change dramatically when after the game we go out to have a few pints at the pub. Our immediate relations to others clearly change. Yet, we continue to engage them in joint attentional ways that remain pragmatic and specifically social. In the noisy pub we may have to depend on custom and gesture, pre-defined social roles, and environmental arrangements, more than clear proposi-tional communication, to obtain the pint and to engage in our celebrations with others. The game changes; the rules change; but the basic capacities of primary and secondary intersubjectivity, including joint attention, continue to give us access to the other person's meaning. This is the case even if the rare puzzling circumstance comes up and I have to employ theory or simulation, for even in such cases the only starting point I have is the ongoing interaction, now perhaps less coordinated than in the football game. But here it becomes clear that the whole story is more complicated.

---

[8] To claim that things are relatively transparent on some levels (everyone knows about everyone's intentions to score goals and to win the game) is not to deny complexity and indeed the large amount of deception involved in the play. The player feints right and goes left as the defense tries to anticipate the move. As Aggerholm et al. (2011) suggest, this is a kind of deceptive creativity. "Performance in high-level football obviously involves intentions and the players certainly have a tendency to perform in specific ways that make sense in relation to the common objective. But no matter how good you are, you always have to move into an open situation and relate and adapt to the social situation of the game as it unfolds" (Aggerholm et al. 2011, 351). To be effective the feint demands a "sensitivity and openness to the dynamic configuration of the social situation" (354). More specifically, one deals with this type of deception by assuming the other's deceit and then attending to and responding to the other player's bodily movements and gestures. One doesn't deal with it by asking in each case whether the player has a hidden intention to deceive. See Gallagher and Ilundáin-Agurruza, 2020.

Back in the cow pasture, when John grabs my arm and shouts and we start to move, I can tell quite readily whether he is shouting because he thinks this is good fun—he may think the situation in which philosophers are being chased by cows to be rather funny—or because he is afraid of being trampled. I will be able to tell this from the grip on my arm, from the intonation in his voice, from the expression on his face, and so on. It may or may not be so easy on the football field; yet, within the game, and given our background knowledge, we will only be able to grasp our opponents' feints and strategies by their postures and movements.

More generally, in joint attention, not only the direction of gaze, but also the emotional expression on the face of the other has a measurable effect. In studies of object evaluation, for example, the gaze of the other person towards an object can draw one's attention to the object. Subjects presented with a face looking towards (or away from) an object evaluate the object as more (or less) likeable than those objects that don't receive much attention from others. When you add an emotional expression to the face, the effect is stronger (Bayliss et al. 2006; 2007). In addition, the quality of the other person's movement is important. Seeing another person act with ease (or without ease) toward an object will influence one's feelings about the object (Hayes et al. 2008). Indeed, my awareness of the gaze of others towards objects or in joint attention influences my perception of objects in regard to motor action, significance, and emotional salience (Becchio et al. 2008). Thus, my actions with respect to the world, and with respect to others, emerge in the context set by those others.

Developmental studies support this view and trace these affect-related processes to the beginnings of joint attention. Infants are highly responsive to attentional and emotional cues as part of their secondary intersubjective abilities. Infants often share emotions—e.g., exchange smiles—when playing with a toy in joint attention with another, and they get visibly upset if the other person they are interacting with assumes a passive face (e.g., Messinger & Fogel 2007). They follow another person's gaze to the appropriate target (Butterworth & Jarrett 1991) and reference the other's emotional expressions to know whether to approach novel objects (Klinnert et al. 1986; Moses et al. 2001). When infants of 12–18 months see a negative emotional expression by a parent toward a particular toy, they later, and in a different context, avoid playing with that toy (Hornik, Risenhoover, & Gunnar 1987). Furthermore, the emotional expressions of one person while watching the action of another (who is showing anger or a neutral facial expression) will influence an 18-month-old infant's inclination to imitate the actions of the second person (Repacholi & Meltzoff 2007; Repacholi, Olsen, & Meltzoff 2006; Repacholi, Meltzoff, & Olsen 2008; also Walden & Ogan 1988).

In effect, neither attending to others nor joint attention is reducible to a mere geometrical relation or a set of lines that connect gaze-gaze-object. Joint attention is invested with interest and affect. These connections between perception of gaze, joint attention, and emotion have been shown to correlate significantly with emotion regulation later in development (Morales et al. 2005). Further, they have been shown to break down in autism where lack of emotional connectedness between young autistic children and others correlates with the lack of engagement with the other's attitudes towards a shared world (see García-Pérez, Lee, & Hobson 2007; Hobson 2011; Hobson, Lee, & Hobson 2007; Sigman et al. 1992).[9]

5.3.2 Joint action

Interactions also include joint actions, mutually generated intentional actions and responses that lead to a build up of meaningful action chains. One intentional movement—e.g., pointing—may motivate movement on the other's part, moving in a specific direction, reaching, grasping, moving back, handing over, taking back, and so on, creating a shared space of affordances.

Joint action is a complex form of social interaction. There are different views in the current literature about exactly what constitutes joint action. Sebanz et al. (2006, 70), for example, define joint action as "any form of social interaction whereby two or more individuals coordinate their actions in space and time to bring about a change in the environment." Although they don't include the notion of shared intentions, they identify joint attention, action observation, task-sharing, and action coordination as cognitive mechanisms through which a successful joint action can be achieved. Coordination patterns, however, are specified to some degree based on the intentions shared by the agents. At the very least, on some level of description, joint actions involve shared intentions (Carpenter 2009), and in part this may be what distinguishes human group activities from those of other animals (Tomasello et al. 2005).

Conceiving of an intention as an internal mental state, however, is problematic for understanding the concept of shared intention. In contrast to some authors who think that a shared or "we" intention is just the summation of two or more internal intentions, each of which belongs to a separate agent, Bratman highlights the idea that a shared intention "is not an attitude in the mind or minds of either or both participants. Rather, it is a state of affairs that consists primarily in attitudes (none of which are themselves the shared intention) of the participant and [intersubjective] interrelations between attitudes" (Bratman 1993, 107–8). Enactivists would think of these as intentional attitudes (Hutto 2011, 313), instantiated bodily to include M-intentions and P-intentions (it is suggestive that the term "attitude" can mean "bodily posture").

A good example of a joint action that depends on intentional attitudes can be found in empirical studies conducted by Lindblom (2015; see Lindblom & Ziemke 2007; 2008). In a frame-by-frame analysis of video images from episodes of spontaneous social interaction captured in situ, Lindblom was able to show the precise dynamics of interaction leading from joint attention to joint action during a novel but well-defined task. The task is to lift a very young horse (filly) onto her legs. The individual, Bob, who initiates the action draws the attention of his two colleagues, not by his vocal instructions, but by his movement toward the horse, his hand-claps, and encouraging words to the horse. There is a large amount of background knowledge about horses that enters into the dynamic. "The situation at hand is obvious, the fact

---

[9] One also finds in autism a lack of social emotions, feelings such as coyness, embarrassment, guilt, pride, jealousy, or shame, as well as empathic concern (Hobson et al. 2007; Hobson, Harris, García-Pérez, & Hobson 2009).

that the filly is unable to rise by herself is obvious, and everybody knowing it is not healthy for a horse to lay down for too long [– all of this leads to the formation of a joint intention to lift the horse]" (Lindblom 2007, 227). They also know that one person on his own cannot lift the filly. Two other ranchers come to Bob's aid, and from that point they set about lifting the horse, but they engage in this joint action with very little vocal communication. Rather bodily actions, facial expression, gaze direction, tone of voice, bodily posture, and gesture communicate the specific movement intentions among the group as they work. Joint attention is maintained through such bodily and communicative movements, and it leads directly to a complex joint action that is guided by the continuing movements, postures, gestures, etc. of all three participants. Here is the sequence of events.

(1) At first, Bob is standing next the filly and begins to bend down at the same time as the filly begins an attempt to rise. As Lindblom notes, it is difficult to say who is influencing whom at this point. Bob might be grasping the filly's intention to rise, and for that reason he bends down to assist her. The filly might notice Bob's downward movement as an intention to help, or may simply move in response to Bob's approach. In any case, together "they create a co-regulated activity with the intention to 'get up'" (227).

(2) This first lifting attempt fails and Bob's two colleagues rush over "with big strides as well as almost in step," but with attention directed toward the filly. Bob, who is just beginning another attempt, notices their approach, and utters "Come on." Together they take up positions for the actual lift. This attempt also fails, "seemingly because they did not really cooperate with each other or did not know exactly how to perform the joint action of lifting, and consequently the unregulated interaction, lasting about 5 seconds, comes to nothing" (229).

(3) The men then back away to assess the situation. An onlooker suggests a strategy of grasping each other's hands underneath the filly. One of the men then aligns his bodily position opposite Bob to indicate readiness to try the strategy. Bob motions for the onlooker to join them (to provide a partner for the third man), indicating by his gestures where she should locate herself.

(4) Bob then demonstrates by way of a lifting gesture: "he lowers his upper body and hands slightly, and then he continues the whole gesture upwards..." illustrating both the common consensus and how the attempt will be made (231). Before Bob lowers his hands, one of the other men who has been looking at Bob, "starts to make a lifting gesture, which is slightly different, as a way of sharing Bob's idea of how to lift, as well as indicating that he actually has understood [from his perspective] what to do in the next try" (232). This gesture combines elements of a first-person perspective, lifting his hands as he would in his own action—indicating he understands his role in the process— immediately followed by a second-person perspective—by overlapping his hands, he represents how his hand will be in relation to Bob's hand.

(5) The following action, with Bob and one co-worker joining hands under the midsection of the filly, the other man at the hind quarter, and the fourth person joining the group and pulling the horse up from the front, is perfectly coordinated and successful.

This is an example of the human capacity to engage in joint attention and joint action directed toward a goal. A common intentionality emerges among the individuals as they enter into the interaction involved in a specific task. This interaction is carried out primarily in spatially and temporally coordinated movements that include action-oriented positioning and postures, and communicative gestures. To understand how this process works, one needs to take the entire group as the unit of analysis. Their shared understanding emerges from a set of embodied movements and actions in the specific context of what they were doing, and it is irreducible to any set of mental states in one individual or even the collection of mental states found in all of them. The meaning of the action transcends any one individual; it is generated in the interaction required for the outcome, which, as Lindblom indicates (2007, 237), is a distributed and collective phenomenon.

Other studies provide some indication of how such coordination works. That individuals show a strong propensity to synchronize their behavior in the presence of others can be seen in experimental arrangements that are highly unlikely to elicit mutual actions. For example, subjects sitting in front of each other on rocking chairs that are shaped so as to bias for different rocking frequencies nonetheless synchronize rocking frequencies (Richardson et al. 2007). In another study (Knoblich and Jordan 2003) subjects share control over a tracking device to keep it aligned with a horizontally moving object—a difficult task that cannot be achieved by any one individual on his own. In this task individual subjects solve coordination problems by anticipating the other person's moves without relying on explicit communication. Likewise, in a "herding sheep" game Nalepka et al. (2015) show how dyadic cooperation comes to be established in a trial-and-error fashion, without well-formed prior intentions, or explicit communication. A joint coordination strategy is discovered as each individual works on the task and enters into a synchronized movement without verbal communication. The "pairs converged on the same two stable states of coordination known to constrain rhythmic intra- and interpersonal coordination in general ... although no verbal communication was allowed, in a few instances a participant would exaggerate their oscillatory movements in what seemed to be an attempt to communicate with their partner" (Nalepka et al. 2015, 1707). More generally, in order for two subjects to synchronize movements, one subject's anticipation and adjustments, on their own, although necessary, are not sufficient for synchronized performance. Anticipation and adjustment need to be bidirectional, or mutual (Konvalinka et al. 2010).

5.4 Of Three Minds

There is more to say about social cognition, and a number of further issues will be explored in the next couple of chapters, but at this point some theorists may be impatient. They may say, at this point, yes, but you have not yet explained what this understanding of the other is—how does all of this bodily activity and interaction amount to anything that would count for an explanation of social cognition? In the ToM framework one expects an explanation in terms of either folk psychology— "Now I have some belief about Harry's belief, which I have formed in some metarepresentational or introspective process"—or some subpersonal process—"Now the

ToM module or the mirror neuron system assigns an output state to the target; the subject infers or projects a mental state to the other's mind." And so forth. Such accounts remain too closely tied to the traditional picture of the mind and to individualist mechanisms that the embodied, enactivist view challenges. In contrast, for IT, the mind is a second-person phenomenon. It still involves both personal and subpersonal processes, but these processes run deeper and into more ambiguous territory than found in the clear-cut space of mental states. The processes are embodied and emotional; they are pragmatic and intersubjective, rather than individual, intellectual, or ideational.

My understanding of another person is action- (or interaction-) oriented, and in some cases it just is the embodied, affective, pragmatic, and intentional attitudes that pull or push me into interaction with her. When I interact with the other person I understand her in terms of my embodied preparation to respond to her, in coordination with or in opposition to her; I have an immediate positive or negative sense; I already find myself in a normative attitude characterized as a pragmatic yes or no, or a more ambiguous "let me wait and see where this is going" which may manifest itself in hesitancy or holding back. Such attitudes are instantiated in processes that are perceptual—the other person's face tells me more than her words—and actionable—she is someone I need to listen to or talk to right now, or she is in need of help—and this constitutes an engaged understanding that is as much (or rather, more) *in the action* or *in the world*, than it is in my head. This kind of understanding is not reducible to a representational state in my brain, or to a set of neuronal patterns, or to a well-defined doxic state of mind, although it is certainly open to my possible reflection and, as we'll see, narrative iteration. If I step out of the action for a second I can say how I feel, or what my belief is. But the fact that I can put things in terms of folk-psychological mental states, or that I can represent the situation in linguistic phrases, does not mean that these mental states or linguistic phrases constitute the explanation, or the proper theoretical level that would account for social cognition. Likewise, if I can explain that my mirror neurons are firing, that does not explain *why* they are firing or what else is going on.

I'll conclude this chapter with a look at how IT avoids the various problems encountered by TT and ST. As previously noted, IT avoids several of the problems associated with the simulation interpretation of the mirror neuron system by proposing an enactivist interpretation of mirror neurons. In this regard there are no claims for *matching* or *pretense* or *instrumental control*, the various aspects that have been tied to definitions of simulation. On the enactivist view our motor systems are not required to go into matching or pretend states to understand another person's action. Rather, as we engage with others in our everyday meaningful contexts, we understand the meaning of their actions in terms of our possible responses; we see them in terms of social affordances. Mirror neurons are activated in an anticipatory, preparatory mode, attuned to my possible responses (see Jacob 2008; more on this in *Chapter 6*).

IT sees no problem with the neural *reuse hypothesis* (see *Section 4.3.8*) understood as an evolutionary principle that explains how the brain comes to function the way it does. Indeed, it can help us understand the plasticity that is involved in both phylogeny and ontogeny, and that applies not just to the brain, but also to the system as a whole—the "metaplasticity" of the brain-body-environment (Malafouris 2013).

An adequate understanding of reuse recognizes that the brain and body co-evolve, and do so in ways that are shaped by various environmental niches and the possibilities for action afforded by the evolving system. Imagine how differently the brain would function if the human body evolved without hands; imagine how different our concept of rationality might be, or how different our mathematics might be (Gallagher 2017a).

IT does not deny that the brain is an important part of the body or that it plays an important role in cognition and social cognition; it does not deny that mirror neurons, motor-control processes, or the notion of reuse may play some role in social cognition. Indeed, we can find an important clue about the nature of social cognition in the concept of reuse. Specifically, the idea that we are reusing certain resources indicates something not only about the new use, but also about the original use and the nature of the resources we are reusing. The clue is that in many cases the original use sets the direction for reuse and how reuse functions. On the reuse hypothesis, for example, our perceptual-motor systems were originally designed primarily for *action*, not for observation—not for mirroring, matching, or simulation. This primacy of action arguably carries through to the reuse of our motor systems in contexts of social cognition. When I see your action I see it as an affordance that motivates my own action—your action is perceived as something that I can respond to, and that is a good part of precisely how I understand your action. A similar principle may govern the emotional realm: when I see your emotional expression I respond to it, and that may happen in a variety of ways that are not necessarily equivalent to contagion or a matching simulation.

The simulation theory, in emphasizing pretense or replication, or, as Jacob (2008) points out, a backward-looking retrodictive grasping of the other's prior intentions, blinds the theorist from seeing that the other's action affords me action-opportunities that may motivate or elicit complementary or cooperative or opposing actions on my part. Mirror neuron processes are forward-looking and predictive, as Jacob rightly argues. They are anticipatory not just of the other's next action, however, but in a way that is preparatory for one's own response to the other's action. Studies by Caggiano et al. (2009; 2011) support this idea. Single-cell recordings of mirror neurons in area f5 of the macaque premotor cortex show differential activations depending on whether the other agent is within peripersonal (reachable) space, or in extrapersonal (unreachable) space. Such differential activations for reachable *versus* non-reachable space suggest anticipatory action-related responses, encoding "aspects of the observed actions that are relevant to subsequent interacting behaviors" (2009, 403). This is not completely irrelevant for understanding the intentions of the other agent; on the enactivist interpretation, even in the case of merely observing the other's action, it indicates an understanding of the other in terms of how one might (or might not) interact with the other, depending on how close (or far) the other agent is.

A portion of these spatially selective mirror neurons…encode space in operational terms, changing their properties according to the possibility that the monkey will interact with the object. These results suggest that a set of mirror neurons encodes the observed motor acts not only for action understanding, but also to analyze such acts in terms of features that are relevant to generating appropriate behaviors.   (Caggiano et al. 2009, 403)

On the enactive interpretation, I understand the meaning of your actions precisely in terms of what I can do in response to your actions. In effect, in the social context, my motor system continues to be pragmatic and enactive, something built primarily for action and reused for interaction, in a way that goes beyond simulation as it is typically understood.

The *integration problem* doesn't arise, as it does for explicit/conscious versions of TT or ST, because interaction is online and real time. As agents, we are part of the agentive situation and not mere observers, and our comprehension of the other's actions tends to flow smoothly unless something goes wrong. At that point we might have the opportunity to pull back and reflect on things, but that type of reflection itself tends still to be situated and often interactional. In some cases, for example, our possible interaction is to ask the other person whether we have misunderstood.

For the second-person interaction described by IT there is no *simple phenomeno-logical problem*; everyday phenomenology reflects a pre-reflective sense of agency for our engaged interactions with others, some part of our affective responses to them, our grasp of contextual meaning, and in some cases our reflective puzzlement about their actions. Furthermore, there is clearly no *developmental* problem for IT. It doesn't try to read intellectualist or adultist ToM processes into infant behavior; rather, it describes processes of primary and secondary intersubjectivity that are consistent with what infants do, and indeed it draws on developmental studies for support.

Placing emphasis on social interaction rather than mindreading leads to a con-ception of the mind very different from that found in the standard approaches. One can begin to see that for IT, the mind, as a second-person phenomenon, is not an internal, unobservable set of mental states. Rather, the mind is "out there" in our actions and interactions, in our gestures and communications, constituted in our engagements with the world and with others. *Second-person minds* are supported by context, situation, and the social roles in which we, as agents, are engaged. In most of our everyday situations we need go no further in order to gain an understanding of the other.

This is not to deny that there is also an important first-person dimension to the mind. The second-person mind is also a *first-person mind*. As I engage in interactions with others, I enter into ecological relations with the world and with others that generate my embodied, pre-reflective first-person experience. In developmental terms, my affective and sensory-motor experiences (the embodied experiences of my movements, my actions, and my interactions) give me a first-order, first-person awareness from the very beginning. On-going bodily processes and second-person interactions combine to shape this awareness and to move us through a stream of experience, from one thing to the next. Even though a good part of it arises in my interactions with others, this is indubitably *my* experience, differentiated from everyone else's experiences, not because it is inaccessibly packaged up in a closed Cartesian mental space, but because my body acts as a principle of individuation (as medieval philosophers used to say). This "mineness" of experience, however, is not a problem for social cognition; it is not the problem of other minds. You do not need to access or mindread my first-person phenomenal experience in order to understand me since much of that first-person experience is being shaped and driven by our interactions in second-person relations where you have perceptual access to my agentively situated bodily movements, facial expressions, gestures, communicative actions, and so on, and thereby to my "second-person mind," or as Sartre (1956) might say, my existence-for-others.

One objection to this interactionist or relational view comes from internalist conceptions of the mind, including the more recent predictive coding models of brain processing. Thus, for instance, entirely consistent with the unobservability principle discussed in the previous chapter, Jacob Hohwy (2013, 254) argues that it is essential that the mind be private and not accessible by others. As he puts it, "consciousness is private so that it can be social." His idea is that just as the individual brain, on the predictive coding model, uses multiple modularly separated sources of sensory evidence to construct a prediction about the world, specifically because multiple sources of information improve its inferences, so also, interacting minds require multiple and independent sources of evidence to construct the best inter- pretation of the world. If all knowledge about the world derived from one source, our communal inferences would not be optimal. Thus, "if we wore our conscious experiences on our sleeves—if they were public and not private—then they could unduly influence other individuals' reports and we would not then benefit from integrating our [competing] reports with theirs" (253). We can certainly grant that such multiple sources of evidence work to our advantage in some circumstances; but it's not clear that the idea that there be multiple intersubjective sources requires that each source be a private mind inaccessible to others, as Hohwy suggests. All it requires is that each source be a *different* mind. To have multiple sources it is sufficient to have multiple perspectives—defined not only in terms of unique embodied egocentric spatial frames of reference at any point in time, but also unique histories of experience, different current affective states, and so on. The fact that I, as an embodied agent, see the world from a perspective somewhat different from yours would be sufficient to provide the multiple sources of evidence that Hohwy seeks, without the need to picture the mind as "invisible and hidden from others" (Locke 1690; cited in Hohwy 2013, 249).

Still less do we need to worry about the mind as it is represented in standard ToM approaches—that is, in terms of belief-desire psychology, as a set of propositional attitudes or mental states. This is what we might call the *third-person mind*. As we experience the world and enter into second-person interactions, we form dispositions and habits. As we *reflect* on these dispositions and habits, and on our first-order experiences, using concepts developed in linguistic and cultural practices, we formu- late a shorthand way of describing ourselves in terms of our beliefs and desires, and because they are already linguistically formed, we can communicate what they are. Such propositional attitudes derive significantly from our second-person inter- actions, but in every case they are just that—derivative, the product of reflection and/or linguistic practice. This derivative conception of the mind is the one that standard ToM approaches start with. Where are these beliefs and desires and intentions and how can we access them? This is the mind that requires mindreading, the mind that seems hidden away, when in fact it is the mind that is most easily expressible in terms of language. To the extent that such mental states do enter back into our second-person interactions, they do so through the fact that we communicate about them. In this regard they are not really hidden away, and they present no real problem of social cognition as long as we have access to some form of communication.

This is not to deny that we are all capable of deception. And if you set out to deceive me, you may well succeed. Yet, the only way I might even suspect that you are trying to deceive me in an interactive situation would be to discover it through your actions, your facial expressions, your gestures, your communications, perhaps the odd dynamics of our interactions, etc. I may also be able to reason some things out, such as inconsistencies between what you say and what you do, or how you act in some contexts. Unless I am constantly suspicious of you, however, I don't think that this would be my usual practice. I would be motivated to try to reason it out only if something in your embodied, intersubjective comportment provided some indication that I should. If and when I do engage in this kind of practice, or in cases where I am puzzled by your behavior, or in some other unusual circumstances, I may put myself in the observational stance. I may try to work it out, through inferences or simulations, or by formulating some reasoned discourse, or more likely a narrative through which I try to figure out your story and your motivations (see *Chapter 7*). In most cases of social cognition, however, we have no need to engage in this type of thing since we have ready access to the other person's behaviors, movements, actions, expressions, and so on, and we take others at face value.

To see how IT resolves two other problems encountered by ToM explanations—the *diversity problem*, and the *starting problem*—we need to develop the account of IT further to include the role played by direct social perception (*Chapter 6*) and communicative and narrative competencies (*Chapter 7*). We might already have discerned a first pass at the starting problem, however. What sets us on the right track and what gets social cognition off the ground (and this would also have to be the case even in the rare and specialized cases of mindreading) are the embodied and contextualized practices of interaction. Assuming typical development, we arrive on the scene, as newborns, already attuned to other people's faces and their emotional expressions; and we come already prepared to interact with others. These are precisely the interactive processes of primary intersubjectivity that IT points to, not only as the starting point developmentally, but also as the continuous starting point for our everyday engagements with others. In social cognitive practices (and even in the exceptional cases of mindreading by theoretical inference or simulation), social interactive processes allow us to avoid the starting problem. They provide the minimal embodied skills, and together with the rich worldly contextualization that comes along with secondary intersubjectivity, and the even richer social and cultural contexts that come along with communicative and narrative practices, they form the "massive hermeneutical background" (see *Section 7.4*) that in every instance continues to get social cognition off the ground.

6

Direct Social Perception

Interaction theory suggests that perceptual processes play an important role in intersubjective understanding. In this chapter I want to clarify and deepen some of the analyses provided in the previous chapters and answer some objections that have been raised against the role of direct social perception in social cognition. First, I'll say more about the idea that we enactively perceive (rather than infer or simulate) the intentions and emotions of others. This idea is not widely accepted, especially when the claim is that the kind of perception involved is direct rather than inferential. As we'll see, however, in a recent, and I think surprising turn, theory theorists have argued that some form of direct perception can give us a sense of the other's intentions and emotions, and that when rightly conceived direct social perception may also be consistent with TT. It is important, therefore, to clarify how perception works in the intersubjective context, and what role, if any, inference plays in social cognition.

It's also important to keep in mind that the account of direct social perception outlined here is only one part of IT, and an explanation of its role in social cognition is not meant to be a full explanation of how we understand others.[1] No one claims that social cognition is fully accomplished by a direct perception of the other's mind. Direct social perception fits into a more comprehensive account that involves

---

[1] For example, Abramova and Slors (2019, 406) identify a direct social perception account as a distinct enactivist approach to social cognition in contrast to a more interactionist approach. My view is that direct social perception is always part of an interaction context. Elsewhere, however, I indicated that "for the most part, in most of our encounters in everyday life, direct perception delivers sufficient information for understanding others" (Gallagher 2008, 540). Some might interpret this as claiming that direct social perception by itself would be sufficient for understanding others. The statement is clearly in need of a *ceteris paribus* clause. In the rich context of typical everyday interactions between neuro-typical agents direct social perception may be sufficient for understanding others, meaning that no mindreading (by theoretical inference or simulation) is necessary. Obviously my interactions with others can involve a variety of cognitive performances—perceptual and non-perceptual. We might, for example, be engaged in action planning and this may involve a secondary intersubjective understanding of the situation and possible strategies we could pursue together. Such cooperative interaction may add to my understanding of your intentions. Michael, Christensen, and Overgaard (2014) rightly point out that even in cases where direct social perception (or aspects of it) may be intact, as in Williams Syndrome, this is clearly not enough to navigate the social world. But whether high-level mindreading, rather than other kinds of cognitive abilities that target contextual and strategic features of social interactions, is required in any of these situations (typical or non-typical) remains an empirical and open question. Furthermore, I am in complete agreement with Castro and Heras-Escribano (2019) concerning the importance of the normative context, without, however, thinking that this makes direct perception less important. Pluralist approaches to social cognition clearly include, among other things, an emphasis on social, cultural and normative practices (see Fiebich, Gallagher & Hutto 2017; Gallagher & Miyahara 2012; Gallagher & Fiebich 2019).

primary and secondary intersubjectivity, and practices that are social, cultural and normative, as explained in the previous chapter.

6.1 Perceiving Intentions and Emotions

The idea that social perception is a form of direct perception is not new. It has its roots in classical phenomenology where Max Scheler is often quoted as a good representative.

> For we certainly believe ourselves to be directly acquainted with another person's joy in his laughter, with his sorrow and pain in his tears, with his shame in his blushing, with his entreaty in his outstretched hands.... And with the tenor of this thoughts in the sound of his words. If anyone tells me that this is not "perception", for it cannot be so, in view of the fact that a perception is simply a complex of physical sensations... I would beg him to turn aside from such questionable theories and address himself to the phenomenological facts.
>
> (Scheler 1954, 260–1)

The idea that we can directly perceive emotions is reiterated and reinforced by Merleau-Ponty, as well as Wittgenstein.

> I do not perceive the anger or the threat as a psychological fact hidden behind the gesture, I read the anger in the gesture. The gesture does not make me think of anger, it is the anger itself.... I perceive the other's grief or anger in his behavior, on his face and in his hands, without any borrowing from an "inner" experience... because grief and anger are variations of being in the world, undivided between body and consciousness...
>
> (Merleau-Ponty 2012, 190, 372)[2]

> In general I do not surmise fear in him—I see it. I do not feel that I am deducing the probable existence of something inside from something outside; rather it is as if the human face were in a way translucent and that I were seeing it not in reflected light but rather in its own.
>
> (Wittgenstein 1980, §170)[3]

IT makes similar claims, not only about emotions, but also about the intentions of others. Such claims motivate three questions: (1) What is an intention if it is something that can be perceived? (2) What is an emotion if it is something that can be perceived? And (3) what is the nature of social perception if intentions and emotions can be perceived?[4]

The latter question is important since according to one sense of "perceiving another's mental states," X perceives Y's mental states iff Y's mental states figure in

---

[2] Or again: "Anger, shame, hate, and love are not psychic facts hidden at the bottom of another's consciousness: they are types of behavior or styles of conduct which are visible from the outside. They exist on this face or in those gestures, not hidden behind them" (Merleau-Ponty 1964b, 52–3).

[3] Or again: "'We see emotion.' —As opposed to what?—We do not see facial contortions and make the inference that he is feeling joy, grief, boredom. We describe a face immediately as sad, radiant, bored, even when we are unable to give any other description of the features. Grief, one would like to say, is personified in the face" (Wittgenstein 1980, §570; see Overgaard 2005, for discussion).

[4] Elijah Chudnoff (2016) raises similar questions and presents a good review of the empirical evidence in support of what he calls the psychological thesis that "Some of our sensory perceptual experiences of other people represent them as being in certain mental states." One further question that I won't address directly is: What other mental states can be perceived? (8).

the content of X's perceptual experience. But then one might argue that neither TT nor ST need deny the phenomenological claim that we have perceptual experiences with such content, since it would be possible for perception at the phenomenological level to have such content while processes at the subpersonal level that deliver such content are inferential or involve some kind of extra-perceptual cognition. The question then becomes whether such perceptual content is delivered by subpersonal processes that involve extra-perceptual and/or inferential processes, or by processes that are perceptual and non-inferential only. As we've already noted, TT and ST suggest that at the subpersonal level extra-perceptual tacit theory or simulation enters into the process. Accordingly, clarifying a sense in which perceptual processes at the subpersonal level do not involve either theoretical inference or simulation will be important for IT. In the following, in order to elucidate what it is to directly perceive intentions and emotions, I borrow from action theory and emotion theory certain conceptions that are consistent with the idea that we can perceive such things directly; i.e., without having to infer or to simulate or to add any other cognitive process to perception.

6.1.1 Perceiving intentions

Phenomenologists have long suggested that there is a kind of bodily or motor intentionality *in* action (Husserl 1989; Merleau-Ponty 2012), and recent discussions in action theory agree that one's motor intentions (M-intentions) and intentions-in-action (P-intentions) (Pacherie 2006; Searle 1983) are just that—intrinsic to the motoric kinematics and the action itself (see *Section 3.2*). M- and P-intentions reflect the fact that the experiencing agent is intentionally engaged with the world through actions and projects that are not reducible to simple internal mental states, but involve an intentionality that is motoric and bodily. Actions have intentionality because they are directed at some goal or project, and this is something that we can see in the actions of others. With respect to understanding the specific claim that in contexts of interaction one can directly perceive the intentions of others (without needing to infer or simulate them), the idea is that the meaning, the intentionality of action, is perceptible. To claim that the meaning of something is perceptible requires that we define perception as a rich, enactive, or as I'll say, "smart" process, and not just as a registration of sensory input (see *Section 6.1.3*).

There is good evidence for direct perception of M- as well as P-intentions since such intentions are actually present in the movements that we can see, and intentional action is almost always in some meaningful context. Studies by Cristina Becchio et al. (2012; 2017) show that even in the absence of contextual information, intentions can be perceived in bodily movement. These studies build on well-known work in kinematics showing that different action intentions specify different kinematic dynamics in movement (Ansuini et al. 2006; 2008; Marteniuk et al. 1987; Sartori et al. 2011a).

The first point, then, is that intention shapes action kinematics. Consider, for example, reaching out to grasp an apple. What you are going to do with the apple (eat it, offer it to someone, throw it) shows up in the dynamics of your reach, and in variations in your grasp. In this respect the relatively immediate M-intention is built into the movement and kinematic details of the action. Second, Becchio et al. show

Figure 6.1 Presented with video clips of just this part of the action of reaching and grasping for an apple, and before the action is completed, subjects are able to predict with 76 percent accuracy whether the agent is going to eat the apple, offer it to someone else, or throw it.

Source: Reprinted from C. Becchio, V. Manera, L. Sartori, A. Cavallo, and U. Castiello, "Grasping intentions: from thought experiments to empirical evidence," *Frontiers in Human Neuroscience*, Volume 6, Article 117, Copyright © 2012 Becchio, Manera, Sartori, Cavallo, and Castiello, Figure 1, p. 2, doi: 10.3389/fnhum.2012.00117, reproduced under the terms of the Creative Commons Attribution-NonCommercial 3.0 Unported License (CC-BY-NC 3.0), https://creativecommons.org/licenses/by-nc/3.0/.

that perceivers are sensitive to these differences in kinematics and can see (with above 70 percent accuracy) the intentions in these movements—for example, they are able to discriminate between cooperative, competitive, and individual-oriented actions (Sartori et al. 2011b) (see *Figure 6.1*). Indeed, "intentions become 'visible' in the surface flow of agents' motions" (Ansuini et al. 2014). Furthermore, subjects are able to discriminate these differences even without specific contextual information—in the dark with point-lights on the wrist and fingers of the agent (Manera et al. 2011; Becchio et al. 2012) (see *Figure 6.2*). Further evidence for the perception of intentions can be found in studies of adult bodily kinematics and the dynamics of social attention and interaction, as in the studies by Lindblom discussed in *Chapter 5* (Lindblom 2015; also see Atkinson et al. 2007).

Someone might still object that these experiments do not rule out the idea that upon seeing what we see of the movement, we still must infer the intention (e.g., Curioni, Sebanz, & Knoblich 2018).[5] But it is not that the M-intention lies somewhere outside or behind the action movement such that we need an inference to get to it; the action movements (the kinematic dynamics) constitute the M-intention. P-intentions (literally, intentions-*in-action*) are just that: *in the action* as it is carried out within specific environments.[6]

---

[5] Curioni, Sebanz, and Knoblich (2018) seemingly take perception to be a simple bottom-up activation of sensory areas. Their objections are based on this conception and the idea that one has to add computational or inferential processes (involving context, prior knowledge, etc.) in order to penetrate to the other person's D-intention. See Gallagher (2017a, Ch. 6); Gallagher (2018b); and below for responses to these types of objections.

[6] The experiments by Becchio and colleagues imposed an artificial constraint in asking subjects to identify one of three possible action intentions: eating the apple, offering it to someone, throwing it. Also,

(a) 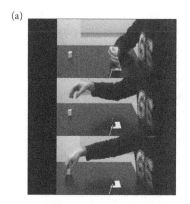   (b)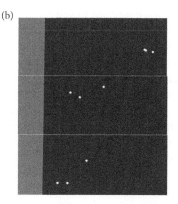

Figure 6.2 (A) Single frames extracted from a video clip representing an individual coopera-tive action sequence. (B) Single frames extracted from a point-light clip representing the same cooperative action sequence. The mean accuracy for the point-light clips = 72 percent of correct responses.

Source: Reprinted from C. Becchio, V. Manera, L. Sartori, A. Cavallo, and U. Castiello, "Grasping intentions: from thought experiments to empirical evidence," *Frontiers in Human Neuroscience*, Volume 6, Article 117, Copyright © 2012 Becchio, Manera, Sartori, Cavallo, and Castiello, Figure 2, p. 3, doi: 10.3389/fnhum.2012.00117, reproduced under the terms of the Creative Commons Attribution-NonCommercial 3.0 Unported License (CC-BY-NC 3.0), https://creativecommons.org/licenses/by-nc/3.0/.

I want to emphasize the importance that context plays in our typical and everyday actions and in social perception. We started (in *Chapter 1*) with the idea that actions come along with their circumstances. In everyday circumstances we are not dealing with the kind of abstractions that we employ in experiments—observing one very short segment of an action in a minimal context, or observing one segment out of context and in the dark lit only by point lights. Most often actions are fully contextualized by physical, social, and cultural affordances. They develop over time and they are characterized by an intrinsic temporality that makes them coherent. Our perception of another's action is often framed by what we know about the other person and her practices, and by the overall sense of the circumstance in which she is acting. Social perception is typically perception in the interaction context, in which the other's actions are in context, and in which perception is also the perception of that context and not just isolated or abstract movement. At a minimum in everyday agentive situations, we perceive not just M-intentions in the kinematics of the other's organism; we also perceive P-intentions in what Dewey calls the organism-environment.

As previously indicated (*Chapter 3*), in many cases of intentional action, there is no prior or D-intention—no deliberative planning out. For example, if I am sitting at

---

subjects were simply observing (on video) and not interacting with the agent. The Lindblom study, cited in *Chapter 5*, however, involved field research rather than lab experiments, and the ecological situation that she studied did not involve artificial limitations in terms of a limited range of possible answers. The subjects studied were interacting with each other on a complex task in a work setting. In the Becchio studies the instructions concerning the choice from a limited number of intentions may substitute for the real-life context that occurs in non-experimental settings (see Gallagher 2018b).

my desk working hard to solve a philosophical problem, I may reach for my cup of coffee to take a drink, even as my attention remains on the problem. This is an intentional action, but I did not first form an intention to take a drink (although, of course, if asked, I could retrospectively formulate a statement of intention or a reason to explain my action). At best, the intention was formed in the movement itself, and there was no intention other than the one you can see in the situated movement. To suggest that we need to go beyond what is just there in the movement in order to infer an intention located somewhere beyond or behind the action, is, in some cases, to invent something (some hidden intention) that does not exist. In these kinds of simple intentional actions, the P-intention may be nothing over and above the M-intention specified by the details of the environment.[7] Furthermore, even in cases when someone has formed a D-intention and we are attempting to grasp that D-intention, perhaps by processes that involve inference or simulation, we do so in many cases only by starting with the M- and P-intentions that we take as (at least) expressing the D-intention. That is, it is only by directly perceiving the M-intention that we can even start to make an inference to the D-intention, if in fact that is necessary at all.

I noted (in *Section 5.4*) that deception is an issue that is often raised in response to claims about direct social perception. Surely (someone will object) we cannot know that another person intends to deceive us without some serious mindreading (Curioni, Sebanz, & Knoblich 2018, for example, raise this objection). But first, deception aside, it's always possible for one to be mistaken about another's intention, and this seems to frame a more basic objection to direct social perception. More generally, it is sometimes claimed that direct perception theories are not able to explain perceptual mistakes. Standard explanations invoke internal mediating representations and the idea of misrepresentation. How is it possible to get something wrong, to mis-perceive another person's intention or emotion if there are no mediating representations involved in perception?

An enactivist explanation suggests that some misalignment in the brain-body-environment system is at fault. Environmental conditions may not be right; the perceiver's physical state may be problematic (she may be fatigued, for example); something may be moving too fast, etc. There are a lot of moving parts and some misalignment among them can lead to getting something wrong in what you see or hear, especially since perception is a temporal process that involves non-linear relations between different timescales (*Chapter 2*), and the object of perception may itself be a changing pattern. Second, despite the possibility of such mis-alignment, the perceptual system has evolved such that in ordinary circumstances it works well. In

---

[7] John McDowell (2011, 1) makes a similar point: "adapting Brian O'Shaughnessy's dual aspect conception of the will, I propose that when one intentionally engages in bodily action, the action's intentional character is an aspect of something that is also bodily through and through. The result stands in contrast with familiar philosophical pictures of the relation between mind and body." He proposes that "[i]f rationality can be in bodily activity as opposed to behind it, we have a vivid contrast with a familiar picture according to which a person's mind occupies a more or less mysterious inner realm, concealed from the view of others. If physical activity can be rationality in action, as opposed to a mere result of exercises of rationality, we have a vivid contrast with the tendency to distance a person's body" (p. 17). For the notion of bodily rationality, see Gallagher 2017a, Chapter 10.

fact it works so well we may recognize deception in the motor behavior of another person without having to take the further, mindreading, step. Some highly attuned perceivers (for example, parents, poker players, police interrogators, and psychotherapists) are already able to detect attempts at deception at the level of M-intentions and P-intentions. "If an actor pretends, say, that a suitcase he is carrying is heavier than it actually is, his movements will have a non-natural kinematics that can be detected by observers" (Pacherie 2005, 9, citing Runeson & Frykholm 1983). Subjects can discern whether activity in staged social actions is intended or not even on the basis of watching point-light displays of the agents' movements (Good 1985). Importantly, these capabilities start to take shape in infancy. 7–9-month-old infants perceive certain ambiguous acts like offering and withdrawing food as playful intentions with different goals and outcomes than when the same actions are interpreted literally as intentions to feed (Legerstee 2005, 124; Reddy 1991; 2008). Third, it's important to note that if indeed another person's behavior motivates a suspicious mindreading about possible deception, it is likely something that we have perceived in their behavior that acts as the motivating factor.

Intentional bodily movements, therefore, have very distinctive properties that reflect intention; they are simultaneously constrained by the agent's goal, by the attributes of the situation, and by a set of kinematic and biomechanical rules that jointly shape their dynamics (Pacherie 2005). The intentional aspects of bodily movements are not extrinsic to those movements—they are intrinsic and are reflected in their organization. Intentional actions have observable characteristics that distinguish them from non-intentional behaviors. Intentional kinematics reflect, not only a distinctive dynamics contingent on the agent's goal, but also specific features of the agentive or social situation. Rearrangement of the physical environment, or a different posture of the agent will lead to an alteration of the kinematics required to perform an action. Thus, an important aspect of both P- and M-intentions concerns the fact that intentional actions, many of which may be habitual or culturally defined practices, are not carried out in thin air—they are always situated in physical and social environments. How I will carry out my D-intention to buy a car, for example, will depend on the various circumstances of who, what, when, where, . . . specific cultural practices involved in such actions, as well as environmental and bodily conditions that may facilitate or hinder my action. Intentions involve feedback-governed processes that extend into the world, and which exhibit, as Robert Brandom puts it,

a complexity [that] cannot in principle be specified without reference to the changes in the world that are both produced by the system's responses and responded to . . . . [Such practices] are "thick", in the sense of essentially involving objects, events, and worldly states of affairs. Bits of the world are *incorporated* in such practices. (Brandom 2008, 178)

Also, as I argued in *Section 5.2*, social perception is enactive. That is, my perception of another's action is already formed in terms of what it affords for interaction, or how I might respond to that action. I see your action, not as a fact that needs to be interpreted in terms of your mental states, but as a situated opportunity or affordance for my own action in response. In the context of interaction, the intentions that I can see in your movements appear to me as logically or semantically continuous with my own, or discontinuous, in support of or in opposition to my task, as encouraging or discouraging, as having potential for (further) interaction or as something I want to turn and walk away from. Merleau-Ponty describes it as a kind of know-how: a "praktognosia" (2012, 141). My own perceptually informed bodily responses to the world or to another person are shaping my perception and are ways of encountering the other that cannot be reduced (or inflated) to a form of mindreading. The perceiver is enactively engaged in perceiving the intentions of others, in such a way that her own motor intentionality contributes to perception and to the meaning of what is perceived. Perception operates on the same principles even in the case of passive observation. That is, even in an observational stance, and even if I know that I am not going to engage with the other, perception is *for action* or *for interaction*, and I see the other's action in those terms; i.e., in terms of how I might respond to it.

To summarize: as we interact with others we can perceive their (M- and P-) intentions in their bodily movements, gestures, facial expressions, in what they are looking at, and what they are doing in the rich pragmatic and social contexts of everyday life. Even if, to some degree, action movements by themselves are under-determined, pragmatic and social contexts add specification. On the enactivist view, one doesn't need to access internal states (propositional attitudes, beliefs, desires, inside the head); rather, on both (or all) sides of social interaction, intentions are in the movement, in the action, in the environmentally attuned responses. In such contexts, we normally perceive another's intentionality in terms of its appropriate-ness, its pragmatic and/or emotional value in the particular situation, or in terms of our own possible responses, rather than as reflecting inner mental states, or as constituting explanatory reasons for her further thoughts and actions.

Is this a form of crude behaviorism? No. The idea of "thick" contextualized behavior, mentioned by Brandom, involves rejecting the view that takes "behavior to be just bodily movement and so strips it of intentionality, relocating all that is alive and intelligent in the hidden mind" (Leudar & Costall 2004, 603).[8] Movement, behavior, gesture, expression, and action are infused with intentionality—not only because they are expressive of or specified by M- and P-intentions, which may reflect D-intentions, but also because they are situated in meaningful contexts. What is out there to be seen is more than thin behavior understood as a series of mere move-ments; rather we can perceive a rich mixture of physical and social contexts, intentions, and meanings.

6.1.2 *Perceiving emotions*

The claim is not that we can directly perceive all, or all kinds of mental states. We may see contextualized behavior that suggests that a person *believes* some particular fact, or is *thinking* in a certain way. In some cases what we call a person's belief is a disposition that is activated in the action that we can see. But the claim is not that in

---

[8] "If we stop thinking of behaviour as something that must be described in 'thin' terms, and recognize that it can also be described in 'thick' terms, then the illusion that the line between 'the observable' and 'the unobservable' is to be drawn along the line of thin descriptions will evaporate, and one will stop thinking that 'the mental' is unobservable, obscured from view by bodily movements and accessible only as a matter of inference" (Sharrock & Coulter 2009, 77).

every case we can see his belief or his thought. Depending on circumstances, we may offer the proverbial penny and simply ask the other person what they are thinking if she is not already telling us; and if that is not possible, and there is some important reason why we need to figure out what that person is thinking or believing in ways that are not revealed in her actions, then we may have to revert to inference or simulation. In contrast, however, just as we can perceive intentions, we can directly perceive some emotions. According to the thin ToMistic view, emotions are mental states that need to be inferred in the light of other mental states; e.g., beliefs and desires (Harris et al. 1989; Nguyen & Frye 1999; Wellman & Banerjee 1991). They may be expressed in bodily ways, but to perceive bodily expressions/behaviors is not to perceive the emotion itself. We require inferences to move from bodily expressions to an understanding of actual emotions. So on the view of direct social perception, how is it possible to perceive emotions?

The claim that we directly perceive emotions is not made by way of a Jamesian move that might reduce emotions (at least in part) to observable bodily expressions; the claim is not that to perceive an emotion is reducible to the idea that I perceive the gestures of the other's body *simpliciter*. Nor is it the idea that I *perceive* the visible expressions and *apperceive* the hidden sides of those expressions (see Joel Smith's [2010] appeal to this Husserlian idea; see Krueger 2012). Rather, if we think of emotions as complex *patterns* of features, experiences, and behaviors—and, as such, as "individuated in patterns of characteristic features" (Newen, Welpinghus, & Jukel 2015)—then emotion perception can be considered a form of pattern recognition (Izard 1972; Izard et al. 2000). J.L. Austin holds a similar view about the nature of emotion.

It seems fair to say that "being angry" is in many respects like "having mumps". It is a description of a whole pattern of events, including occasion, symptoms, feeling and manifestation, and possibly other factors besides. It is as silly to ask "What, really, is the anger itself?" as to attempt to fine down "the disease" to some one chosen item [. . .]. That the man himself feels something which we don't (in the sense that he feels angry and we don't) is [. . .] evident enough, and incidentally nothing to complain about as a "predicament": but there is no call to say that "that" ("the feeling") is the anger. (Austin 1979, 109)

On this pattern theory of emotions, particular expressions and expressive actions may be constitutive features of a specific emotion but not necessary components of all instances of the emotion. Emotion, accordingly, is a cluster concept, characterized by a sufficient number of characteristic features, although no one of them may be necessary to every instance. What we do perceive when we perceive an emotion is a package (a gestalt, or what Mitchell Green [2010] calls "an interrelated set of phenomena" or a "systematically related set of components") that includes a number of different constitutive aspects of the emotion pattern—not necessarily all aspects— but enough of its significant constituent features to count.[9]

---

[9] This kind of emotion pattern perception fails in some cases of autism and schizophrenia where subjects have a propensity to view the face as an array of unrelated details; they miss the pattern/gestalt and fail to recognize the emotion. "While most people perceive the face or body of another as a familiar whole imbued with life, subjectivity, and expression, schizophrenia patients will sometimes focus on individual parts or the purely material aspect of the person before them" (Sass & Pienkos 2015). We might also

Again some see the threat of behaviorism looming in this view. Pierre Jacob (2011) has objected that the idea that we directly perceive emotions or intentions leads to a crude behaviorism. The dilemma that Jacob puts forward is that if the direct social perception account argues that bodily expressions are constitutive of emotional or cognitive states, if they can be identified with patterns of observable behavior, then advocates of direct social perception must embrace an unattractive behaviorist position. This, however, does not follow. It is possible to maintain that some bodily actions are expressive of and partly constitute mental phenomena (in the sense that they actually make up their proper parts), without *reducing* psychological states *to* expressive behavior (Krueger & Overgaard 2012). The claim is simply that embodied mental states are only partly constituted by perceptible behaviors. As Green (2007) puts it, if we accept that we sometimes perceive objects by perceiving their parts, then it is also acceptable that we can perceive intentions and emotions although they entail other components that are not fully perceptible (for a differing view see McNeill 2012).

Furthermore, the perceptual aspects of the complex pattern of an emotion are not reducible to purely bodily expressions. We also need to add (consistent with John Dewey's [1895] critique of James) a situational aspect—where the fact that emotional experiences and behaviors are situated in specific ways is part of the pattern (Mendoça 2012). This is to take seriously the phenomenological point that emotions involve intentionality, something that helps to disambiguate emotional expressions. Including situational aspects as part of the perceptual pattern of an emotion also suggests that one can perceive complex, and not just basic emotions. Certain postures and gestures and the style of certain glances may be perceived as jealousy, but only when enough of the context is also perceived.[10] In any case, outside experimental situations, the face on which we see joy or fear is never just a free-floating face disconnected from the rest of the body, or from the surrounding situation; and those other parts of the pattern allow us, in most cases, to resolve what otherwise might be an ambiguous expression.

The idea that emotion, as a perceptual object, is a pattern of aspects or factors is meant to respond to the question: What is emotion if it is something that can be perceived? This answer motivates the idea I just mentioned, that the perception of emotion is a kind of pattern recognition. In some sense this is true, but it is not the whole story. As Beatrice De Gelder (2006) has pointed out, to perceive an emotion, as a bodily expression, is not simply to recognize an object or a pattern, as if the task was

consider the case of what is perceived by non-human animals. Overgaard (2019, 143) suggests that "Eagles, dogs, cats, monkeys (and so on) can see human facial contortions, fist-clenching, and the rest, and so ... are able to see (components of) human emotions. But surely they cannot see them as the emotions they are." The question should be whether they can see a sufficient amount of the pattern that would constitute an emotion. Dogs, I suggest, seem to be able to see some basic emotion patterns as the emotions they are.

[10] This is just a sketch of the pattern theory of emotion (see Newen, Welpinghus, & Jukel [2015], for a more detailed account). Goldman and Sripada (2005) provide a simulationist account of face-based emotion recognition, emphasizing that non-perceptual processes might be necessary "to elaborate purely perceptual information." This need not contradict the idea that we directly perceive emotions since that idea does not deny that "elaborating" on perceptual information can involve cognitive (non-perceptual) processes. The issue considered here, in any case, is not about elaboration.

one of mere recognition. This may often be the way that emotion perception experiments are set up. A subject is presented with a picture or video of a face or a body and asked to identify the emotion. In contexts of real interaction with others, the task is not the observation of and identification or recognition of an emotion; it rather concerns how one responds. To perceive an emotion, as De Gelder puts it, is to experience significance. It is to become attuned to a valence that manifests itself affectively and has an effect on the perceiver. If I see an angry person coming towards me—displaying the typical facial and movement pattern of anger—I don't remain a neutral perceiver who simply identifies the emotion he sees. My perception is not just the activation of retinal and cortical neuronal processes that lead me to believe that the other person is angry. My entire system is activated in its own affective way involving heart rate, respiration, hormones, and so on, all of which have an effect on my perception (Gallagher 2017a, Chapter 8).

The idea that perception is merely the identification or recognition of an object or a pattern of features remains an overly intellectualist and incomplete explanation. In the same way that, at some level, it *affects* you (in the strong sense of "affect") when you experience the gaze of the other person directed at you, your perception of the other's emotion *affects* you, even if this affect is not consciously recognized. Thus, even in an observational stance within an experimental setting, when presented with masked, subliminal images of angry or happy faces or bodies, one's autonomic and peripheral systems register the emotion and respond (Tamietto 2013), and this response is part of the organism's perceptual process. The effect is much greater if there is the potential for interaction—that is, if one is gazing into the eyes of a real person who is gazing back—in this situation it includes a synchronization of specific brain areas across the brains of both subjects (Hirsch et al. 2017); but it also includes a more full-bodied, affectively rich intercorporeity. The perception of emotion is an affective perception. This does not rule out the idea that one might have an affective response to some inanimate object (as, e.g., in the aesthetic experience one might have in looking at a beautiful stand of trees, or in looking at the aftermath of clear-cutting a forest), but the affective perception of another person's emotion is defined by a particular set of social affordances that trees don't offer. Trees don't hug back.

6.1.3 Non-inferential perception

In the philosophy of mind, the notion of direct perception is suspect because it has traditionally been associated with the idea that it cannot be mistaken. If there is no representation that mediates perception, then we cannot account for error or illusion. Norman Malcolm (1953), for example, considers G.E. Moore's claim that one can have a direct perception of an after-image in a way that one cannot have a direct perception of an environmental object, and he ends up thinking that the impossibility of error is "the main feature of the philosophical conception of direct perception." But taking an after-image or a visual illusion as an example of something we can directly perceive, and concerning which we cannot make a mistake, is, I think, a mistake. Dealing with this issue would take us too far afield, however, so let's put things differently.

By direct perception we mean perception that does not involve a certain kind of inference, but can still involve error. Theoretically, however, perception has been said to involve inference in one of two ways: in either intra-perceptual processing or extra-perceptual processing. Here I'll argue against the latter view;[11] i.e., that:

1. we perceive (or sense) X, but X is meaningless unless we add something to perception, and
2. what gets added to perception is an inference—a very fast inference (or some other cognitive process like simulation) to make sense of X.

Going back to the idea that we can directly perceive M- and P-intentions, and the evidence for this provided in the experiments by Becchio and colleagues, one might object that from the claim that a perceiver understands that p is the case solely on the basis of perceptual *stimuli* (e.g., the M-intention in the action), it is not legitimate to conclude that the perceiver understands that p is the case based solely on perceptual *processes*, or more specifically that the subpersonal processes are entirely perceptual. Rather, the objection might go, perception of an intention is underpinned by both perceptual and extra-perceptual subpersonal processes. On some versions of TT and ST something like an extra-perceptual inference (or simulation) is added to the perception because perception by itself is characterized as an impoverished form of observation, detached from action (or interaction). On this view there is a disconnection between my perception and anything that might involve my own action. It follows that if I were to remain with only what I literally perceive of your apparent behavior I would seemingly be in the dark, or totally perplexed, or at least puzzled by it.

In contrast to this view, the enactivist approach argues that direct social perception, without any extra-perceptual inferential processes involved, can grasp more than just surface behavior—or to put it precisely, it can grasp behavior as meaningful. In this regard it is a kind of *smart* perception (Gallagher 2008). In the case of a not-so-smart social perception I open my eyes and I see a body moving in a meaningless way, flailing her arms for example, and I have to make sense of it in some non-perceptual way. My eyes are working fine; my visual cortex is processing all of the visual information, but what vision delivers is relatively meaningless, "thin" behavior, which I then have to interpret in some further cognitive steps that involve inference. In contrast, in the case of smart perception, in the very same situation, when I open my eyes I see a person engaged in an exercise routine at her gym. I do not see meaningless behavior and then infer that it is a form of exercise—and I don't have to call on inference unless she is doing something out of context or something that consists of weird or inappropriate movements. Part of what makes smart perception smart is that it is always contextualized; I perceive actions with their circumstances, and other bodily comportments such as facial expressions in their context. In addition, my perception is obviously informed by my prior experience, so if I never encountered yoga before then I might start to wonder and to make inferences when I see the other person in a certain yoga position. Likely I may even have to ask someone what she is doing.

---

[11] For arguments against the former view, that perception is itself an inferential process (a view that goes back to Helmholtz and is defended in current models of predictive coding) see *Section 6.2.3*.

On the smart perception view there is no denial that subpersonal processes in the brain contribute to perception. Even Gibson's notion of direct perception does not deny that subpersonal brain processes are involved in our ability to see affordances in the environment. In the case of smart social perception, the brain actively contributes—more precisely, the organism, including the brain, is engaged, and has something to contribute to the shaping of perception. Perception involves complex, dynamical processes at a subpersonal, sensory-motor level—but these processes are part of an enactive engagement or response of the whole organism, rather than additional, extra-perceptual, inferential, or simulative processes.

For example, the fusiform "face area" of the brain is activated, not only for face perception, but also when we look at the front (grill, headlights) of cars (Gauthier et al. 2000; Xu 2005). The significance of this is that the neural processes that underpin direct social perception are plastic and can be tuned by (social and cultural) experience. This activation (part of what constitutes the perception I have of my car if in fact I am looking at its front end) is not the underpinning of some additional inferential cognitive act. I do not perceive and then go through some other process that correlates to the activation of the fusiform face area; rather, fusiform activation helps to constitute the way that I perceive the car, or the other person's face, etc. Importantly, perception of another's face activates not just the face recognition area and ventral visual stream, but also the dorsal (action-related) visual pathway—suggesting that we perceive affordances in the face of the other (Debruille et al. 2012). Faced with the face of a real person, the perceiving subject, at a minimum, makes eye contact with very subtle eye movements. Accordingly, face perception presents not just objective patterns that we might recognize as emotions. It involves complex interactive affective and response patterns arising out of an active engagement with the other's face—not a simple recognition of facial features—but an interactive perception that includes my own affective response to the other's emotion.

Meaningful perception of any sort may rely on activation of association areas outside very early sensory-processing areas. But let's note two things in this regard. First, even neuronal activity in the earliest of perceptual-processing areas, such as V1, reflects more than simple feature detection. For example, V1 neurons are activated in ways that anticipate reward if they have been tuned by prior experience (Shuler & Bear 2006). This is not perception first, followed by an additional neural or cognitive function that registers the possibility of reward. The reward aspect is part of how the perception is organized in this case, even at the level of neuronal patterns in early visual processing. This is most likely the result of neural plasticity, and as such it is not the underpinning of some additional inferential cognitive act. My perception is what it is, not because I add top-down inferences generated in other parts of the brain to sensory-motor perceptual processes, but because those sensory-motor processes have been shaped by prior experience and are functioning within a system of brain-body-environment.

Second, most if not all neuroscientists accept that subpersonal neural underpinnings of perception are extremely plastic and can be tuned by (personal, social, and cultural) experience. The neural networks of perceptual systems, including association areas, are set up by previous experience, and the various influences of those prior experiences shape ongoing and forthcoming experience. Perceptual areas are, as Jesse Prinz puts it, "set up to be set off" (2004, 55) by prior experience and plastic changes. The activation of association networks has also been tuned by prior sensory-motor experience, and has a function not of associating sensory and motor information (as Hughlings Jackson had suggested), or forming a representation, but of being part of the ongoing perceptual activation or response. On this view, in perception, the network (of primary and association areas) is set off as a dynamical whole (rather than as a train of hierarchically arranged inferences) in response to worldly happenings.

More generally, the enactivist idea of sensory-motor contingencies (e.g., Noë 2004) is only part of the story; enactivism is even more embodied when we take into account bodily affect, as well as the role that intersubjective interaction plays in shaping perception (Colombetti 2014; Gallagher 2017a; Gallagher & Bower 2014; Varela, Thompson, & Rosch 1991). Perception involves complex, dynamical processes at a subpersonal, sensory-motor level—but these processes are part of an enactive engagement or response of the whole organism, rather than additional, extra-perceptual, inferential, or simulative processes.

Even on the subpersonal level the story is not only about brain processes, but must also include the peripheral and autonomic systems. We can see this when we consider disruptions of bodily movement, perception, and social cognition in the case of Autism Spectrum Disorder (ASD). In contrast to ToM accounts of autism which suggest that the core problem with social cognition is a lack of mindreading ability (e.g., Baron-Cohen 1995), IT has pointed to early developing sensory-motor problems that disrupt primary and secondary intersubjective processes and the kind of interaction that is essential for typical development. For some time we have known that individuals with (or later diagnosed with) ASD have problems with motor control and movement (e.g., Teitelbaum et al. 1998; Damasio & Maurer 1978), and it has been suggested that such problems interfere with social interaction and the enactive perception of the intentions of others (Gallagher 2004a; 2005a). Recent research into the fine neuroscientific details of movement confirms this view and reinforces the type of analysis of intention perception found in Becchio's experiments mentioned above. Elizabeth Torres (2013; Torres et al. 2013) demonstrates that motor intention is mapped out in very specific patterns that involve the integration of efferent signals and online proprioceptive/kinesthetic feedback. Natural bodily movement includes both intention-related proprioception correlated with goal-related voluntary actions, and proprioception that correlates with spontaneous, non-goal related, sometimes reflex movements that may be embedded in actions. In typical agents, these two streams of proprioception are more or less segregated and the system is able to discriminate between them (although the complexity of this process is immense, see Brincker and Torres 2013). This is important for motoric anticipation and control of the sort discussed by Susan Hurley (see Section 4.3.8). In ASD (across the spectrum) these two streams are "blurred" so there are disrupted patterns in re-entrant (afferent, proprioceptive) sensory feedback that usually contributes to the autonomous regulation and coordination of motor output. "[T]ypical volitional control is highly compromised often with a striking disconnect between the intentions and the actions of the affected individ-ual" (Torres et al. 2013, 2).[12]

The implication is not only that the autistic subject has difficulty in moving, and carrying out (or even forming) intentions, but that just such problems disrupt timing and certain factors essential for engaging in social dynamics, and for perceiving intentions in others (see, e.g., Zapata-Fonseca et al. 2019). In typical development, the maturity of the proprioceptive system brings with it gains in motor control that involve higher predictability (i.e., higher predictive power based on prior movement),[13] higher reliability, and a broader scope of possible movements that adds to efficiency. In contrast, in all subjects with ASD tested by Torres, there were significant differences in noise-to-signal ratios in these processes, differences in peak velocities, and a lack of diversity of kinesthetic input—"Proprioceptive input was random, (unpredictable), noisy, (unreliable), and non-diversified in ASD" (2013, 16–17). Moreover, in the experiments conducted by Torres et al., these problems with movement correlated with poorer performance in cognitive decision-making (discriminating and pointing to a specified target), and it's likely that subjects with ASD would have further problems discriminating intentions in the movements of others, making sense out of their gestures, or making fine-grained discriminations of emotional facial expressions of others during real-time social interactions (Torres et al. 2013, 18–19). The fact that kinesthetic reafference is noisy and unstable in subjects with ASD means that they have difficulty mapping between their own movements and their kinesthetically informed visual perceptions of the move-ments of others.

The specificity found in Torres' research lends support to an embodied-interaction approach over a ToM approach. But one important question that requires further research is whether kinematic disruptions in autistic subjects are different from those found in other disabilities (e.g., cerebral palsy, ADHD, cerebellar ataxia). Indeed, one objection could be that not all cases of motoric abnormality lead to autistic problems with social cognition (see Cook, Blakemore, and Press 2013; Gallagher & Varga 2015).

---

[12] "Parts of the peripheral information involving position, movement, touch, and pressure along with their patterns of variability are routed through general somatic afferent (GSA) fibers: some flow through the so-called 'conscious' proprioceptive channels that reach the neocortex via the thalamus, whereas others flow through 'unconscious' proprioceptive channels with targets at the cerebellum, striatum, and limbic systems.... Typically there is balance and flexible exchange between these re-afferent forms of feedback that facilitate central regulation, anticipatory planning, and predictive control of the motor output and its consequences. In autism it is very unlikely that this balance and flexibility remains" (Torres et al. 2013, 3).

[13] "In the language of Bayesian statistics, such acquired 'priors' allow the agent to make meaningful categorizations and sense unexpected internal and external disruptions through their own movements. We have also found that mature TD micro-movements can be separated into functional classes with different levels of intentionality. They operate at different time scales in their latencies to reach critical points (e.g., maxima) along the kinematic trajectory" (Torres et al. 2013, 18). The bottom line here is that what predictive-processing accounts call priors are not just in the brain; they extend to include what Brincker and Torres (2013) call "motor priors" in the peripheral nervous system, and beyond that as well (see the discussion of Barrett and Bar [2009] in the following section; also Gallagher and Allen 2018; Gallagher 2017a).

Can the "wide" and "smart" embodied features of perception—i.e., those broader embodied and motoric processes that tie perception directly to action in typical development, together with the important neural processes that, *via* experience-based plastic changes, make habitual, affective, valence-related, environmentally attuned aspects intrinsic to perceptual experience—account for the seemingly strong claim that we perceive meaning? This is a concern raised by Søren Overgaard (2017; 2019). For example, he writes: "Even if something is literally perceptible, it does not follow that human perception does (or even can) arrive at, or disclose, the *meaning* or *significance* of that something (or the *kind* of thing it is). Extra-perceptual inferences may well be required for us to get at the meaning" (2019, 142). Although Overgaard rightly qualifies the objection with some reference to the idea that perception is "smart," it still seems that he construes perception as something that is not so smart. He makes the point that someone with ASD may see precisely the emotional expression on another person's face but fail to recognize it as a particular emotion. That is, the person with ASD may perceive that element of the other's emotion, and therefore literally perceive the emotion, but fail to perceive it as meaningful. This, however, is not precise. Because of the various problems associated with ASD detailed above, we should say that the person with ASD fails to perceive the emotion-*pattern*, and in that sense fails to perceive the emotion. That a facial expression falls upon the perceiver's retina and activates neurons in the visual cortex doesn't mean that she gets to the point of pattern-recognition and perceives the emotion. Clearly, the idea that perception is smart is more complicated than that.

I think that it is perfectly correct to say that even if I perceive the other's intention or emotion (and in many cases I perceive both, and not always as distinct things, but likely as integrated into a more holistic pattern), I perceive it as meaningful, precisely in contrast to the way that someone with ASD may not be able to see it. I see it as anger or as joy or as an intention to throw the apple, or to throw it angrily —and such things are meaningful, and I understand them as such.[14] This is not to say, however, that I comprehend its full meaning. I may not be able to perceive *why* someone is angry or overjoyed, or why someone is doing what she is doing. Overgaard is right that to gain more hermeneutical depth more than perception may be involved.

6.2 The New Hybrids

In the wake of IT's challenge to the ToM approaches to social cognition, several theorists have argued that direct social perception is not an alternative to ToM, but is in fact consistent with TT and/or ST (Bohl & Gangopadhey 2013; Carruthers 2015; Lavelle 2012; Overgaard and Michael 2015). I've used the phrase the "new hybrids" to

---

[14] I think Overgaard's (2017) example of the bicycle works against the point he wants to make. He suggests that if someone has never seen a bicycle before and doesn't know what a bicycle is, he may be able to see the bicycle, but he won't be able to see it *as* a bicycle—it would not have that meaning. I think that is absolutely right. But that just means that learning and brain plasticity are parts of the larger story. If the person becomes familiar with bicycles (let's say he lives in Copenhagen for a time and sees all of the bicycle action there), then I don't think he would have any problem seeing a bicycle *as* a bicycle. The same applies to emotions, at least for those that may not be hardwired.

refer to those theories that propose that direct social perception is actually compatible with TT or ST (Gallagher 2015a). On the one hand, it may be contentious to use the phrase "new hybrids" since these theorists maintain that there is nothing *new* or *hybrid* about the idea that TT or ST can easily incorporate direct social perception as an element of social cognition. On their view, and despite some supposedly counter indications, ToM accounts have always been consistent with the idea of direct social perception. On the other hand, some theorists, including myself, think that the claim that direct social perception is consistent with TT or ST is a surprising turn.

6.2.1 *When UP is down*

According to new hybrid theories, the idea of direct social perception is not, and has never been, a problem for theory theorists. There are two issues to consider in regard to such claims. The first is whether there is some truth involved in the historical part of the claim. As one might expect, given older debates about direct perception (see, e.g., Malcolm 1953; Fodor and Pylyshyn 1981), it has not been smooth sailing for theories of direct perception *vis-à-vis* standard theories of cognition or social cognition. Critics of direct perception have denied that there is any such thing.

This first question concerns the "unobservability principle" (UP), discussed in *Section 4.1*; i.e., the idea that minds are exclusively intracranial and perceptually inaccessible or unobservable. It is precisely because this principle has been so closely associated with TT and ST that the idea that these approaches can now embrace direct social perception seems a surprising turn. Carruthers (2015), for example, admits that "theory-theorists often introduce their work by emphasizing that mental states are abstract and imperceptible," and that this is part of the motivation for requiring the need for theoretical inference to such mental states. I've already cited examples of theorists who endorse UP (e.g., Leslie 1987; Mitchell 2008; Epley & Waytz 2010). There are plenty more. Tooby and Cosmides, for example, suggest that "no human has ever seen a thought, a belief, or an intention" (in Baron-Cohen 1995, xvii). Likewise, Karmiloff-Smith (1992, 138) contends that theory of mind "involves inferences based on unobservables (mental states, such as belief)...." Gopnik and Wellman (1992, 148) characterize ToM as involving an appeal to "abstract unobservable entities"—i.e., mental states. Or consider:

Mental states, and the minds that possess them, are necessarily unobservable constructs that must be inferred by observers rather than perceived directly. (Johnson 2000, 22)[15]

On the basis of such statements, and others like them, UP seems to rule out direct social perception. To argue that direct social perception is consistent with TT or ST, UP has to be relaxed or dismissed or put down in some way. This seems to be what happens when Carruthers (2015) argues that some mental states are perceptible and

---

[15] Jacob (2011) agrees: "On the standard approach, another's expressive behavior should be sharply distinguished from her psychological states, including her emotional and affective experiences: the former cannot constitute the latter. Nor could one observe or perceive another's emotional or affective experiences: one can only perceive (or observe) another's expressive behavior."

that TT would not deny this. Bohl and Gangopadhyay (2013)[16] and Lavelle (2012) explicitly deny that UP is a doctrine of TT or ST. Setting aside the issue of historical accuracy concerning claims that ToM approaches have traditionally either accepted or denied UP, let's take a closer look at the appeal to perception in these new hybrid theories.

6.2.2 *Perception and extra-perceptual inference*

Generally the notion of the directness of perception is opposed to the idea that perception is inferentially mediated (Fodor & Pylyshyn 1981). I indicated above that perception could involve inference in two ways: in either intra-perceptual processing or extra-perceptual processing. Let's continue our examination of the latter idea.

At least on some ToM accounts, one perceives behavior and then some extra-perceptual inference (or more generally, some extra-perceptual cognitive process; e.g., a simulation) is added to perception in order to allow the observer to go beyond perceived behavior and to attribute mental states to the other person. This implies a two-step process: perceptual observation plus extra-perceptual cognition (inference or simulation). The extra-perceptual process does not have to be conscious—it can be instantiated in subpersonal neural activation in ToM areas or the mirror system. On these theories, perception is not sufficient or direct; it needs to be supplemented by processes that instantiate a non-perceptual mindreading operation.

Shannon Spaulding (2017b), for example, grants that it may be possible to directly perceive M-intentions in the actions of another person. Even if this is the case, she argues, this amounts to a banal fact since no one would deny this—even a theory theorist could accommodate this sort of banal view of direct social perception. "In fact, a modern-day Cartesian could perfectly consistently accept this idea. Moreover, the idea is compatible with the view that access to our own minds and other minds is indirect and inferentially mediated" (Spaulding 2017b, 165). Spaulding here cites Carruthers. Carruthers (2013, 144n3) suggests, "the phenomenology of much everyday mindreading is that we just see someone as being about to act in some specific way in pursuit of a presumed goal, or hear the intent behind what they say." Direct social perception is compatible with an inferentialist view as long as one accepts the directness as merely a characterization of perceptual phenomenology or phenomenal experience, and accepts that all the real inferential action of social cognition is located at the subpersonal level and is inferential. Accordingly, it *seems as if* we directly perceive M-intentions, for example, but, for theory theorists like Carruthers and Spaulding, the controlling processes are inferential and occur on a subpersonal level.

On the one hand, to the extent that the theory theorist would treat the perceptual aspect as merely phenomenal or, indeed, epiphenomenal or banal, direct social perception really plays no significant role in social cognition. It simply delivers the

---

[16] In contrast, Gangopadhyay and Schilbach (2012) state: "Theories of mind-reading, such as TT and ST, have traditionally stayed away from the discussion of perceptual knowledge of other minds mainly due to the underlying assumption, of a Cartesian sort, that mental states, being separate from bodily behavior, are not given in the perceived bodily behavior" (2011, 411).

results of the deeper mindreading process, which is the real work of social cognition. Perception by itself is not sufficient to do the job.

On the other hand, a theory theorist could take perception a bit more seriously, as an essential part of how a mindreading process works on the subpersonal level. Carruthers (2015), for example, argues for a kind of integration or binding of perception and conceptual inferential process. The mindreading process includes extra-perceptual inferential process that are quickly integrated into perceptual processes. As he indicates, the integration is an online binding between ToM concepts and the perceptual system; not a reconfiguration of the latter, but a kind of cognitive penetration. Conceptual representations interact "deeply and pervasively in perceptual processing" (2015, 502) and are thus integrated into the results of that processing. According to Carruthers: we now know that "concepts interact with visual processing at early (pre-attentive) stages, influencing the resulting perceptual contents and perceptual phenomenology" (2015, 501). The only limit to this binding is the speed with which the concept can be processed.

[C]onceptual information will need to be processed within the window of a few hundred milliseconds that elapses between presentation of a stimulus and its subsequent global broadcast. The only limit will be whether mindreading inferences can be drawn fast enough for binding to take place. Since many forms of mental-state awareness are seemingly simultaneous with awareness of the behavior and/or circumstances that cause them, we can presume that ordinary mindreaders can draw the requisite inferences quickly enough.   (2015, 504)

The concepts that are bound to the perception process are implicit ("tacit") theoretical generalizations about mental states; "provided that the mindreading system can operate swiftly enough for its output to be bound into the content of the perceptual states that provide the basis for its interpretations, and globally broadcast along with the latter, then it will be possible for mental states to be perceived" (504). He suggests that there is a "back-and-forth processing taking place between the mindreading system and its perceptual input" (504n4), and this results in an integrated perceptual-mindreading state. The hybrid theory (combining TT and direct perception) is predicated on a hybrid perceptual-mindreading state produced by fast inferential processing.

Sulin Lavelle (2012), who also defends the idea that some mental states may be perceptible, distinguishes between two interpretations of direct social perception: a strong one and a weak one. She argues that TT is consistent with the weak view, and that the strong view is untenable. What precisely is the weak view? According to Lavelle, the weak view of direct social perception is that "information about other's mental states is available in our conscious experiences of them and we need not add an extra step to our experience in order to know such information. The weak version is silent on the processes facilitating our conscious experiences" (2012, 219–20). Lavelle argues that we need not add an extra step (an explicit inference) to our *conscious* experience; but that's because, according to TT, which is not so silent about the subpersonal processes, the extra step is already in the mix—it's already added at the subpersonal level. Specifically, the subpersonal processes are inferential, in contrast to the strong version of direct social perception (which is the enactive, IT version) where subpersonal processes that subtend social perception are not inferential or theory-like or an instantiation of folk psychology. As Lavelle notes, TT rejects this strong version.

To characterize direct social perception Lavelle cites Dretske's (1969) distinction between epistemic and non-epistemic seeing. Epistemic perception is fully informed by theory-laden inferential processes on the subpersonal level. That an inferential process is theory laden is a concept borrowed from the philosophy of science, and it is clearly the right way to put it in the context of science and philosophy where there is a lot of theorizing going on. In the realm of folk psychology, however, it means that a person's concepts or beliefs are informing her perception.

In some sense it may all come down to an understanding of neuroscience and how we conceive of the working of perceptual networks. There definitely is "split second" processing involved in the complex, dynamical neural activations of social perception. A dynamical super-fast interplay of bottom-up and top-down processes "elicit" parallel and concurrent activations and lateral inhibitions (Freeman & Johnson 2016). The question is whether we should interpret these neural activations as one set of sensory/early perceptual processes plus the addition of a second set of top-down mindreading processes that through inferential processes shape the end result (in line with the weak version of direct social perception and new hybrid theory), or as a coherent distributed processing that already includes more than sensory processing and is characterized by network plasticity (consistent with the strong direct perception view). The data show that perceiving the face of another person, for example, involves a distributed activation of neural circuits in "a neural network for flexible split-second social perception, including the fusiform gyrus (FG), orbitofrontal cortex (OFC), and anteriortemporal lobe (ATL)" (Freeman & Johnson 2016, 363). That there is a dynamical integration of top-down and bottom-up processing doesn't necessarily mean that we can draw a line to distinguish perceptual processes on one side and mindreading processes on the other, or that this integrated processing somehow means that perception is less direct.

Indeed, there is good evidence that perceptual processes at the subpersonal level are already shaped, *via* mechanisms of plasticity, by bodily (enactive) and environmental (including social and cultural) factors and prior experience. Consider, for example, the difference between the way Westerners and Asians perceive and attend to visual objects and contexts (Goh & Park 2009). One can also find, not only brain processes that are different relative to the use of different cultural tools and practices, but also cultural variations in brain processes specifically underlying person perception and emotion regulation (Kitayama & Park 2010). For example, relative to European Americans, Asians show different neural processing in response to images of faces that represent a social-evaluative threat (Park & Kitayama 2012). It's important to keep in mind that perception is more than just neural processing. Perception employs active movement so that by way of motoric behavior we seek sensory targets. Perceivers actively engage in perceiving objects and other people, moving their head or body to better hear, for example. Eye tracking shows that perceivers target different visual aspects of the perceived object depending on interest (Yarbus 1967). This applies to face perception as well, and, cultural differences affect where we look on the face of the other person. Thus, for example, East Asians focus on the eye region to gain a sense of the other's emotion, while Europeans distribute their gaze more evenly across the face or may focus on the mouth area (Caldara 2017; Jack et al. 2009). This cultural difference in perceiving facial emotional expressions starts as early as 7 months of age (Geangu et al. 2016). Accordingly, in very specific ways, social and cultural factors have a physical effect on bodily comportment and brain processes that shape basic perceptual experience and emotional responses. Rather than cognitive penetration, perception is set up by cultural permeation (Hutto et al., 2020).

Along this line, Lavelle herself cites Cecilia Heyes' (2010) proposal that the mirror system is formed through associative processes rather than by inferential processes. Current sensory activation—e.g., in the visual cortex—may activate a network that includes other sensory (non-conceptual) associations (in association areas) that specify aspects of the current perceptual object—a certain facial pattern, for example, can be informed by previous perceptions of angry behavior so that I see the face as angry. Those sensory associations, in networks that have been attuned by prior perceptions, can be non-conceptual yet still sufficient to contribute to a direct perception of the other person's embodied emotional state. If it is possible for my response to the other to get further informed by some separate folk-psychological conceptual contributions, it's not clear that this is a necessity in all or even most cases.

A new hybrid theorist, by sticking to the idea that a perception of another person's intention or emotion must, through an inferential process, incorporate extra-perceptual folk-psychological information, seemingly rejects the notion of neural plasticity and reiterates a model of the mind where meaning would be added, top-down, piled onto the perceptual vehicle to form a new representation. This is the perspective reflected, for example, in Lavelle's rejection of Gallese's idea that we "don't need to suppose an over-arching top-down influence in order to have a neural mechanism that maps the goal. We already have it in the premotor [or parietal] system. We don't need to imply a further mechanism that maps the goal" (Gallese 2006,15; also see Michael et al. 2014). *Pace* any simulationist explanation of this process, I think Gallese is right.

Lavelle, in the end, concludes: "The moral is that while theoretical entities [i.e., mental states] need not be unobservable, one requires a theory in order to observe them" (2012, 228). She sees perception playing some role in social cognition, but like Carruthers she discounts personal-level phenomenology and places all the real action of social cognition in subpersonal processes where theory informs a weak perception. In doing so, however, she seemingly has to discount neural plastic effects in the sensory-motor system.

Bohl and Gangopadhyay (2013) also argue that social perception needs to be supplemented by theoretical inference or simulation. This is because they take perception to be simply the sensory registration of the properties of objects or people. "There is something more to the awareness of a mental state, even in face-to-face encounters, than the mere contact with the colour or the shape or any other sensorily accessible property of an object" (2013, 11). This, however, is clearly not the concept of direct social perception found in IT. Direct social perception is *not* reducible to a simply passive picking up of sensory properties; rather, it involves an enactive process that responds to intentions and emotions.

On a more positive note, Bohl and Gangopadhyay (2013) propose a Husserlian solution, adopting a position developed by Joel Smith (2010) on the basis of Husserl's notion that we perceive the full presence of an object (even the sides that we do not literally see) by incorporating the notion that those unseen sides are "apperceived" or co-presented, where apperception is an aspect of perception. Applied to social perception, the idea is that while we perceive the observable physical behaviors of others, we apperceive the unobservable mental states in some fashion. As Bohl and Gangopadhyay, following Smith, correctly point out, social perception is certainly different from object perception where we can fulfill (or disconfirm) our apperceptions by walking around or manipulating the object and actually seeing the previously hidden sides. Rather than being able to do that in the case of our perception of others, however, Husserl suggests that we can fulfill our apperceptions of others' mental states by a continued perception of anticipated consistent behavior (1960, §52). Perception, after all, is not instantaneous; it can develop over time and fulfill (or disconfirm) the perceptual expectations of further behavior. But if Smith takes this to be a direct social perception account, Bohl and Gangopadhyay quickly retreat from that position. They defend a ToM supplement for perception because they treat direct perception as a mere sensing of sensory properties (where direct perception could pick up only the redness of the other person's face rather than her embarrassment). Accordingly, they see the potential for a hybrid in terms of supplementing a not-so-smart perception with theory. "The anticipations structuring the content of perceiving other minds as co-presented may well be integrated with situated and context-dependent folk psychology which informs perceptual experience. This line of thought opens up a space for fruitful discussions between perceptual accounts and ToM accounts of social cognition" (Bohl & Gangopadhyay 2013, 13). They provide no account, however, of how the supplementation works, although one can presume that they would appeal to processes similar to the inferential ones described by Carruthers or Lavelle.

6.2.3 Predictive processing and new hybrid theories

A second way to understand the role of inference is to think that subpersonal inferential processes are intrinsic to perception itself. This infra-perceptual role for inference goes back to Helmholtz and still has currency in predictive processing models. In regard to this second way of understanding the role of inference, there are three questions:

(1) Is the complex neural processing that subtends perception necessarily inferential?
(2) If so, is that process of such a kind that one can define it as theoretical (or simulational), as required by TT (or ST)?
(3) If so, does that mean that perception is not direct?

With respect to the first question, much depends on how we understand the neuroscience. Helmholtzian neuroscientists would endorse the idea that the neural processes underlying perception are themselves inferential processes (Helmholtz 1867). And in terms of social perception, the theory theorist might be tempted to say that such subpersonal inferential processes just are the theoretical inferences that allow us to mindread. But the theory theorist cannot easily claim that Helmholtzian inferences that underpin perception are the ones underpinning mindreading. First, Helmholtzian inferences (if there are such things[17]) are characterized as very basic processes involving, for example, the visual perception of edges, colors, shapes, and so forth, and are meant to answer very basic questions about how we perceive anything as a visual object. It's not clear how such processes would be related to folk psychology. Helmholtzian inferences, at least in the classic sense, are not rich enough to underpin mindreading. Second, if TT did make this claim, it would be tantamount to the claim that mindreading just is the *perception* of whatever Helmholtzian inferences would allow, perhaps, at best, a perception of behavior—e.g., I see the agent reaching for the cup. One would need to add to perception some other kind of subpersonal, extra-perceptual, extra-Helmholtzian inferences to get anything like the full-blown mindreading that TT has in mind. That would bring us back to the idea of not-so-smart perception plus some other cognitive process.

We might say the same of any Bayesian predictive processing account that treats perception and object recognition as an inferential process (Friston 2012, 248). It's obviously important to understand the real dynamics of how the brain works. More generally, we've known for a long time that anticipatory processes are hugely important for perception and action. In neuroscience we have the work of Alain Berthoz, who draws in part on Husserl's phenomenological account of intrinsic temporality (see *Section 2.2*). Predictive coding models provide an account of how neural processing participates in these pervasive dynamic anticipatory processes. But again there are questions of how to interpret such processes. In predictive models (Hohwy 2013; Clark 2016) the assumption about visual perception, for example, is that the brain has no direct access to the outside world, so it has to interpret or decode sensory input in light of a top-down generative model or "prior." If you think of this in terms of inference, then the brain is seemingly inferring to the best representation of what has caused a particular pattern of neuronal activation. Since a given pattern could be caused by any number of different stimulus configurations, the task involves using probabilistic inference to minimize prediction errors or "surprisals."

This kind of Bayesian predictive model of perception seems more sophisticated than the Helmholtzian one, but the question is whether it scales up to a point where one can say that the prior actually involves a theory of the folk-psychological kind. Karl Friston (2012) thinks it can. Understanding motor behavior as depending on

---

[17] There are significant objections to the Helmholtzian idea that perception involves subpersonal inferences (see Bennett & Hacker 2003; Hutto & Myin 2013; Orlandi 2012, 2014). Moreover, there is some suggestion that the notion that brain processes are inferential is really only metaphorical (see Hatfield 2002 for review). Even Helmholtz (1867, 430) suggests that the processes of perception "are *like* inferences" (Helmholtz 1867, 430). And Stephen Palmer, with reference to Fodor and Pylyshyn, states: "Using the term 'inference' to describe such a process may seem to be somewhat metaphorical and thus to undercut the force of the claim that perception works by unconscious inference. But, as we said at the outset, unconscious inference must be at least somewhat metaphorical, since normal inference is quite clearly slow, laborious, and conscious, whereas perception is fast, easy, and unconscious. The important point for present purposes is that perception relies on processes that can be usefully viewed as inferences that require heuristic assumptions" (Palmer 1999, 83).

predictive processing, he states: "At a more abstract level, predictions about how we will physically move are composed and generated in a way that determines how we behave. Perhaps the most important determinants of our behaviour (and their underlying predictions) are beliefs about the intentions and behaviour of others. This necessarily requires an internal model of self in relation to others and an implicit sense of agency" (Friston 2012, 249). In some predictive accounts of social cognition, however, understanding the other's intentions does not mean understanding M- and P-intentions, but is assumed to mean understanding D-intentions as distinguished from goal, kinematics, and muscle activity (Kilner, Friston, & Frith 2007). Moreover, in contrast to the studies of kinematics cited above (e.g., Becchio et al. 2012), some models of predictive processing assume that "[i]n the specific case of action-observation the same kinematics can be caused by different goals and intentions" (Kilner, Friston, & Frith 2007, 161). Whether this is a matter of granularity, where at some level of detail different intentions may correspond to different kinematics, and at another level they don't, is not clear. In any case, just by such assumptions, one might then be led to the idea that these details require resolution by inferential processes rather than by direct perception.

Likewise, Teufel, Fletcher, and Davis (2010) adopt a predictive model that seems consistent with Carruthers, where "social perception is subserved by an interactive bidirectional relationship between the neural mechanisms supporting basic sensory processing of social information and the theory-of-mind system" (2010, 376). The bidirectional dynamics is what makes this a hybrid theory that depends on both bottom-up perceptual processes and top-down ToM processes. On the predictive-processing model, the ToM system not only depends on perception as an information source, but also the ToM system feeds forward to influence sensory processing. Teufel et al. call this a "perceptual mentalizing"—or one might say, a mentalizing of perception—in which beliefs about the other person's mental states shape perceptual processes. They show experimentally that an observer's belief about whether another person can see or cannot see (through a pair of either transparent or opaque glasses) will have an effect on the way the observer perceives the other's direction of gaze (signaled in terms of the direction in which the head is turned). On Teufel et al.'s interpretation, the automatic tendency to follow the gaze of the other to locations where they are looking is top-down modulated by ToM. This modulation depends on (1) the observer's prior experience of wearing either the transparent or opaque glasses and (2) the ToM attribution of the other's mental state of seeing or not seeing. Yet, as Teufel et al. make clear, "the neural mechanisms of perceptual modulation by ToM are uncertain" (p. 378), although they identify gaze-sensitive neurons in the superior temporal sulcus (STS) as involved in this kind of perception, and hypothesize that the ToM frontal areas (e.g., the medial pre-frontal cortex) have "a knock-on effect" in the STS. This process, however, could easily be modeled on a kind of predictive dynamical attunement, or associative process, rather than on a set of inferential processes.

To be clear, for predictive models there may be several ways to answer questions about (1) the generative model that informs predictions; (2) the target to be understood; and (3) the status of inference in the perceptual process. Concerning the generative model, instead of the strong ToM interpretation just mentioned, Clark

(2016, 151ff), focusing on the role of mirror neurons, takes the top-down generative model to be predicting on the basis of (prior learned) contextual information rather than folk-psychological beliefs. In more enactive terms consistent with the idea that the generative model is formed in a self-organizing process that includes active inference—i.e., active exploration of the environment—it can be understood as instantiating the perceiving agent's attunement to a particular environment. In contrast to the ToM assumption that the target to be understood is the other person's distal intention, belief, or some other hidden mental state, the target may be the agentive situation (which includes ourselves). That is, the generative model includes the tracking of the organism's own behavior (Ramstead et al. 2019). Finally, even if predictive processing accounts conceive of perception itself as inferential, one can still ask whether the concept of inference necessarily rules out a direct grasp of the situation. Kirchhoff and Robertson (2018) propose a non-representational concept of inference that they put to work in the predictive processing context. In this context "inference" just means that the dynamics of the agent's self-organization is described in a Bayesian mathematical framework, a concept of inference related to the physics of information that does not imply a cognitivist or representationalist interpretation. In effect, what is described as a "Bayesian" process or as inferential is in actuality a kind of dynamical adjustment process in which the brain, as part of and along with the larger organism, settles into the right kind of attunement with the environment—an environment that is physical but also social and cultural.[18]

Consider, for example, that what we see in the present incorporates an affective sense associated with relevant past visual perceptions. By carefully mapping the connections between different anatomical structures within the brain and examining the reaction times of the different parts of the orbitoprefrontal cortex (OFC) during visual processing Barrett and Bar (2009) have shown that visual perception is already informed with affective value from the start. Their *affective prediction hypothesis* "implies that responses signaling an object's salience, relevance or value do not occur as a separate step after the object is identified. Instead, affective responses support vision from the very moment that visual stimulation begins" (2009, 1325). These affective processes start only milliseconds after visual sensations register on the retina (p. 1326). Simultaneous with the very earliest part of visual perceptual processes, the medial OFC is activated and initiates a host of muscular and hormonal changes throughout the body. The activated sensory-motor patterns include "interoceptive sensations" from organs, muscles, and joints associated with prior experience. These are integrated with current exteroceptive sensory information and help to guide the ongoing response and subsequent actions. Barrett and Bar suggest that changes in, for example, the perceiver's breathing, muscle tension, or stomach motility have an effect on perceptual experience, more or less recessively (2009, 1326). Somatic priors, conjointly with visual and affective processes, modify the system's response. In other words, and consistent with what we said in the previous section, in the perceptual process, the perceiving body is configured into overall peripheral and autonomic

---

[18] My thanks to Micah Allen and Maxwell Ramstead for discussion of these ideas; also see Gallagher and Allen (2018).

patterns that have prior associations with the object (or person) from past experi-ence. This configuration contributes to seeing the object (or person) as something (or someone) that we recognize and that makes sense in the overall experiential context. We literally see objects and persons through their affective value for us. In terms of the predictive-processing model, priors are not just in the brain, but involve a whole body adjustment.

On the enactivist view, brains play an important part in the dynamical attunement of organism to environment. Social interaction, for example, involves the integration of brain processes into a complex mix of transactions that involve moving, gesturing, and engaging with the expressive bodies of others; bodies that incorporate artifacts, tools, and technologies, that are situated in various physical environments, and are defined by diverse social roles and institutional practices. Brains participate in a system, along with all these other factors, and brains would work differently, because the priors would be different, and therefore the surprisals would be different, if these other factors were different (Gallagher 2017a; Gallagher & Allen 2018). Whether or not we should think that such cognitive and affective states enter into subpersonal processes in terms of predictive models, it's an open question about how the neural (synaptic-inhibitory) processes described by such models are best characterized— whether as inferential or a kind of dynamical attunement, or in terms of plasticity where sensory-motor neurons have become attuned by associative processes and prior experience. After all, if empirical priors are cashed out in terms of neuronal activations shaped by prior experience, that doesn't necessarily translate into beliefs or theories. Embodied affective attunement seems far removed from the idea that folk-psychological concepts are penetrating perceptual processes.

Clearly, however, it's not far-fetched to think that one's beliefs and values, as well as one's affective states and cultural perspectives, can shape the way that one quite literally sees the world, and in fact there is good empirical evidence that they do (Gallagher & Varga 2014; see *Section 6.3*). But how should we conceive of such things? It's not clear that such beliefs, values, and cultural perspectives are strictly speaking theoretical (rather than, say, of narrative or pragmatic origin); and it is also not clear that they target the mental states of others, rather than situations, expected behaviors, and anticipated interactions. One can conceive of such phenom-ena playing pragmatic roles in shaping our own actions, our responses to, and our interactions with others rather than playing any theoretical or narrowly folk-psychological role. Accordingly, a new hybrid view that sets out to characterize the nature of direct social perception as complex and informed by beliefs, etc., may also need to change some of the central tenets of TT. Whatever the cognitive and affective states that might subserve our direct perception of others, they are not necessarily theoretical or propositional belief states about the mental states of others. Rather, they may target the other's bodily comportment and the physical and social situations that define her actions; and they may serve (or limit or enhance) the perceiver's own (positive or negative) affectively informed responses and the extra-individual interactive processes that define the situation of social cognition.

In this regard, one might think that a simulationist interpretation of the mirror system would be closer to a direct social perception view, and that on this basis a new hybrid view could be formulated without depending on the notion of theory or inference. Palumbo and Jellema (2013) outline this sort of hybrid view. They distinguish basic perceptual processes that may include contrast/context effects, adaptation, and representational momentum, from a low-level mindreading (simulation) mechanism involving emotion anticipation (the involuntary anticipation of the other person's emotional state), and they suggest that the latter may bias perception. This is very much in line with the proposal of Teufel et al., except that Palumbo and Jellema propose a simulationist mechanism rather than a higher-order theory view. Again, however, taking a more enactivist interpretation of mirror neuron activation, or taking a more associationist approach (Heyes 2010), or even following Gallese's insistence on plasticity (*sans* simulation), one can easily think of such mechanisms as an integrated sensory-motor, perceptual process.[19]

The same challenge can be directed at Teufel et al.'s (2010) interpretation of imitation studies that, as they contend, demonstrate the influence of top-down mental-state attribution on the automatic processes involved in imitation. Again, they think that such processes simply reflect the influence of ToM input on the perception of another's actions. As evidence they point to studies that show changes in an observer's perception of the temporal onset of another individual's action, depending on whether they believe that the same movement is intentional or is achieved *via* an external motorized apparatus—there is an intentional binding effect for the intentional action (Wohlschläger, Engbert, & Haggard 2003; Wohlschläger et al. 2003 also see Haggard et al. 2002). Teufel et al. interpret this as a top-down influence of intention attribution on perception. On the direct social perception view, however, one's sense of the difference between intentional and non-intentional action is not necessarily based on a mental-state attribution; and intention is not something that needs to be inferred: it's a kinematic difference that one can see in the movement itself, even in cases where the contrast is not the clearly visible difference between human and machine movement. Intentional binding is not the result of an inference; it's part of the structure of the perception of intentional action.

Indeed, Teufel et al. (2010) hint at an alternative, non-ToMistic interpretation. Indicating that processes in the superior temporal sulcus (STS) are the controlling ones, rather than processes in the mirror system (which depends on information from STS), they suggest:

---

[19] Di Bono et al. (2017) use a paradigm similar to the Becchio studies to show differences in kinematics and brain activity that correlate to differences in action intention (social action *versus* individual action). On the one hand, they suggest that their findings "support the fact that social intentions are accessible to perception." On the other hand, they take differential activation of the medial prefrontal cortex (a purported ToM area) during the social task to suggest a hybrid simulation plus theoretical inference model that combines a fast direct social perception with a slower, reflective ToM process. They also show that mirror system activation is different between the reach-grasp aspect of social action (grasping in order to hand the object to someone) *versus* individual action (grasping to place the object in a different location). It's important to note, however, that there is more involved than just differences of intention in such cases. There are differences in expectation. At the very least, the agent is expecting something different in accomplishing the social task—a possible response from the other person (at a minimal, the other's acceptance of the object). Activation of the mirror system, in this case, reflects not only the "encoding" or "representation" of the intention, but also the anticipation of a possible response from the other.

Intriguingly, it is the STS that codes this information.... In other words, the STS is tuned to the sensory characteristics of biological, animate and intentional motion and only observed movements that are perceived as exhibiting these sensory characteristics engage the mirror neuron system via the STS, a proposal that is also suggested by neurophysiological evidence from single-unit recordings.   (379)

If indeed the STS is perceptually tuned to just such intentional movement then it's not clear what ToM modulations add to the process. Teufel et al. address this question by focusing on process. They suggest that ToM modulations may either facilitate or suppress (although they also suggest that ToM "supplements") STS processes depending on the context. This would be consistent with a predictive-processing model, as explained above, but it's also perfectly consistent with an account other than one involving theoretical inference. Teufel et al. assume that ToM involves "explicit beliefs...about the intentionality of a movement" or, more generally, about mental states (2010, 379). But, as I suggested above, the beliefs, values, affects, and cultural perspectives that shape perception may target situations, behaviors, future interactions, etc., rather than mental states. In this regard, what Teufel et al. call ToM may really be more like pragmatically and culturally specific attunements that "fine tune" STS and the mirror system to M- and P-intentions and the various affective patterns that make their appearance in the perceiver's environment.

6.3 Over the Top: Some Concerns from Social Psychology

Andreas Roepstorff and Chris Frith (2004) expand the notion of top-down control within the context of experimental behavioral science by pointing to the social aspects of the experimental setting and the effects that the interaction between the experimenter and the experimental participant have on control of action in the experiment. Scripts and instructions given to experimental subjects are at the top of the top, the "top-top." This constitutes a shared interpretive frame that defines the experimental context and often substitutes for what would be the everyday context of a particular kind of action. Even over and above the specifics of this experimental context, however, there are always the wider everyday bodily, social, and cultural factors that enter into experimental settings since neither experimenter nor subject ever fully leave their lifeworld as they enter the lab (Vinson et al. 2016). This wider lifeworld context is full of biases that can distort perception and action—and that's why experimenters try to control for them using scripts and instructions.

Here we are led to a possible objection to the concept of direct social perception from the perspective of social psychology, related to empirical findings about phenomena like "dehumanization" and "implicit" racial bias (Gallagher and Varga 2014). One might object, based on these findings, that social perception is not direct since it obviously depends on a body of cultural beliefs that operate along the lines of a culturally relative folk psychology. In addition to defending against this objection, I'll suggest more generally that studies in social psychology help us to see that an adequate account of social cognition requires going beyond the relatively narrow realm of current theorizing in cognitive science. This may be surprising since the study of social cognition in cognitive science is often thought to be a good example of wide-ranging interdisciplinary research, involving cognitive and developmental psychology, neuroscience, and philosophy. One can argue, however, that there is still something missing from an understanding of social cognition if we leave out insights developed in social psychology and more generally in social philosophy. These insights involve in-group and out-group distinctions that manifest themselves in various ways in ideological constructs, cultural narratives about otherness, class relations in societies, and so on. Indeed, issues concerned with in-group *versus* out-group effects are just the tip of the iceberg, and I'll suggest in subsequent chapters that one of the severe limitations of current theory in social cognition is that it remains ideal theory. In ideal theory, as Charles Mills defines it: "A general social transparency will be presumed, with cognitive obstacles minimized as limited to biases of self-interest or the intrinsic difficulties of understanding the world, and little or no attention paid to the distinctive role of hegemonic ideologies and group-specific experience in distorting our perceptions and conceptions of the social order" (Mills 2005, 169).[20] The following remarks are just a start towards a more critical discussion of such limitations.

There is no shortage of research in social psychology on in-group and out-group relations.[21] Yet such research has not found its way into the debates between TT, ST, and IT. Some of this evidence from social psychology may seem to put the idea of direct social perception into question. It is well known, for example, that individuals are more accurate at recognizing the intentions and the emotions of members of their own culture *versus* those of other cultures (Elfenbein & Ambady 2002a & b; Matsumoto 2002). Subtle differences in emotional "dialects" across cultures reduce cross-cultural emotion recognition (Elfenbein et al. 2007). Research also shows that the in-group advantage in emotion recognition is largely independent of biological or ethnic factors; that is, individuals make best sense of emotions expressed by a member's own cultural group, regardless of race and ethnicity (Elfenbein & Ambady 2003). On the one hand, it's not clear that this constitutes a challenge for the view of direct social perception proposed here. If emotions are best thought of as complex patterns of experiences and behaviors, and if emotion perception involves a form of pattern recognition, then it makes sense that the cultural differences between these patterns might make it harder for individuals to recognize the emotions of individuals from other cultures. Something similar might be said about intentions insofar as there are culturally typical ways of doing things, and culturally typical things to do.

On the other hand, research also shows that independent of "dialects," one's *beliefs*, and most strikingly one's negative beliefs about out-group members, can

---

[20] To be clear, the issue is not about using ideal theory as a methodological strategy, but rather about ending up with ideal theory, with its presumptions and distortions, as a result.
[21] On general issues see Bain et al. (2009); Bastian & Haslam (2010); Brewer & Silver (2000); Brewer et al. (1993); Fiske (2004); Haslam et al. (2005, 2007, 1991); Leyens et al. (1994); Likowski et al. (2008); Tajfel et al. (1971). A study by Hamlin et al. (2013) suggests that these biases run deep into affective dimensions even in infancy.

interfere with one's ability to recognize emotions (Gutsell & Inzlicht 2010). In these cases making sense of the emotions of others is not constrained by differences in emotion patterns, but by specific beliefs about the out-group member. It seems that whether X is able to recognize the emotions and intentions of Y crucially depends on X's beliefs about the racial or ethic group to which Y belongs. On some conceptions it is not just a matter of "having a belief" but of having a set of beliefs or a set of platitudes about the out group that constitutes part of folk psychology, or, in effect, a theory.

Furthermore, the possibility of *dehumanization* shows that being able to experience the other as a human being, and to grasp her intentions and emotions, are to a large degree contingent socio-cultural phenomena. Dehumanization, a phenomenon often found in contexts of war and genocide, refers to processes in which individuals or groups are simply understood as somehow lacking full humanity (see Ataria & Gallagher 2015 for an extreme example of this—the *Muselmann* phenomenon in Nazi concentration camps). Others are understood as lacking characteristics that in-group members take to be characteristically human (a sense of morality, civility, higher cognitive abilities, emotional warmth, etc.). In-group members occasionally perceive people of a certain ethnicity as animal-like (animalistic dehumanization) or as automatons (mechanistic dehumanization). In extreme cases, such out-group members are met with disgust and perceived as somehow non-humans or sub-humans, as beings *without an inner life* (Haslam 2006). It seems that in such cases perception completely fails to grasp the other, and some basic empathic grasp of another as a fellow human is missing. In situations of extreme conflict this helps overcome revulsion against killing; but moderate versions of this phenomenon are present in subtle everyday processes (Haslam 2006; Haslam & Bain 2007; Haslam et al. 2005, 2008a & b; Bain et al. 2009; Bastian & Haslam 2010; Fiske 2004, 1991; Goffman 1986).

Such phenomena seemingly challenge the idea of direct social perception. Indeed, dehumanization can manifest itself in bodily processes usually connected with primary intersubjectivity. For example, non-conscious processes of automatic mimicry of others' expressions, gestures, and body postures are less frequent for dehumanized out-group members (Likowski at al. 2008). Also, motor-resonance mechanisms that may support social perception of intentions and emotions are modulated by cultural factors and inextricably bound to group membership. A study by Xu et al. (2009) dramatically demonstrates the neural effects of implicit racial bias and shows that empathic neural responses to the other person's pain are modulated by the racial in-group/out-group relationship. fMRI brain imaging showed significantly decreased activation in the anterior cingulate cortex (ACC), an area thought to correlate with empathic response, when subjects (Caucasians or Chinese) viewed racial out-group members (Chinese or Caucasian respectively) undergoing painful stimulations (needle penetration) to the face, compared with ACC activation when they viewed the same stimulations applied to racial in-group members.

We are simply less responsive to out-group members and we display significantly less motor-cortex activity when observing out-group members (Molnar-Szakacs et al. 2007). Most strikingly, in-group members fail to understand out-group member actions, and this is particularly prominent for disliked and dehumanized out-groups. The more dehumanized the out-group is, the less intuitive the grasp of out-group member intentions and actions (Gutsell & Inzlicht 2010).

The evidence from studies of dehumanization and implicit racial bias thus seems inconsistent with direct social perception, and shows that mechanisms of social perception are constitutively dependent upon historical-cultural situatedness and group membership. While the argument for direct social perception draws on empirical findings concerning primary intersubjectivity and enactive interpretations of resonance processes, it seems that social psychology and cultural neuroscience raise questions about exactly such processes. Recent studies of such processes (as in Xu et al. 2009) deliver evidence for our basic understanding of others being constitutively dependent on culturally sanctioned beliefs or values. In light of these findings, one may ask: should such cultural beliefs and values that enable and disable social cognition not be seen as a form of "theory"? And, if the recognition of emotions and intentions depends on such a "theory" would this then not contradict direct social perception and support TT?

The answer is no. First of all, keep in mind that the idea that we have direct social perception of another's intentions and emotions is part of the larger *interaction theory* of social cognition which draws on evidence that our basic understanding of others is enabled by innate or very early developing embodied capabilities and by interaction itself (see De Jaegher et al. 2010). The term "innate" here signifies those capabilities that have developed prenatally as a combination of genetic and prenatal experiential factors. The newborn comes already prepared for interaction with others, as evidence for primary intersubjectivity suggests (see Trevarthen and Aitken 2001; and Meltzoff & Moore 1989 for cross-cultural studies). To disrupt a common metaphor, however, this does not mean that the infant comes "hardwired." Rather, it means that the newborn infant has some circuits already working, but even these circuits are open to plastic reorganization; they are either reinforced or they deteriorate depending on subsequent experience;[22] generally speaking, they are reshaped by social and cultural experiences.

Although interaction theorists, in their critique of TT and ST, focus on primary embodied processes, they also grant that social and cultural contexts are important for a full understanding of the other. IT maintains that we are not only action-oriented in our pragmatic dealings with the world, we are also, from the very beginning, *interaction*-oriented in our encounters with others. Thus, as we saw, beyond the embodied capacities of primary intersubjectivity, IT acknowledges the importance of secondary intersubjectivity (starting with joint attention in the first year of life, and including the pragmatic understanding of others in highly contextualized situations) and of communicative and narrative practices (see *Chapter 7*). The stories that we listen to as children, or that we see enacted (in various media), or play-acted, and even the parables, plays, myths, novels, films, television, etc.[23] we are

---

[22] Evidence along this line can be found in what is sometimes considered induced autism as the result of extreme social deprivation in orphanages (see Hobson 2002).

[23] Richard Rorty (1989, xvi) suggests "the novel, the movie and TV program have, gradually but steadily, replaced the sermon and the treatise as the principle vehicles of moral change and progress"

exposed to as adults, are not neutral with respect to how we perceive the world. Cultural narratives, as well as our own culturally situated experiences with others, bias our expectations in regard to their actions and, as the science shows, can bias perception itself. While it was once thought that such biases were automatic and more or less immune from change, it is now accepted that the manipulation of the social context can moderate in-group racial bias, down to the level of perceptual processes (Barden et al. 2004; Bargh 1999; Blair 2002). Thus, IT can and does acknowledge that social and cultural forces play an essential or constituting role in social perception and particularly in the understanding of emotions and intentions.

Moreover, this kind of evidence puts into question accounts of social cognition that assume we are hardwired to intuitively grasp others as "fellow human beings" by means of innate, modularistic ToM mechanisms or pre-programmed mirror systems operating in a top-down, automatic, and context-independent fashion, yielding culturally independent capacities of the sort described by Segal (1996) and Scholl and Leslie (1999; quoted in *Section 4.3.2*).[24] Evidence from studies of dehumanization is simply inconsistent with these ideas, and shows that mechanisms of social cognition are constitutively dependent upon historical-cultural situatedness and group membership. This suggests that the fundamental perceptual level of understanding others as agents or persons is essentially context dependent—an aspect that any theory of social cognition must account for.

To deny that cultural factors have such effects on perception would only make sense if one were to accept the thesis of the "cognitive impenetrability of perception" (Pylyshyn 1999) which is no longer universally accepted (Siegel 2011). The frequent example in discussions of cognitive penetrability involves the effects of beliefs. When you know that bananas are yellow, this knowledge affects your color perception for bananas, so that an achromatic banana will appear to be yellow (Gegenfurtner, Olkkonen, & Walter 2006). This leads too quickly, however, to the idea of top-down penetration or that perceptions are theory laden.

In fact, both sides of this debate (cognitive penetrability *versus* impenetrability) tend to conceive of the problem in the same way; that is, they conceive of cognition, operating on the upper floors of the system, and as either inferentially injected, or not, into early perceptual areas of the brain—as if developmental and learning processes had an effect only on prefrontal or higher association areas and somehow by-passed perceptual and motor areas without lasting effect. As I've been arguing, we

---

(1989, xvi). We should add video games to this list. As research shows, prolonged play of such games induces changes in various cognitive functions, including hand-eye coordination, spatial visualization, visual anticipation, reaction time, and attention (Latham et al. 2013). Such changes involve brain plasticity; they are not induced because players change their theories or improve their inferences.

[24] Scholl & Leslie (1999, 140) add that "It is certainly the case that these basic ToM abilities may eventually be recruited by higher cognitive processes for more complex tasks, and the resulting higher-order ToM activities may well interact (in a non-modular way) with other cognitive processes, and may not be uniform across individuals or cultures." On this view, higher-order cognitive elaboration does not affect perceptual or basic ToM processes. On the enactive view proposed here, cultural practices, including communicative and narrative practices, go deeper and affect embodied perceptual processes and action possibilities. The research suggests that cultural factors can also lead to the loss or diminishment of the ability to understand others.

| 100% Black | 80% Black | 60% Black | 40% Black | 20% Black | 0% Black |
| 0% White | 20% White | 40% White | 60% White | 80% White | 100% White |

Figure 6.3 The face on the left is exactly the same skin color as the face on the right.

Source: Reprinted with permission from D.T. Levin and M.R. Banaji, "Distortions in the perceived lightness of faces: The role of race categories," *Journal of Experimental Psychology: General*, Volume 135, Issue 4, pp. 501–12, Copyright © 2006 by the American Psychological Association, Figure 2, p. 502, doi: 10.1037/0096-3445.135.4.501.

should rather think in terms of cultural permeation rather than cognitive penetration (Hutto et al., 2020).

Evidence about context sensitivity puts the very idea of cognitive penetration as it is traditionally conceived into question. Context-sensitivity rather than knowledge-based inference can explain why we see a banana as more yellow than it actually is, or why subjects (including Caucasians and African-Americans) see African-American faces as darker than Caucasian faces even when they are exactly the same skin color (Levin & Banaji 2006; Orlandi (2014, 192ff) (see *Figure 6.3*). In the latter case, for example, it is not because we *know* factually that one face is African-American and infer that skin color must be comparatively darker, and so see it as such. Rather, we see it as such because we never see skin color all by itself; we see skin color along with shapes of noses and mouths—elements of a face pattern that we may associate with darker skin color because of statistical regularity.

If this were the result of knowledge-based inference, then we would expect the perceived difference to disappear once we knew that the skin color was identical—but it doesn't. Accordingly, this is not cognitive penetration as typically conceived by the inferentialists. At the same time it's not clear that this sends us back to the idea of cognitive impenetrability or information incapsulation of the perceptual system (see Firestone & Scholl 2015, 2016). Rather, in terms of cultural permeation, not only a variety of perceptual aspects (e.g., facial patterns), as in this case, but also, more generally, cross-modal effects and action- or affordance-related changes—i.e., changes related to body schematic control—can change visual receptive fields (Graziano & Botvinick 2002; Witt et al. 2016). These changes, in turn, can be modulated by much wider cultural contexts (e.g., Soliman & Glenberg 2014; Vinson et al. 2016). Indeed, effects related to one's prior experience within a particular culture seem much more pervasive, and they operate in a way that modulates neuronal firing patterns, perception, bodily postures, behavioral habits, everyday practices, and intersubjective interactions (Gallagher 2017a, Chapter 6). As Soliman and Glenberg put it:

[C]ulture enters the scene not as a self-contained layer on top of behavior, but as the sum of sensorimotor knowledge brought about by a bodily agent interacting in a social and physical context. As such, culture [permeates] the web of sensorimotor knowledge, and can only be arbitrarily circumscribed from other knowledge.... [Cultural biases are] acquired and maintained through immersion in environments with different patterns of interpersonal interactions.... These interactions "tune" the sensorimotor system...By tuning, we mean a process of neuroplasticity, or learning.   (2014, 209–10)

Likewise, moods, traits, habitual practices, and skills also can modulate perception. For example, for someone without the skill to read Russian a sheet of Cyrillic script looks different than it looks to her after she becomes literate in Russian; to a vain performer, the faces in the audience never look disapproving, while to a performer who lacks confidence, the same audience may look displeased (Siegel 2011). In a kind of circular way, and as Siegel points out, in a way that can be epistemically pernicious, "penetrated" perceptions are confirmatory of the beliefs, moods, and traits of the perceiver. In the case of cultural biases, they can also be neurologically pernicious since they can reinforce neuronal firing patterns and result in the plastic changes discussed above. More generally, they can reinforce embodied practices and postures, behavioral habits, and intersubjective interactions.

None of this, however, counts against the idea that my perception of another's intentions and emotions are direct, requiring no extra-perceptual inference that would take us beyond what we perceive. All such changes, pernicious or not, are not additions to perception, an added-on set of inferences; rather, they transform the perceptual process itself. In the case of dehumanization, for example, one is not trained to make bad inferences; one is conditioned to directly perceive others as non-persons.

Accordingly, the findings offered by social psychology studies concerning "dehumanization" and "implicit" racial bias, far from threatening the idea of direct social perception seem to clearly contradict the idea of innate or hardwired ToM modules. This suggests that it is important that the science of social cognition take into account the role of ideological constructs, stereotypes, cultural narratives about otherness, phenomena concerning in-group and out-group dynamics, as well as class and power relations in societies—topics currently neglected in the mainstream social cognition literature found in philosophy of mind, cognitive psychology, and neuro-science. Too often, in this mainstream literature, social cognition is portrayed as dependent on internal mechanisms that belong to a neutral observer of another person's behavior, *simpliciter*, without taking into consideration that social-interaction processes are shaped by forces external to the individual, and by social and institutional practices that impact intersubjective understanding to the extent that they form and sometimes deform perception, as well as any further cognitive processes involved in our understanding of others. We return to these issues in *Chapter 8*.

7

Communicative Actions and Narrative Practices

In *Chapter 4* I presented reasons to doubt that the standard ToM accounts can give an adequate account of our everyday intersubjective abilities for understanding the intentions and the behaviors of other persons. In this chapter I want to continue to build the more positive account (started in *Chapter 5*) of just these everyday intersubjective abilities and show that they are not reducible (or inflatable) to ToM-istic mindreading or mentalizing.

It is quite likely that at this point the theory theorist or the simulation theorist will stand up and say, "Yes, this is all well and good, and we don't deny that the aspects of primary and secondary intersubjectivity that you have mentioned are indeed important—but all of these factors are mere precursors to the real action, which is the kind of mindreading found in adults and even young children. Clearly something different happens starting around 4 years of age. To get at the more subtle and sophisticated aspects of social cognition you need more than embodied interaction; you need what TT and ST offer: mindreading."

We should decline the offer. There is an alternative—one that is not so esoteric that it needs to appeal to invisible mental states, propositional attitudes, mental representations, and so forth; one that remains embodied and, to use an odd piece of language, "en-languaged." I'll refrain from using that awkward word and just say that the alternative involves language in a way that extends the IT account to include communicative actions and narrative practices.

As I have attempted to show, ToM approaches miss some basic and important processes of social cognition. Yet, acknowledging the important role of processes that define primary and secondary intersubjectivity—the embodied, sensory-motor, affective processes that enable us to perceive the intentions of others, and the perceptual and action capabilities that enable us to understand others in the pragmatically contextualized situations of everyday life (starting in the first year of life)—is not sufficient to address what are clearly developmental changes that occur around the ages of 2, 3, and 4 years. The "elephant in the room" around the age of 2 years is, of course, language. Focusing on communicative and narrative practices does not mean that the embodied and interactive processes of primary and secondary intersubjectivity are left behind (cf. De Bruin & De Haan 2012). Communicative action is itself interaction and clearly involves bodily movement, alignment, synergistic processes, etc.; and narrative is about actions and interactions and is tied to contextualized particulars. There is continuity rather than disconnection between interaction and the social practices that involve language. Indeed, if language development itself is something that depends on some of the processes of primary and secondary intersubjectivity, language also carries these processes forward and puts them into service in much more sophisticated social contexts.

7.1 Communicative Actions and Interactions

Again I'll appeal to developmental studies because it is often clearer to see things as they begin. Language acquisition is often said to occur around 15 months to 2 years. That's when children begin to speak words and then sentences. But of course things are not as simple as that. Before their first word, infants make intelligible vocalizations, and typically developing infants hear speech, perceive movement, and move themselves.[1] Not all movement is language, but all first-order language, as it is generated, is movement—movement of vocal cords, tongue, lips, and hand gestures being the primary examples. Some of language is propositional; some is not. Pre-propositional language is not a placeholder until propositional language develops; it doesn't disappear when propositions appear. Movements like head nods and pointing continue to form part of meaningful communicative practices, along with pre-predicative vocalizations.

Here I take three pointers from Merleau-Ponty's analysis of language. First, as Merleau-Ponty (1964c, 40) puts it, we are born into a "whirlwind of language." From the beginning, perhaps even before birth, the child hears speech, and is spoken to. For example, newborn infants already have a preference for their mother's voice and the rhythms of her speech (DeCasper & Fifer 1980). Second, as Merleau-Ponty (2012) explains, language accomplishes thought. He points to the common experience of the speaker not knowing what he is going to say until he says it. In first-order speech we do not first think things through, and then simply externalize our thoughts. To say that language accomplishes thought is not to say that there is first something inside one's head that then gets put out or expressed, but rather to say that the expression is the thought, and that language generates meaning. Through it we discover what we, and others, mean. Likewise, we can say the same for gesture; gesture accomplishes thought (Cole, Gallagher, & McNeill 2002). Third, Merleau-Ponty (2012) suggests that language transcends the body. This does not mean that language can be accomplished without the body, without movement, but neither is it reducible to physical movement. In the same way that semantics is not reducible to syntax, the meaning that is generated in language is never reducible to the physical markers and movements that generate language.

The idea that language transcends the body also reminds us of the hermeneutical principle that the text, or let us say, the communication always goes beyond the author/agent/speaker, just as we said of interaction itself. This is meant, not just in the sense that language signifies something other than the speaker, but in the sense that as one is involved in communication, one is involved in a process that is larger

---

[1] Oller et al. (2019) have shown that as soon as infants can breathe independently (even 2-month premature infants) they are capable of vocalizing protophones (early precursors to speech). Also see Gallagher 2017d for a discussion of social cognition in blind-deaf children.

than an individual speech act, or a collection of speech acts. Language not only accomplishes thought, it accomplishes other things too. In its pragmatics, it is pragmatic. Speech acts and gestural acts and communicative actions of all kinds get things done, and often have unintended consequences. Examples of this abound in politics.

First-order communicative practices—that is, gestures (body language in general) and speech acts—are second-person practices. The infant's motor responses towards other agents are different from their motor responses towards non-agentive objects. In the case of social interaction their gestures are *for-others*, and in cases where they are not for others (e.g., in cases where I speak or gesture to myself) they are derivative from the social context. The infant responds to motherese and child-directed speech, where intonation and rhythm emphasize emotional meaning. And then the caregiver responds to the infant's response. Turn taking ("cyclic proto-conversation") emerges very early, by 6 weeks of age, and there is a certain rhythm to it. Engaging in vocalizations often involves whole body movements for the infant, in "dance-like enthusiasm," and these movements can facilitate the mutual regulation of feelings (Trevarthen et al. 1998, 94). Imitation, attention, emotional expressions, hand gestures, movements of the lips and tongue are all part of this original tango of communication.

In regard to social cognition, communicative practices are solutions. One does not need TT or ST or IT to explain that I can make myself understood through language. Assuming that you are reading this, we are involved in such a process right now. I can say or write things like "Social cognition involves the problem of how we understand one another." You can ask, in person or via e-mail, "What do you mean?" The only way to continue and to get you to understand what I mean is by way of more language. Some aspects of this are more difficult and some easier if the language is written rather than spoken. In first-order oral communicative practices, too, some aspects are more difficult and some easier than if language is written. There are plenty of things to say about such things, but my task here is not to develop a theory of communicative action. Rather, it is simply to point out how communicative practices are solutions to problems of social cognition.

In solving such problems language takes different shapes: from proto-conversation to a more formally structured conversation where there may be specific rules for turn taking; from simple commands to formal communiqués; from bare statements of facts to full narrative structures. Conversation, in its complex details, is clearly a form of social interaction and depends on the same kinds of dynamical processes found in interaction more generally. This idea is very much in line with what Charles Goodwin has shown in his empirical studies on the situated pragmatics of conversational interaction. To provide some detail and to indicate the complexity involved in what might first seem a simple scenario, I want to cash out these ideas using one of his examples. Goodwin (2017) shows that meaning emerges at the intersection of social, cultural, material structures, and their dynamical changes in the environment where action and interaction occur. The factors involved include vocalization, gesture, postural orientation, and the use of items in the local environment. Meaning, including what we can understand of the other's actions, is accomplished, not just *via* a linear set of speech acts (the traditional focus of analysis) but, by drawing on "different kinds of semiotic resources" (Goodwin 2000, 1490) available in the environment and in whole body pragmatics.

Goodwin, for example, provides a detailed analysis of a dispute between two young girls over a game of hopscotch. There is an interactive organization of various phenomena that have to be considered to understand the full encounter. "For example, spoken language builds signs within the stream of speech, gestures use the body in a particular way, while posture and orientation use the body in another, etc." (2000, 1494). Goodwin emphasizes the "visible, public deployment of multiple semiotic fields that mutually elaborate each other" (2000, 1492). Factors in these fields are varied and include, for example: the temporal flow/rhythm of high *versus* low, and hard *versus* soft vocal intonation of speech; speech acts, some of which have a deontic rather than descriptive force; the set of instituted norms involved in the game of hopscotch—i.e., the rules of the game; and deictic reference to a completed action (throwing a marker on one of the squares). One girl intentionally moves and stands in the way of the other girl, interrupting the game. The bodily orientations of the two girls, which allow for eye contact and joint attention toward the hopscotch pattern on the ground, as well as the ongoing temporal modifications in those postures, create meaning as the encounter unfolds. In the communicative actions, hand gestures integrate with the speech, but also with the changing body positions of both girls.

Carla [one of the girls] has to use her body in a quite precise way while taking into account the visible body of her co-participant. She is faced with the task of using not only her talk, but also her body, to structure the local environment such that her gestures can themselves count as forms of social action…. Unlike talk, gestures can't be heard. [This means] Carla actively works to position her hand gestures so that they will be perceived by Diana [the other girl]…. Carla's hand is explicitly positioned in Diana's line of sight…thrusting the gesturing hand toward Diana's face twists Carla's body into a configuration in which her hand, arm and the upper part of her torso are actually leaning toward Diana (Goodwin 2000, 1498).

(See *Figure 7.1*)

How close is the gesture to the other girl's face? That proximity has meaning, as does its timing *vis-à-vis* the speech act. If it were not a gesture, but a touch, how hard

Figure 7.1 A game of hopscotch.

Source: Reprinted from *Journal of Pragmatics*, Volume 32, Issue 10, C. Goodwin, "Action and embodiment within situated human interaction," pp. 1489–522, Copyright © 2000 Published by Elsevier B.V., Figure 1, p. 1494, with permission from Elsevier: https://www.sciencedirect.com/science/article/abs/pii/S037821669900096X

or soft, and where the touch occurred, would also have meaning. The gesture is meant to be attention grabbing, forcing the other to orient to the point being made in what Carla is saying, or to a point of joint attention towards something in the environment—a grab could do the same thing. This is not one-sided: Diana, the other girl, is standing on one foot, attempting to finish her jump through the hopscotch squares, attempting to ignore the challenge made by Carla, and the accusation of cheating.

The interaction, the conversation, is not confined to vocalization and gesture—reference is made to the physical environment, with glances to the hopscotch squares under discussion. This is an example of distributed communication, which builds on material aspects of the environment and the context of the game. Joint attention is broken when one girl looks away. This also is meaningful and shows that the accomplishment of meaning involves two-way interaction and is not under the control of just one individual. In another moment, Carla stomps her foot in a gesture that hits three semiotic points:

- Where Diana is looking
- On the hopscotch square in question
- On the object that Carla is iterating in speech

The social understanding involved in this encounter between two young girls builds on precisely the complex integration of primary and secondary intersubjective capacities, situated within pragmatic and social contexts, supplemented with and supporting communicative and narrative processes. In such interactions, agents enter into dynamical relations that constitute a system extending across different timescales and beyond what each individual agent brings to the process (De Jaegher et al. 2010; Kalampratsidou & Torres 2018). The physical and social affordances presented by the pragmatic and social contexts, are relational and depend on the possibilities opened up by interaction itself. One girl's attempt to understand or communicate with the other, whom she knows, and with whom she is interacting, is not reducible to her observation of the other in her situation; rather, she is already part of the other's situation, as the other becomes part of hers. It's a shared agentive situation; a shared context within which they encounter each other. In interaction, contexts are relational.

Consider, then, the wealth of resources that an agent can draw on from the communicative context, beyond the vocalized words:

- The gestures and facial expressions of the other person
- Their bodily movements, postures, and proximity
- The intonation of voice
- The other's attention—the means to grab it for joint attention
- The temporal flow/rhythm of interaction
- Instituted norms
- Social rules, roles, and identities
- Knowledge of completed actions
- Knowledge of person-specific traits, preferences, attitudes, etc.
- The rich material environment

Goodwin adds an important qualification, if vision and "getting in each other's face" are important aspects of this example of dynamical interaction, "this is by no means a fixed array of fields. Thus, on many occasions, such as phone calls, or when participants are dispersed in a large visually inaccessible environment (e.g., a hunting party, or a workgroup interacting through computers), visual co-orientation may not be present" (2000, 1500). Contexts change over time; they may be enriched or impoverished, but they always count towards the production of understanding or misunderstanding (Duranti & Goodwin 1992).

One can see from this kind of analysis that live communication is not reducible to a simple set of alignment processes, although it does include such processes. The notion of intersubjective alignment itself is defined in different ways by different authors. Some researchers equate it with simple matching, imitation, or entrainment and distinguish it from other more intentional coordination processes (e.g., Rothwell, Shalin, & Romigh 2017); others define it as more than mimicry, and as including more complex forms of coupling (Tollefsen, Dale, & Paxton 2013). It is clear from the research on conversational analysis and communicative interaction, however, that there is a broad range of embodied and ecological processes integrated into such events, and that different circumstances (e.g., how structured or unstructured the immediate environment might be) and different intentions elicit different dynamical balances among these processes.

All of these semiotic resources, and the linguistic practices that go with them, help to clarify and complicate our social understanding of others. Narrative practices especially are worthy of further consideration since they tell the story of how cultural factors come to inform the pragmatic and socially structured contexts where we encounter one another.

7.2 Narrative Practices

There is a developmental story to tell about gaining narrative competence. Around the age of 2, children are in secure possession of "an early intentional understanding of persons having internal goals and wants that differ from person to person" (Wellman & Phillips 2001, 130; Bartsch & Wellman 1995). Young children are already practiced in understanding things as other people understand them in pragmatic contexts, and when the processes of primary and secondary intersubjectivity are combined with language ability, young children are ready to understand things and people in emerging narrative structures. Narratives can take us a long way toward the more nuanced and sophisticated understanding of the adult, without resorting to mindreading in the form of theoretical inference or simulation, or the folk-psychological framework per se.

Among developmental psychologists one often finds the idea that narrative is rooted in proto-narrative activity. Jerome Bruner, for example, suggests that "Narrative structure is even inherent in the praxis of social interaction before it achieves linguistic expression" (1990, 77). Although we learn to form linguistic narratives through interactions with others—specifically when caregivers elicit accounts of just-past actions or events and when as young children around 2–3 years we appropriate the narratives of others for our own (Bruner 1996; Legerstee 2005; Nelson 2003a & b;

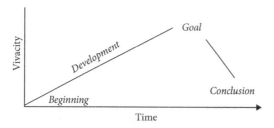

Figure 7.2 Four phases of action.

Reddy 2008; 2012; Trevarthen 2013) – the contours of our narratives are shaped by the structures of the actions and events themselves. Primarily we narrate our actions and the actions of others (see *Section 2.5*). Actions take time to unfold; they have a beginning, they develop, they accomplish a goal, and they conclude. Delafield-Butt and Trevarthen (2015) find the origins of narrative in the earliest forms of intentional (planned) movements, in which, eventually, we can identify distal goals and social meaning. Narratives are reflective of "the innate sensorimotor intelligence of a hypermobile human body" (2015, 1). They reflect the fourfold structure of action itself (*Figure 7.2*).

This is not a static structure; it is dynamic and affective. It integrates bodily arousal and points of focused intensity, expressive movements, heart-rate, respiration-rate, affective responses; it reflects the same "vitality dynamics" found in play in infancy (Stern 2010)—all factors that ground experienced meaning. Importantly, these dynamics, at least at first, are embedded in intersubjective interactions, and only in such contexts can we speak of an emergence of meaning—a meaning that emerges in the interaction itself. Such movements are further shaped in "early proto-conversations and collaborative play of infants and talk of children and adults" (Delafield-Butt & Trevarthen 2015, 1).

A good example of this can be found in the emergence of pointing behavior in the 9-month-old infant. If we follow Vygotsky's (1986) analysis, a spontaneous reaching movement by the infant for an object that is out of reach becomes an expressive movement of pointing only if a caregiver is present to interpret it as such. The reach begins as instrumental, but in the presence of the other it becomes expressive, and this is reinforced for the infant by the action of the caregiver, who moves the object to within reach, or gives the object to the infant. Through ongoing practice and repetition, the infant's reach takes on the interpreted meaning—pointing for a desired object—for the infant herself. Meaning emerges from movement, a move-ment that forms an instrumental action with a goal, and, perceived as such in the intersubjective context, becomes a request for help.

The child's first attempts at narrating typically "occur *in action*, in episodes of symbolic play by groups of peers, accompanied by – rather than solely though – language. Play is an important developmental source of narrative" (Nelson 2003a, 28; emphasis added; see Richner & Nicolopoulou 2001). In pretend play, the plot thickens in the action of the play, in what the child is doing in pretense; the language that goes along with the play process is not narrative itself, but is performative vocalization. Here's an example from Hutto and Gallagher (2019). The mother takes the toy car, for example, and says "Zoom, zoom, zoom." She is not narrating the car; she is driving it in pretend play. The child then takes a turn. The vocalization, and gradually, the words, become part of the narrative that captures the pretend action. The mother says, "The car goes zoom." She is now initiating a narrative about the car. Later she says, addressing the child, "You played so nicely with the car this afternoon, didn't you?" The mother is leading the child into a kind of narrative. Later the child says, "Car goes zoom. I play with car." The child is beginning to narrate his action. Even without the proto-conversation, intentional, goal-directed actions exhibit structure, as Delafield-Butt and Trevarthen (2015) suggested (see previous discussion of this point in *Section 2.5*). Narrative comes to reflect that structure of action as it represents the action. In this sense, narrative structure derives from action structure.

When do we start to tell stories to children? My unscientific bet is that before a child in English-speaking countries reaches first birthday, they have heard the nursery rhyme "This little piggy" a hundred times. You probably know the rhyme.

> This little piggy went to market,
> This little piggy stayed at home,
> This little piggy had roast beef,
> This little piggy had none.
> And this little piggy went...
> "Wee wee wee" all the way home.

My own mother who grew up in a beautiful but poverty stricken region of Ireland substituted "bread and butter" for "roast beef" in a telling reflection of her own culture. Notably, this little rhyme with its narrative structure is performed in motherese (it's comic if you say it in business-like fashion) and it is performed on the child's body, normally by pulling on the child's toes as the child squeals and wiggles with delight. It's a fully embodied narrative. According to another narrative by Jerry Seinfeld, the last line is the only reason evolution has given us the little or "pinky" toe (*Seinfeld*, Season 5 Episode 21; this implies that the rhyme is much older than its publication date of 1760, however). It doesn't take long to go from "This little piggy" to the well-known fable of "The Three Little Pigs," and we can tell children this story before they understand the words by pointing to pictures. What Horst Bredekamp (et al. 2009) calls "picture acts" (*Bildakten*) can help the child understand that the speech acts are telling a story. In this example we see that children learn quite early about how the extended mind (Clark & Chalmers 1998) works, with narratives played out on our bodies and in external representations.

We learn to make sense of persons (others as well as ourselves) in dramatic and narrative ways as young children. When children listen to stories, or (re-)produce them in play-acting (and the same applies to adults who are exposed to myths, parables, plays, novels, etc.) they become familiarized with different characters and with a range of ordinary or extraordinary situations, and the sorts of actions appropriate to them, all of which helps to shape their expectations about people and their behaviors. When children play-act narratives, they produce and reproduce them, and in so doing are interactively engaged with them.

Moreover, children are well supported in this process. They may be provided with running commentaries on stories that teach them not only which actions are suited to particular situations but also which reasons for acting are acceptable and which are not (Gallagher & Hutto 2008). By absorbing such standards we first learn how to judge an action's appropriateness (though, of course, in time such standards are sometimes questioned and sometimes overturned). An education in narratives of many sorts—even of the more general and less personal variety—provides knowledge of what actions are acceptable and in what circumstances, what sort of events are important and noteworthy, and what accounts count as reasoned accounts of action. Quite generally, stories—real or fictional—teach us what others can expect from us, but just as importantly, what we can expect from others in particular situations. This is not just coming to know what others ought to (and thus are likely to) do, but what they ought to (and thus are likely to) think and feel, as indexed to the sort of people they are and what social roles they play. Through narratives we learn the *norms* associated with the social roles that pervade our everyday environments—shops, restaurants, homes, theatres, etc. These narratives are not set aside from everyday life, they leak into our everyday engagements and conversations with each other, sometimes providing typical patterns that help us make sense of another person's actions.[2] Furthermore, "conversations about written and oral stories are natural extensions of children's earlier experiences with the sharing of event structures" (Guajardo & Watson 2002, 307). Through them children discover why characters act as they do in particular cases, becoming accustomed to standard scripts, scenarios, characters, plots, etc.

To appreciate such stories children must be initially capable, at least to some degree, of responding emotively, just as they do in basic social engagements. Engaging with narratives is not a passive affair: it presupposes a wide range of emotive and interactive abilities. The kind of emotional resonance that one finds already in infancy, in primary intersubjectivity, plays an important role in gaining narrative competency. Decety and Chaminade (2003) have shown this connection as it plays out in the adult brain. In their fMRI study subjects were presented with a series of video clips showing actors telling sad and neutral stories, as if they had personally experienced them. The stories were told with either congruent (e.g., frowning during the telling of sad stories) or incongruent (e.g., smiling during the telling of sad stories) facial and motor expression of emotion. Subjects were then asked to rate the mood of the actor and how likable they found that person. Watching

---

[2] A good example of this is found in the cultural practice of evening visitation in rural Irish villages up through the last century—neighbors going from one home to the next, engaging in conversation and storytelling. Some of the stories were standard cultural narratives (often ghost stories), but most were personal stories about adventures and misadventures of neighbors and friends who went out on fishing boats or into pubs, and so forth. At a certain point in the 1980s I witnessed an interesting change taking place in this practice in one small village, but a change that I'm sure was repeated in many villages. The first television in the village appeared in one of the houses that had been one of the liveliest for conversation. As the local neighbors continued to visit that house the conversational practice changed. The conversation was turned off when the television was turned on; the local narratives stopped as the televised narrative (e.g., the show *Dallas*) captured everyone's attention. When the television was turned off, conversation began again. But the conversation was about JR or some of the other characters on the show *Dallas*, and such conversations started to replace the local storytelling.

sad stories versus neutral stories was associated with increased processing activity in emotion-related areas (including the amygdala and parieto-frontal areas, predominantly in the right hemisphere). These areas were not activated when the narrator showed incongruent facial expressions. The reasonable hypothesis is that incongruency between what we sense as the emotional state of the other person, simply on the basis of seeing their faces, body postures and actions, and the narrative content they present, is disruptive to understanding. Whatever is going on in the brain correlates not simply to features of action and expression (and the subjectivity of the other person) but to the larger story, the narrative scene, or the circumstance of the other person, and how features of action and expression match or fail to match those circumstances. If the emotional character of the other person is not in character with the narrative framework it is difficult to understand that person, the story, or both.

7.3 The Landscape of Action

Possibilities for intersubjective interaction and understanding that start with primary and secondary intersubjectivity develop along a route that in most ordinary cases exploits communicative and narrative competencies rather than procedures associated with traditional ToM accounts. Some have argued the other way around, however. Janet Astington (1990), for example, has argued that acquiring narrative competency requires having a theory of mind first. Citing Bruner's concept of the landscape of consciousness ("what those involved in the action know, think, or feel, or do not know, think, or feel" [Bruner 1986, 14]), she suggests that to understand narrative we need access to the characters' minds, and to have the latter requires us to have a theory of mind. But Bruner himself offers some experimental evidence against the necessity of the landscape of consciousness for understanding narratives, or the portrayed actions.

Feldman, Bruner, et al. (1990), in a study of narrative comprehension in adults, presented two different versions of the same story to two groups, respectively. The first and original story mentioned the mental states of the characters as the story develops, and so reflected a rich landscape of consciousness. The second story was the very same story stripped of mental terms, leaving only the "*landscape of actions.*" The results showed no significant differences (1) in subjects using reader-related mental verbs when they recount the narrative; (2) in recounting the facts of the stories—"the retellings were virtually indistinguishable"; (3) in recounting the order of events; and (4) when providing a meaning summary (or gist) for the story: "there is no version difference in the kind of gist given." In effect, we get a good amount of meaning without having to frame the narrative in ToM terms.

A likely explanation of these results is that the structure of narratives about persons, as revealed explicitly in action plots, can be identified, responded to and described on several levels and in several ways. It is possible to be alive to the major events in a drama without always being able to or needing to decipher, with full clarity, the *reasons* why a protagonist will have acted. If it's a drama on stage, the only way to get to such reasons is by following the action and conversation. In a written text, the narrator or author may or may not make reasons explicit. In any case it's possible to have some sense of what is going on in an unfolding drama without understanding it in terms of an internal drama. This is apparently a common experience for those first encountering Shakespearean plays (see Hutto 2006).[3] Often we simply find meaning and reason in the contextualized actions and speech acts of the characters. Because of our exposure to narratives, we become familiar with actions of a standard sort, and their meanings, without having to get into the minds of the characters.

To be clear, it's not just Shakespeare, and not just staged or written narratives. These considerations apply equally to the narratives of everyday life that we encounter with our neighbors and friends. A narrative understanding of the other's actions and reasons is not necessarily a matter of characterizing the other's "inner" life—if this is understood as a series of causally efficacious mental states. What we understand is something much richer; it is the other's actions and reasons, set out in a landscape of action as they figure against a background context and history, and perhaps the larger set of projects that characterize a person's life history. Such things are best captured in a narrative form. Coming to understand another's reasons for acting should not be understood as designating their discrete "mental states," but rather their intentional attitudes, dispositions, and responses as whole situated persons. I encounter the other person, not abstracted from their circumstances, but in the middle of something that has a beginning and that is going somewhere, even if that somewhere is uncertain. I see them in the framework of a story in which either I have a part to play or I don't. Such narratives are not primarily about what is going on inside their heads; they are rather about their life events, and the way they respond to such events—the events going on in the world around them, which is typically the world that we share with them.[4]

Crucially, coming to appreciate the other's story—to see why they are doing what they are doing—does not require a capacity for mentalizing inferences or simulations. Our understanding of others is ordinarily not based on attempts to get into their heads; typically we do not need to access a landscape of consciousness since we already have access to a landscape of action, which is constituted by their embodied actions and the rich worldly contexts within which they act—contexts that operate as scaffolds for the meaning and significance of their actions and their expressive movements.[5]

---

[3] My daughter Julia was 4.5 years old when, during a stay in Cambridge, we attended touring productions of *Twelfth Night* and *A Midsummer's Night Dream*. I doubt that she could follow the detail of the Shakespearean language; nonetheless, she was enthralled by the characters and actions on stage, which may in part explain her decision to pursue an acting career. See Gallagher and Gallagher (2019) for a discussion of empathy and acting.

[4] This is not to deny that some narratives are more psychological than others—those of James Joyce or Dostoyevsky, as Jordan Zlatev suggests (private correspondence). Luckily Joyce, Dostoyevsky, and other novelists put us inside the heads of their characters and we do not have to theorize or simulate our way in there. There is no denying that human beings are complicated psychological creatures, or that the psychological lives of Stephen Dedalus or Raskolnikov are fascinating in ways that outstrip an understanding in simple folk-psychological terms. The issue, here, is how we come to understand people in our everyday interactions with them.

[5] The idea that narrative understanding does not rest on or presuppose ToM abilities *per se* (including simulation capacities that involve making belief/desire predictions and explanations) is in line with

How do we get this sort of complex and nuanced understanding of why people do what they do? Off the football field, and outside institutions, people don't always wear their reasons for acting on their sleeves. Many times we may not be in a position to grasp their meaning, for example, if we are not in a position to interact or to communicate with them. In such cases we seem not to have a starting point. Yet, the pervasive presence of narrative in our daily lives, and the development of specific kinds of narrative competency, can work around the starting problem we found in TT and ST, and provide a better way to account for the more nuanced understandings (and mis-understandings) we have of others. In this regard Daniel Hutto has developed what he calls the *narrative practice hypothesis* (Hutto 2008a; 2007a & b; also see Gallagher and Hutto 2008). Reliance on narrative practices, together with communicative practices, provides a good answer to those who would insist that theoretical inference or simulation is the only game in town.

Hutto defines the narrative practice hypothesis as follows.

The core claim of the Narrative Practice Hypothesis (or NPH) is that direct encounters with stories about reasons for acting, supplied in interactive contexts by responsive caregivers, is the normal route through which children become familiar with both (i) the core structure of folk psychology and (ii) the norm-governed possibilities for wielding it in practice, knowing *how* and knowing *when* to use it.   (Hutto 2008, 117)

Consider the following example (from Gallagher & Hutto 2008). Someone might ask: Why is Laura going to India? If I don't really know Laura, and if I've never heard her say why she is going to India, then I may attempt to get at her reasons from a third-person perspective. This is surely something we do occasionally. This sort of speculative attempt at folk-psychological explanation might run as follows. Laura is a young, American college student. Why do young, American college students travel to India? Some think that India is a romantic place where one can learn about meditation practices and have an adventure. So Laura might desire to go to India for such reasons. One reaches this conclusion by calling on background knowledge (involving some set of assumptions and biases)—general knowledge or beliefs about what American college students tend to think and value as well as one's knowledge about widely held beliefs about India. The attributed reason may be correct or incorrect in Laura's case, but lacking detailed information about Laura, one is forced to appeal to generalizations informed by knowledge of an impersonal sort.

Two things are worthy of note. First, this kind of speculation is not likely to be very reliable in most interesting cases. Second, there is no obvious reason to think that the background knowledge in question is theoretical. To say that one is operating

---

Gregory Currie's (2007) claim that our skills in comprehending narratives involve the adoption of frameworks through which we identify with (and are effectively "asked to" take on) certain *personas*, which can be understood as embodied "stances" that particular narratives invite us to adopt. The activity of framework adoption is quite distinct from understanding a story's content—as detailed in its plot or *fabula*. As Currie characterizes it, adoption or attention to a narrative framework activates our subpersonal mechanisms for imitative and emotional responding—thus it is something that engages us viscerally. He contrasts this with the idea that attention to the narrative framework involves developing a "theory" (even if a not very explicit one) about the *persona* embedded in narrative; although he does not wholly reject the latter proposal since he acknowledges it may have a role when it comes to communicating about narratives.

with theories about India and theories about the belief-forming tendencies of American students in such cases is surely to stretch the notion of theory beyond reasonable limits.

Let's modify the example slightly. If I know Laura, but do not know precisely why she is going to India, I will be able to make a more informed guess about her reasons. Laura is the kind of person who really wants to help impoverished children, and she once told me about an organization in India that offered such help, so that is *probably* why *she* is going to India. I will have learnt this about her from my previous exchanges with her, or on the basis of what others have told me about her. In this case too, my attribution is knowledge-based but the knowledge in question this time is particular and personal, something gained through specific communications. What I have gained through such communications is not the Laura Theory. Rather, it is specific knowledge about Laura that is clearly narrative in nature. My attribution is hardly theoretical; it remains particularistic and narratival.

Here's a third version. If I know Laura I may already know her reason for going to India or I might get at it by much more reliable means. I may know why she is going because she may have already told me. If not, I could always ask her. Of course, she may be lying or she may be deceiving herself about this, but even acknowledging those possibilities, direct communication is undeniably my most secure route to her reasons.

It is important to stress that in each of these cases our capacity to understand Laura's actions or intentions is framed by the activity of checking to see if *her reason*, as it were, makes sense within the framework of one of several possible narratives. Learning of a person's reason is only a small part of the story of our everyday understanding of why others act. It is also necessary to situate and evaluate reasons in wider contexts and against certain normative assumptions. Would it make sense for anyone to go to India for that sort of reason? In particular, does it make sense for Laura to go? Is doing so in line with her character, her larger ambitions, her existing projects, or her history? What does it say about her? Does it make her a generous person, a naïve idealist, a person who habitually acts on her moral instincts? Understanding reasons for action demands more than simply knowing which beliefs and desires have moved a person to act. Understanding intentional actions requires contextualizing them, both in terms of cultural norms and the peculiarities of a particular person's history or values.

This ability to understand another person is about more than just getting the meaning content of their narrative. Narrative gives us a form or structure that we can use in understanding others. Gaining narrative competency means that we start to make sense of the others' (as well as our own) actions *via* implicit narrative frameworks. That is, we learn from narrative practices how to frame an understanding of others. We start to see others, engaged in their actions, not simply in terms of the immediate and occurrent context that might be listed as a set of facts. We start to see them as engaged in longer-term (plot-like) projects that add meaning to what they are doing. In the same way that an isolated gesture (a gesture that has no context) has little meaning, but gains in meaning as we see it performed in context, so an action takes on meaning when we see it in terms of a broader narrative. In our earlier example, a waving hand on its own might mean a variety of things, but it will take on a specific meaning when a police person is waving at me as I drive toward her; so also a specific action for which we have no narrative framework may have less meaning than one that fits into an extended and storied pattern of activity. Even when I am not in a position to know, or if I see some perplexing behavior, the question is likely, "What's his story?" rather than "What's going on in his head?"

This doesn't mean that our understanding of others requires an *explicit* narrative storytelling; but it does require the ability to see/to frame the other person's action, and the intentions and circumstances that come along with it, in a detailed pragmatic or social context, and to understand that context in a narrative way. As Alasdair MacIntyre (1981) suggested, for an observer, or for a participant, an action has intelligibility when it can find a place in a narrative.

In this light, reasons for acting are best thought of as "the *elements* of a possible storyline" (Velleman 2000, 28). As such, making explicit a person's narrative is one medium for understanding and evaluating reasons and making sense of actions. Such narratives allow us to understand a person's "rationale" when this is not immediately obvious. Through narratives we gain a shared knowledge about roles and rules in our common world; we learn how we ought to behave in various circumstances, and at the same time we learn how others ought to behave as well, *ceteris paribus*. Our expectations concerning others' actions are the result of our becoming accustomed to local norms, coming to embody them, as it were, through habit and practice. This implicit way of framing events and actions, in the form of diverse narratives, rather than the wielding of theoretical generalizations, or the imposing of overly homogeneous simulations, is the crucial backdrop against which we make sense of reasons for action.

Competency with different kinds of narratives thus enables us to understand others in a variety of ways. According to the narrative practice hypothesis, distinctive kinds of narrative encounters are what first allow us to develop our folk-psychological competence.

[C]hildren normally achieve [folk-psychological] understanding by engaging in story-telling practices, with the support of others. The stories about those who act for reasons—i.e. folk psychological narratives—are the foci of this practice. Stories of this special kind provide the crucial training set needed for understanding reasons. (Hutto 2007b, 53)

Children thus acquire competence in understanding reasons and mental states through exposure to and engagement with narratives and when appropriately and actively supported by their caregivers. Caregivers frequently prompt a child to answer certain questions in terms of the landscape of consciousness as they jointly attend to the narrative and co-attend to what motivates the agent. Children thus learn how and why these attitudes matter to the protagonists of such stories, providing them with specific normative expectations about the other's behavior.[6]

---

[6] Children's fairy tales, where characters act for reasons, can be and are told in the landscape of action format, and not just as folk-psychological narratives in the landscape of consciousness. In Gallagher and Hutto (2008) we stated: "Folk psychological narratives – as exemplified by *Little Red Riding Hood* – are distinguished by being about agents who act for reasons." Hutto (2008) provided a more detailed discussion of this story where he quotes the version found in Lillard (1998). "Little Red Riding Hood *learns* .... She *wants* ... and she *thinks* ... " etc. Of course, this may be one version of the story as it is told to

The fact that 4-year-olds can pass classic false-belief tests may be tied to the development of narrative practices. Controlled studies have shown that narrative training is responsible for improving performances on false-belief tasks, which suggests to theorists who adopt a ToM perspective that narrative is an effective tool for "at least modest improvements in children's theory of mind development" (Guajardo & Watson 2002, 320). In fact, however, many false-belief tests are presented in the form of a narrative and could be interpreted as tests for a certain level of narrative competency rather than ToM on the TT or ST models.

This is not to use theoretical inference, as in TT, but to engage in a narrative practice, drawing on what we have learned from our exposure to narratives. Folk-psychological narratives give us a way to frame things reflectively in terms of beliefs and desires, and to explain other people's actions in those terms when the focus is on reasons, and when the landscape of action is not sufficient to tell the whole story. In some cases we come to understand another person's action by locating it in the landscape of actions, through the use of implicit narrative frameworks; in other cases, if required to explicate or explain that action, we may be able to make the landscape of consciousness more explicit in a folk-psychological narrative.

On an enactivist IT view, narrative competency enables an interpretation of the other's actions and intentions without the mediation of folk psychology. In many cases the landscape of action—encountering another's action in significantly contextualized situations that we can easily frame in narrative—is all we need to understand their reasons. And their reasons need not be understood in terms of mental states. When I see someone eating gelato and thoroughly enjoying it, I can understand that in terms of the gelato having just the right taste as this person is taking a summer evening stroll with friends. I don't have to appeal to folk psychology at all. Folk-psychological explanation is just one kind of narrative practice, and I don't always gain very much by going that route. An explanation that tells us that she *believes* gelato is good and *wants* to eat it adds nothing to what I already know from her actions.

Accordingly our narrative practices tend to focus on the landscape of action and we do not use folk-psychological narratives nearly as often as the ToM approaches suppose. As Bruner points out: "When things 'are as they should be,' the narratives of folk psychology are unnecessary" (1990, 40). Generally folk psychology only comes into play in cases where the actions of others deviate from what is normally expected and we encounter difficulty understanding them, or in the rare cases where we are challenged to explain or explicitly predict another's action. By and large, since most everyday social interaction takes place in familiar (and normalized) environments, we get by without having to make folk-psychological attributions and without seeking explanations.

some children. The Charles Perrault (1697) version as translated in Lang (1889, 51–3) contains significantly fewer mental state words (five altogether); and neither the Italian/Austrian version (Schneller, 1867, no. 6, 9–10), nor the French version (*Conte de la mère-grand*) contains any mental state words. All versions can be found at http://www.pitt.edu/~dash/type0333.html, translated/edited by D.L. Ashliman, 1999–2018. Thanks to Leon de Bruin (personal communication) for pointing this out.

7.4 The Massive Hermeneutical Background

I suggested in the previous chapter that one way to avoid the starting problem is to acknowledge that social cognition depends on the kind of embodied interactive processes described in primary and secondary intersubjectivity. Communicative and narrative competencies clearly provide another part of what we need in order to avoid the problem; namely, a great deal of background knowledge—a massive hermeneutical background (MHB; see Bruner & Kalmar 1998; Gallagher 2011). Neither TT nor ST tells us much about this idea. On a nativist view of TT, where a certain innate ToM module for social cognition simply comes online (around the age of 2 years, or possibly earlier) and allows us to reason our way into an understanding of others (e.g., Carruthers 1996; Scholl & Leslie 1999), solutions to the starting problem remain entirely mysterious. We simply have the capability, and we start using it when our brains are sufficiently developed. On a more empiricist view of TT one might argue that there is a natural connection between what I'm calling the narrative-based MHB and folk psychology. On this view one might conceive of folk psychology as a set of generalizations based on the MHB. We gain the MHB through exposure to narratives, and in lots and lots of interactions with others. Then, on this supposition, we simply abstract from the MHB, through an inductive process, the general rules of human behavior that constitute folk psychology. Gopnik and Meltz-off (1998), for example, argue that young children are like scientists, constantly doing experiments (having experiences, playing, observing others) and generalizing across those experiments. On this view, folk psychology, as Spaulding (2017a, 304) defines it, "a rich body of information about how mental states relate to other mental states and to behavior," would be considered an abstract set of principles generated from the particularities of the MHB. Accordingly one can simply draw on that background—the kind of very particular knowledge that comes from narrative exposure and our experience of how people behave—to set the stage for the application of folk-psychological rules.

One might make a similar argument about simulation skills. On this view we could consider the MHB to consist in a learned set of narratives and skills including practical knowledge of how to engage in simulation routines. Thus, for either TT or ST, I know what rule or principle to apply, or what simulation to run, for any particular situation, because I draw on the particular knowledge or set of skills I have in the MHB.

There are some conceptual problems with this way of thinking, however. For example, if these empiricist accounts explain how we acquire the MHB to support folk psychology or, *mutatis mutandis*, simulation skills, they seem to presuppose that already within the MHB there is an implicit understanding of others. If there were not an intersubjective understanding already implicit in the MHB, then it's not clear how we could rely on it to specify a relevant folk-psychological rule or how it could be the basis for activating a simulation. If the MHB actually does address the starting problem, then it would have to offer at least the degree of intersubjective understanding that would satisfy, for example, Goldman's first step in the simulation routine: "First, the attributor creates in herself pretend states intended to match those of the target" (2005, 80). If this is the case, however, if there is an intersubjective understanding already implicit in the MHB, then it undermines the universalist claim that typically goes along with TT or ST—namely, that folk-psychological mindreading or simulation is the primary and pervasive way that we understand others. Rather, the intersubjective understanding that is already implicit in the narrative-based MHB would be developmentally primary. Moreover, if we rely on the MHB to get mindreading inferences or simulations off the ground, then MHB would be as pervasive as folk psychology or simulation is claimed to be. In that case, rather than primary and pervasive, mindreading inferences or simulations would be secondary, and likely put into use only in situations where our interactions with others break down and the resources of the MHB and narrative practices are not sufficient to deliver a working understanding of others. Furthermore, if there is already an intersubjective understanding implicit in the MHB, then it is not clear whether folk psychology would be simply a continuation, by way of abstraction or generalization, of this kind of understanding, or whether it would constitute something different, and if the latter, what that difference is.

These issues suggest that we should take a closer look at the MHB and ask about its status in our everyday interactions with others. I will argue that the kind of understanding of others implicit in the MHB is not a precursor that is somehow replaced by folk psychology or by a set of simulation skills (see, e.g., Baron-Cohen 1995; Currie 2008), nor is it a form of theoretical inference or simulation. Rather, it is closely related to the set of ongoing embodied interactions and narrative practices that we have described as characterizing most of our everyday encounters with others.

There are a number of conceptions of what we are calling the MHB. John Searle (1978, 1992), for example, considers the "Background" to be a set of pre-intentional capacities, skills, and abilities which constitute a general know-how and which allow us to function in everyday life. For Searle, intentional phenomena "such as meanings, understandings, interpretations, beliefs, desires, and experiences only function within a set of Background capacities that are not themselves intentional" (1992, 175).

The idea that the background capacities are not intentional (understood in the Brentanian sense of intentionality) is motivated by the following thought. Any one intentional state (e.g., having a belief) is always part of a larger network of intentional states, but neither an intentional state on its own, nor a set of intentional states is self-interpreting or self-applying. This is similar to what I've called the starting problem, which is similar to what in AI is called the "symbol grounding" problem or the frame problem. The question Searle is trying to answer is: What determines the conditions of satisfaction for any intentional state or any network of intentional states? His intuition is that the conditions of satisfaction for any intentional state are determined by a non-intentional set of capacities; for example, a set of sensory-motor capabilities. Searle offers an example from Wittgenstein. We look at a picture of a man walking uphill; but nothing in the picture itself seems to specify that the man is walking uphill rather than sliding back down the hill. What grounds our interpretation is our own experience of walking. If an intentional state is not cashed out in terms of some background capacity, skill, or practice, it would lead to an infinite regress in terms of trying to understand the meaning of the intentional state, much in the same way that in using a dictionary one can be led from the meaning of one word to the meaning of another, and from there to the meaning of another word, etc. etc. ad infinitum.

Searle's argument is based on linguistics and most of his examples come from language use. "Sally gave John the key, and he opened the door" (1992, 181). This, like any sentence, is underdetermined with regard to its meaning. We understand the sentence to mean that Sally first gave John the key, and he then used it to open the door. But this understanding involves unstated content that we seemingly have to add to the sentence to make sense of it—minimally, that keys open doors. This cannot be accomplished by adding more words to the sentence; that would simply introduce more underdetermined elements. Rather, the meaning is fixed by our practices and our know-how about how keys and doors work. Practices and know-how are not simply other sentences or propositional attitudes; they involve moving around the world and doing things—real motoric attitudes (cf. Stanley 2011; Gallagher and Aguda, 2020).

There are some issues here that I will set aside for purposes of this chapter, but let me note that Searle changes his mind about the non-intentional status of the background (1992, 186ff); the background, Searle decides, includes both intentional and non-intentional states. Again, for our purposes we can set this issue aside and simply say that the background includes all kinds of capacities, practices, skills, and some finite range of knowing-how and knowing-that, where the latter takes the form of very particular knowledge in narrative form. Whether we want to say that all of these things are intentional (on a wide definition that would include things like motor intentionality) or not, shouldn't matter for our purposes here.

Another issue concerns the question of whether we should think of the background as somehow reducible to brain processes, as Searle does. The background (or the MHB), however, includes cultural elements, and elements that are tied to specific social practices, and it is not clear how this might be reducible to neurophysiological capacity.[7] One way to see this is to think of how the background comes into our everyday practices. In this regard Pierre Bourdieu's (1990) notion of *habitus* is useful. We can think of *habitus* as an individual's particular background. As such, *habitus* is a system of long-term, acquired dispositions (habits, schemas) of perception, thought, and action. These are embodied, affective, and pragmatically situated dispositions that are not necessarily consciously manifest in our practices, but they function prenoetically; that is, they shape our experiences without our being aware that they are doing so (Gallagher 2005a). They are formed in response to physical and social environmental factors, and they continue to depend upon and evolve in tandem with those factors; in this respect, they are not reducible to neurophysiological states.

Consider some basic somatic aspects of *habitus*. Physical skills, for example, are not unrelated to posture and gait. The latter, however, are not simply a matter of a functioning basal ganglia and connected brain areas, but depend in essential ways on specifics of the body—flexibility of the joints, muscle tone, bone structure, physical size, etc.—as well as immediately present and long-term factors of the physical,

---

[7] Searle is an internalist who thinks that all factors that contribute to cognition must be cashed out in neurophysiological terms; he writes: "The occurrent ontology of those parts of the Network that are unconscious is that of a neurophysiological capacity, but the Background consists entirely in such capacities" (1992, 188).

social, and cultural environments (Gallagher 2005a, 2017a). These factors—brain, body, environment—are all part of one system. Walking around different geographical environments (compare living in the mountains *versus* living in the desert or the city) will affect my physical condition and way of moving. If I live immersed in a hip-hop culture, it is very likely that my gait is culturally affected; if I am a ballet dancer, or a military officer, my posture is likely quite different from that of the general population. More generally, what I am able to do and the particular skills I have are enabled and limited by the particular culture that I live in, which contributes to and in specific ways sets my *habitus*. It may also be that the basal ganglia, and many other areas of the brain of the ballet dancer are somewhat different from the same areas of the desert nomad, or the Cornell cosmologist living a sedentary life next to a waterfall. But it is not that difference in basal ganglia that would constitute the full story of one's posture or gait or specific capabilities and skills. One's movement history is not inscribed like a text in the motor areas of the brain—no one can simply read it off from a perfect brain scan—although it is clear that one's movement history has literally (physically) shaped parts of the brain and have specified some of the details of how they function.

Likewise, one's life-narrative is not inscribed like a text in one's brain, yet the details of one's life, in broad strokes, do have serious effects on various aspects of neural function. What precisely does the pre-frontal cortex look like in a person raised in an apartheid regime and told throughout his life that he is incapable of helping himself, and, as a result, has become convinced by this message and is unable to see any other possibilities? Whatever the answer to that question, the complete structure of this way of being-in-the-world is not something that can be explained by neurophysiology. Indeed, it goes the other way—the neurophysiology is explained by these different ways of being-in-the-world.

The background, having its effects through a particular shared *habitus*, instantiates a normative force that plays an essential role in regulating social practices, and contributing to social reproduction. Through deep educational processes, including formal educational practices which are themselves shaped by background conditions, individuals learn to act in ways that are tied to the possibilities provided for them. On Bourdieu's analysis, they learn to expect nothing different. Such dispositions tend to generate the same dispositions in others, and thus a certain normative order.

The background, considered not as narrowly neurobiological, but as widely embodied and embedded in practices that are not only physical, but also social and cultural and normative, is deeply hermeneutical, in the sense that it shapes the way that individuals interpret themselves and others. The shaping process is both constraining and productive, reflecting principles well defined by the hermeneutical tradition (see Gadamer 1989; Gallagher 1992). To put things most succinctly, the massive hermeneutical background, as it relates to an individual's capacity for intersubjective understanding, finds its beginning in intersubjective interactive practices, and, through communicative and narrative practices, is further built up to expand social and cultural norms.

In order to understand others in circumstances instituted by such complex social practices and normative formations, and to engage in such practices, much depends on our basic perceptions, emotions, and embodied interactions, but we also need something more. As I have been arguing, we do not turn to folk psychology or simulation at this point. Rather we extend our developed abilities for understanding others, through communicative and narrative practices. At best, we can then think of folk psychology as an abstracted version of the massive hermeneutical background, put to use in certain rare situations as one way to understand another's reasons for acting.

7.5 Empathy

Empathy, as I will argue, is something that depends on all of the various interactional and action-oriented aspects of social cognition that we have been discussing—primary and secondary intersubjective processes, direct social perception, communication, and narrative practices. But it is not reducible to any one of these. We can clarify this view by contrasting it to some recent simulationist accounts of empathy. Simulation theory conceives of empathy as closely related to, if not identical to simulation. Does the simulationist account of empathy hold up, even if a simulationist account of social cognition does not? In answering this question I'll return to the *diversity problem* and show how our narrative practices can address it, even if they cannot solve it.

Simulation theories of empathy fall into two types: those that argue that empathy is equivalent or closely tied to what is considered the default form of everyday social cognition (Decety 2005; Gallese 2001; Goldman 2006; Stueber 2006), and those that argue that empathy has a special status which makes it distinct from everyday social cognition (Vignemont & Singer 2006; Vignemont & Jacob 2012; Jacob 2011). I'll argue that both types of simulationist theories encounter insurmountable difficulties. I'll then propose, as an alternative, an account of empathy informed by interaction theory and narrative practice.

7.5.1 Empathy as mindreading

Much of the contemporary debate about empathy is driven by the neuroscience of mirror neurons. Some theorists associate empathy with mirroring or motor-resonance processes themselves. According to Vittorio Gallese, for example, this lived bodily motor equivalence between what we observe others doing, and the capabilities of our own motor system enables a fast, automatic empathic understanding that fits with the elementary timescale (see *Section 2.3*) of neuronal activation. "I submit that the neural matching mechanism constituted by mirror neurons... is crucial to establish an empathic link between different individuals" (Gallese 2001, 44). Following ST, he extends this model to include expressive aspects of movement that give us access to the emotional states of others (e.g., Gallese & Goldman 1998). One aspect of Gallese's account is that he equates empathy with what would count as a standard action or emotion understanding. Empathy is nothing more than the phenomenological level of his "shared manifold hypothesis" correlating with simulation on the functional level, and the activation of mirror neurons on the subpersonal level. Accordingly, since the mirror system is activated in most cases when we observe another person engage in intentional action, empathy is a basic, common, and everyday occurrence.

Jean Decety (2004, 2005, 2011), in contrast to Gallese, contends that empathy is not simply action- or emotion-resonance. It also requires a minimal and more explicit comprehension of the *mental states* of the other person. He does not deny, however, the importance of resonance systems, especially in early infancy, and he accepts that we have an innate capacity to feel that other people are *"like us,"* and that this is related to the possibility of experiencing empathy. But we also quickly develop the capacity for a simulation-based mindreading which allows us to put ourselves *mentally* in the place of others (Decety & Grèzes 2006). Decety rightly emphasizes that in this process difference is just as important as similarity. Empathy is founded on our capacity to recognize that others are similar to us, but to do so without confusing ourselves with the other.

According to Decety, then, three fundamental components interact to create empathy:

1. A component of motor resonance, the activation of which is generally automatic.
2. Insight into the subjective mental perspective of the other which may be controlled and intentional.
3. The ability to differentiate between self and other. (Decety 2005; also Decety & Jackson 2004)

The major difference between Gallese and Decety concerns the second component. For Gallese, this component is not something *more* than what the resonance system already delivers, automatically; for Decety, this is the "something extra" that is needed for empathic understanding. This second component would push us beyond the elementary timescale into the conscious integrative timescale. For both Decety and Gallese, however, empathy is equated with everyday social cognition—either basic motor resonance or a basic form of mindreading.

The "something extra" that Decety requires equates to a higher-level simulation, and one could interpret that as a conscious or introspective process, involving imaginary enactments (e.g., Goldman 2006, 2005, 1989). For Goldman high-level simulation involves self-reflective, conscious processes (2006, 147–8). He explains high-level simulation as a form of pretense, which he calls "Enactive" or E-imagination. To avoid confusion with an enactivist conception of social cognition, I'll re-label it S- (for simulative) imagination. S-imagination just is that type of process that generates pretend states which, according to ST, resemble the mental states of the other person.

If, however, as Goldman proposes, simulation describes a standard strategy for our everyday social cognition, is this equivalent to empathy? Goldman often equates simulation and empathy, calling ST "empathy theory" (2006, 17); "interpersonal mental simulation [is] also called empathizing" (2006, 205; also 291). Goldman (2011, 32) endorses the idea that the term "empathize" is roughly equivalent to intersubjective simulation and that "empathy is a key to mindreading…the most common form of mindreading." In other places, however, he recognizes that empathy may be distinguished from mindreading. Thus, he poses the question: "What is the relationship between mentalizing and other forms of social cognition? For example, how is it related to empathy…?" (2006, 21). Goldman's usual answer seems to be that mentalizing or mindreading just is empathy, but to make this equation he subtracts certain things that other theorists might want to include in a definition of empathy: "mindreading is an extended form of empathy (where this term's emotive and caring connotation is bracketed)" (2006, 4). Thus he can qualify other forms of empathy as affective or emotional empathy.

Karsten Stueber also equates empathy with simulation and claims that empathy is central and "epistemically essential" to our understanding of other agents (Stueber 2006, 131; 2012). Like Goldman's distinction between low-level and high-level simulation, Stueber distinguishes between basic and re-enactive empathy—the first is a form of empathy that operates on a subpersonal elementary timescale, the second involves the integrative timescale. Basic empathy is a perceptual phenomenon that "allows us to directly recognize what another person is doing or feeling" when observing her facial expressions or behavior (Stueber 2006, 147). Like Gallese, he argues that basic empathy is linked to the activity of the mirror system. Basic empathy, however, is not sufficient to "explain and predict a person's behavior in complex social situations" or to provide "a full grasp of all mental concepts that we attribute to the typical adult" (ibid.). Accordingly, in a similar way to Decety, Stueber contends that we require something more; namely, re-enactive empathy. The "something extra" that comes along with re-enactive empathy is identified as involving more sophisticated mindreading abilities. This requires a higher-order simulation of thoughts or mental states taken as reasons for action.

For all of these theorists, then, whether or not they distinguish between low-level, neural simulation and high-level simulation of the explicit mindreading sort, there seems to be no good distinction between our ordinary everyday processes of social cognition and empathy. Mirror neuron activation seems to be involved in providing a basic, automatic, simulative understanding of the immediate bodily expressions of the other person, and some kind of more explicit simulation routine apparently allows us to grasp the mental states that motivate the other person's actions. In all cases, this is meant to be a description of our everyday understanding of others, and this is equated with empathy at one level or the other, or both levels. Social cognition is, by default, a form of empathy. Yet, in our ordinary way of speaking, saying that I empathize with you suggests more than just understanding your mental state.[8]

7.5.2 Empathy distinguished from mindreading

In contrast to the thinkers already mentioned, Frédérique de Vignemont, Tania Singer, and Pierre Jacob (Vignemont & Singer 2006; Vignemont & Jacob 2012; Jacob 2011) clearly distinguish empathy from everyday mindreading. Their analysis depends on something "more" than elementary processes of mirror neurons, and like Decety, Goldman, and Stueber, they locate empathy on the integrative timescale where neural underpinnings are integrated into conscious affective states.

---

[8] Dan Zahavi (personal correspondence) has rightly pointed out that the term "empathy" came into existence as a relatively recent (early twentieth century) translation of the relatively young German term *Einfühlung*. The original meaning of *Einfühlung* is much closer to the very basic, automatic processes that Gallese and many phenomenologists describe. If we stick to that original sense, then the very low-level contagion-like processes of mirroring, or a certain kind of direct perception, may be more appropriate to describe empathy. Still, this is not the contemporary common understanding of the term.

Vignemont and Singer offer the following definition in terms of a set of collectively *sufficient* conditions for empathy.

There is empathy if: (i) one is in an affective state; (ii) this state is isomorphic to another person's state; (iii) this state is elicited by the observation or imagination of another person's affective state; (iv) one knows that the other person is the source of one's own affective state.

(Vignemont & Singer 2006, 435)

The second condition seemingly distinguishes empathy from sympathy. Empathy involves being in the same or similar affective state as the other; sympathy involves being in a different affective state (e.g., I feel *sorry* that you are in *pain*). Jacob specifies the second condition further as *the interpersonal similarity condition*, "arguably the major assumption of the simulation-based approach to empathy" (Jacob 2011, 521).

The third condition, specifies the affective state as a vicarious experience—e.g., in empathy I feel vicarious pain or "as if" pain, rather than real, physiological pain caused by bodily injury. Vignemont and Jacob contend that the capacity for creating vicarious experiences is based on S-imagination, which, as we've seen, involves running off-line, high-level (i.e., explicit, conscious) simulations (Vignemont & Jacob 2012; Jacob 2011). The fourth condition, which Jacob calls the "*ascription condition*," distinguishes empathy from emotional contagion, which typically happens unbeknownst to the subject. Taken together, the second, third, and fourth conditions make empathy a form of simulation consistent with ST. The first condition, however, which Jacob calls the "*affectivity condition*," distinguishes empathy from standard mindreading: "in a standard process of mindreading [e.g.,] another's pain, one forms the belief that another is in pain. Believing that another is in pain is different from experiencing empathetic pain" (Jacob 2011, 523–4).

Vignemont and Jacob add a fifth condition: the *caring condition*: in empathy one must care about the target's affective life. As Jacob explains this, empathy depends on a consideration of context; it is not the *default* response to my simple awareness of your affective state. Rather, empathy depends on a top-down modulation and requires that the empathizing subject cares or is concerned about the other. Empathy is *other-directed* in this regard.

For clarity, let me summarize these five conditions.

1. *The affectivity condition*: there is no empathy unless both target and empathizer experience some affective state. The affectivity condition distinguishes both empathetic and sympathetic experiences from standard mindreading.
2. *The interpersonal similarity condition*: there is no empathy unless the target's and the empathizer's affective states stand in a similarity relation to each other (i.e., both experience pain or both experience fear).
3. *The vicarious state condition*: the empathic state involves an "as if" or vicarious affective state, generated by the empathizer's imaginative portrayal of another person's affective state.
4. *The ascription condition*: there is no empathetic understanding unless the empathizer knowingly ascribes the affective state to the target.
5. *The caring condition*: the empathizer must be led to care about the target's affective life because of context.

We've already seen (in *Chapter 4*) some specific problems with the simulationist concept of mindreading in ST. They include the matching problem, the starting problem, and the diversity problem, among others. It would seem that if empathy were equivalent to or something close to a simulationist concept of everyday social cognition or mindreading (as in Gallese, Decety, Goldman, and Stueber), then the problems we earlier identified with regard to simulation as a form of mindreading would also be problems for a simulationist view of empathy. Alternatively, if we follow Vignemont, Singer, and Jacob and make a clear distinction between everyday mindreading skills, as they are portrayed in the ST literature, and empathy—that is, if we reject the view that empathy is a kind of default mindreading and yet still retain the idea that empathy is a form of simulation—then the question is whether the critique of ST extends to this view of empathy.

Jacob (2008, 2011) addresses the matching problem. In his critique of the mirror neuron version of low-level simulation he notes that simulation-based approaches to mindreading overemphasize interpersonal similarity. He argues that interpersonal similarity (matching) is neither necessary nor sufficient for mindreading. However, he rightly insists, "acceptance of a S-B (simulation-based) model of *empathy* does not amount to acceptance of a S-B model of *mindreading*" (2008, 10). In other words, it is one thing to reject the simulation-based approach to mindreading, and something quite different to reject the simulation-based approach to empathy. While matching or interpersonal similarity may not be necessary for mindreading, it does play an important role in empathy.

Vignemont, Singer, and Jacob can thus accept some of the criticisms of ST's conception of mindreading, but since they distinguish mindreading from empathy, they can argue that these criticisms don't go all the way through to the simulation account of empathy. ST may overemphasize intersubjective similarity when it comes to everyday mindreading, but the idea that similarity or matching is not the case in those contexts does not mean that a simulative matching state cannot characterize cases that involve imitation or empathy. Moreover, any worry about the empirical evidence against matching at the neural level is simply not an issue since, for these theorists empathy involves a high-level simulation rather than an automatic mirroring. Hence, on this score at least, the matching problem is not a problem for the *interpersonal similarity condition*.

There is, however, another issue concerning condition (2)—"the major assumption of the simulation-based approach to empathy" (Jacob 2011, 521).[9] *The interpersonal similarity condition* is framed in terms of an isomorphism of affective states, which is supposed to distinguish empathy from sympathy. Zahavi and Overgaard (2012) have suggested that this is not sufficient to distinguish between empathy and sympathy. If A feels sad for his friend B because of some injustice done to her, but B feels angry about it, on condition (2) this would be a case of sympathy but not empathy since A and B are in different affective states. If, however, B starts to feel sad about the injustice, then condition (2) would lead to a recategorization of A's feeling as empathy. Zahavi and Overgaard suggest that this is wrongheaded since A is in exactly the same affective state whether B is angry or sad, and they reason that it would be odd to say that A is empathizing in one case but not in the other, since the only change is in B.

One response to this objection is to think of empathy as an intersubjective relational phenomenon. That is, empathy is not defined as simply an individual's internal mental or affective state in isolation from the other; it involves the wider context, so that a change in the other's particular state will make a difference to our empathic relation. Furthermore, it's not clear that we should understand similarity purely in terms of the *phenomenal* aspects of the affective experiences (e.g., the feeling of sadness as a phenomenal state as similar in A and B), rather than in terms of *intentionality*. On this alternative view the wider context includes the intentional object that should be the same for both A and B's affective experiences. For example, A's sadness or anger may be *about an injustice done to B*. But it would hardly be empathy if A was feeling sadness or anger about that injustice while B was upset for some other reason about which A knows nothing. In other words, empathy requires a form of *co-intentionality*. Even when the intentional structures of A and B's affective states line up, however, they will not be perfectly isomorphic since A and B are in different situations: B has actually suffered the injustice B is sad about, while A has not, and this can easily entail differences in affective states. For example, a sadness tinged with anger in B will be somewhat different from an empathic sadness not tinged with anger in A. It may be that even some non-similar affective state, plus co-intentionality, may be sufficient for empathy. If A is outraged (but not sad) about the injustice that B has suffered, knowing that B is simply sad (but does not feel outrage) about the injustice, it would seem odd to claim that A is not empathizing with B. A is outraged; B is sad. In both cases, however, it's about the injustice done to B. Is this not empathy on A's part? This reinterpretation of condition (2) highlights the significance of understanding the *situation* or *circumstance* of the other person, and not just her internal affective state. Understanding the situation or the context of the other person seems essential for empathy.

On the simulationist account we are considering, however, S-imagination doesn't come close to addressing the issue of context. S-imagination simply generates pretend states that resemble the mental states of the other person (Goldman 2006, 48). I think we need to look elsewhere. The realization that the similarity condition concerns the *intentionality* of the affective state points us in a specific direction. It focuses attention on the *situation* or context of the other person rather than on the phenomenal character of their affective states. Understanding the other's situation is, I will argue, facilitated more by narrative than by simulation abilities.

7.5.3 Empathy on the narrative timescale

Even before the age of 2 years, when, according to Decety and Jackson, a child's capacity for empathy starts to emerge[10] a number of important developments

[10] Decety and Jackson (2004, 78) note: "It is around the 2nd year that empathy may be manifested in prosocial behaviors (e.g., helping, sharing, or comforting) indicative of concern for others. Studies of children in the 2nd year of life indicate that they have the requisite cognitive, affective, and behavioral capacities to display integrated patterns of concern for others in distress.... During this period of

contribute to the beginnings and the growth of narrative competency in the child. At 9–18 months we see the development of secondary intersubjectivity when children start to grasp the meaning of objects in terms of shared pragmatic goals. Children begin to make sense of the world through their interaction with others. Around this time the ability for mirror self-recognition emerges, and this provides the child with a more objective sense of self, an important development in providing a more concep-tual self-other distinction, which, as Decety correctly insists, is important for empathy. In addition, sometime between 15–24 months, children acquire language, or as Merleau-Ponty (2012) puts it, language starts to acquire them, which leads to advances in their communicative capacities. Finally, between 18–24 months, children start to manifest ability for episodic and autobiographical memory (Howe 2000).

Along with a growing linguistic competency, a developing conceptual sense of self, and the interactions associated with secondary intersubjectivity, the development of episodic memory helps to kick-start narrative abilities during the second year of life. It may be that 2-year-olds work more from scripts than from full-fledged narratives; their narratives have to be elicited by questions and prompts (Nelson 2003a & b, 2009). But from 2 to 4 years, children fine-tune their narrative abilities by means of a further development of language ability and memory skills. Through narratives we also learn from others and engage more fully in intersubjective sense making. Around 4 years of age children start to represent the views of other people in their narratives, contrasting what they know about some events with what others know about the events (Nelson 1992; Perner 1992).

The development of narrative competency contributes to the capacity for a form of narrative- or N-imagination, which involves understanding people in their particular circumstances rather than, as in S-imagination, understanding mental states in a person's head. N-imagination provides a way to narratively frame the other person's experience. As indicated above, this doesn't mean that our understanding of others requires an occurrent or explicit narrative storytelling. Our ability to frame actions and situations in narrative can happen in an implicit fashion in ways that attune our perceptual abilities, so that we can often times just see what the situation is, or implicitly N-imagine the circumstances of the other person. It is this capacity for N-imagination that gives us the kind of understanding of the other's situation required for empathy.

Jacob (2011), in defending his simulationist view of empathy, however, raises some objections to this narrative view. In response to the claim that we gain ability in understanding others through narrative practice, he points to the developmental literature which shows that young infants (at 13 months, and even younger), and therefore without narrative competency, pass "spontaneous" false-belief tests, where violation of expectation is measured by average looking times or where the expected correct answer is measured by anticipatory looking in that direction (Southgate et al. 2007, 2010). The question posed by Jacob is this: How could narrative competency explain capacity to pass false-belief tasks in young infants?

---

development, children increasingly experience emotional concern 'on behalf of the victim,' comprehend others' difficulties, and act constructively by providing comfort and help . . . ."

There are three points to be made in response to this question. First, no one claims that narrative competency is required for this kind of early performance on spontaneous false-belief tasks. Narrative, as noted above, may be involved in many of the "elicited" false-belief tests given to 3–5-year-olds, and narrative competency may be required to pass those tests, at least in the sense that the child has to be able to follow the narrative to understand the question. But this clearly does not apply to the kind of task at stake in the experiments with young infants. Second, with respect to the question of what capacity does explain the ability of young infants in these experiments, there is ongoing debate. Some propose a form of low-level simulation (Herschbach 2007); Carruthers (2009, 2013) suggests that infants at this age already are capable of metarepresentation and inference; Perner and Ruffman (2005) appeal to the infant's use of behavior rules (e.g. "people look for objects where they last saw them") gained *via* statistical learning abilities. Alternatively, one can offer an enactivist account of the infants' behavior on these tests (Gallagher 2015b; see Gallagher and Povinelli 2012). Perhaps we can agree that the jury is still out on this question. Third, to be clear, whatever the correct answer is, with respect to the issue of empathy, we can set aside this issue about young infants and false beliefs, since, according to Jacob himself, as well as Vignemont and Singer, it has nothing to do with empathy. They claim that empathy is not a matter of low-level processes (of whatever kind), which are surely the processes involved in early false-belief tests.[11] Thus, these experiments are not directly related to the claims made here about empathy or narrative. Again, no one has suggested that 13-month-olds are employing narratives. Within the framework of Jacob's own simulationist theory of empathy, the question about false-belief paradigms in infants falls into the category of mindreading or contagion, and is therefore beside the point.

Does a narrative theory of empathy help to address the diversity problem in ST? The diversity problem concerns the fact that, since simulation depends narrowly on one's own first-person experience as its basis, it seems inadequate when faced with the variety of ways people respond to situations. If we depend on our own prior experience in order to sense what the other person may be thinking in a particular situation, the question is whether we really attain an understanding of the other or are merely projecting ourselves. Faced with the diversity of people we encounter, how can our own relatively narrow experience be the basis for understanding them?

This is a problem that pertains to both high- and low-level simulations. Simulation is often described in the following way: "In all cases, observing what other people do or feel is transformed into an inner representation of what we would do or feel in a similar, endogenously produced, situation" (Goldman 2008, 27; see Keysers & Gazzola 2006, 390). But, as we asked in *Chapter 4*, how does knowing what *we* would do help us know what someone else would do? Given the vast variety of actions, beliefs, experiences, and feelings that people experience, it seems presumptuous to suggest that one's own limited first-person experience is capable of capturing

[11] Unless one wants to claim that high-level mindreading might be possible for the infant, as hinted by Goldman who suggests that the early false-belief data may motivate some revision in defining high-level mindreading as "late" developing (Goldman 2006, 146, n. 20). Even in this case, one would have to decide whether we should call this empathy rather than mindreading.

that diversity. There are thus two points to be made: (a) consistent simulation would introduce a consistent first-person (or in group) bias into our understandings of others—i.e., we would be led to think that others must do what we would do, or experience what we would experience; (b) our own experiences, no matter how extensive, can never meet the diversity of experiences had by the many others that we encounter, even in our own culture.

On the one hand, the answer to the diversity problem may simply be "yes," it is in fact a real problem. As indicated in *Chapter 6*, various studies show that we are more inclined to empathize with people who are closer and more like ourselves than with those who are more distant and more unlike ourselves (see Boltanski 1999; Chouliaraki 2006; Gutsell & Inzlicht 2010). Call this the "*real* diversity problem." The idea that empathy is a form of simulation may actually explain why this is a problem. But it would make it an unsolvable problem if simulation were the unavoidable default, or the only way in which we empathize.

On the other hand, we can still explain the real diversity problem if empathy depends on narrative practices, and if we are exposed to only a narrow set of narratives reflecting our own local cultures. We can more readily empathize with those who are close and similar to us because we already know the general lines of their stories. We have an easier time placing them in a familiar narrative framework. Yet it does seem possible in some cases to empathize with those who are not like us. We can empathize with monsters or aliens from other planets, as portrayed in film, and we can empathize with humans who live in far-away lands and who are very different. This is possible, however, only when we know their stories—only when we can frame their behavior in a narrative that informs us about their history or their situation.[12]

Narratives, however, are not miracles, and I don't want to claim that they necessarily promote empathy or caring attitudes (cf. Nussbaum 1997; Pinker 2011), or that reading literature will necessarily improve our capacity for understanding others (cf. Kidd & Castano 2013; Decety & Cowell 2015; Oatley 2016). In this respect, there are two points to make. First, it's clear that we sometimes fail to understand others, and this may be due to a failure of narrative to provide the proper resources in particular cases, or indeed, that we are equipped with the wrong narratives. Breaking out of some narratives and into others in these contexts involves communicative competency, and narrative competency once again. A retreat to simulation, if we take that to mean reliance on one's first-person experience, will not necessarily work. It seems clear, however, in many intersubjective contexts the other person can tell us their story, and one can ask questions and seek responses from those concerned, and out of this communicative practice one can start to reframe a narrative that will allow for understanding.

Second, it also seems right to say that empathy involves more than what Robert Hogan calls "the intellectual or imaginative apprehension of another's condition or

---

[12] Studies of altruistic behavior motivated by empathy bear this out. Empathic reactions are stronger when we understand the personal situation of an individual than if we have abstract, detached, theoretical, or merely statistical information about the plight of others (Slovic 2007; Small, Loewenstein, & Slovic 2007; also see *Section 9.3*).

state of mind" (Hogan 1969, 308), even if that is based on appropriate narratives. I can understand you and the circumstance you are in, but that doesn't necessarily mean that I am empathizing with you. For empathy there needs to be an affective component (cf. Vignemont et al.'s affectivity condition). One way to think that some affective state must be involved in empathy is to think that the empathizer's affective state is, at a minimum, an irreducible empathic affectivity. Isn't empathy, regardless of whatever other affective state it may involve, itself an affective state? That is, one can understand empathy not as necessarily taking up a secondary affective state— e.g., the sadness or outrage I feel along with you—but as being its own primary and irreducible affective state—the complex state of feeling empathy which may itself modulate other secondary affective states.[13]

In this regard empathy is a kind of intersubjective, relational affect similar to the feeling of solidarity. Whereas the feeling of solidarity may involve my feeling of being with you in the spirit of a certain project, the feeling of empathy involves my feeling of being with you with respect to your situated experience. Solidarity, however, unlike empathy, may involve the expectation of reciprocity; if I feel solidarity with you, then I would expect you to feel solidarity with me. Also, solidarity may be transitive—if I feel solidarity with you, and you feel solidarity with a third person, then, as long as the solidarity is about the same type of project, I should also feel solidarity with the third person. Empathy involves neither reciprocity nor transitivity. That empathy involves its own primary and irreducible affective state of feeling-*with*-another frees it from necessarily involving some secondary affective state—e.g., the real or simulated copy of the other person's affective state of sadness, outrage, etc. For example, one could experience empathy for another person's intellectual difficulty in solving a mathematical problem, and this empathy would itself still be a feeling.

Stueber (2008) suggests that the importance of narrative is simply to provide "hints and clues" to enhance the simulation (empathetic re-enactment) process. In this section I've moved the argument one step further: understanding the nature of narrative competency gives us good reason to give up the standard simulationist account of empathy altogether. This requires a shift away from thinking that empathy is about simulating or re-enacting mental or affective states (*via* S-imagination), towards thinking of empathy as involving an attitude that primarily involves an affective understanding of the other person's situation based on a co-intentionality accomplished *via* N-imagination.

In this respect, narratives, including cultural narratives (fairy tales, theatre, film, etc.), provide the possibility of understanding diverse contexts; they provide part of the massive hermeneutical background (*Section 7.4*); they can give us access to contexts that are broader than our own circumstances and that allow us to understand a broad variety of situations. Empathy does not float in thin air like a balloon on a thin string of first-person experience—it is tied to the ground by the particular

---

[13] Accordingly the idea of empathy as an affect is different from what Stueber (2008) calls "affective empathy"—the vicarious sharing of an affect, which would be consistent with Vignemont and Jacob's interpersonal similarity condition. The fact that the feeling of empathy is not experienced by the person with whom one empathizes complicates the simulationist claim about a phenomenal matching of affective states.

contextualized details that are reflected in narratives, which are stories about actions and interactions which are always situated. They tell us about people in specific situations, what they do, how they interact with others, and they sometimes indicate the motives people have for doing what they do. Through such narratives we gain interpretive insights into the actions of others. Through a diversity of narratives I can be open to the experience and the life of others, in *their* context, as I can understand it, rather than in terms of my own narrow experience. Narratives can also help to shape our sense of different possibilities (I'll return to this point in *Chapter 9*).

PART III
A Critical Turn

8

Recognition and Critical Interaction Theory

In this chapter I explore how we might move from considerations that focus on social-cognitive issues to understanding their implications for concepts that are basic to the development of a critical theory that addresses social and political issues—basic concepts of agency, autonomy, and recognition. Debates about the nature of social cognition, like the debates about embodied, enactive approaches to cognition, have stayed within the walls of philosophy of mind and cognitive science. However, if social interactions, involving not only primary and secondary intersubjectivity, but also communicative and narrative practices, play an essential role in understanding others and in the co-constitution of the shared lifeworld, and if some aspects of cognition and social cognition are constituted by processes that occur in the physical and social environment, including social, cultural, and institutional practices, then these debates hold some important implications for larger themes in the social and political realm.

It's notable that Colwyn Trevarthen has indicated numerous times that his distinction between primary and secondary intersubjectivity was motivated by a reading of Habermas (e.g., Trevarthen 2008, ix). One could argue that Axel Honneth (2008a, 2012), who makes reference to Trevarthen's distinction between primary and secondary intersubjectivity, has reincorporated this enriched account of intersubjectivity back into critical social theory. How the concept of primary intersubjectivity gets reappropriated, or indeed, re-cognized in Honneth's conception of recognition, however, is linked to questions not only about child development, but also to historical-philosophical issues about whether one should understand recognition in terms of a summons (*Aufforderung*), following Fichte, or in terms of a struggle, as Honneth, following Hegel, suggests, or in terms of a gift, as Ricoeur, following Hénaff suggests. I'll start with a brief tracing of the philosophical history of the concept of recognition, beginning with Fichte, and then follow a few twists and turns through Hegel, Honneth, and Ricoeur. This initial reading is organized around questions of development with respect to how recognition takes hold in life. I'll then look more closely at Honneth's analysis of recognition.

8.1 The Roots of Recognition

8.1.1 *The summons*

In his *Foundations of Natural Right* (1796) Fichte argues that mutual recognition (*Anerkennung*), as a relation between free rational beings, is a necessary condition for the possibility of each subject's self-consciousness and autonomy. In order for me to be a free agent—to be aware of my freedom and to act freely—I require being recognized as free by others and I must recognize others as free. The autonomy of an individual subject depends on an intersubjective mutual recognition, such that if we deny the freedom of others, we short-circuit our own agency. For Fichte (2000) an autonomous agent is a self-positing reflective self-conscious agent, and this gets expressed in the agent's rational deliberation about reasons for action. Not only is our agency limited by our capacity for self-reflection, but also our self-reflection is limited by the types of actions and interactions in which we can engage, and specifically by relations of intersubjective recognition.

Recognizing agents other than myself involves recognizing them as summoning me to self-conscious agency. The subject is determined as "self-determining" through "a summons [*eine Aufforderung*] to the subject, calling upon it to resolve to exercise its efficacy" (Fichte 2000, 31). The other person summons me to action, or to refrain from action, in what Stephen Darwall (2005) suggests is a second-personal address. Michael Nance describes it as follows:

When someone makes such a demand on us, it occurs to us that we may choose how to act on the basis of reasons. It is up to us to conform to the summons or not, and just this realization is the first moment of awareness of oneself as an agent. An experience of such a summons is a necessary condition for the I to posit itself as an agent; it is no coincidence that Fichte uses the term *Erziehung* ("upbringing" or "education") to describe the process of summoning at the level of ordinary experience. (2015, 612)

The notion of *Erziehung* introduces the idea that the summons and mutual recognition take time to emerge over a course of development and upbringing. According to Fichte, the agent cannot assume the existence of other agents "without positing itself as standing with those beings in a particular relation, called a relation of right [*Rechtsverhältnis*]" (2000, 39), which just is a developing relation of mutual—i.e., reciprocal—recognition. Thus the relation of free beings to one another is a relation of reciprocal interaction that takes place through a developing intelligence and freedom. One cannot come to recognize the other if the recognition is not mutual; and one cannot treat the other as a free agent, if both, the one and the other, do not mutually treat each other as free (Fichte 2000, 42).

If we ask how mutual recognition gets off the ground, for Fichte the notion of the summons appears to be central. Do I come to recognize the other's autonomy and my own autonomy through the other's summons directed at me, or do I first have to recognize their autonomy for the summons to count as significant? To avoid a problematic circularity here, Nance (2016), following Siep (1979), suggests that the summons is a "one-sided recognition" that transitions us into mutual recognition.

Mutual recognition is not presupposed by the summons; rather the summons, which is by definition a recognition of me as an agent, is the initiation of my own reflective self-consciousness of that agency, and my reflective consciousness of the other as an agent. Franks (2005) argues that this emergence of mutual recognition is a natural event that happens automatically and regardless of any practical response that I make (to answer or to ignore the summons). Recognition gains a normative purchase only later in development in socio-political or legal contexts. As Nance

(2015, 612) points out, however, this interpretation draws a distinction that Fichte doesn't make—namely, between the analysis of a natural recognition as a summons, which "turns out to have more to do with child development and up-bringing (*Erziehung*) than with rightful political relations," and a normative recognition that is part of a theory of right.

In light of Fichte's analysis of recognition, I want to emphasize four strongly connected points that I think are important for any theory of recognition, regardless of the debates about how to interpret Fichte, although these points are clearly consistent with Nance's interpretation.

(1) the notion of the summons is central to the emergence of mutual recognition;
(2) this emergence concerns child development and upbringing;
(3) to the extent that autonomy emerges in such intersubjective relations, autonomy is relational; and
(4) it is achieved in a gradual way.

On this last point, Nance (2015, 622) explains: "the extent [or degree] to which one engages in relations of reciprocal recognition with other free agents determines the extent to which one can be free oneself."

8.1.2 *The struggle*

Although Hegel was critical of Fichte for providing only a formal approach to natural law, Hegel, as Honneth points out, found Fichte's concept of recognition to be a model for thinking about "the internal structure of those forms of ethical relations that he wished to presuppose as a fundamental first of human socialization" (1995, 167). As Honneth suggests, however, there is a contrast between Fichte's analysis of recognition in *The Foundations of Natural Law*, with its transcendental and formal start, including its application to legal relations, and Hegel's analysis, which introduces psychological considerations and opens up multiple dimensions. Hegel is concerned to understand a "practical intersubjectivity in which the movement of recognition guarantees the complementary agreement and thus the necessary mutuality of opposed subjects" (Honneth 1995, 16). Thus, in Hegel, Honneth argues:

Within the framework of an ethically established relationship of mutual recognition, subjects are always learning something more about their particular identity, and since, in each case, it is a new dimension of their selves that they see confirmed thereby, they must once again leave, by means of conflict, the stage of ethical life they have reached, in order to achieve the recognition of a more demanding form of their individuality. (Honneth 1995, 17)

In contrast to Fichte's account in which mutual recognition may gradually, and perhaps even automatically, emerge from the other's summoning, for Hegel there is a conflict or tension that involves a struggle for recognition constrained by the particularity of the subject's distinctive identity. The struggle, as Honneth indicates, also implies a constant transcendence or movement and reconciliation with the other.

According to Honneth, Hegel thus uses "a theory of conflict to make Fichte's model of recognition more dynamic. Hegel gains not only the possibility of providing a first determination of the inner potential of human ethical life but also the opportunity to make its 'negative' course of development more concrete" (1995, 17). The struggle is not the Hobbesian struggle for self-preservation within a state of nature, but already a struggle that involves ethical and psychological identity (Taminiaux 1985). Hegel's most famous analysis is found in his master–slave dialectic in the *Phenomenology*. Hegel shows that when intersubjective interaction involving two-way reciprocal relations is eliminated, as in slavery, even a one-way recognition is undermined; this is destructive not only for the victim, but also self-destructive for the victimizer. In denying the autonomy of the slave, the autonomy of the master is compromised because the master refuses to recognize the other, the slave, as an autonomous subject. The slave, who is treated as a reified object and denied status as a subject, is then in no position to recognize the master's status as master; that status depends, as such, on just that possibility of recognition.

For Honneth, denials of recognition can be just as real in our everyday lives, in our relations with others, as well as in reifying bureaucratic, administrative, and institutional arrangements that are externally imposed, deliberately or not. Such arrangements are reflected in just those cases where, as Honneth puts it, social relationships give way to a "climate of cold, calculating purposefulness" where an artisan's care for her creations gives way "to an attitude of mere instrumental command; and even the subject's innermost experiences [seem] to be infused with the icy breath of calculating compliance" (2008a, 17). For Honneth, cases of reification are social pathologies because they freeze or at least distort social interactions and rob individuals of autonomy.

The origins of recognition and its pathologies, for Honneth, and for Hegel too, can be traced back to the early development of first relations.

Hegel initially describes the process by which the first social relations are established in terms of the release of subjects from their natural determinations. This growth of "individuality" occurs in two stages of mutual recognition, which differ from each other in the dimensions of personal identity that receive practical confirmation. In the relationship between "parents and children"... subjects recognize each other reciprocally as living, emotionally needy beings. Here the component of individual personality recognized by others is "practical feeling", that is the dependence of individuals on vitally essential care and goods. The "labour" of raising children... is directed towards the formation of the child's "inner negativity" and independence, so that, as a result, "the unification of feeling" must be "superseded". Hegel then follows this (now superseded) form of recognition with a second stage, still under the heading "natural ethical life", of contractually regulated relations of exchange among property owners.

(Honneth 1995, 19)

What is important, for both Hegel and Honneth, is the transition from "the practical relations to the world that subjects had in the first stage" to a "second stage" as a realm of universal (less particularistic) legal relations. Honneth dwells on the first stage more than Hegel does. He also enriches his analysis with insights from George Herbert Mead's social psychology, and he makes reference to developmental psychology, including the work of Trevarthen, to gain some empirical ground. Furthermore, he links the analysis of the transition from the first stage to the second, through Donald Winnicott's psychoanalytic approach.

I'll argue in the next section (8.2) that Honneth's account of recognition starts too late in the developmental story; that is, it starts with joint attention and secondary intersubjectivity, which suggests that he discounts the role of the embodied dynamics of social interaction that begins in primary intersubjectivity.[1] This happens, I'll argue here, because of the way that he characterizes primary intersubjectivity.

As characterized in previous chapters, following Trevarthen, primary intersub-jectivity includes unmediated sensory-motor and emotional aspects of behavior and basic activities that are apparent from the very beginning of postnatal life. Infants enter into embodied and affective interactions with their caregivers, responding to movements, gestures, facial expressions, etc., that they not only directly perceive but to which they also enactively respond in dynamic ways. Honneth conceives of primary intersubjectivity differently. First of all, he characterizes it as a stage through which an infant passes. In contrast, according to interaction theory, it's not a passing stage since primary intersubjectivity continues to characterize human interaction throughout the lifespan. One does not transition out of primary intersubjectivity into secondary intersubjectivity; rather, secondary intersubjectivity builds upon primary intersubjectivity. Secondary intersubjectivity includes joint attention and joint action with others in pragmatic and social contexts that involve reference to a common world. Whereas primary intersubjectivity is paradigmatically dyadic (self-other), secondary intersubjectivity is triadic (self-other-world). It involves precisely what Honneth calls "the practical relations to the world" that emerge sometime during the first year of life and are found typically in joint-attentional contexts where the infant perceives and starts to understand the world and the various objects in its environ-ment through the behavior and actions of others.

Honneth changes his account a number of times across his developing and complex theory of recognition. In his book *Struggle for Recognition*, for example, as cited above, what he identifies as the "first stage" seems to be described in terms that fit secondary intersubjectivity. In later works, however, he recognizes primary inter-subjectivity as a prior stage of emotional attachment, but takes it to be a necessary antecedent to recognition, a stage on the path to what he takes to be primary in recognition—the disclosure of a world: "it is through this emotional attachment to a 'concrete other' that a world of meaningful qualities is disclosed to a child as a world in which it must involve itself practically" (2008a, 45). Even in these later works, then, there is a consistent downplaying of primary intersubjectivity insofar as he equates it with a specific conception of emotional attachment as a form of undifferentiated identity.

[T]he individual's learning process functions in such a way that a small child first of all identifies with its figures of attachment and must have emotionally recognized them before it can arrive at knowledge of objective reality by means of these other perspectives.   (2008a, 46)

One possible reading of this is that Honneth distinguishes between emotional attachment (which he equates to primary intersubjectivity), emotional recognition

---

[1] My disagreement with Honneth concerns his starting point, and, of course, the effect of that start on the rest of his analysis. There have been other criticisms of Honneth that also complain about his starting assumptions, although with reference to the end point. Thus, as Martin Jay explains, Alexander Garcia Düttmann contends that "Honneth rigs the outcome of the struggle for recognition in advance by positing an ideologically idealized norm of anticipated and desirable reconciliation" (Jay 2008, 10; see Düttmann 2000, 156). Likewise, Italo Testo (2012) suggests that Honneth overlooks Hegel's conception of natural recognition developed in his Jena writings. Also see Deranty (2005).

(as a transition to secondary intersubjectivity), and knowledge of objective reality (based on secondary intersubjective relations). Furthermore, he focuses his analysis on the status of the self or self-relation, more so than on social interaction per se—specifically, he distinguishes in recognition aspects that involve self-confidence, self-respect, and self-esteem (Honneth 1995, 131; see Honneth 1998, 2007, 2008a; also see Varga & Gallagher 2012).

Here I want to focus on a second aspect of Honneth's characterization of primary intersubjectivity, and how this plays into the notion that there is a struggle for recognition. Honneth's analysis of this struggle takes over a concept from Winnicott. Specifically, not only is primary intersubjectivity a stage that we move beyond, but also Honneth associates primary intersubjectivity with the classic psychoanalytic notion of undifferentiated oneness, which he finds in Winnicott: "One can plausibly assume that every human life begins with a phase of undifferentiated intersubjectivity, that is, of symbiosis" (Honneth 1995, 98; emphasis added; see Winnicott 1989).

This initially experienced behavior unit, for which "primary intersubjectivity" has established itself, raises the central question that occupied Winnicott during his life: how are we to conceive of the interactional process by which "mother" and child are able to detach themselves from a state of undifferentiated oneness in such a way that, in the end, they learn to accept and love each other as independent persons? ... Since both subjects are initially included in the state of symbiotic oneness in virtue of their active accomplishments, they must, as it were, learn from each other how to differentiate. (Honneth 1995, 98–9)

On this view, in primary intersubjectivity, mother and child "are incapable of individually demarcating themselves from each other"—or, at least, during "the first months of life, the child is incapable of differentiating between self and environment" (Honneth 1995, 99). Indeed, there is some indication that Honneth does not take primary intersubjectivity to be a form of *inter*-subjectivity at all. "It is true that infants' early experiences of fusion [*Verschmelzung*] do not have an intersubjective structure owing to the fact that they lack a sufficiently differentiated partner with whom a relationship would need to be formed; but paradoxically, we can only grasp this early state by employing the concept of primary intersubjectivity" (2012, 229). For Honneth it is paradoxical to call it primary "intersubjectivity" precisely because, on Winnicott's view, it is not intersubjective. Moreover, Honneth again characterizes this "phase" as something that the child gets over—something that finally comes to an end when the child gains the capacity for "cognitive differentiation between self and environment" at around 6 months of age (Honneth 1995, 100). At this point there begins a transition to secondary intersubjectivity.

Accordingly, there is a clear contrast between Honneth's view of primary and secondary intersubjectivity and these concepts as they are found in Trevarthen, and interaction theory more generally (see Meehan 2011; Varga & Gallagher 2012). First, as Trevarthen construes it, even in primary intersubjectivity there is a very basic self-other differentiation, and that's the only way there can be genuine interaction between mother and child. Interaction, per se, depends on differentiation. This self/non-self differentiation, understood in its most minimal terms, can be found in non-human animals, and in the human fetus (Castiello et al. 2010), because it is built into bodily movement—specifically the proprioceptive and efferent differences between being moved and moving oneself – self or autonomous movement. It's also built into touch, so that the sensory-motor system of the infant can register the difference between someone else's hand touching its face (eliciting the rooting reflex) and its own hand touching its face (no rooting reflex) (Rochat & Hespos 1997). Thus, we also find characteristics of primary intersubjectivity in, for example, the specific reversibility implicit in one's vocal utterance,[2] in turn-taking in proto-conversation, and differential kinematic responses to self versus non-self (Reddy 2008). Second, as already indicated, the embodied (sensory-motor) processes of primary intersubjectivity do not constitute a phase or stage that a human goes through and leaves behind; they continue as an important part of social interaction throughout one's lifetime.

Honneth's Winnicottian interpretation of primary intersubjectivity, which fails to acknowledge the embodied dynamics of dyadic intersubjective interaction, supports his conception of recognition as involving a struggle. Recognition is accomplished only after struggling through the phase of undifferentiation; that is, only as the child gets beyond the indistinguishability between self and other. This is precisely the most basic idea of the struggle for recognition (Honneth 1995, 101). Recognition is accomplished in transition from undifferentiated fusion to secondary intersubjectivity, which, for the infant, is a struggle for independence—an independence from undifferentiated unity and an establishment of an identity differentiated from the other. In later works, to be sure, Honneth (2012, 222) revises his view of undifferentiated oneness, citing Stern's view of the empirical evidence. He qualifies the notion of infantile fusion, claiming that it is not absolute, and there are always moments when differentiation breaks through (2012, 226). Nonetheless he retains the idea that recognition begins in the child's struggling transition out of primary intersubjectivity, taken as an undifferentiated state of existence. There is also good reason to think that Honneth gives up the idea that primary intersubjectivity (understood as fusion) is a stage that one transcends once and for all, since Honneth proposes to extend Winnicott's concept as a model for the intersubjectivity of groups (2012, 210). In certain aspects of group behavior, we seemingly fall back into the fusion of childhood experiences: "the intersubjective life of the group is generally marked by regularly occurring, episodic states that lead to a more or less intense fusion between the group members.... [Accordingly] intersubjective life in the group will constantly be marked by tendencies towards fusion" (2012, 210–11).

Honneth thus further advances his interpretation of Hegel by making the intersubjective aspect more apparent and by his continued appeal to Winnicott (e.g., Honneth 2012, 13ff). Indeed, this carries over into his account of more complex forms of recognition involved in institutions, for example. If institutions were simply externalizations or extensions of my individual mind (in Hegel's terms,

---

[2] In Hegel too one finds an emphasis placed on proprioception and communication, including the idea that the voice has a kind of reversibility (in the sense indicated by Merleau-Ponty) where it is both felt internally and experienced as an objective/external auditory expression that is communicative. "The individual becomes as such immediately another to itself, and what it becomes, its simple voice, breaks itself [into two]: it hears what it says; the voice reflects itself in itself insofar as it realizes itself in another" (Hegel 1975, fragment 13, 239, and 239n, translated in Testa [2012, 186–7]). Honneth finds this thought in Herder and Gehlen, as well as Mead (Honneth 1995, 73–4).

manifestations of objective spirit), the only problems we might run into would be cases that involve self-deceit or self-contradiction. But what we find are differentiated responses to our actions from others. Winnicott shows this to be the case even in early development. He shows that the mother or other caregiver will respond to the infant's actions, sometimes by showing understanding, other times by showing disapproval or indifference. The infant learns that the other's response will depend not entirely on what the infant will do, but on the other's own intentionality, situation, or emotional state. Honneth suggests that this motivates a transition from desire to recognition, which incorporates a reciprocity, which in Hegel's terms involves negativity or a restriction. "In the encounter between two subjects, a new sphere of action is opened in the sense that both sides are compelled to restrict their self-seeking drives as soon as they encounter each other.... [I]n the process of interaction both subjects undergo a transformation" (2012, 15). As Honneth notes, Hegel calls this "recognition," "the reciprocal limitation of one's own egocentric desires for the benefit of the other" (2012, 17).

8.1.3 The gift

Paul Ricoeur, in his book *The Course of Recognition*, draws on both Jacques Taminiaux and Honneth: specifically, Taminiaux's commentaries on Hegel's Jena writings, and the historical summary in Honneth's *Struggle for Recognition*, devoted to the "systematic reactualization" of themes dealt with by Taminiaux.[3] There is a complex history here.

In his work on Hannah Arendt, Taminiaux offers a critique of the later Sartre's notion of recognition. Sartre's concept of *praxis* is, Taminiaux claims, modeled on *poiêsis*, and accordingly is thoroughly modern (i.e., non-Greek). This is Sartre's "idea that the total unbridling of laboring activity and the production of abundance in consumer goods would lead to a properly human interaction" (Taminiaux 1997, 55). When scarcity is removed, we gain autonomy and become "the author of our history to the same extent that the maker is the lucid master of the work." Yet, in *poiêsis*, plurality is not essential, and this determines Sartre's concept of recognition. As Sartre suggests: in recognizing the other, plurality is inessential and "the unity of praxes as such is what is Essential" (Sartre 1976, 131). Taminiaux, in effect, rejects a concept of recognition that either diminishes the individual (the *sine qua non* of an intersubjectivity that would issue in some form of autonomy) or reduces it to a form of economic sameness (where *praxis* is reduced to *poiêsis*), or social fusion. In agreement with Arendt, Taminiaux emphasizes that *philia*, as well as other social and political phenomena of plurality, are agonistic—nothing near a fusion or full harmony (Taminiaux 1997, 177). He favors a view of human affairs as "an adventure experienced by humans in their interaction" rather than "a fabrication process carried out by a single one" (Taminiaux 1997, 55).

This adventure is not necessarily a *struggle* for recognition, even if there are agonistic features involved. Ricoeur (2005) finds inspiration here in Taminiaux, as

---

[3] Ricoeur (2005, 174). Marcelo points out that the attentiveness with which Ricoeur read these two authors "is proven by the personal copies of the books we can find at his library, now at the *Fonds* Ricoeur. They are heavily underlined and commented on the margins" (Marcelo 2011, 117).

well as in the Greeks, and in Hannah Arendt's notion of pardon and reparation. Arendt sees the possibility of an intersubjective plurality that is never fusion or undifferentiated unity, or an identity that either motivates struggle or resolves struggle. This is in contrast, not only to the later Sartre but also to Hegel who describes "[t]he reconciling 'Yes' in which the two I's renounce their exclusive and opposing existence as an existence of the I which has been expanded into a duality, and therein remains identical with itself" (Hegel 1997, 409). In contrast to any such fusion, for Arendt, forgivenness/releasement, the "remedy against the irreversibility and unpredictability of...action," allows for reconciliation—but this is possible only in conditions of sustained intersubjective plurality, since it depends "on plurality, on the presence and acting of others, for no one can forgive himself...." (Arendt 1958, 237; see Williams 1992, 208 ff., for discussion on this point).

Ricoeur thus brings us back to the Fichtean concept that autonomy is not only relational, but also a matter of degree. A finalized or complete mutual recognition is never entirely possible. Accordingly, the self-recognition that Fichte makes central for autonomy "requires at each step, the help of others, in the absence of that mutual, fully reciprocal recognition that will make each of those involved a 'recognized being'" (Ricoeur 2005, 69). Ricoeur here rejects the concept of the struggle of recognition because it leads to unending demands for recognition; he questions "the importance of the idea of struggle at each stage along the way" because it leads to a "bad infinity" (Ricoeur 2005, 216, 218).

The thesis I want to argue for can be summed up as follows: The alternative to the idea of struggle in the process of mutual recognition is to be sought in peaceful experiences of mutual recognition, based on symbolic mediations as exempt from the juridical as from the commercial order of exchange. (Ricoeur 2005, 219)

Ricoeur, in contrast to Hegel and Honneth, and building on notions of *philia* (Taminiaux) and forgiveness (Arendt), prefers the model of the gift, as he finds it developed in Marcel Hénaff, which, in other terms, is not the model of justice, but of *agapê*, where one gives or bestows recognition without the demand for recognition in return.

But do we have to go so far as to believe in or hope for *agapê* in order to find a model for a workable interaction? I think not. Williams (2008) and Marcelo (2011), for example, suggest that Ricoeur's "interpretation of recognition as gift-exchange is strikingly similar to Fichte's *Aufforderung*." Marcelo continues: "This interpretation is not without merit, because this notion of 'summons' in Fichte indeed assumes the character of an injunction that invites the other to respond but does not necessarily force a response" (Marcelo 2011, 116; see Williams 2008).

A gift, as Ricoeur characterizes it in agreement with Hénaff, is "without price" (2005, 235). Alternatively, I want to suggest that we can cash out the notion of *Aufforderung* in the relatively affordable terms of primary intersubjectivity properly conceived—that is, interpreted not as undifferentiated unity (on the Winnicott-Honneth reading), but according to Trevarthen's conception which involves self-other differentiation. This nonetheless seems consistent with Ricoeur since, as Marcelo (2011, 116) notes, for Ricoeur mutuality never involves a state of fusion.

More than this, primary intersubjectivity gives us the four points that we found in Fichte's notion of summons:

(1) Primary intersubjectivity is central to the emergence of mutual recognition. It does not presuppose mutual recognition; it begins with an initial response to the other that is immediately (and in some cases automatically[4]) met with another response that moves gradually to the possibility of mutual recognition.

(2) Although primary intersubjectivity operates in our social interactions throughout our lifetime, this response is found first in infancy and is the driving force in development.

(3) The autonomy that emerges in such intersubjective relations is relational (see *Section 8.3*).

(4) And it is achieved in a gradual way. Clearly, in early development the infant is not independent in any real sense; but this changes only through interactions with others that allow the infant to develop independence—not as an escape from an undifferentiated unity, but as something that develops only within an interdependence with others. A caregiver is, in principle, just that—someone who gives care and nurturing which in turn allows for the gradual achievement of autonomy that continues to require others to be sustained.

What we get in primary intersubjectivity is not a model of perfectly reciprocal recognition achieved by some dialectical struggle that leads beyond an imagined indifferentiation towards well-defined individuality (defined well, perhaps, in dimensions of self-confidence, self-respect and self-esteem, as Honneth would have it), and then onward to a utopian politico-economic justice. Rather, with primary intersubjectivity, we get a way of finding ourselves where we are, summoned to interact with one another in imperfect relations that sometimes require giving recognition and sometimes require receiving forgiveness, and sometimes just living with the fact that there can be no repayment. Not a bad infinity that demands something we cannot give; but perhaps a good infinity of a continuous response to others.

8.2 Recognition Redux

Critical theorists have recently returned to the idea that recognition is an important principle in regard to how we live our everyday lives, as well as in regard to philosophical questions of justice. Axel Honneth especially makes this a central theme of his work. As we've seen, Honneth, as in almost all contemporary discussions of this concept, takes his bearings from Hegel's discussion of recognition in the *Phenomenology of Spirit*, along with references to his early Jena manuscripts and his

---

[4] As we've seen (*Chapter 5*) according to some explanations primary intersubjectivity is hardwired in the activation of mirror neurons, so that a basic motor resonance or a basic empathy is automatic. I've suggested that for the young infant, whether or not the response is spontaneous or automatic, it involves a process that draws the infant into what eventually becomes full-fledged intersubjective interaction. As Reddy (2015) suggests, as the infant develops, she (the infant) comes to recognize the other's response as a response to (or recognition of) her.

late *Philosophy of Right*. What Hegel shows is that when intersubjective interaction is eliminated or compromised (as in slavery), recognition and autonomy are too. One can see the connection between interaction and autonomy in the definition of interaction provided in *Chapter 5*.

> Interaction: a mutually engaged co-regulated coupling between at least two autonomous agents, where (a) the co-regulation and the coupling mutually affect each other, and constitute a self-sustaining organization in the domain of relational dynamics, and (b) the autonomy of the agents involved is not destroyed, although its scope may be augmented or reduced.
>
> (See De Jaegher et al. 2010)

In the case of slavery, the social institution not only distorts interaction, but also undermines it since it does not allow for co-regulation; both recognition and autonomy are compromised on both sides of the relation.

To get a sense of the depth of the affective significance of the elimination or disruption of social interaction, one need not go back to Hegel, or the extreme example of slavery. Rather, we can get a good sense of it in an experiment conducted by Murray and Trevarthen (1985, mentioned above in *Section 5.2*). They show the importance of live interaction between caregivers (in this case, mothers) and 2-month-old infants in a "double TV monitor experiment" in which mother and infant interact by means of a two-way live video link. Despite the intervention of the communicative technology, the infant and mother engage in lively interaction in this situation similar to when the mother and child are in non-mediated contact. When presented with a recorded rerun of their mother's actions, however, the infant quickly disengages and becomes distracted and noticeably upset. This change in behavior occurs despite the fact that the visual stimulation has remained precisely the same as what the child had seen during the live action. What's missing is the dynamical contingency of interaction, and the child notices it almost immediately. The experiment indicates that agents, even very young infants, are not primarily passive observers or mindreaders, but that they actively (enactively) engage with others. The infant responds not just to the mother's expressive behavior (which appears in both the live circumstance and the recorded replay), but also to the fact that the mother's movements are contingent on the infant's own movements—that is, the infant responds to the dynamics of the interaction.

This is an instance of primary intersubjectivity. During live interaction the infant is enactively coupled to the mother. The idea of enactive coupling means, in this context, that (1) it is a dynamical process (i.e., one in which a co-dependent reciprocal causality is established between the coupled systems such that what happens in or to one system is partly dependent on the situation of the other); (2) the recurrent engagement with the other person leads to a structural congruence between self and other (Thompson 2007, 45); and (3) that the engaging agents maintain their autonomy (their own internal self-organization).[5] Accordingly, although one can still talk of individuals who engage in the interaction, a full account of such interaction is not reducible to mechanisms at work in the individuals *qua* individuals.

---

[5] For a more formal account of dynamical coupling, see Di Paolo and De Jaegher (2012, 163).

The lack of interaction dynamics between infant and the videotaped mother registers, in the infant, as a lack of recognition of the infant by the mother, and causes emotional consternation. Just as in Hegel's master–slave dialectic, the failure of the "external" relation translates immediately into "internal" decline. "External" and "internal" are here abstractions from what turns out to be a failure of dynamical coupling at the level of the intersubjective system that would typically be constituted by the interaction.

As reflected in the definition of interaction, in interactional dynamics recognition depends on autonomy and is undermined by reification; that is, treating the other as an object observed from a third-person perspective. At the same time, individual autonomy diminishes without social interaction; and interaction doesn't exist if the autonomy of any of the participants is denied. Interaction, autonomy, and recognition dissipate in cases of slavery, torture, or terrorism.[6]

It is also important to note that interaction has its own autonomy. On enactivist versions of social interaction, the *autonomy of interaction* means that, for example, in a dyadic relation of two dynamical systems (two individuals), a new dynamical system is formed. New processes emerge from the interaction and constitute meaning that is irreducible to the sum of individual actions. Complex coordination patterns that result from the mutual interaction of a social encounter, as such, are not simply inputs to individual mechanisms. Such coordination processes can acquire a momentum of their own and can pull participants into further or continuing interaction. Interaction in intersubjective contexts goes beyond each participant; it results in something (the creation of meaning or an autonomous level of organization) that, at the level of the relational dynamics, goes beyond what each individual qua individual—that is, on their own—can bring to the process.[7]

I'll argue below that the autonomy of the individual within such interactions depends on the autonomy of interaction—that is, to the extent that the individual can participate in the autonomy of interaction, there is the possibility of an increase or decrease of his or her autonomy, depending on the nature of the interaction. Individual autonomy varies, positively or negatively, in relation to the individual's positive or negative interactions.

Slavery and terrorism, reification and the denial of autonomy, are real enough at the political level of nations and subnational groups, but they can be just as real in our everyday lives, in our relations with others, as well as in the externally imposed bureaucratic, administrative, and institutional pathologies that Honneth points to as involving "cold" and "calculating compliance" (2008a, 17). Reified and pre-packaged ways of interacting lack dynamic spontaneity, impose a mechanistic order, and can undermine the autonomous processes implicit in genuine forms of interaction; accordingly, they also distort intersubjective understanding. Mild forms of this can be found in everyday practice. Sometimes reification is reflected in simple things,

---

[6] On one account, terrorism involves the closing down of any possible response from the victim(s) (see Lyotard 1984). But see Erlenbusch-Anderson (2018, Ch. 1) for difficulties in defining terrorism.

[7] See De Jaegher et al. 2010. As Di Paolo, Rohde, and Iizuka (2008, 279) put it, "interaction can dynamically create phenomena that do not directly result from the individual capacities or behaviors of any of the partners if investigated on their own."

such as established hierarchical seating arrangements or meeting protocols, and other times, perhaps when electronic communication on social media is substituted for face-to-face interaction.

This critical interpretation, of course, can be overplayed. One might feel liberated by the possibilities of electronic communication, which can be spontaneous and thoughtful. Moreover, it is sometimes possible to break through dehumanizing bureaucratic arrangements, to meet and to recognize each other as humans and not just as cogs in a mechanistic system. Yet, to be sure, abusive relationships still exist, slavery still exists, as do various scales of torture and political terrorism. Many of these cases require a form of intervention or action that goes beyond communicative action in order to re-establish humane forms of social interaction.

A lack of interaction does not necessarily entail reification. There are situations in which recognition, and even mutual recognition, may be possible without interaction. A recognizes B, but leaves well enough alone and keeps a safe distance. Is there a difference between this divorced or detached recognition and a recognition that is intrinsic to interaction itself? Honneth (2008a, 24) describes a change of perspective from empathic engagement to detached observation. The latter tends toward a reification of others and can be found in attitudes that commodify relationships and in what Lyotard (1984) called the attitude of performativity. Honneth, however, suggests that the detached, observational relation may in fact be a necessary strategic stance required in developed societies to deal with some aspects of the business of everyday life. This kind of detached stance may have a "perfectly legitimate place" in some situations (2008a, 28). The question, then, is whether there is a form of recognition appropriate to this kind of stance, something that saves it from falling into a reifying attitude. If there is, it could be only a formal and empty kind of interaction-impoverished recognition—*détente*—something that maintains the peace, perhaps, but does not promote or support interaction.

This realization, or something like it, motivates Honneth to turn to a pragmatism that emphasizes engaged action. In effect, all of our relations cannot be of the strategic observational kind since our primary stance toward the world is to deal with it in a pragmatic, hands-on way, "from the perspective of the participant," rather than the distant observer.[8] Honneth, however, immediately puts this in terms that come close to a simulation theory of social cognition, referring to it in György Lukács's terms of "empathetic engagement."

In other words, human subjects normally participate in social life by placing themselves in the position of their counterparts, whose desires, dispositions, and thoughts they have learned to understand as the motives for the latter's actions. If, conversely, a subject fails to take over the perspective of another person and thereby takes up a merely detached, contemplative [theoretical] stance toward the other, then the bond of human interaction will be broken, for it will no longer be maintained by their reciprocal understanding of each other's reasons for acting. The elements characterizing the so-called participant's perspective thus consist of the act of taking over the perspective of another person and the resulting understanding of the other's reasons for acting. (Honneth 2008a, 34)

---

[8] Honneth (2008a, 34); making reference to Habermas (1979).

In this text, at least, Honneth seemingly favors ST (putting oneself in the other's place) over TT (taking a theoretical stance) as a model of mindreading mental states (desires, motives, reasons for acting). Tellingly, Honneth, even as he retains the phrase "empathetic engagement," also recognizes something problematic with the emphasis on attempting to understand the other in terms of motives and reasons. Here Honneth engages with Dewey's pragmatic view: the idea that our "understanding of the world is always already bound up with a holistic form of experience, in which all elements of a given situation are qualitatively disclosed from a perspective of engaged involvement" (Honneth 2008a, 36).

I note as a matter of terminology, however, that Dewey (1958) uses the term "interaction" to signify something broader than social or intersubjective engagement. For Dewey, following a broadly understood sense of the term, we interact with things as well as with people. Honneth moves us away from this word by substituting the word "recognition" directly for Dewey's term "interaction" (Honneth 2008a, 36). Yet to the extent that he retains Dewey's concept, "recognition" seemingly signifies something different from just the dynamics of social interaction; it involves engagement with the world, empathetic engagement with both things and people.[9] I'm focusing on these twists and turns in Honneth's texts and terminology primarily to indicate some obstacles to avoid in working out the right concept of recognition. There are three of them here, two of which I've already mentioned.

First, on one reading, recognition seemingly applies equally to things and to other persons; there seems to be no distinction between an engaged involvement with things and one's engaged, two-way interaction with others. It's not clear that Honneth makes that distinction strong enough. To be sure, recognition as it applies to things in our natural surroundings is, for him, derivative from our recognition of others. It involves the transfer of value that others place on things, to the things themselves (2008a, 63). Although such relations with things may be important in many ways (see, e.g., Malafouris 2013), and may be involved in processes of secondary intersubjectivity—including joint attention and joint action (Gallagher & Ransom 2016)—it is also important to note that our relations with others are essentially different from our relations with objects. Accordingly, on a terminological level it would be beneficial to reserve the terms "recognition" and "interaction" for the intersubjective. I believe this is more consistent with the philosophical tradition from Hegel to Levinas (see below).

---

[9] This is reinforced to the extent that Honneth (2008a, 38) ties the concept of recognition closely to Dewey's concept of "practical involvement" but also Heidegger's notion of "care," which Honneth interprets in terms of *Zuhanden*, practical or instrumental involvement, and Lukács's "engaged praxis." I'm emphasizing here the connection between Honneth's term "recognition" and a pragmatic or instrumental attitude. On a related point, there are other more blatant terminological difficulties with the word "recognition." In English (and in the French *reconnaissance*) it clearly has cognitive associations (e.g., with memory), both in etymology and in its use in experimental psychology. The German word *Anerkennung* involves identification as a form of knowledge, and being able to label something. Ricoeur (2005, 23) looks closely at the lexicon to discover all relevant meanings of *reconnaissance*, and he cites the Robert dictionary first of all: "To grasp (an object) with the mind, through thought, in joining together images, perceptions having to do with it; to distinguish or identify the judgment or action, know it by memory." Both Honneth and Ricoeur want to break free of this overly intellectualist connotation of "recognition"—but it's not clear they are successful in this regard.

This first point may be more than just terminological, however. There is a current debate within critical theory concerning whether and how one's intentionality with respect to self, to another person, and to thing (world), respectively, is the same or different or in some regard related (Varga 2010). Let's note three aspects of this debate:

(1) The intentionality at stake involves, at the extremes, recognition and reification, where these are taken in some sense as opposites.
(2) Most of the debate focuses on the question of whether self-consciousness and intersubjectivity are intricately related (whether one has a priority over the other, or can be thought to be equally primordial), and whether the relations are necessary or simply empirical.
(3) One common strategy is to distinguish a primordial (pre-linguistic) intentionality from a more developed (linguistic) form.

Although, as we noted, Honneth (2008a), following Dewey, does not make a strong distinction between recognition of the other person and a pragmatic engagement with worldly things, he criticizes Lukács's failure to distinguish between different forms of reification, and claims that there is no necessary connection between reification of self, other persons, and things. Whether there might be an empirical connection is left an open question. Still, Honneth qualifies this claim by asserting a necessary connection running from the reification of the world to the reification of others, since, "reification of the objective world . . . must be understood as a mere derivative of the forgetfulness of our recognition of other humans" (2008a, 77). This latter idea seems consistent with the idea that recognition of the world is derivative from our recognition of others.[10]

The second obstacle involves taking a simulationist view. To emphasize the role of interaction, especially with respect to primary intersubjectivity, it will be best not to confound it with a simulationist view of "taking over the perspective of the other" if that is understood to be a form of mindreading. Here Honneth (2008a, 41) is right to reject the idea that recognition is simply a matter of taking a stance that searches for motives and reasons (mental states) in the minds of others. There is, of course, a role for perspective taking; namely, in the service of understanding the surrounding world. Here Honneth appeals to developmental psychology and the "triangulation" of joint attention that begins around 9 months of age, and he rightly emphasizes the emotional aspects involved: "emotional identification with others is absolutely necessary in order to enable the taking over of another person's perspective, which in turn leads to the development of the capacity for symbolic thought" (2008a, 42). This is, at best, secondary intersubjectivity, specifically to the extent that it serves to understand the other person's actions in terms of their relations to things.

---

[10] Somogy Varga, commenting on Honneth's criticism of Lukács, proposes to move back to Lukács's idea of an essential or necessary connection between different modes of reification, although he brackets the difference between a necessary and merely empirical connection, and he focuses on an example involving self and other people. "Does for example the reificatory objectifying treatment of others not necessarily involve some objectifying stance toward oneself?" (Varga 2010, 23). He cites the example of racism as involving denigration or reification of the racist as much as of the other person.

This, however, is a third problem that we find with Honneth's conception of recognition, at least in some of his texts. It starts too late: "The starting point of these investigations consists in the same transition from primary to secondary intersubjectivity that the cognitivist approaches also have in mind"—that is, it starts with joint attention and secondary intersubjectivity (2008a, 43). In doing so it overlooks, or at least discounts, the embodied dynamics of social interaction that begin in primary intersubjectivity. At best, and with respect to the emotional attachment found there, Honneth points to primary intersubjectivity as a necessary antecedent to recognition. Again, to raise the right question here, we need to keep in mind that the processes of primary intersubjectivity are not only descriptive of early infancy, or antecedent to a more cognitive stance, but continue to characterize social cognition and are sustained throughout the lifespan.

To summarize, Honneth, in attempting to identify the most basic form of human relationship, which he calls "recognition," does not sufficiently or clearly distinguish this relationship as uniquely or specifically intersubjective. He characterizes (or comes close to characterizing) the social-cognitive relationship at least in some regard as a form of simulation; and he starts at a developmental point too late to acknowledge the role of primary intersubjectivity. This last point is closely connected to his characterization of primary intersubjectivity as a developmental stage that involves an undifferentiated fusion (à la Winnicott), and his characterization of recognition in terms of a struggle.

As an alternative to Honneth's analysis, I propose to focus on the intersubjective relation that is characterized by the dynamical social interactions of primary intersubjectivity, by engagements that are enactive rather than simulative, and that, developmentally, predate joint attention, but are nonetheless sustained in later development. Perhaps, however, what I propose may be consistent with a second possible reading of Honneth that would put him closer to this alternative by making the term "recognition" synonymous with primary intersubjective processes, at the expense of claiming that he is neither clear nor unambiguous in his definition of the concept. As we saw, Honneth clearly identifies the starting point of his analysis as concerned with joint attention, and the infant's engagement with the world of objects. His qualification of this, however, was that even prior to joint attention one has to consider the emotional aspects of intersubjective attachment, something that we could associate with primary intersubjectivity. On this alternative reading, Honneth could be said to slide from making this a mere qualification to equating emotional intersubjective attachment with recognition. As he put it (to quote a passage previously quoted): "a small child first of all identifies with its figures of attachment and must have emotionally recognized them before it can arrive at knowledge of objective reality by means of these other perspectives" (2008a, 46). Here the hint is that recognition is really the emotional attachment to the other that precedes secondary intersubjective processes. We can find some support for this interpretation in his later use of the concept of elementary recognition (2008b).

It's clear that there is a great deal of complexity in Honneth's concept of recognition. He distinguishes three different forms of intersubjective recognition, but focuses his analysis more on the status of the self (or self-relation) within these contexts than on social interaction. Specifically, we noted that he distinguishes in recognition aspects that involve self-confidence, self-respect, and self-esteem (1995, 1998, 2007). In later texts he associates "elementary recognition" with primary intersubjectivity (2008b). Accordingly, we could take Honneth to be advocating a two-level account of recognition, in which elementary recognition is placed at a more fundamental level than the types of recognition involved in categories like confidence, respect, and esteem. Elementary recognition precedes, both ontogenetically and conceptually, second-order and more normative patterns of recognition where the other person's particular characteristics are affirmed.

The normative forms of recognition are expressions and further articulations of the elementary recognition involved in immediate self–other relations. The use of the term "recognition" to encompass both the elementary aspects and the more developed normative aspects of social interaction, however, has concerned some commentators, who have univocally criticized Honneth's account, maintaining that the elementary level of recognition is depicted as a positively loaded condition, which involves an overly optimistic anthropology and an ideal theory (Butler 2008; Geuss 2008; Lear 2008).

To be clear, however, Honneth emphasizes that elementary recognition should not be understood in strictly positive terms; the term "elementary" is meant to convey that positive and negative attitudes, and even indifference toward others, depend on this prior recognition. When responding to his critics, Honneth emphasizes the "non-epistemic," non-cognitive, and pre-normative character of elementary recognition, which involves a kind of existential affectivity (2008b, 151–2). It is on this notion of elementary recognition that I want to focus, and to get some distance from the terminological issues I propose to call this *elementary responsivity* rather than recognition.

8.3 Responsivity

The term "responsivity" is meant to reflect the fact that interactive relations are more akin to emotive or agentive processes than to strictly cognitive ones; elementary responsivity is implicated at the very beginning of interaction, and I mean to associate it with the kind of embodied interactive relation that we find in primary intersubjectivity, while again keeping in mind that we find primary intersubjectivity throughout the lifespan.[11]

We can certainly learn a good number of things from Honneth about the concept of recognition, one of which is that it may be helpful to reserve the term "recognition" for the more complex normative aspects of human relations. Here again, Honneth himself, influenced by Hegel, continues to explicate what Ricoeur calls "an ordered plurality of models of recognition" (2005, 175); he continues to use the term to apply in legal contexts and contexts that involve institutional arrangements (Honneth 2012).

---

[11] This concept of responsivity is close to what Italo Testo (2012) attempts to reconstruct from Hegel's Jena writings—a conception of recognition as developing out of the more embodied and natural aspects of interaction.

Let me note, however, that having made a seemingly neat conceptual (and terminological) distinction between elementary responsivity and other forms of recognition, anything like pure (non-normative) elementary responsivity even in infants may be non-existent once interaction gets under way. We shouldn't think that primary intersubjectivity in infancy is bereft of normative aspects; from the perspective of the adult caregiver or parent who is interacting with the infant, the interaction is already part of an instituted, normative practice—and that defines important aspects of the interaction. Engaging with the infant is not only what parents do; it's what they are supposed to do, and there are various proper and improper ways to do it.

Honneth associates love with the notion of recognition involved in self-confidence, and therefore as already a normative relation beyond elementary responsivity. In this regard, then, we should think about recognition as involving degrees (as well as various kinds) of normativity, from basic forms involved in love, respect, and esteem, to more complicated forms that are involved with formalized social institutions, such as the legal system. Even for the developing infant, as I indicated, and certainly for those beyond infancy, it's never possible to speak of a pure (norm-free) elementary responsivity; each response may already involve a basic emotion, like love,[12] and, therefore, may already be subject to what Ian Hacking (1995) calls a "looping effect" involving some degree of normative recognition. That's because the other (e.g., the caregiver) is already engaged in cultural practices in his or her response to the infant.

Nonetheless, one can clearly contrast the notion of elementary responsivity, associated with the perspective of the participant in primary intersubjectivity, to the notion of recognition that might be involved in the *détente* or the divorced observational perspective that, as Honneth suggests, may sometimes be required in developed society. To the extent that recognition is involved in the latter, it remains formal and relatively empty of affective valence. It may be what is required by a purely procedural or economic rationality, but it is not sufficient for everyday interaction or communicative action. In contrast, the more basic, existential sense of elementary responsivity, on the enactive-interactive approach, is tied to first-order face-to-face interaction.

As the enactivist approach makes clear, a participant in interaction with another person is called to respond if the interaction is to continue. My response to the other, in the primary instance, just is my engaging in interaction with her—by responding positively or negatively with action to her action. Although research on primary intersubjectivity provides a detailed model of elementary responsivity, it may also be useful to consider Levinas's (1969) analysis of the face-to-face relation in order to explicate what this research tells us.

For Levinas, what I see in the other's face is irreducible to its objective properties, its physiognomy, shape, color, or morphological features. Rather, I see significance that transcends any such properties. The other person, resists being simply a physical object, and at the same time resists being simply an epistemological subject. The other transcends this subject-object categorization. This also means that the other is

---

[12] Not everyone lists love as a basic emotion, but some do; for example, Shaver et al. (2001).

not equivalent to an invisible mind, a set of mental states that we might be able to reach through processes of inference. Nor is the other composed of a set of mental states that are like mine, analogically displaced in another body. Rather, according to Levinas, the face-to-face relation primarily registers in an ethical order: the other, in her alterity, is such that she makes an ethical demand on me, to which I am obligated to respond.

I experience the transcendence of the other "when the face has turned to me, in its very nakedness. It is by itself, and not by reference to a system" (Levinas 1969, 75). In contrast to Heidegger who might speak about a system of involvements that constitute the pragmatic world (characteristic of secondary intersubjectivity), Levinas describes a direct embodied encounter with the other. In contrast to Hegel, the face-to-face is not oppositional; "totalized" oppositional arrangements are disrupted by the transcendence of the other. Levinas associates opposition (war, control, slavery, or manipulation) with the concept of totality (a complete system, the opposite of a never complete infinity). "War renders morality derisory" (1969, 21). It involves a reification of the other in practices that include covering or ignoring the other's face.[13] This kind of dehumanization or denial of the face reduces the other to a component of a complete system; such reification excludes the possibility of further interaction. Competitive or instrumental systems can only be derivative, secondary disorders of the primary ethical relationship.

In the circumstance of gazing at the other's face the other's vulnerability shines through, independent of context, and elicits a response from me. The other, in such circumstances, is characterized by both proximity and distance at the same time. When the other is close to me, she is so not merely (if at all) in physical geographical terms, the way an object, artifact, or instrument might be. Intersubjective closeness demands a response "that could range from a passionate kiss to a punch, or some less extreme and more polite behavior of moving away or asking for space" (Gallagher 2014a). Even in the other's closeness, however, there is a distance insofar as I cannot fully grasp the other. This is specifically the transcendence that is most apparent in the other's face. Something irreducible in the other always escapes my gaze. It is something that is "beyond understanding" (déborde la compréhension—Levinas 1991, 18). The face (or more generally, the body) is never the totality of the other. It's not a matter of me seeing the other's face, simpliciter, but of seeing the other seeing me. My perception of the other's gaze when her gaze is directed at me is precisely not something that can be subsumed into a strictly visual representation of eye direction since it has an affective impact on my own system that sets me up for further response.[14]

The virtue of Levinas's analysis, which also carries over to the interactive analysis, is that the other person, in her otherness, resists being simply an entity—resists

---

[13] Seeing the face of the other in battle has profound inhibitory effects on violent behavior directed towards the other. See Grossman (1996); Protevi (2008).

[14] Recent neuroscientific experiments confirm this. Hirsch et al. (2017) show significant and specific activation in numerous areas of the brain, including language centers, when there is direct eye-to-eye contact between two individuals with potential interaction, compared with looking at someone's gaze in a photograph. Mutual eye-to-eye gazing also generates synchronous activation across both brains.

reification. To frame this in terms of enactivist interaction, recall (from *Section 6.1*) that the perception of another's face activates not just the brain's face-recognition area and ventral visual pathway, but also the dorsal (action-related) visual pathway—suggesting that we perceive affordances in the face of the other (Debruille et al. 2012). This suggests that we perceive the other in the mode of the "I can" (or "I cannot")—that is, we perceive affordances for possible responsive actions in the face of the other. Or again, as argued in previous chapters, face perception presents not just objective patterns that we might cognitively [re]cognize as emotions. More importantly, it elicits complex response patterns arising out of an active engagement with the other's face; not a simple [re]cognition of facial features—but an interactive perception that includes a responsive attitude to the other's emotional expressions.[15]

Because facial expressions play a large role in intersubjective interaction, we anticipate facial responses and when they do not occur interaction can be disrupted in terms of its dynamics and affectivity, leading to confusion or feelings of social discomfort. This occurs, for example, in cases of Möbius Syndrome, a form of congenital bilateral facial paralysis resulting from developmental problems with the sixth and seventh cranial nerves (Briegel 2006; Cole 1999; Cole & Spalding 2009). Indeed, part of the problem for subjects with Möbius is not the neurophysiological condition itself, but the way others regard the person with Möbius. Specifically, others often fail to respond because they see no facial response in the subject (Gallagher 2014a; Krueger & Michael 2012).

Levinas (1969, 46) emphasizes the asymmetrical demand of the other on me. Yet, we could think that the elicitation to respond involved in elementary responsivity is generated in the mutual (even if not necessarily symmetrical) turning toward each other. What is important is that the other looks back at me, as I meet her gaze with my own. This mutual engagement is an aspect of primary intersubjectivity. It doesn't matter whether the other is one's caring caregiver, the stranger behind the store counter, the player on the opposing team, or one's torturer—if we make eye contact, if we come face-to-face, something—some affective thing (negative or positive)—is at stake, and there is something more involved than just the physicality of some "thing."

In this respect, I suggest, it is possible to associate what Levinas calls the *transcendence* found in the face of the other, with the transcendence involved in the autonomy of interaction. Rather than conceiving of this experience as something mysterious, as reaching for the unreachable in or beyond the encounter, or the other's face, it is possible to conceive of it as generated or enacted in the autonomy of interaction, which transcends individuality. The most basic and elementary response to the other is in this face-to-face, which sets into play the trajectory of subsequent interactions, and the possibility of transcendence (moving beyond just myself). Elementary responsivity, as it gets shaped in intersubjective interaction, leads to a transcendence that carries participating agents beyond the meaning of their individual actions. The meaning that emerges or that is established by the

---

[15] The use of the term "recognition" in this literature on face recognition is, of course, not equivalent to Honneth's use of the term. The notion of a summons (Fichte's *Aufforderung*) reverberates in the concept of social affordance and is reflected in Kurt Lewin's concept of the "demand character" (*Aufforderungscharaktere*) of emotion (see Lambie 2020).

8.4 RELATIONAL AUTONOMY AND SOME POSSIBLE DISTORTIONS   207

interaction, in turn, calls for further response, in the form of ongoing interaction, or communication, or interpretation. The ethical, to the extent that it is about our way of living with others, is built around this kind of interaction—and around it we start to build certain practices.[16]

Here's the point I want to make, with the help of Levinas. In matters of degree there is neither the possibility of transcendence nor the possibility of reification without interaction. Transcendence is not a feature of the other person, something that belongs to the person as an objective or essential feature. Nor is it tied to some object or subject that can be observed from a third-person perspective. The transcendence of the other—the transcendence that I encounter in the other's face—just is the other's ability (or possibility) to return my gaze—to gaze back at me—and to encounter the same transcendence in my face. Transcendence is not an absolute fact; it's a relational contingency enacted through interaction. Likewise, the failure to enact that transcendence, as when we simply objectify or reify the other person, is also a possibility of relational contingency.

8.4 Relational Autonomy and Some Possible Distortions

The possibility of experiencing the kind of transcendence that comes from inter-action is important for working out a concept of autonomy. Traditional conceptions of autonomy focus on self-sufficiency, self-legislation, or self-determination. Kant is the *locus classicus* for this view. For him, autonomy means giving oneself the law, and the law is an a priori universal law that one can find within oneself. Autonomy, in this regard, is an individualistic concept, self-enclosed in an abstract consciousness. As John Christman notes, "traditional conceptions of the free, autonomous individual put undue emphasis on the ideal/assumption of rational self-awareness and cognitive mental operations and have ignored the importance of embodiment, affect and instinctive (and socially embedded) action" (2009, 13). Hegel offers a critique of Kant that has the potential to address this problem, by emphasizing the concept of socially embedded action. For Hegel a subject is autonomous if, as Honneth puts it, the subject "directs its efforts towards finding itself in a world whose structure is an expression of the subject's own will" (2012, 23). In this regard, autonomy involves action and externalities—finding the right fit between self and world. Hegel writes in the *Philosophy of Right*, "A person must translate his freedom into an external sphere in order to exist as Idea" (1952, 40). For Hegel, importantly, the external sphere is also social.

If Hegel goes some distance toward a conception of autonomy that is more social and relational, it takes something of a hermeneutical push to get him closer to a concept that would relate autonomy and recognition, as Honneth makes clear. It's

---

[16] There is much more to be said about the ethical, but it would take us beyond the scope of our considerations here which are focused on a set of preconditions that are nonetheless relevant to the ethical.

precisely the notion of reciprocal recognition that leads Honneth to the concept of relational autonomy.

> [W]e achieve autonomy along intersubjective paths by learning to understand ourselves, via others' recognition, as beings whose needs, beliefs and abilities are worth being realized. However, this will only be possible if, at the same time, we recognize those who recognize us.... Therefore, if individual autonomy is to emerge and flourish, reciprocal intersubjective recognition is required. We do not acquire autonomy on our own, but only in relation to other people.... Autonomy is a relational, intersubjective entity, not a monological achievement.
>
> (2012, 41)

We find the concept of relational autonomy most clearly developed in feminist critiques of traditional conceptions of autonomy (see Mackenzie & Stoljar 2000 for a good summary; I take my bearings on this topic from their Introduction). For our purposes, Annette Baier's idea that "persons are second-persons" is a good starting point. "Persons are essentially successors, heirs to other persons who formed and cared for them, and their personality is revealed both in their relations to others and in their response to their own recognized genesis" (Baier 1985, 85). Baier in effect argues against an ontological individualism and against traditional descriptions of autonomy that downgrade social ties, usually, in this context, considered to be positive phenomena such as trust, friendship, loyalty, or caring. Agents are not abstract entities; they are embedded in intersubjective relations with others from the beginning (Code 1991). Thus, Virginia Held can point to early development as a critical time when:

> [... A] need for recognition and a need to understand the other... are created in the context of mother-child interaction and are satisfied in a mutually empathetic relationship.... Both give and take in a way that not only contributes to the satisfaction of their needs as individuals but also affirms the "larger relational unit" they compose. Maintaining this larger relational unit then becomes a goal, and maturity is seen not in terms of individual autonomy but in terms of competence in creating and sustaining relations of empathy and mutual intersubjectivity.
>
> (Held 1993, 60)

The "larger relational unit" emerges in interaction and, I would argue, involves the autonomy of interaction, experienced as the transcendence described in the previous section. At the same time, the transcendence and the establishment of a larger relational unit depend on the preservation of the autonomy of the agents involved. The relational autonomy of interaction involves both relatedness to, and differentiation from, others. It promotes a sense of agency in a world of interacting and interpersonal agents and, as Evelyn Fox Keller puts it, a sense of others "as subjects with whom one shares enough to allow for a recognition of their independent interests and feelings – in short, for a recognition of them as other subjects" (Keller 1985, 99). The autonomy pictured here is not a static state where the other is seen in opposition to self; it is a relational autonomy where self and other are engaged in some form of reciprocal responsivity and recognition. The autonomous self, on this view, is more like an intersection or integration of relations with others.

This conception of relational autonomy has to wrestle with problems that seem implicit in the notion of socialization and which have the potential to distort autonomous action and interaction. Here it is helpful to consider the difference between *procedural* and *substantive* accounts of autonomy (Mackenzie & Stoljar 2000, 13ff.). For procedural (seemingly content-neutral) accounts, which do not prescribe in any positive way what one's life should be, some model of critical reflection is essential. Mackenzie and Stoljar (2000) distinguish between structural, historical, and competency approaches to procedural accounts. Each account, as an instance of ideal theory, runs into hermeneutical limitations. A *structural* approach, such as Harry Frankfurt's (1988) conception of autonomy as a capacity for a reflective use of second-order desires (or intentions) in evaluating first-order desires might be challenged by asking what makes second-order desire autonomous. If our second-order desires are themselves shaped by our social relations, that would seem to place limits on autonomy. On the *historical* account, critical reflection needs to be independent of historical accidental formation (Dworkin 1988), or at least not influenced by negative historical formation (Christman 2004). The problem here, however, is that someone who is thoroughly embedded in their historical perspective is not necessarily in a position to recognize what would count as negative for autonomy. Finally, the *competency-based* concept of autonomy requires reflection and skills of self-direction/self-realization. Here, too, any such reflective skills are learned as practices within social and historical settings.

The response to these issues should be that although they appear to be problems for non-relational accounts of autonomy, they are not necessarily irresolvable problems for relational accounts since relational accounts recognize that autonomy is always a matter of degree and is always relative to the particular social and agentive situation in which a particular agent finds herself. That is, an account of relational autonomy should fully accept the historical and hermeneutical limitations as definitive for a limited autonomy, in contrast to anything like an abstract, absolute individual autonomy. Critical reflection, for example, is not something that happens on an internalist conception of a purely "in-the-head" process. It, like many other types of cognitive events, can be an intersubjective, interactional accomplishment that takes place in communicative practices. Accordingly, any degree of autonomy traced to this kind of critical reflection will already be delimited by social and normative practices.

Amongst substantive accounts, some are stronger and more ideal than others. On a strong account, one requires a context-free knowledge of right and wrong based on rationality. One has to be in a position to be able to distinguish correct from incorrect behavior, and to be autonomous one needs to choose the right or correct way to live (Benson 1994; Wolf 1990). On this account, there's no such thing as an autonomous criminal or terrorist. On a weaker account, autonomous subjects must be free to choose the right way to live (even if they don't), and having made a choice, their social situations should not be oppressive to the point of taking away self-respect, self-trust, or competence to judge from a rational perspective. Even a criminal can be autonomous if she has the wherewithal to make rational judgments about her life.

From the perspective of relational autonomy, such demands for rational judgment are too ideal and narrow, since agents in the lifeworld are in fact not just rational minds. Mackenzie and Stoljar summarize the kinds of issues that are at stake in these different approaches.

[P]ersons are socially embedded and...agents' identities are formed within the context of social relationships and shaped by a complex of intersecting social determinants, such as race, class, gender, and ethnicity.... [A]n analysis of the characteristics and capacities of the self cannot be adequately undertaken without attention to the rich and complex social and historical contexts in which agents are embedded.... [We] need to think of autonomy as a characteristic of agents who are emotional, embodied, desiring, creative, and feeling, as well as rational, creatures. (2000, 4)

If we think of relational autonomy as involving the "larger relational unit" that results from intersubjective interaction, so that there is no individual autonomy without the kind of interaction that involves an extra-individual autonomy, then this would need to be the beginning point for a more prescriptive model of social-relational autonomy. John Christman finds this, for example, in Marina Oshana's concept of relational autonomy, which he describes as follows.

[A]utonomy obtains only when social conditions surrounding an individual live up to certain standards. In addition to allowing the person to develop critical reflective abilities and procedural independence (of the sort internalists demand), the surrounding social conditions in which the autonomous person resides must allow her significant options, they must ensure that she can defend herself against psychological and physical assault when necessary or against attempts to deprive her of her rights, she must not be forced to take responsibility for others' needs unless agreed to or reasonably expected, and they must allow her to pursue goals different from those who have influence or authority over her.

(Christman 2004, 150; see Oshana 1998)

Christman (2009, 14), who is critical of this kind of account of relational autonomy, worries about its strong substantive aspects. If a person freely chooses to give up her freedom to make alternative life choices—for example, if someone choses a life of obedience and gives up all other alternatives for religious or other reasons—then isn't this still an informed exercise of autonomy? Christman argues that a person's authentic choice, based on a free deliberation, to adopt an oppressed or subservient social status reflects autonomy and deserves respect. On this view, the exercise of freedom has to be authentic. Autonomy depends on a reflective deliberation that allows the person to realistically choose otherwise "were she in a position to value sincerely that alternative position" (Christman 2004, 154). On Christman's conception of authentic reflection, relational views, like Oshana's, sometimes stray when they include conditions that rule out the free choice of a life that involves limiting one's freedom.

In considering such issues, I think it helps to appeal to the idea that autonomy is not only relational but also always a matter of degree; clearly any claim that someone is only autonomous if she can completely escape a life structured by authoritarian rule is misleading. Christman holds for a weaker condition; namely, having the ability to adequately reflect on one's life and embrace it. Autonomy, however, as indicated above, is not simply hinged to one's reflective judgment, where one seemingly gives oneself the law, since the law or the order that one chooses, and in some sense, one's reflective capacity itself, are things that depend on others. Reflective ability is limited or enhanced by social relations and arrangements. Reflection may be literally a social accomplishment if it involves communicative practices and deliberations with others. Such communicative practices are never perfect since our lives are always circumscribed by a mix of private and social practices within contexts of personal relations and local institutions. It's difficult (and perhaps impossible) to attain a third-person, purely rational reflective attitude, since we are immersed in and shaped by our everyday dynamical interactions with others. Accordingly, any procedural framework that supports or advances autonomy is already relational and socially embedded.

How does this look from the perspective of a critical interaction theory? Relational autonomy is not only a matter of degree, it is also a compound autonomy, because one agent's autonomy is always defined (constrained or enhanced) not only by others, but also by another (extra-individual) autonomy—that of the larger relational unit. Accordingly, the autonomy of the individual is interdependent with the autonomy of interaction. That is, to the extent that the individual can participate in the autonomy of interaction, the possibility exists of an increase or decrease of his or her individual autonomy.[17] The individual's autonomy, which is a relational autonomy, varies, positively or negatively, in relation to the individual's positive or negative interactions, the valence of which will depend, in part, on the individual, in part on the others with whom she interacts, and in part on the structural features of the specific practices or institutions within which she interacts. The idea that autonomy is relational, moreover, again emphasizes the importance of elementary responsivity, which is the initiation of interaction, and the forms of recognition, which are carried by and constrained by various social practices.

[17] I think it's possible to provide a measure of autonomy in terms of the quality and quantity of physical, social, and cultural affordances that are available to an individual, agentively situated in intersubjective contexts. See *Section 10.3*.

9

Telling Actions: Institutions, Collective Agency, and Critical Narratives

The concept of socially extended cognition (Gallagher 2013) has some relevance for understanding how social and cultural practices shape not only our cognitive processes, but also our actions and interactions. What I've called "cognitive" or "mental institutions" (Gallagher & Crisafi 2009; Slaby & Gallagher 2015) are not only institutions that support cognitive processes, but are also such that without them these specific cognitive processes would not exist. Examples include legal systems, schools and universities, government agencies, and cultural institutions. Indeed, science itself, understood as an instituted practice, is an important example.

In the previous chapter we saw that much of the contemporary discussion of recognition has drawn on Hegel. Despite the fact that Hegel is rarely mentioned in contemporary discussions of the philosophy of mind and cognitive science, he also has relevance for understanding cognitive institutions as they relate to the concept of extended mind (Clark & Chalmers 1998; Clark 2008). Joel Anderson provides some insight on this in a note to his translation of Habermas.

> The notion of "objective mind" (which stems from Hegel, where it is often translated as "objective spirit") is used to refer to social institutions, customs, shared practices, science, culture, language, and so on—those entirely real parts of the human world that are neither held within one individual's mind nor physically instantiated independently from humans. In this sense, then, recent discussions within philosophy of mind and cognitive science regarding "situated cognition" or the "extended mind" are also about the "objective mind".
>
> (Habermas 2007, 42–3n5)

In this chapter my concern is neither to work out an interpretation of Hegel, nor to extend the discussion of the extended mind.[1] Rather, I want to focus on the profound effects that cognitive institutions have on most of our everyday actions and interactions. I'll suggest ways in which narrative practices can establish and support such institutions, and how they can also operate as the basis for a critique of such institutions.

---

[1] I endorse a liberal enactivist version of the extended mind idea. Some authors (including Clark 2012; Wheeler 2014; Thompson & Stapleton 2009) view enactivism and the extended mind hypothesis to be in opposition with each other. Again, my aim in this chapter is not to take up this debate, but see Gallagher (2018d) for discussion.

9.1 How Institutions Shape our Actions and Interactions

Cognitive institutions include a range of cognitive practices that are produced in specific times and places, and are activated in ways that extend our cognitive processes and affect our social interactions when we engage with them. Just as we might use pencil and paper to do some math, or a notebook or piece of electronic technology to assist with our memory—all nice examples of the idea of the extended mind (Clark & Chalmers 1998)—so also we might rely on other people to do the math for us, or to store or retrieve our memories (Sutton et al. 2010). When we organize with others to engage in such cognitive practices we have examples of socially extended cognition. We may, for example, form a committee to study a problem and make a decision based on what we learn. Such a collection of people might also decide on a set of rules or a set of practices that they will follow for the sake of efficiency or fairness. A committee, a group, a team—but also a set of established rules or practices designed to solve problems or form agreements—may get instituted and take on a structure that goes beyond its original ad hoc status. In this respect a cognitive institution is established, in some cases informally, and in others more formally.

The legal system is a good example. Consider, for example, a contract or legal agreement which is in some real sense an expression of several minds externalized and extended into the world, instantiating in external memory an agreed-upon decision, adding to a system of rights and laws that transcend the particularities of any individual's mind. Contracts are institutions that embody conceptual schemas, which, in turn, contribute to and shape our cognitive processes and our actions. They are not only the product of certain cognitive exercises, but are also used as tools to accomplish certain aims, to reinforce specific behaviors, and to solve specific problems. Institutions of property, contract, rights, and law not only guide our thinking about social arrangements, for example, or about what we can and cannot do, but allow us to think in ways that would not be possible without such institutions. Insofar as we cognitively engage with such tools and institutions we extend and transform our cognitive processes, and we shape the way that we act and interact with each other.

The legal system is constructed in part by these cognitive processes. Legal practices, the formation of legal judgments, the administration of justice, the application of law to particular cases, are, among other things (such as exercises of power), *cognitive*. They do not, however, happen simply in the individual brains of judge, jury, officers of the court, etc. Of course we do usually think of judgments as happening in the privacy of one's own head. But some judgments depend on extra-neural (often social) practices and the technical processes that guide them or that allow the manipulation and management of a large amount of empirical information. In a court of law, for example, testimony is produced according to rules of evidence; and judgments are made following a set of rules that are established by the system. The process in which judgments get made will depend on a number of people remaining cognitively engaged with a set of practices, and a body of law, the relevant parts of which come to the fore because of the precise particulars of the case, as the proceedings develop.

Consider an example that involves three different scenarios. Alexis is given a set of facts and is presented with a collection of evidence, and she is asked to judge the legitimacy of a certain claim that is being made.

(1) In the first scenario she is asked to make her judgment on the basis of her own subjective sense of fairness, weighing the evidence entirely in her own head.
(2) In the second scenario experts specify the kind of questions or considerations she can address, although she still forms the judgment in her own reflections.
(3) In the third scenario experts further provide possible answers and a set of rules to follow in making her decision.

In the first scenario Alexis seemingly does all of the work in her own head. In the second, there may be less cognitive effort on her part since she did not have to draw up or decide which questions to consider; and in the third scenario the possible answers were already provided and she was given a procedure for deciding among them. Yet, it's clear that in all of the scenarios, even the first, cognition is socially extended across specific institutional practices. In the first scenario Alexis is presented the evidence (by someone else, and supposedly in line with what is allowed as evidence in this system) and given a task predetermined by others. She doesn't think these things up on her own. In none of these cases can Alexis' thinking be reduced to strictly "in the head" processes. What she considers and her cognitive strategies are specified by others and by practices that are beyond just what she might think on her own. The cognition involved is distributed. There is a distribution across a number of participants—including the experts, where the distribution is different in each scenario. In (3) we might think that there is less cognitive effort going on in Alexis' head—she not only doesn't have to draw up the questions and possible answers, she doesn't have to produce the principles or rules required to make the judgment. There may be less cognitive effort going on in the heads of the experts too, since what they provide to Alexis (answer types and rules) may be pre-established in the legal system, instituted by previous practice. Indeed, we could say that such questions, possible answers, and rules create the tracks along which the cognitive processes must run to keep it, literally, legitimate. The answer types and the rules are part of a system; they are, so to speak, stored in a system—a system previously established in cognitive processes, and maintained in textual, technological, and institutional procedures and cultural practices. The relevant elements of the system were previously established in processes that we would certainly call cognitive, and likely depend on a more wide-ranging set of (cognitive) justifications. When individuals like Alexis and the experts become engaged with the system in the right way, the system does some of the cognitive work.

Judgments, then, are not necessarily confined to individual brains, or even to the many brains that constitute a particular court or legal system. They emerge in the workings of a large and complex institution. Yet these judgments and legal proceedings are cognitive processes that then contribute to the continued working of the system in the form of precedents. The practice of law, which is constituted by just such cognitive and communicative processes, is carried out via the cooperation of many people relying on external (and conventional) cognitive schemas and rules of evidence provided by the legal institution itself.

Judgments made in such contexts, and the specific kind of judgments that are made, are forms of cognition that depend on a large and complex system without which they could not happen. Indeed, these cognitive practices are such that in principle they could not happen just in an individual's head. Even in the case of a highly trained attorney who seemingly does her legal reasoning in her head, what she does, and what makes it the kind of cognition that it is, depends not only on the fact that she has previously engaged in the workings of the legal system (receiving her training and tuning her cognitive abilities in law school by following specific practices of that educational institution), but also on the *ongoing* workings of the legal system since what she engages in—i.e., the particular cognitive process of forming a legal judgment—*is what it is* only in that system. It's not difficult to imagine a specific kind of question that would never even come up if there were no legal system. The legal system in effect helps to generate certain cognitive events, sometimes creating perplexities and problems of a purely legal nature, and sometimes helping to resolve them. An individual required to make judgments about the legitimacy of certain arrangements thus engages with the legal institution and interacts with others in such contexts forming a coupled system in a way that allows new cognitive processes to emerge—cognitive processes that would otherwise not be possible. Take away the external part of this cognitive process—take away the legal institution—and "the system's behavioural [and cognitive] competence will drop, just as it would if we removed part of [the individual's] brain" (Clark & Chalmers 1998, 9).

If according to the extended mind hypothesis it is right to say that working with a notebook or a calculator is mind-extending (Clark & Chalmers 1998), it seems equally right to say that engaging with the legal system (for example, in the practice of legal argumentation, deliberation, and judgment, or any cognitive processes involved in the administration of law), or with the institution of science, etc., are mind-extending too. Importantly, extensive cognition is not a simple one-way process that makes use of tools, technologies, and institutions, but it is often the case that technologies and institutions shape our cognitive processes; such things make our brains work in certain ways, and may even elicit plastic changes in neuronal structure.

The picture just painted is still oversimplified and somewhat ideal since the legal system does not function in isolation from other institutions, and may be subject to a variety of extra-institutional (but still social/cultural) constraints, so-called "institutional entanglements" (Slaby & Gallagher 2015). Generally, this can be said of any such institution. Consider, for example, the cognitive work involved in scientific research. Would it be possible—or would science even be what it is—without the kinds of things—labs, instruments, scientific practices and procedures (including current publication practices that specify stylized sections in the standard journal article)—that allow for collaboration, and that carry scientific thinking forward? It is possible to list a large set of institutional practices that make instances of cognition scientific cognition. This would be a study in itself (see, e.g., Latour & Woolgar 1979; Slaby & Gallagher 2015). To be clear, however, we know that research questions and decisions in science are not determined purely by scientific procedure, and scientific results are not strictly confined to scientific labs. Accordingly, to fully understand the ins and outs of scientific practices one must consider not only the institution of science, but how precisely this cognitive institution is related to other cognitive institutions (such as governmental, medical, military, media-related, and/or legal institutions) and how it is embedded within the ambient society at large. Once we open discussion to include broader cultural factors, any institution we are considering, including the legal system, will be shown to be less ideal and less stable than, for example, the legal system considered abstractly on its own.

Importantly, these socially established institutions sometimes constitute, sometimes facilitate, and sometimes impede, but in each case enable and shape our interactions with other people. Furthermore, as discussed below, the notion of a cognitive institution is itself a helpful tool for developing a critical stance that allows us to scrutinize current institutional practices and to ask important questions about their aims and directions. For example, whether these processes improve (or impede, or distort) our understanding, our communicative practices, our possibilities for action, our recognition of others, our shared and circumscribed freedoms, and so forth.

Marc Slors (2019), in an analysis of cognitive institutions, relies on the distinction between functional integration (where there is close causal coupling between agent and external resource) and task-dependency (where much of the work is done by structural coupling among external elements that coordinate according to well-defined tasks). Using this contrast he distinguishes between:

(1) *extended cognition* (characterized by high functional integration and low task-dependency);
(2) *distributed cognition* (characterized by high functional integration and high task-dependency); and
(3) *symbiotic cognition* (characterized by low functional integration and high task-dependency).

Slors argues that cognitive institutions are best conceived in terms of the third form. Here he thinks that the legal system is a good example of a symbiotic cognitive institution where there is strong structural coupling but weak functional integration.

[S]ocial institutions such as legal systems, educational systems, and systems of cultural conventions typically involve a very high degree of holistic inter-defining of roles and tasks. The tasks of judges, barristers, clerks, prosecutors, etc. are inter-defined, as are the roles of teacher, head of school, and pupil, and the roles of host, guest and waiter.   (2019, 1192)

At the same time, according to Slors, there is no essential reason for the individual agent to be causally coupled to the legal system in any way similar to the example of doing math with pencil and paper.

To limit the notion of cognitive institution to the symbiotic form, however, may be too constricting. A different example pushes towards a slightly different way of thinking about this (see Gallagher, Mastrogiorgio, and Petracca [2019] for more detailed discussion). Specifically, Andy Clark points to the idea of cognitive institutions in his remarks on markets and economic reasoning.

Institutions, firms and organizations seem to me to share many of the key properties of pen, paper and arithmetical practice.... [Like pen and paper] firms and organizations provide an external resource in which individuals behave in ways dictated by norms, policies, and practices; norms, policies, and practices that may even become internalized as mental models.

Daily problem solving, in these arenas often involves locally effective pattern recognition strategies that are invoked due to some external originating prompt...discharged in a present manner, and that leave their mark as further traces...in the overarching machinery of the firm.   (Clark 1997, 269, 279)

Here I think it's important to distinguish between different conceptions of cognitive institutions. Clark, for example, follows Denzau and North (1994) who define institutions as "the rules of the game of a society [consisting] of formal and informal constraints constructed to order interpersonal relationships.... [T]he institutions are the external (to the mind) mechanisms individuals create to structure and order the environment" (1994, 4). For Denzau and North, however, the order is defined by shared mental models, such that "ideologies and institutions can then be viewed as classes of shared mental models" (ibid). Clark takes this to be consistent with the functionalist integration found in the extended mind idea—the same sort of tight agent-resource causal integration that characterizes use of paper and pencil to do math. Alternatively, one can think of economic reasoning as more strictly scaffolded by market structures; i.e., external structures that constrain and enable agents' behavior, rather than involving internal mental states or models. The idea of "market design" (Vulkan, Roth, & Neeman 2013), for example, which stays with an information-based conception in economics (Mirowski & Nik-Khah 2017), aims to design markets where it's possible to off-load much of the market participants' cognitive burden onto the rules of the market, to the extreme of promoting "zero-intelligence" traders (Gode & Sunder 1993). Conceived in this way, a market would be an institution designed to order interpersonal relations according to impersonal relations by relying on high degrees of task-dependency (structural coupling among elements of the system), in contrast to functional integration.

The idea, then, is that cognitive institutions are not always characterized by symbiotic cognition or high task-dependency but can be characterized by different degrees of functional integration and task-dependency across the categories of extended, distributed, and symbiotic processes. If the legal system is a good example of an institution with low functional integration and high task-dependency (although this may vary across different elements and functions of the legal system), a market may not be so easy to classify. Although Clark describes the market institution as similar to extended mind conceptions of arithmetical practices with paper and pencil integrated with mental models, he also recognizes that, depending on circumstances, it could also approximate a "highly scaffolded" market design that reduces agents to zero-intelligence traders.

Strong constraints imposed by the larger scale market structure result in firm-level strategies and policies that maximize profits. In the embrace of such powerful scaffolding, the particular theories and worldviews of individuals may at times make little impact on overall firm-level behavior. Where the external scaffolding of policies, infrastructure, and customs is strong and (importantly) is a result of competitive selection, the individual members are, in effect, interchangeable cogs in a larger machine.   (1997, 274)

More generally, recognizing the variability of institutions across these different categories will give us a way to ask critical questions about how they work, and how they might be adjusted or transformed with a view to reducing reification,

218 TELLING ACTIONS: INSTITUTIONS, COLLECTIVE AGENCY

increasing autonomy, and addressing institutionally generated distortions in inter-subjective interactions.

9.2 Narrative Practices and Collective Agency

Within a group or institutional framework, individuals may jointly reflect on what they are doing or what they plan to do; that is, on their joint actions, shared goals, and shared intentions. They can do this by engaging in communicative practices that are supported by narrative. These so-called "we-narratives" about what they are doing, have done, and will do, or what they ought to do and want to do, can play a number of different roles in the formation and maintenance of the group or institution (Gallagher & Tollefsen 2019). Specifically, narratives can support the attribution of joint agency, the formation of group identity and group stability, and can provide a framework for understanding group responsibility.

9.2.1 Attribution of joint agency

In the case of an individual actor Graham and Stephens suggest that the attribution of self-agency originates at higher-order levels of retrospective reflection, understanding this in terms of "our proclivity for constructing self-referential narratives." Such narratives allow one to explain one's behavior retrospectively (1994, 101; see *Section 3.2*). On this view one attributes self-agency for an action if it fits coherently into one's self-narrative.

This type of self-attribution involves a retrospective judgment of agency that reinforces the individual's sense of agency. David Velleman (2000, 2005, 2006), in contrast, describing what he calls "narrative authorship," emphasizes the *prospective* function of narrative. He argues that narrative provides a framework both for testing one's formation of prior (D-) intentions and for the continued guidance of actions, and so considers it to be a means of self-governance underpinning autonomy. For Velleman a rational autonomy depends on forming intentions that are consistent with one's narrative understanding of oneself. We attribute agency most properly to just such autonomous subjects. In the individual this involves gaining a reflective distance from oneself, which allows for what Charles Taylor (1989) calls "strong evaluation," a critical stance that one might take toward one's own intentions. Just as narrative practices of reflection allow for this reflective distance in the individual case, it also allows for the same kind of reflective distance in a group or institutional context.

Although in the individual case a sense of agency may be based in part on pre-reflective aspects tied to sensory-motor processes (see *Chapter 3*), an individual's retrospective attribution of agency and prospective action planning may be based on narrative. This suggests that, in the case of joint action, beyond the idea that individual participants can have an experiential or phenomenal sense of joint agency (Pacherie 2012), a group itself may collectively attribute agency to itself via both prospective and retrospective narrative processes, where narratives are formed in a collaborative way. Narratives, in conjunction with intentions, can be, and often are, formed collectively in communicative practices. Joint projects, understood as a set of joint actions that may add up to certain instituted practices, rituals, etc., integrated or distributed across place and time, require something more than just the individual participants' prospective and retrospective cognitions. Insofar as retrospective and prospective narratives are collectively instituted, and can guide collective intention formation, they can ground the reflective attribution of joint agency that is irreducible to individual experiences of agency, since such group/institutional narratives may extend beyond any passing set of participants. Narratives themselves can become instituted and can continue to be formative from one generation to the next.

9.2.2 Group identity

Likewise, a group, by means of communicative practices, can prospectively work out and reach agreement on a narrative that makes it clear to others who they are in terms of group identity. Groups and institutions typically need something that can support and speak to identity over time—where the identity can be continuous even through a changing series of participants. One can think here of corporations, universities, or other types of institutions where people come and go over long time periods. In part, identity is formed in collective memories, and these are framed and perhaps documented in narratives. This is what happens in the creation of retrospective narratives during distributed practices of remembering, for example (Barnier et al. 2008; Coman et al. 2016). Groups, institutions, and communities develop and store collective memories, beliefs, and norms in narrative form. Coman et al. (2016), for example, show that mnemonic convergence (measured by the degree of overlap among community members' memories) is accomplished in part through communicative practices. Narrative structure can facilitate this process (Donald 1991; Nelson 2003b; Wertsch 2008a,b).

Accordingly, communities, as well as individuals, have narrative identities, as Ricoeur (1988, 246ff) notes.

> The notion of narrative identity also indicates its fruitfulness in that it can be applied to a community as well as to an individual. We can speak of the self-constancy of a community, just as we spoke of it as applied to an individual subject. Individual and community are constituted in their identity by taking up narratives that become for them their actual history.
>
> (Ricoeur 1988, 247)

Importantly, Ricoeur notes that narrative identity is not "a stable and seamless identity"—it is always possible to tell different (or even opposed) narratives about the same events. Each narrative may be a dialogue between a history of fact and fiction. Also, he suggests, narrative identity "does not exhaust the question of self-constancy" (249).

Cassie Striblen (2013) offers an important distinction with respect to this kind of identity construction. Specifically, with respect to group identity, she distinguishes between internal and external construction. In the case of internal narrative construction:

> Over time, in loose coordination, individual group members generate the group narrative by recounting origins, writing histories, defining goals, values, and norms for the group, contrasting themselves with other groups, highlighting prominent members and events, and so on.
>
> (2013, 159)

In contrast, external construction involves non-members who "contribute to the group's narrative as well, perhaps contesting the values or details promoted by the standard narrative" (ibid). The resulting complex narrative, internally and externally formed,

provides a morally significant identity for the group and its members, an explanation of who members take themselves to be as a persisting collective, including what values they hold, what traits they possess, what actions they have taken and what goals they pursue. The group narrative might then factor into the practical reasoning processes of group members, just as individual narrative does at the individual level.   (Ibid)

Identity narratives—of who we are and who we want to be—can facilitate prospective activities of future planning in various group and institutional contexts. This shows the close tie between identity, agency, and intention formation, but it also shows that questions of identity over time, specifically in group or institutional contexts, involve the formation of distal-intentions in narrative timescales. For example, M-intentions in two different individuals are not (and cannot be) identical as we engage in a jointly intended joint action. Even in the case of contagion or mutual imitation, for example, dancing or swimming in sync, M-intentions are not identical, precisely because we have different bodies that in strict motor detail (on the elementary timescale) move differently. Similarly, as Searle (1983) indicates, shared P-intentions (intentions-in-action that operate on a more integrative timescale on the order of seconds) may have a goal in common, but do not necessarily have the means in common. As we engage in joint actions towards a common goal, our actions and individual P-intentions cannot be identical because, most basically, we occupy different positions in a shared environment. Thus, the phenomenon that makes for collective identity involves reflective D-intention formation and is found on the narrative timescale. Accordingly, we, as members of the same group, may share the same narrative, in part or in whole, and that narrative expresses the collective D-intention and constitutes it as a collective intention.[2]

9.2.3 Stability

Participants in a joint action might form shared intentions, but for different reasons. This raises a worry about stability: what is it that binds the group such that the members have some reason for continuing their participation in the joint action? Bratman (2006) suggests that any theory of shared agency needs to solve this issue of stability. He appeals to the notion of mutual assurance and norms, and he considers the norms of stability to be built into the shared intention. Gilbert (2013) offers a theory of shared agency grounded in joint commitments. On this view, the idea of commitment provides a normative integration that binds people together and

---

[2] This doesn't mean that M- and P- intentions and their differing timescales are irrelevant. Asking what happens on all three scales may provide a way to talk about a dynamics of collective agency, since social interactions among participants involve all three timescales. Interactional dynamics that include relations to external environmental elements, for example, can involve entrainment, which can be expressed in a set of attentional dynamics. Collective attentional processes emerge out of such entrainment processes. Evidence for this can be found in studies of the dynamics of human collective attention (e.g., Fusaroli et al. 2015).

maintains stability. Either or both of these theories may be true, but they don't tell us how commitments or normative assurances come about.

One explanation is that for both long-term planned coordinated projects and even longer-term coherency of institutions, narrative can provide stability (Tollefsen & Gallagher 2017). First, it specifies what it is that we are mutually assuring ourselves about, or what we are committing to. That is, a narrative specifies the content of commitments and assurances. Second, explicitly or implicitly, with respect to means and norms, narrative may indicate a way to proceed—a direction for joint action. Narrative can express both means and goals of future actions, and, although not as formally as a legal contract, agreement with the narrative can signal assurances and commitments in ongoing communicative actions. The narratives we tell about our joint projects contribute to the development of stability in the group. At the same time, if we intend to change our group plan or our commitments in any way other than simply walking away from the group, this would likely be reflected in a changing narrative.

David Carr (1986a,b) also suggests that a stable community is established *via* communicative practices that include the formation of narratives. In some cases, however, differing stories can come into conflict, suggesting that identity and stability are never absolute or absolutely settled.

Both individuals and communities can fly apart if these conflicting stories are not resolved. No community is entirely free of conflicting versions of what constitutes its life-story, its origins, tasks and prospects. But some communities are more coherent than others. In any case such coherence is never settled once and for all, but is a constant process of reciprocal narration, persuasion, negotiation, revision.   (1986a, 529)

In this context, it's helpful to distinguish between narrative formation and narrative endorsement. Narrative formation is a complex process, occurs over varying lengths of time, and as Carr notes, involves reciprocal communicative processes, persuasion, negotiation, and revision. Such processes, however, do not presuppose a unified perspective, although it may indeed contribute to establishing a group identity that various members may endorse to varying degrees. In the case of an already established group identity, a new member of the group may simply endorse the narrative, adopting it as an understanding of what the group is about. Narrative endorsement may vary by degree in the sense that someone joining the group may identify more or less with the group and its narrative. Indeed, one's endorsement of a group's narrative may be based on a different perspective or orientation than another group member's endorsement. As members of a particular group, for example, we all may acknowledge our group's history, but each of us may interpret that history from different perspectives (giving different weights to different aspects), and we may thereby have different reasons for belonging to the group and for endorsing the narrative.

All three of these issues—joint agency, identity, and stability—are relevant to the concept of an institution, or what Tollefsen (2015) calls a "corporate" group, as distinguished from an aggregate (a collection of people not acting together) or a plural group (short-lived, constituted in one action, for example, you and me moving a table together).

Corporate groups are those that have a structure, an organization (sometimes hierarchical), and a decision-making process. Their identity does not change with a change of membership. A group that acted only once would not be a corporate group. Corporate groups require a pattern of behavior that exhibits a unity of agency over time.   (Tollefsen 2015, 47)

Narrative, at the very least, reflects the structure of the group and of collective actions taken by the group, and may be what makes that structure explicit and functional. Furthermore, narrative may be involved in the decision-making process in some cases, where making a strategic decision may simply mean changing the narrative, and then acting accordingly. Narrative provides a reflective capacity (as a social/communicative practice) that can underpin prospective intention formation and retrospective attributions of agency. Such a narrative capacity can shape the actions of the group, constitute an instituted rationality, and, in turn, constitute an autonomy (of the institution) that would go beyond and possibly place limitations on the autonomy of the individual members.

9.2.4 Responsibility

Narrative may also serve an important role with respect to collective or shared responsibility. Striblen (2013) considers a narrative framework to be neutral relative to specific conceptions of responsibility, and she takes this to be an advantage for thinking of group responsibility. Kantian theories that emphasize the notion of an individual autonomous self, relying on universal reason, for example, would suggest that "one's group memberships ought not to impact one's moral decision-making" (Striblen 2013, 150). In contrast, communitarian conceptions of the individual rely heavily on social relationships in moral decision-making, and attribute a high degree of group responsibility. Narrative theories are meant to be more descriptive, even if what they describe are the normative standards by which groups come to attribute responsibility.

Striblen (2013, 160) rightly indicates that the group narrative does not operate above or independently of the group members. She suggests a necessary interdependence between the group and its members and contends that there would be no group narrative if there were no members. Although this is clearly correct, there is also something more to say in this regard. The narrative, which may be formed over time by many individuals, transcends those individuals and may persist beyond them. It may persist across changing generations of group members. Not only can a narrative lead us to attribute intentionality to the group, the processes connected with narrative formation—communicative and reflective processes that may emerge collectively and accomplish more than any one individual could—can also be treated as constituting aspects of the collective that are not reducible to the minds of the individual members. Likewise, the attribution of responsibility would require a distribution reflected in part in the degree that individuals formulate and/or endorse the narrative.

This way of understanding collective intentionality pushes us away from the traditional sorts of analyses that reduce such intentionality to individual mental states. Instead, we can point to the real processes involved in communicative practices, intersubjective deliberations, narrative formations, and endorsements that lead to actions—processes that define a group's identity, and that allow a collective to maintain some degree of stability over time. Collective intentionality and agency are distributed across such processes, and the idea that we can explain such things in terms of beliefs or intentions, as when we say that we or they believe in X and intend to do Y, is grounded in just such processes.

With respect to group identity and responsibility, one might challenge the idea that narrative is the right thing to look at since a group's narrative may be nothing more than "public relations," a smoke screen, or propaganda—deceptive and not reflective of the real identity of the group. From a critical perspective, we need to look for hidden narratives—or give more weight to Striblen's notion of externally constructed narratives. Ultimately, we may have to judge narratives and measure identity by the group's actions.

There is a deeper issue. To the extent that the narrative, even if formed over time by many individuals, transcends those individuals and persists beyond them, a less optimistic picture than that painted by either Striblen or Carr might be justified. Striblen (2013, 160) suggests that the group narrative "does not operate above or without its members. There is a necessary interdependence...." And Carr (1986a, 532) maintains that the "community ... is not opposed to the individuals who make it up but exists precisely by virtue of their acknowledgement of each other ...." Even if these claims are, to some extent, correct, it's also true that narratives can take on a life or a power of their own; they can transcend individuals and come to conservatively support an instituted structure, as well as oppress or dominate (in explicit or subtle ways) the intentions of the individuals that belong to the group. It's just here that the idea that narratives can, in some cases, operate in implicit ways, shaping the way that we see and understand and act in the world, becomes relevant.

Narratives, much like intersubjective interactions themselves, as they are shaped in both extended institutional and technological structures and practices, can be positive in allowing us to see certain possibilities, but at the same time, they can blind us to other possibilities, and carry our intentions and cognitive processes in specific directions. Accordingly, we need to take a closer and critical look at how social and cultural practices, institutions, and the narratives that support them, either productively extend or, in some cases, curtail individual autonomy and shape our intersubjective relations. The forces and power structures that receive support from narratives can play dominating roles that distort democratic processes, and can affect an extensive range of social, legal, and political practices. Since narratives, along with certain technologies and media, as they are strategically used for consciously determined objectives by various institutions for various purposes, can manipulate and move us to action, we need to ask what such things do to us as subjects of cognition, agents, and group members.

9.3 Critical Theory and Critical Narratives

The idea of socially extended cognition motivates a critical normative perspective not usually taken up in the cognitive science literature. Cognitive processes that are shaped in social-cultural and institutional structures and in technological practices can allow us access to certain possibilities even as they block other possibilities. These structures and practices can expand or limit the quality and quantity of affordances available to us. Such considerations lead us back to the issue of autonomy. If the externalities of institutional structures, and social and cultural practices—including, for example, those of legal systems, bureaucracies, markets, corporations, and even local social groups to which we belong—can shape our cognitive processes and social affordances from the outside, is there much room left for the notion of individual autonomy? Such structures and practices can have profound effects on us, on our thinking, and on our social interactions. Again, it is important to ask what institutions do to us as agents and as subjects of cognition. I think that these kinds of questions fall squarely into the concerns of critical social theory.

Consider, for example, that cognitive studies of decision-making show that even if one seems to be engaged in solitary mental reflection, decision-making is really a matter of embodied, emotion-rich, environmentally modulated processes. Even if we are trained as hard-nosed rationalist philosophers, or no-nonsense business executives, or data-driven scientists, research has shown that our decisions are influenced by various institutional practices. Sometimes the effects are unintentional and are accidental features of the institutional environment; sometimes they are the result of an institution's strategic planning. Examples can be found almost everywhere. They include the spatial arrangement of supermarkets for merchandizing purposes, the architectural design of churches, the rules of evidence and the structure of allowable questions in a courtroom trial, and a variety of rituals and practices designed to manipulate our emotions.

A good and relatively innocuous example of how institutions may use different media to manipulate our cognitive processes and change our behaviors can be found in studies of altruistic behavior. Empathic reactions are stronger when we understand the personal situation of an individual than if we have only abstract, detached, theoretical, or merely statistical information about the plight of others (Slovic 2007; Small, Loewenstein, & Slovic 2007). The kind of information provided to potential charitable donors will affect not only their decision to act altruistically by making a donation, but will determine the amount that they donate. It's known, for example, that a higher number of victims involved in a major disaster or in genocide will not necessarily generate more altruistic behavior than a smaller number (*Figure 9.1*).

When someone is presented with a set of statistics, representing the cold although convincing facts about the enormity of the problem to be addressed, they show less altruistic behavior (make less donations) than when they are presented with an image and/or personal story of one individual involved. Alternatively, when presented with the personal narrative concerning the suffering of an individual person, people experience a variety of emotional reactions and show a higher degree of altruistic behavior (*Figure 9.2*). This is an example of how different media can enter into our cognitive processes, and how institutions may use media to elicit certain behavior. Our decision-making process changes, indeed is manipulated, when one set of external factors is introduced rather than another—that is, when images plus narrative are part of the process rather than just statistical data.

The objective of the charitable organization that exploits such practices for the sake of raising money may be noble, and the outcome, a certain amount of altruistic behavior, may be good for everyone, but one can easily think of other organizations,

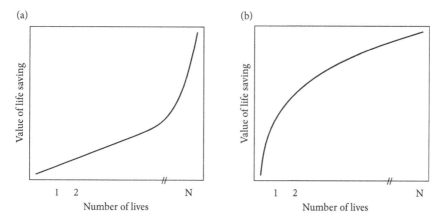

Figure 9.1 Graph A represents a normative utilitarian model that suggests that the larger loss of life will motivate a greater degree of altruism. Graph B represents something closer to actual behavior. The greater the loss of life the more abstract and emotionless it becomes with only slight increases in altruistic behavior after the first few cases.

Source: Reprinted from P. Slovic, "'If I look at the mass I will never act': psychic numbing and genocide," *Judgment and Decision Making*, Volume 2, Issue 2, pp. 79–95, Copyright © 2007 American Psychological Association, Figures 3 and 4, pp. 84–5, reproduced under the terms of the Creative Commons Attribution 3.0 Unported License (CC-BY-3.0), https://creativecommons.org/licenses/by/3.0/.

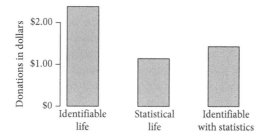

Figure 9.2 Mean donation in cases when subjects were told that donations would help support a particular individual vs. when subjects were told that donations would support relief efforts addressing problems summarized by a set of statistics, vs. when they were presented with both the statistics and the individual case.

Source: Reprinted from *Organizational Behavior and Human Decision Processes*, Volume 102, Issue 2, D.A. Small, G. Loewenstein, and P. Slovic, "Sympathy and callousness: The impact of deliberative thought on donations to identifiable and statistical victims," pp. 143–53, Copyright © 2006 Elsevier Inc., Figure 3, p. 149, with permission from Elsevier: https://www.sciencedirect.com/science/article/abs/pii/S0749597806000057.

other objectives, and other outcomes that may not be so innocuous. The point is, however, faced with such institutional practices, we ought to understand, not only from an efficiency perspective how precisely they improve (or impede, or distort) cognitive processes of decision-making or problem-solving, or how we can improve their efficiency—these seem to be questions already addressed by various studies in cognitive science. We also need to ask from a critical perspective whether these processes improve (or impede, or distort) our communicative practices, our possibilities for action, our recognition of others, our shared and circumscribed freedoms, and so forth.

It is clear from the previous chapter that autonomy is not necessarily increased when interaction ceases or when we attempt to step outside social institutions. When possibilities for interaction are closed down, individuals can lose their freedom. This is the case where one person or group totally dominates another (as in totalitarian arrangements, or slavery). In such cases, interaction may cease or get greatly curtailed. This fits well with Iris Marion Young's definition of oppression: "Oppression consists in systematic institutional processes which prevent some people from learning and using satisfying and expansive skills in socially recognized settings, or institutional processes which inhibit people's ability to play and communicate with others or to express their feelings and perspectives on social life in contexts where others can listen" (1990, 38). In a similar way, terrorism can be defined as an attempt to bring the mutual dynamics of interaction to a halt.

Institutional arrangements and the various possibilities for extending cognition through social and cultural practices can facilitate interaction or can thwart it. Interaction is not facilitated in one-directional actions or cognitive exercises where, for example, one group employs surveillance technologies to control other groups. Control of this sort does not have to be explicit, and, as Foucault learned from Hegel, and everyone else learned from Foucault, exercises of power that are not explicit gain in potency.[3] Moreover, such effects do not have to be deliberate, where someone or some group explicitly decides to act against another. They may be unintended effects, or they may simply happen by chance.[4] In any case, our engagement with cognitive institutions may, on the one hand, help to reduce cognitive load and increase productivity, but, on the other hand, may restrict the scope of individual action choices and curtail our cognitive scope. Institutional structures and arrangements may lead cognitive processes in directions not anticipated, and can easily distort cognitive and communicative processes.

Research by Edwin Hutchins (1995), for example, showed that time-related details of communicative practices can introduce unexpected confirmation biases into outcomes. More communication, or early communication, is not always better than less or later communication. This applies to the example of a jury. On the one hand, if jury members are allowed to communicate with each other early in a trial process, there is a strong motivation to secure a shared interpretation of the information they have. As a result, Hutchins points out, they rush "to the interpretation closest to the center of gravity of their predispositions, regardless of [any further] evidence" given to them (1995, 259d; see Clark 1997). All further evidence is interpreted to confirm their initial view. On the other hand, if early communication is restricted, individuals in the jury tend to balance their own predispositions against the evidence presented, and the group confirmation bias is reduced. "Such results

---

[3] For Foucault the constraints imposed by institutions and social practices affect embodied processes that in turn are involved in intersubjective interactions (see Erlenbusch-Anderson 2015).

[4] Clark (1997, 276) cites a good example of how VHS recording technology gained market share in spite of the superior Betamax technology based on early market biases.

suggest that the collective advantage of a jury over an individual decision may dissipate proportionally to the level of early communication between members" (Clark 1997, 286). In other words, in the same way that a legal system organizes rules of evidence to push cognitive processes toward fair judgments, so also the way it organizes the rules of communication among jurors will affect the judgments of the individual members, and the jury as a whole.

When structural features of cognitive institutional practices are exclusionary, closing off possibilities, or when such practices are designed so that whoever uses them comes to be dominated by them, with the result that their thinking is narrowed and determined, then again autonomy, not just of the individual, but of social interaction is compromised. There's an old saying: when God closes one door he opens another. We could also say, in some contexts, when technologies or institutional arrangements open one door they close another, or perhaps several others. It continues to be a real question, for example, whether our now firmly established information and social networking technologies dominate by closing off possibilities, or liberate by creating more possibilities. It's an empirical question of where, in any particular case, such processes fall on a scale between the extremes of performativity and paralogy, to put it in terms defined by Lyotard (1984). That is, we should be able to place particular institutional practices somewhere on a scale that at one end defines value in terms of strict measures of efficiency (performativity), and at the other end describes a creative explosion of possibilities (paralogy).

Critical theory, of course, already targets these kinds of things in its projects of cultural critique. In this respect, what I suggest here is twofold. First, that the cognitive-science informed analyses of interaction theory and socially extended cognition which offer insight into these processes and how they operate in institutional practices and procedures can inform critical theory. Second, since the cognitive science of such phenomena focuses on narrow questions about *how* such things work rather than on the broader consequences of such practices, we need to give cognitive science a critical twist. In this respect, what we can say quite clearly is that most cognitive theories, theories of action and interaction and social cognition, tend to be "ideal theories" in Charles Mills' sense of the term (see *Section 6.3*). Theories of cognition and social cognition presume "an idealized cognitive sphere" that ignores the effects of social constraints, especially those that involve race, gender, class, and specific oppressive structures, and considers biases to be a matter of "self-interest or the intrinsic difficulties of understanding the world, [with] little or no attention paid to the distinctive role of hegemonic ideologies and group-specific experience in distorting our perceptions and conceptions of the social order" (Mills 2005, 169).

Standard accounts of action and interaction abstract away from the specifics of everyday life; they ignore the circumstances that are framed by social and instituted practices that often lead to structural distortions and injustices. An idealized account of action forgets that actions always carry along their full circumstances. An idealized account of social interaction typically starts with the concept of agents as the "abstract and undifferentiated equal atomic individuals of classical liberalism" and then proceeds to ignore differences that result from "structural domination, exploitation, coercion, and oppression, which in reality, of course, will profoundly shape the [social] ontology of those same individuals, locating them in superior and inferior positions in social hierarchies of various kinds" (Mills 2005, 168). On ToM models, for example, agents engage in idealized forms of rationality that are seemingly unaffected by their affective states or social positions. Differences in some social affordances available in western industrialized societies based on racial or gender differences, for example, with few exceptions[5] are simply not considered. Theories of social cognition need to consider such issues. For critical theory these are issues that pertain to social justice; for cognitive science, however, these same issues pertain to how we actually do the science, and to the question of whether we get it right when we explain social cognition in abstract and idealized terms.

What role do narratives play in this kind of critical project? Narratives, to the extent that they support the formation of institutions, traditions, practices, etc. can be rigid protectors of the status quo, and promoters of corporate and national interests. For this reason some critical theorists (e.g., Habermas 1987) are suspicious of narratives. I'll argue here that, without downplaying this suspicion, our abilities to develop a critical perspective on the institutions and the narratives that shape us, are themselves dependent on a narrative competency tied to collaborative communication processes. In the end *we*, by collectively and critically reframing our narratives— that is, by the use of a critical narrative practice—will be able to change our institutions and thereby change who *we* are.

In Habermas's critical theory we find a strong endorsement for the importance of interaction. In his critique of action theory, for example, Habermas emphasizes this importance.

[Analytic action theory] is limited to the atomistic view of action by an isolated actor and does not consider the mechanisms for coordinating action through which interpersonal relations come about. It conceptualizes action on the presupposition of exactly one world of existing states of affairs and neglects those actor-world relations that are essential to social interaction. As actions are reduced to purposive interventions in the objective world, the rationality of means-ends relations [i.e., instrumental rationality] stands in the foreground.   (1984, 273–4)

Instrumental rationality falls far short of the kind of communicative rationality involved in the practices that enrich and further the development of interaction.

Communicative acts – that is, speech acts or equivalent nonverbal expressions – take on the function of coordinating action and make their contribution to building up interactions.... Communicative action is dependent on situational contexts, which represent in turn segments of the life-world of the participants in interaction.   (1984, 278–9)

Habermas, however, stops short of recognizing the contribution of narrative practices to this development. So here let me outline how the concept of narrative competency as developed in interaction theory fits into a critical theory context. I suggest that a consideration of narrative competency can in fact contribute to a better conception of the kind of communicative practices that Habermas and Honneth, and more generally, critical theory, champion. Indeed, narrative practices must be understood as essential to making thematic just those "actor-world

---

[5] Cutting and Dunn (1999) come close to an exception. Their focus is more on family background and language differences. A number of studies of empathy have explored racial and gender differences.

relations," situational contexts, interactions, and lifeworld events that critical theorists find important because they are tied to questions about recognition and justice.

Here I leave aside specific issues that involve the differences between an empirical account of those practices we actually use in understanding others, and a normative account that prescribes how such practices ought to be. How one diagnoses existing communicative practices or prescribes for more critical ones will certainly be affected by the model one takes as the empirical account of human interactions (TT, ST, IT, or some other theory). Where the line is drawn between the empirical and normative is a difficult issue, however. For example, Honneth (following Lukács) suggests (as an empirical claim, which nonetheless seems to be a normative diagnosis as well) that our everyday affairs are characterized by reification and an accompanying observational attitude. Are social relations, as they have come under the influence of commodification and contemporary social and communicative practices, so shaped by such practices that they start to fit theories of social cognition that take their starting point with third-person observation (e.g., some versions of ToM), rather than the more embodied accounts of interaction theory? We at least need to think that how communication ought to happen is constrained by how it can happen. Understanding how communicative practices start to take shape in normal developmental terms may be a good starting point for understanding how distortions enter into the process.

As I have been arguing, to get a good account of the more sophisticated and nuanced aspects of adult social cognition and interaction, there is no need to view theoretical inference or simulation as the primary and pervasive mode of understanding others. Rather, in addition to the kind of embodied processes of primary and secondary intersubjectivity, one should look to contributions from communicative and narrative practices. Consider what we have said about narrative in previous chapters. We become thoroughly familiar with stories very early, and we learn to use the narrative framework to make sense out of our own actions and the actions of others, as well as our joint actions. Narratives are focused on action and they translate actions into language. I've suggested that at least in some cases the narrative framing of actions tends to loop back and invade our everyday intersubjective engagements and conversations, sometimes providing normative templates to help us make sense of another's behavior. We listen to stories, or we act them out; we can see them acted out in play and in plays, on television, in our family house, or on the street. Everyday personal narratives, as well as cultural narratives, are formed and understood *interactively*—and they help to form us in our self-understanding. Narratives (which are much more particularistic and closer to our lifeworld than theory or folk psychology) help to frame specific situations and their meaning in a way that gives us an understanding of what others in those situations are about. They contribute to, and shape, the massive hermeneutical background necessary for understanding ourselves and others; they teach us what to expect or not expect; what is appropriate or not appropriate; they provide knowledge of what actions are acceptable and in what circumstances, and when, and by whom, and what sort of events are important and noteworthy, and what kind of explanations constitute the giving of good reasons.

It's not clear, then, that we can easily step outside our everyday narratives. Yet Habermas, for example, has very little to say about narrative in the context of critical communication. The closest he comes to saying anything promising in this regard is in one footnote. He makes a clear distinction between propositional discourse (i.e., theory) and narrative.

There is in fact an intuitively accessible distinction between thinking in propositions in abstraction from speaker–hearer relations and imagining interpersonal relations. In imagining stories in which I – the imagining subject – have a place in a context of interactions, the roles of participants in the first, second, and third persons – however internalized – remain constitutive for the sense of what is thought or represented.   (1984, 440–1, n. 42)

This suggests that even in working out theoretical solutions to problems in the lifeworld, the propositional thinker will need recourse to narratives in which to imagine different scenarios. Narratives are tools, and can be critical tools for problem-solving.

For the most part, however, Habermas treats narrative as a force that reproduces traditions and reinforces the established power structures. For enlightenment thinkers, more generally, narrative is a weak cousin to scientific discourse. Narrative "is seen as limited, conservative and unreliable in its purchase on knowledge" (Wells 1996, 32). This seems to be the way Habermas thinks of it, and why narrative is not a resource for his views on communicative action. According to Habermas, narrative maintains the lifeworld's "culturally transmitted and linguistically organized stock of interpretive patterns" (1987, 137). Habermas seems to think that our attitude toward what I have called the massive hermeneutical background needs to be a hermeneutics of suspicion. Susan Wells provides a good analysis of Habermas' attitude towards narrative.

Those interpretive patterns shape everyday life, family relations, and the repertoire of face-to-face interactions in the life-world, a domain of customary relations.... [Narrative] coexists with system, where relations are regulated outside language, by money and power.... Habermas's theory, then coheres with traditional understandings of narrative as conservative, prereflective, and socially integrating.   (1996, 33–4)

All of this is beyond doubt. Narratives can scaffold the oppressive prejudices embodied in gender roles, race relations, and class distinctions. As Sally Haslanger puts it, these prejudices take the form of "unconscious patterns of behavior that reinforce the role in oneself and others and enable one to judge others by its associated norms. And in order for large groups of people to internalize similar or complementary norms, there must be a cultural vocabulary—concepts, narratives, images, scripts, cautionary tales—that provide the framework for action" (Haslanger 2012, 11).

But certainly narrative can also offer some critical possibilities, since narratives serve to mediate intersubjective relations. They can map out the immediate and deeper contexts of action and understanding, provide detailed descriptions of events, objects, and persons, help to coordinate complex tasks, define the identities and roles of individuals and groups, and express agreement among individuals. Critical narrative practice can also generate a reflective attitude about new or different possibilities. There is dialectic and sometimes surprise or revelation in our self-understanding when we are forced to confront the different worlds that the narratives of others open up, or find in our own narratives differences from what may be the more dominant cultural narratives. Consider, for example, what W. E. B. Du Bois (2007), in his *Souls of Black Folk*, calls 'the strange experience' of finding out who you are when you find out that you are 'a problem' in the eyes of others because of the color of your skin.[6] This realization takes shape not only in his narrative, but in us as we read his narrative and as a different experiential world opens up and challenges us when we start to see from his perspective. This confrontation with a critical narrative (and its perspective) which shows us in some aspects what our world really is can motivate an attempt (by means of action) to form a new narrative. Narrative literature (like art generally) often plays this critical role. Narratives provide one important source for staking out new social arrangements, and for pushing the boundaries of what is acceptable and what is not.

If criticism (which can involve a theoretical stance) "illuminates the life-world by making explicit what is latent in narrative texts" (Wells 1996, 34), that illumination itself usually takes the form of another narrative. I've been suggesting that narratives serve communicative purposes, and here I want to argue that they play a central role in the kind of communicative rationality that critical theory prefers over instrumental rationality. Can we not think of narrative practices that seek to resolve communicative problems—narratives that themselves constitute a form of critical reflection? It is surely right to say that narratives can be conservative, but they can also serve a critical function. They can be the keepers of memory, but they can also represent the blueprints of change. In any case they can tell us about who the others are, and who we are.[7] In this respect, narrative may in fact involve a form of recognition, as suggested by Hannah Arendt.

According to Arendt, action discloses who we are and at the same time "produces" stories whether we intend for them to do so or not (1958, 84). We don't do this alone, however; we tell who we are to others and meaning gets constituted in a "web of relationships." As Habermas and McCarthy (1977) note, however, this is a piece of ideal theory insofar as Arendt describes "unconstrained communication," and ignores strategic action, "another form of social interaction (which is, to be sure, not oriented to reaching agreement but to success)" (1977, 17).[8] Setting this aside, however, for Arendt, for this revelation of oneself and the other to work (in action and narrative), it requires a form of recognition—specifically mutual consideration as

---

[6] Thanks to Jasper St Bernard for calling this text to my attention.

[7] Wells thus suggests: "Just as Habermas's theory of language overlooked the work of interpretation, so his treatment of narrative divorces narration from reflection, as if readers and writers [as well as speakers] were unable to reflect as they read [or speak, or interact], as if the structures of narrative were spontaneously generated in a natural outpouring of language" (1996, 34). Habermas's conception of narrative undermines his own project since anything that approaches the genuine consensus that he aims for can only take place when each party understands each other's backgrounds and normative assumptions. Harrist and Gelfand (2005, 225) argue that: "As a form of hermeneutic dialogue, life history dialogue serves as a model for how we come to understand ourselves, know each other, and may serve as a forum for cultivating understanding."

[8] Seyla Benhabib (1986), building on Habermas, distinguishes four modes of action: communicative (the goal of which is mutual understanding), expressive (which aims at self-realization in a competitive fashion), instrumental (which concerns making or doing things with objects), and strategic (which aims to manipulate others).

we enact our stories together, and the possibility of making promises and offering forgiveness. This is required due to the boundlessness, unpredictability, and irreversibility of words and deeds enacted within an intersubjective plurality: "Since we always act into a web of relationships," Arendt explains, "the consequences of each deed are boundless, every action touches off not only a reaction but a chain reaction, every process is the cause of unpredictable new processes" (Arendt 1987, 41).

In this regard narratives play an important role in enabling both recognition and responsiveness to the extent that they capture something that goes beyond a purely formal or reified relationship. It's one thing to say, for example, that we ought to treat all humans as ends, and never as mere means, thereby recognizing the dignity of the human person. But it is quite another to encounter someone in the highly contextualized situations of everyday life and to recognize and acknowledge them for who they are. We can do that only when we have a narrative that we can use to make sense of them, or when they, or others give us the narrative that constitutes their own story. The more normative forms of recognition, as they get applied, are particularistic, constrained by particularistic practices and institutions; as a result, we often fall short of recognition in circumstances that can be ambiguous and unfair. Should recognition in such circumstances involve the evaluative judgment of others? Maybe it should, or maybe it should not; but in many cases it just does. And many times these judgments are biased one way or another. Ideally, we recognize others as persons who deserve respect; but if they are accompanied by a narrative about their abusive behavior, their enslavement of others, their terrorist activities, then that complicates *how much* respect we owe them.

Specifically, with regard to communicative action, it helps to know with whom we are communicating and what their interests are. Since speech situations are never ideal, but always call for interpretation, it's best to put all narratives on the table. How, otherwise, would we be able to diagnose the kind of communicative distortions that critical reflection is supposed to address? The Rawlsian idea of the original position behind a veil of ignorance, in which the participants know neither their own story nor anyone else's, like Habermas' notion of an ideal speech situation, may be a regulative idea that would abstractly define certain principles of fairness or justice, but it is not a practical model of democratic communication. Our evaluative perspectives and affective attitudes are always shaped by life forces. Gadamer's observation is important: "Long before we understand ourselves through the process of self-examination, we understand ourselves in a self-evident way in the family, society, and state in which we live" (1989, 276). But we should say too that self-understanding is not so self-evident, and that the families and communities and institutions in which we live shape our perceptions and our abilities to evaluate. Dropping a veil of ignorance over deliberations of justice will not negate or eliminate the biases that shape our cognitive processes. Putting our narratives on the table can go some distance towards this goal.

In real communicative settings the other person's story can make a large difference. Giving equal voice to an impoverished woman who has missed out on educational opportunities is not equal to giving equal voice to a privileged male CEO who has studied at the best universities. Things are not so black and white. The inequity may only become apparent in the communication process itself, but the reasons why there are such inequities in any particular case only become understood when their personal narratives are laid out on the table. Only then are we in a good position to employ critical reflection to address such inequalities. Only then can we avoid a simulation-style reduction of the other's narrative to the model of one's own self-narrative. Putting myself in the other person's shoes will be difficult if the other person doesn't own a pair of shoes. The diversity problem appears once again, and will be a problem for any critical theory that takes simulation as a model for social cognition and communication.

So the suggestion is that narrative can be put to a reflective and critical use. Of course, just as the lifeworld can be colonized by systems (for example, just as economic market forces can shape or misshape our lives) so systems can invade narratives and put them to the service of established relations. But systems can do the same with theory. Theory has no advantage over narrative in this regard. Moreover, if the force of such colonization depends on most of it remaining hidden (the less we know of it, the more power it has) then the capacity for narrative to set out and explicate such hidden powers will be a critical capacity, and will itself support recognition.

Importantly, narrative is better able to do this in the very language of the lifeworld—in terms that focus on people, and events, and actions, and interactions—and in a way that avoids the abstractions and the often reductionist leanings of theory. In that case, a critical narrative practice will run less of a risk of dehumanizing and alienating the participants—which is, of course, what critical theory is trying to avoid in the first place. What we need to do in critical reflection is to stay close to everyday experience—we need to capture the everyday interaction as it really happens among people; and what we need to avoid are the reifying and reductionistic abstractions and generalizations that often characterize philosophical theory, whether it's action theory or theory of mind.

I've insisted that our understanding of others is not a matter of mental states flying through thin air between minds; human feelings, intentions, thoughts, and beliefs are deeply embedded in backgrounds and contexts, and embodied in social interactions and communicative practices in the everyday lifeworld, and all of these phenomena are characterized by a great many differences that need to be recognized and acknowledged. Just because these backgrounds and contexts are rich and complex, narrative is a relevant and unavoidable tool for understanding others. Competency with different kinds of narratives enables us to understand others in a variety of ways, as they live in a diversity of situations. Narrative needs to be part of what critical theorists call critical reflection, which should include the recognition of difference and the sometimes irreducible nature of such differences. The aim of critical narrative practice would be to level the playing field, not by eliminating differences, but by making intelligible where people are located on that field so that differences can be addressed by institutional rearrangement or by other means.

9.4 Imperfect Consensus and Critical Practice

Theory involves setting things out in neat patterns, and ideally it involves formalizing these patterns in terms of algorithms or mathematical formulae. The dream of theory, as someone has likely said before, is a perfect accounting. Following Habermas, critical theory is a theory that runs on a certain set of practices—communicative practices that involve critical reflection informed by scientific explanation. There are at least two parts to these practices, as Habermas indicates in his notion of depth hermeneutics. The hermeneutical part involves the attempt to understand ourselves and others in the particularity of our shared or sometimes our very different situations. The scientific or explanatory part attempts to explain how and why these situations exist—how social, economic, institutional, and political forces shape our lifeworld. The reality, and not the ideal, is that science itself is hermeneutical and situated, and that, as an institution itself, it also succumbs to social, economic, and political forces (Slaby & Gallagher 2015). Because science is practiced by humans who gain their third-person perspective from the meshing of first- and second-person lifeworld perspectives the hermeneutical part of critical reflection gains importance. Here it's a matter of understanding others, and understanding others in our everyday interactions is neither reducible nor inflatable to providing theoretical explanations.

At the same time, however, taking a critical stance with respect to understanding others is different from our involvement in everyday interactions. It involves taking a critical reflective attitude, which, as Gadamer (1989) pointed out in his well-known debate with Habermas, is also hermeneutically situated. In these critical practices there is collaboration, but also tension, between scientific explanation and intersubjective understanding. The tension is most clearly seen as one between Enlightenment-style universalizing tendencies in theory (when science stops being scientific and becomes scientistic), and the insistence on the inescapable particularity and diversity of our everyday situations as we attempt to understand ourselves and others.

Narrative practices fall on the hermeneutical side. They attempt to capture the particularity of our situations. That has to be the starting point for any critical practice. Here is the situation. I live here in country A, which has this history; I live in this culture, and I've had this upbringing, and my gender and race and ethnicity and position and social and economic status are such and such. I aspire to this other position, and I have these intentions and plans. You live in the same country but with a somewhat different cultural background, and have had a very different upbringing. Your gender, race, ethnicity, position, social and economic status are such and such, and very different from mine. Perhaps you aspire to stay where you are. Or perhaps you feel trapped and unable to move; perhaps you are oppressed, or depressed, or disabled and moving is near impossible. To level the playing field one first has to define what the playing field looks like. It's littered with things, artifacts, possessions, buildings—some things that can't be easily rearranged. It's not difficult to see that making it level in even a few places is difficult. One then needs to bring in ladders and ramps, and whatever else might be needed. But we don't really see the field until we bring all of the narratives out into the open and examine them. We have to specify in significant detail the *this* and *that*, the *such and such*.

Habermas and Gadamer agreed on one thing: that communication or dialogue is essential. What Albrecht Wellmer says about Gadamer's conception of dialogue, however, applies equally to Habermas' conception of communicative action.

The Enlightenment knew what a philosophical hermeneutic forgets – that the "dialogue" which we, according to Gadamer, "are", is also a context of domination and as such precisely no dialogue. . . . [T]he context of tradition as a locus of possible truth and factual agreement is, at the same time, the locus of factual untruth and continued force.

(Wellmer 1971, cited in Habermas 1980, 204–5)

From Habermas' perspective, hermeneutical dialogue and narratives are too trusting since they fail to take into account extra-linguistic factors and the objective and hegemonic force of cultural traditions, economic arrangements, class structures, race, gender, etc. What the ideal critique requires, however, and what Gadamer rules out, is an escape from the constraints imposed by those hegemonic factors by means of a methodological, scientific reification. Since critical reflection is itself situated in the same mix of forces, it does not escape the distortions introduced by these forces.

This does not mean our interactions and communicative actions are fully determined. Merleau-Ponty (2012, 410) emphasized the very aspect of language that Gadamer came to recognize, and that Habermas requires as the *sine qua non* of critique; namely, the aspect of transcendence. Language operates as a constraint, but also as an enabling condition. Gaining a critical perspective will not be accomplished in a total escape from the forces that constrain our communicative processes. It will always involve an incomplete transformation or partial transcendence accomplished within these processes.

Accordingly, our communicative processes can never resemble an ahistorical conversation behind a veil of ignorance, or between absolutely autonomous minds. What Habermas calls the "unlimited interpretive community," a consensus "achieved under the idealized conditions of unlimited and control-free communication," not only cannot be "permanently maintained," but, given the nature of intersubjectivity, language and interpretation, is impossible to attain. Even if this ideal is conceived of as a formal, regulative measure, in practice it cannot be instantiated except in a set of communicative actions with all of their constraints; it cannot be instantiated outside of a hermeneutical-agentive situation constrained by particular forces, and in which we always already exist. Which is just to say, that as an ideal, it cannot be instantiated.

The task of critique, as a form of action and interaction, is not something that can ever be finished. There are no easy transformations, nor total revolutions; no unambiguous appropriations of traditions, nor complete escapes from them. History is, as Merleau-Ponty (1973, 225) insisted, an open dialectic. Critical practices are irreducible to either trouble-free conversations or context-free speech acts, because there will always be contestation within history. There will always be irreducibly different perspectives. Not only because of the nature of communicative practices, but also because of the nature of history, there is no possibility for perfect consensus.

From our considerations about action and interaction, however, we learn to reverse Wellmer's emphasis, or at least to set it in balance, without disputing the appropriateness of the intentions of critical theory. The setting for communication is not exclusively a locus of factual untruth and domination; it is also, and at the same time, a locus of possibilities for cooperation and joint actions, as well as limited or incomplete truth. There are events that include responsiveness and transcendence,

and occasions of recognition. Due to the inescapable ambiguity of historical existence, however, even in critically informed practices recognition, agreement, or
consensus will never be perfect, since, as Merleau-Ponty indicated, historical reality
is "the excess of what we live over what has already been said" (1964a, 83). Even
imperfect consensus, however, may improve a situation and may reduce the degree of
domination or exploitation to a level that, even if not absolutely emancipatory, is
somewhat acceptable. Nothing, not even emancipation, is exempt from this ambiguity.

All of this may be obvious, or it should be obvious from the analyses in the
previous chapters, and from what we see in our everyday lives. Interaction is always
embodied, which means it is always situated and shaped by cultural forces and the
various constraining factors involved in communicative practices. The mother's
gesture to the infant already speaks in the language of her personal history, her
race, her gender, her economic status, her culturally defined role. Recognition, which
starts in elemental responsiveness, is already constrained by those forces that are
never fully external to experience. Needless to say, all of this takes place, and is in
place, long before the infant is in a position to raise a critical question. Twenty years
later, if the infant is lucky, the question might come up. In the meantime, institu-
tionalized and imperfect forms of recognition support our survival. Recognition is
accomplished only in such imperfect intersubjective interaction contexts. This means
that in taking a critical perspective we cannot look merely at individualistic phenomena to account for either the possibility or the failure of recognition. Failures of
recognition and the occurrence of social pathologies are not attributable simply to a
failure of simulation processes or the absence of a feeling of mutual sympathy
(Honneth 2008a, 122).

Honneth draws the following conclusion.

In the last three decades, social criticism has essentially restricted itself to evaluating the
normative order of societies according to whether they fulfill certain principles of justice.
Despite its success in justifying some normative standards and despite its efforts at differentiating the various fundamental aspects involved in the act of defining such standards, this
approach has lost sight of the fact that violating generally valid principles of justice is not the
only way in which a society can show itself to be normatively deficient. Recent social criticism
has not only failed to pay sufficient attention to those deficiencies that are still best described by
the term "social pathologies", but it has even failed to establish plausible criteria for judging
certain social practices to be pathological.

Neither social nor individual pathologies are reductively biological or merely neurological. All of the forces of culture can come to play a role here. Responding to others,
interacting with them, and recognizing them within the variety of human
institutions—these are all embodied and enactive practices; they are also embedded
and extended in narrative practices and in the social and cultural forces that
characterize human existence in different times and places. Recognition, as a way
to resist reification, or to address social pathologies, is more than cognitive, it is also
affective, as Honneth makes clear; but it is also more than affective experience, since
it depends on arrangements that go beyond the individuals involved.

The task of critical theory is to investigate all instances where institutional, social,
and cultural factors—whether they are overly rigid bureaucratic and performative

practices, or cognitive tools, media, technologies, or cognitive institutions that curtail our social interactions, or fail to regulate them properly, or established narratives that rigidly preserve the *status quo*—impinge on our lives in ways that lead to reification, pathologies of recognition, or serious limitations in our cognitive-affective and intersubjective lives.

Because social interactions more than any other aspects of human existence make us what we are, and because they provide the ground on which we build all of the institutional and cultural practices that shape our lives, then without limiting the diversity that can be found in our world, our judgments about those institutions and cultural practices should concern *first* whether they distort our interactions or even prevent them from happening. What kinds of interactions we prefer over others would require further criteria that we can only work out through continued inter-action and further narrative practices. These ought to be criteria that would be constrained and guided by some concept of justice.

10

A Practice of Justice

Rather than attempting to work out principles of justice as they might derive from or pertain to the abstractions of original positions or ideal situations of communication, or as they might apply to large-scale social-economic-political regimes, I propose that we ask what justice is as it pertains to immediate embodied intersubjective interactions, and how it extends from there to institutionally mediated social interactions. Are there criteria to be found within the analyses of action and interaction that would define the practice of justice or a set of just practices? By focusing on the *practice* of justice my aim is not to provide an ideal or necessarily universal notion of justice, but to ask whether there is a conception of justice already at work in our everyday practices. Admittedly, justice in practice may be imperfect, less than universal, and often found alongside injustice. Even if that ambiguous mix of justice and injustice characterizes our everyday interactions, it does not preclude rearrangements that would lead more in the direction of justice.

10.1 Justice in the Wild

Reading *A Theory of Justice*, an influential book by the contemporary philosopher John Rawls, I cannot escape the feeling that rather than describing a human innovation, it elaborates on ancient themes, many of which are recognizable in our nearest [non-human] relatives. (Frans De Waal 1996, 161)

In traditional philosophical discussions of justice, one starts either abstractly by inventing an original or ideal situation in which to formulate principles of justice, or, just as abstractly, with a conception of the state of nature. In the latter case, social contract theories picture either a struggle for existence (Hobbes) or a benign setting that emerges into some kind of trade-off of nature with civil society (Rousseau). We don't need to invent a state of nature, however; we have some scientific data from ethologists and developmental psychologists about situations "in the wild," even if so far this gives us only glimpses into real states of nature.

In discussing the most basic interactions of non-human animals, Mark Bekoff and Jessica Peirce (2009, xiv) consider data from the study of animals in the wild and suggest that a basic sense of justice is interwoven with cooperative behavior (including a cluster of behaviors that reflect altruism, reciprocity, honesty, and trust) and empathy (including neighboring phenomena of sympathy, compassion, grief, and consolation). Although it still may be controversial to think that non-human animals engage in practices that can be considered moral or just (Bekoff and Pierce offer evidence for this claim; also see Rowlands 2002),[1] clearly some of these aspects of cooperation and empathy are to be found in the earliest intersubjective interactions among humans. Much of the evidence cited in previous chapters supports the idea that infant-caregiver interactions involve a reciprocity from the earliest moments, and that basic empathy, altruistic behavior, and consolation emerge quite early in human infants. We can also say that in almost every case where something starts to vary from such typical interactions (at least before a specific age, and excluding some developmental disorders on the side of the infant) the cause lies with the caregivers, typically adults who must deal with their own physical and affective circumstance and perhaps the pressures and social distortions that shape their own lives.

Justice, in such contexts, is not rational in any sense connected to the notion of *ratio* or proportion or equity. Bekoff and Pierce cite experiments with the "ultimatum game" by Keith Jensen and his colleagues, where participants are asked to divide some goods to share with others. Jensen tested chimpanzees; the goods were raisins. Chimpanzees differed from adult humans in the way they played the game. The chimpanzees, without getting upset, accepted any offer, even a very low one from a partner who kept most of the raisins for herself. Bekoff and Pierce do not agree with Jensen's conclusion that chimpanzees, in contrast to humans, are not sensitive to fairness, but they do agree with Jensen that what one might consider a fair (i.e., equal) distribution is not necessarily rational: "the behavior of these chimpanzees is considered more rational in pure economic/game-theory terms" (Bekoff & Pierce 2009, 110). That is, it is economically reasonable to accept anything more than zero; and it makes sense to keep the most for oneself in most cases. Jensen's experiments, in any case, were not conducted in the wild, and this may affect the behavior studied.

If we look into the philosophical origins of the meaning of justice we are led back to Anaximander who, in one of the oldest, if not the oldest fragment in Greek philosophy, conceives of justice in the natural order of things, as a kind of "structured arrangement" in the ecology of how things rhythmically respond to each other over some course of time (Curd 2016; Oppermann 2003). Without claiming that Anaximander had anything like human interaction in mind,[2] the notion of a quite basic natural justice as a dynamical arrangement of responses, or of a back-and-forth giving and taking, seems to capture the type of rhythm described by Colwyn Trevarthen and other developmental psychologists in their characterization of primary intersubjectivity. Of course, Anaximander's is not a positive conception of justice as it relates to legal or political issues. Nor is it a conception of justice that concerns the distribution of goods. But, reading it through the notion of primary intersubjectivity, it is relevant to understanding how we treat others, and how they ought to be treated. It's not clear that this always comes down to fairness, or a sense of justice based on a sense of fairness. Indeed, if Bekoff and Peirce are right that a sense of justice "seems to be an

---

[1] Bekoff and Pierce rehearse a significant amount of empirical evidence for this kind of claim. I don't try to summarize all of that evidence here since my point is not to substantiate such claims but to take the idea of justice in the wild as one possible starting point for the wider-ranging discussion that follows.

[2] There's a tradition of abstruse interpretations that go along with the seeming poetic nature of Anaximander's fragment, starting with Theophrastus. See, e.g., Heidegger's 1946 essay, *Der Spruch des Anaximander* (Heidegger 2015, 296–343); Derrida (1994, 23–9).

innate and universal tendency in humans" (2009, 114), and continuous with certain tendencies in some non-human animals, a more basic sense than the sense of fairness may be at stake—a sense, perhaps, of just being able to respond, or being able to join in the back-and-forth arrangement of responses. As we've already seen, and as Bekoff and Pierce suggest, "before they can sit or walk, human babies are able to assess another person's intentions, and these social evaluations are important in deciding who's a friend or who's a foe" (ibid)—or, more basically, what type of action they might anticipate from the other person, and how they might respond to it. On this reading, there is injustice (or a disruption of justice) when the structured, dynamical arrangement of (friendly) interaction gets disrupted, something that occurs, for example, in the still face experiment, or in Murray and Trevarthen's (1995) experiment when the dynamics of interaction are undone by a recorded video of the mother.

It's not clear that the concept of justice as a structured arrangement or ecology, as in Anaximander's fragment, involves fairness. Plato introduces the notion that justice is a kind of balance—a balanced arrangement. The idea that justice is more than (or at least different from) fairness or this sense of balance, however, can be seen in the link between justice and friendship (philia) in Aristotle. "How man and wife and in general friend and friend ought mutually to behave seems to be the same question as how it is just for them to behave" (2009, 1162a29–31; see also 1159b25–6). Yet, he also states: "When men are friends they have no need of justice" (1155a26–7). And, likewise: "Each of the [political] constitutions may be seen to involve friendship just in so far as it involves justice.... But in the deviation-forms, as justice hardly exists, neither does friendship" (1161a10–30). This seems to mean, not that justice is something over and above friendship, but that it is something already built into friendship.

Aristotle's notions of justice and friendship are complex, primarily because there are many different kinds of friendship, and justice may mean different things within different friendships (Curzer 2012, 276). And if a perfect/equal friendship is one in which we find ourselves mirrored in our friends, there is also the important kind of unequal friendship—of parent and child, for example—where, even if one can reciprocate, it is never an equal reciprocation. The parent always gives more than the child can pay back. This is consistent with Aristotle's idea of general justice or justice as complete virtue, which "is complete not absolutely, but in relation to others" (2009, 1129b25–7; 1130a32–b2; 1130a10–13). Curzer's (2012, 224) gloss on this is to understand "in relation to others" to mean that "general justice consists simply of those aspects of all of the other virtues which pertain to other people." General justice can lead to more precisely defined practices that rule how we treat each other as friends, which we find in Aristotle classifications of rectificatory justice, economic justice,[3] and distributive justice. These different categories define practices that derive from and instantiate justice in specific circumstances. They concern

---

[3] Aristotle calls this "reciprocal justice" and describes it as follows: "Reciprocal justice holds exchange associations together, on the basis of proportionality and not on the basis of equality" (2009, 1132b32). This is a form of justice in exchange and financial dealings. I'll refer to it as "economic justice" here simply because I want to reserve the term "reciprocity" for more basic processes.

righting wrongs, trading goods, and how to treat (equally or unequally) others in these matters. But none of these categories explicate absolute rules since part of any circumstance is the kind of friendship involved.

> The duties of parents to children and those of brothers to each other are not the same, nor those of comrades and those of fellow citizens, and so, too, with the other kinds of friendship.
>
> (Aristotle 2009, 1159b35–1160a2; see also 1165a14–33; 1162a31–3)

> Each friendship fleshes out Aristotle's right rule for distributive justice in a different way. This explains why Aristotle takes our responsibilities toward different people to vary according to the nature of our friendships with them…. Generalizing, people have different justice-duties in different friendships because different friendships have different goals. Therefore they have different values, different definitions of "equal", and different rules for distributive justice.
>
> (Curzer 2012, 278)

The details of how we ought to treat others in varying circumstances clearly fall within the broad category of justice as well as the derivative forms of justice. But before one can specify anything about different justice-duties in categories of rectification, exchange, or distribution, one needs to determine precisely what the justice-relation is in the first place, such that it can change or lead to different treatments in different cases. "To inquire how to behave to a friend is to look for a particular kind of justice, for generally all justice is in relation to a friend" (Aristotle 2012, 1242a19–21). If we follow Aristotle on this, then, justice should not be simply equated with one or some addition of these derivative or particular kinds of justice-duties. Justice, for example, is not equivalent to some appropriate distribution even if it leads to some distributive arrangement.

The justice relation concerns the relation between friends. Honneth will suggest that this relation is one of recognition, but, as I've argued (*Section 8.2*), any of the developed forms of recognition that he describes are, like issues that pertain to legal rectification, economic exchange or distribution, derivative from an elementary recognition or, as I've termed it, elementary responsivity. Such a relation is ruled out in the case where interaction is impossible, where autonomy and the possibility of response are cut off, and recognition is undermined, as in the case of slavery (Aristotle agrees that there cannot be friendship or justice in the master–slave relation per se—and Hegel's analysis is consistent with this).

Returning to the wild, Bekoff and Pierce point to the occurrence of interactive play in non-human animals as a place to see the emergence of justice. They conceive of play, however, in terms of a set of rules accompanying a sense of fairness, social expectation, and equality (2009, 120–1). I think that play (or what we might call free play) should be distinguished from games, where rules are pre-determined or already instituted. In free play there may be implicit taboos, but they do not emerge or get defined as rules until something goes wrong; and this gets signaled by pausing the play, or stopping it full stop, or transitioning into something that is no longer play. Play involves action and interaction and the ability or possibility of the participants to continue in play. It's defined by a set of interactive affordances. When one animal starts to dominate in playful interaction, closing off the other's affordance space (or eliminating the autonomy of the other), the interaction and the play stop. What a participant can do in this basic kind of play is not determined by a pre-established rule or norm; it is limited only by what the other will allow and how the other responds. The initiation behavior of some forms of non-human animal play (e.g., the bow in the dog) is not an agreement like a social contract that comes along with a set of rules. It's a request (based on a species-specific natural rather than learned posture) for a certain kind of response; a signal that the action is not an aggressive attack. "A dog asks another to play by crouching on her forelimbs, raising her hind end in the air, and often barking and wagging her tail as she bows. [A bow also comes] right before biting... and right after vigorous biting..." (Bekoff & Pierce 2009, 121). Self-handicapping (e.g., not biting as hard as the dog can) is a response to the other's vulnerability as the action develops, based on an immediate sense of, or an attunement to what would or would not cause pain rather than on a rule.[4] Role-reversal (where the dominant animal makes itself more vulnerable) creates an immediate affordance for the continuance of play.

We don't have to say (*pace* Bekoff and Pierce) that these aspects of play exist to maintain *fair* play. Just as in rat play, as Bekoff and Pierce indicate (following Pellis), there is ongoing assessment, monitoring, and fine-tuning of responses to maintain the play mood (2009, 124); this does not mean that there is rule following for the sake of maintaining fairness. Things might change, however, if something about the affective aspect of the interaction goes off, which would bring along a change in whatever the ongoing dynamical reciprocity had been. In this regard, I think Bekoff and Pierce are correct to mention that *trust* is important "in the dynamics of playful interactions" (ibid). Primarily, trust in such close embodied interactions would be attuned more to a pleasure-pain standard than to a fair-unfair standard. If in a friendly playful interaction one player gets hurt, becomes uncomfortable, or is pushed beyond her affective limits, this can generate an immediate feeling of distrust for the other. That would constitute a disruption of the friendship, a break in this very basic sense that is prior to measures of fairness, exchange, or retribution. Robert Solomon captures this idea at the right scale: "Justice presumes a personal concern for others. It is first of all a sense, not a rational or social construction, and I want to argue that this sense is, in an important sense, natural" (1995,102; cited in Beckoff & Pierce 2009, 132). Beckoff and Pierce then rightly note this "suggests that justice, like empathy, is a sentiment or a feeling, and not only or even primarily an abstract set of principles" (2009, 132).

Should we call this a "basic justice" in the way that one speaks of basic action/activity, or basic empathy, to be differentiated from justice in a more complex sense? Is basic justice in this sense anything more than the interactions of friendship such that unfriendly interactions may involve a basic injustice? In considering the notion of basic justice in Anaximander and Aristotle, and in interactional play "in the wild," a vocabulary starts to take shape: structured arrangement, trust, friendship, response, autonomy, affordance space, and so on.

---

[4] One can think here of the differences in kinematics in the prenatal twin study where each twin adjusts the force of its touch depending on whether it is touching the wall of the womb *versus* the other twin *versus* its own face (Castiello et al. 2010). The latter two touches are more gentle (involving longer movement duration and prolonged deceleration time) than the first.

10.2 Beyond Distribution

This very basic, natural sense of justice may be of little interest to theorists of justice who explore institutional, legal, and political conceptions of fairness, exchange, or distribution. But if the roots of justice are somehow entangled in such basic inter-subjective interactions, this may nonetheless have implications for larger and more standard discussions of justice. In this regard, Axel Honneth (2012) has, I think, provided an insightful analysis of what he calls the "fabric of justice." Here I want to rehearse his analysis and relate it to what we have discussed in previous sections.

Honneth's initial worry is that contemporary theories of justice have little application to social and political practice. This motivates his critical examination of those theories. In his analysis he finds three elements that seem common to all liberal theories of justice.

1. A proceduralist schema
2. The centrality of distribution
3. The appeal to state administration

Honneth challenges each of these elements and offers his own account appealing to the notion of recognition.

What is at stake in such standard accounts of justice is individual autonomy: "what we call social justice has its measure in the guarantee of our personal, purely individual autonomy" (Honneth 2012, 37), and this is conceived in terms of the least amount of imposed limits and the highest degree of independence from others. In the standard account, "social bonds can generally be regarded as limitations on individual freedom.... This has given rise to the influential idea that creating a just society means conceding all subjects a form of self-determination that allows them to be as independent as possible of their partners in interaction" (37). This idea, which downplays the role of intersubjective interaction, and which Honneth rightly questions, is what leads to the idea of distribution as central to the notion of justice.

Because our dependency on others is viewed as a threat to our individual freedom, the latter can only be secured if every individual possesses sufficient means to achieve his or her life plans.   (2012, 37–8)

Justice is, accordingly, equated with just distribution. As Honneth indicates, however, what counts as just distribution is, according to such theories, to be determined by some procedural schema. One can easily think of Rawls' notion of the original position as such a procedure through which a group of seemingly autonomous individuals come to determine the principles of distribution through a voting procedure. Here we start to see that, from the perspective of someone like Rawls, the idea of embodied, enactive interactions that characterize our everyday primary and secondary intersubjective encounters with others are seemingly part of the problem rather than a source of a solution. In the original position, precisely the details of embodied engagement and situated social contexts are to be bracketed by dropping a veil of ignorance around the participants. To arrive at a completely neutral judgment about distribution we need to hide all details, not only about who our neighbors are, but also about who we are—what our embodiment is like.

Are we tall or short? Strong or weak? Are we white or black or some other color? Are we male or female? Are we fully abled? Can we stand up and gesture? Do we believe X or Y or Z? Do we have any special social status? Do we engage in religious practice? Do we belong to specific institutions? All of these details that may shape our real intersubjective interactions are set aside, neutralized, in order to guarantee fairness. The principles of justice that emerge from this arrangement would seemingly be perfectly appropriate for disembodied, non-social beings.

Honneth points to another issue. The idea that we are looking for a distribution schema at all presupposes that we have a conception of which aims and goods are worth pursuing (Honneth 2012, 40), and such goods are likely to include not just material things, but other kinds of arrangements about which we will have learned only through intersubjective, social interactions. To suggest that distribution some-how captures all aspects of value is similar to the reduction of a good life to economic utility (see Amartya Sen 1999 for a critique of this view). More basically, Honneth suggests, the idea that we are able to pursue worthy ends already presupposes the idea of autonomy. But autonomy is not something that can be bestowed by a distribution of goods or opportunities.

> Instead we achieve autonomy along intersubjective paths by learning to understand ourselves, via others' recognition, as beings whose needs, beliefs and abilities are worth being realized. However, this will only be possible if, at the same time, we recognize those who recognize us.... We do not acquire autonomy on our own, but only in relation to other people who are willing to appreciate us just as we are willing to appreciate them.   (2012, 41)

This brings us to the main point of Honneth's analysis. If autonomy, understood as relational, depends on intersubjective interaction rather than distribution, and justice in some sense depends on autonomy, then "current theories of justice completely fail to grasp the structure of justice" (41). Autonomy is not something that can be distributed.[5] "What helps us to acquire autonomy is not cut from the same cloth as a good that can be distributed" (41). This shows proceduralism to be the abstraction that it is. Likewise, it suggests that autonomy and the conditions of justice depend on bottom-up processes—the arrangements of everyday intersubjective interactions—rather than top-down state administration functions concerned with the distribution of goods and opportunities.

If, on these points, we come into alignment with Honneth's analysis, it's not clear that we should follow what seems to be his Hegelian strategy of positing the negation of each proposition in order to advance his positive proposal: distribution is replaced by recognition; proceduralism is replaced by "a reconstruction" of the basic moral norms of recognition; and the state is replaced by non-state actors and organizations. Rather, we can stay with what I take to be his central insight; namely, that justice is not about distribution, but relates to autonomy, which we understand to be relational and compound.

---

[5] As we'll see in the next section, autonomy is something like, or related to what Amartya Sen calls a functioning. Functionings are "features of the state of existence of a person, and not detached objects that the person or the household happens to 'produce' and 'own'" (1999, 10). I'll suggest a slightly different reading of this notion, however.

10.3 Is Justice Just This?

If I reach for a glass and miss or knock it over, my action is not unjust in itself. Justice or injustice is not about the arrangement of what we called (*Section 1.4*), following Hornsby, basic activity coming into line with one's intentions, or one's intentions lining up in the right way with one's actions. In large measure, and above a certain threshold, however, these alignments have to happen if our practices are to be just, and some disturbance in these intrinsic action-alignments can undermine justice. For example, I do not act justly if my intention is good but my action conflicts with my intention or is only accidentally linked to my intention. Justice enters into my individual action, however, only if it involves *inter*action; one's individual actions are only derivatively just or unjust. Justice, like autonomy, is relational. I cannot be just or unjust on my own. So an action is just or unjust only in the way it fits into the arrangements of intersubjective and social interactions.

Accordingly, justice depends on an arrangement in the register of situated inter-actional dynamics. Consider a dyadic interaction. Assume that there is an alignment of capability or skill, basic activity, intentions, and actions for each individual—a coherency, above a certain threshold, in each participant's individual action. "Above a certain threshold"—we can call this a principle of imperfection, meaning, simply, that no action is perfect in its details; for example, in most cases of interaction it doesn't matter in regard to justice that a glass gets accidently knocked over—and in most cases an individual's action within interaction will be more or less coherent, more or less careful. It doesn't have to be perfect. This coherency itself will, in the case of an action contributing to social interaction, depend on the interactional dynamics; an action determined as a specific part of an interaction and playing a role in a gestalt or pattern of interaction. But even if there is action coherency in both participants, and coherency in the interaction (a meshing of intentions, for example), this is not sufficient to make the interaction just. In the case of one or both participants, their intentions, and what they will accept from the other person as a satisfactory arrangement, may be subject to distortion due to agentive situational factors, or due to other interactions or other structured, intersubjective/social/insti-tutional arrangements. The criteria that determine whether the arrangement is just, however, are not determined outside or external to the dynamics of the actions and interactions themselves. It rather concerns the degree of autonomy that is generated in the actions and interactions. I take autonomy, as relational and compound, to be enacted in social interactions and therefore not an external measure.

Justice consists in those arrangements that maximize autonomy in our practices. To this we should add, not only that autonomy is relational, but also that autonomy is compound since in interaction it is never just one person's autonomy that is at stake. In dyadic interaction there are two individual autonomies, plus the autonomy of interaction. As we indicated (*Section 8.4*), one agent's autonomy is always defined (constrained or enhanced) not only by others, but by another (extra-individual) autonomy—that of the larger relational unit. The autonomy of the interaction itself depends on maintaining the autonomy of both individuals. Justice (like friendship) involves fostering this plurality of autonomies (this compound autonomy); it is a positive arrangement that instantiates or maintains some degree of compound relational autonomy. An individual can be more or less autonomous depending, for example, on whom she is interacting with, or on, as John Dewey once put it, "the circumstances of action and the conditions of life" (1929, 592). "Some degree" of compound relational autonomy, however, is not something that can be precisely measured; indeed, it's not clear that it can be quantified, or that it is an additive sum. Still a person may be able to say that she has more or less autonomy in this rather than that circumstance, or when interacting with this rather than that other person.

To suggest that justice involves maximizing autonomy leads to this worry that it is difficult (or perhaps impossible) to measure or quantify autonomy. If a person can say that he has more or less autonomy depending on circumstances, does he make this judgment on anything more than a comparative intuition? Here, if only in some limited fashion, the notion of affordances can be of help in specifying (i.e., giving us a way to talk about) autonomy, even if not strictly quantifying it. We can say that maximizing autonomy translates into maximizing affordances. In a different context I've suggested that we can measure autonomy by evaluating the quality and quantity of affordances provided in the agentive situation (see Gallagher 2018c; Gallagher & Janz 2018). This does not deliver a precise measurement, however, and is complicated by judgments about quality. Recent work on affordance theory (discussed in *Section 1.1*) helpfully suggests that affordances regarded as relational, are not only relative to an individual agent; social and cultural affordances may be defined relative to a form of life (Rietveld & Kiverstein 2014). The suggestion is that, relative to a form of life, they gain in objectivity at least to the extent that we can identify and inventory specific practices that are open to agents participating in a particular culture or cultural practice. If it is difficult in many circumstances to actually count affordances, or to evaluate the quality of the affordances available, in some circumstances it may be easy to see that the number or quality of one's affordances has changed, or that one's affordance space has contracted, reflecting a constriction of autonomy (see de Haan et al. 2013).

Amartya Sen (1999, iii, 17) suggests that a person's well-being can be indexed in terms of that person's functioning—what she "can do." His notion of "functioning vector" is, I suggest, a way to operationalize or track the notion of affordance in economic terms. A set of a person's feasible functioning vectors "represents the freedom that a person has in terms of the choice of functionings, given his personal features…and his command over commodities…" (9). Sen argues that the totality of all the alternative functioning vectors the person can choose from, conditioned by a variety of contingent circumstances, reflects the person's capabilities, which would include bodily skills, but also things like current bodily state (e.g., health, nutrition), and social status, and would be conditioned by surrounding circumstances. He also allows that the functioning vector may depend not only on the capacities of the individual but also on the functioning of others (1999, 8, n.4; also see Sen 2009, 231ff). "Basically, the claim builds on the straightforward fact that how well a person is must be a matter of what kind of life he or she is living, and what the person is succeeding in 'doing' or 'being.' The exercise must, in one way or another, take the form of valuing the functioning vectors reflecting the 'doings' and 'beings'" (1999, 19). Focusing on the possibilities of "doing" in action and interaction, and specifically on what the person "*can* do," ties this concept directly to affordances.[6]

This does not mean that functioning vectors will give us a measure of autonomy, or an exact way to compare a set of affordances. As Sen indicates, the evaluation of well-being will be inherently partial or incomplete. "It can quite easily be the case that while functioning vector A represents a higher level of well-being than B or C, the latter two may not be rankable vis-a-vis each other. There is nothing illegitimate or defeatist in recognizing that the valuation rankings of well-being may have gaps" (1999, 21). It's also the case that maximizing one's own individual well-being may not be the only motive for acting on an affordance. Sen suggests that there are other possible objectives and "possible 'deontological' requirements (related, say, to one's obligations to others)" that can guide individual action (1999, 9), and this introduces additional problems evaluating or measuring affordances or autonomy.

We've seen, however, that there are clear extremes. If, in my encounter with you, for example, the set of affordances available to me, i.e., a rough measure of my autonomy, is, relative to you, 0 (i.e., if I am your slave)—then interaction with you (in the sense defined in *Section 5.1*) is impossible and interactional autonomy is 0; but that means that your autonomy, relative to me is also at 0. This is the extreme of Hegel's master–slave dialectic. It is also an abstract situation since both master and slave are likely involved in other relations where autonomy and recognition (and other affordances) exist to some degree. Even the slave may have a partner or a friend and may engage in just interactions with others. It is also the case that dyadic relations tend to be parts of larger systems of relations. Impinging on dyadic relations we find constrictions and limitations placed on communication and association in societies arranged according to castes, rigid class systems, instituted authoritarian systems (including family and state), religious tyranny, and so forth. As Dewey points out, these are arrangements that lack justice and lead to an alienation that "contradicts the very purposes for which institutions were originally founded" (1973, 92).[7]

Here the discussion of distorted autonomy in (*Section 8.4*) is relevant. Structural features of the specific practices or institutions within which individuals interact can distort human relations in ways that subtract from total autonomy and reduce the overall interactive affordance space. This would be the obvious problem, as Dewey

---

[6] I intend this as a shift away from any focus on the notion of capability *simpliciter*. The notion of affordance, as relational, includes reference to the agent's capabilities, but also includes reference to characteristics of the external (physical, social, cultural) environment. Alternatively, one might think of capability, which Sen (2009, 19) defines as one's "power to do something," as already presuming the notion of affordance, since one doesn't have the power (potential) to do something unless there is the something that one can do. This shift, or at least refocusing, also avoids any possibility of reducing the issue to one of distribution—both affordance and autonomy are relational concepts and, as Honneth suggests with respect to recognition, they resist the idea that they can be reified and distributed like objective goods. Compare this point with Fraser's criticism of Young, where Fraser thinks of capabilities in terms of distribution (Fraser 1997, 191).

[7] Arendt (1958, 202), credits Montesquieu with this thought, that "the outstanding characteristic of tyranny was that it rested on isolation, on the isolation of the tyrant from his subjects and the isolation of the subjects from each other through mutual fear and suspicion – hence, tyranny was not one form of government among others but contradicted the essential human condition of plurality, the acting and speaking together, which is the condition of all forms of political organization" (1958, 202).

understood, if the principle were to be justice for each according to "what he can get through his ability, his shrewdness, his advantageous economic position due to inherited wealth and every other factor which adds to his bargaining power..." (Dewey & Tufts 1932, 454).[8] It may be less obvious in the case of institutions that are supposedly designed to foster communication and free exchange, but which either intentionally or unintentionally establish arrangements that undermine those very aims. In such cases we have the problems we discussed under the headings of *procedural* and *substantive* accounts of autonomy (*Section 8.4*).

If we arrange things in such a way that people cannot be guaranteed appropriate access to healthcare or education, except by bargaining or by making a deal,[9] then the distortions that come along with other factors (not only of social advantage/disadvantage, but of social and institutional arrangements) will undermine autonomy. Distribution, in this regard, is not entirely irrelevant since in a real sense distributive practices are social practices that have an effect on social affordances. Although there is no way to eliminate, or even to track all distortions, or in other words, because there is no perfect society, and because whatever we do to address such distortions we have to do through interaction, we are always in situations of imperfect justice.

It would be Platonic, idealistic, and utopian to say that society has to be arranged in a perfectly just manner in order to get just interactions; and it would be idealism from another direction to say that all interactions have to be perfectly arranged in order to have a just society. It is possible for individuals in an unjust society to enter into just interactions; and it is possible for individuals to enter into unjust interactions even in a just society. Still, one can say there is a kind of dialectical dynamics where, above a certain threshold, just social arrangements depend on interactions being just, and vice versa. Even in a set of unjust social arrangements the achievement of just interactions can have an effect on the whole—can start to move that threshold and perhaps cross it. The threshold is determined historically, and relative to all other practices in a culture.

If this is the case, and if it calls clearly for a kind of bottom-up activism where each of us attempts to maintain our social interactions within the bounds of friendship, and in instances where we cannot do that, at least pay heed to others and do them no harm, this does not rule out a top-down role for institutions, including the state. Indeed, large-scale infrastructures (including healthcare, transportation, and educational systems) are (for better or worse) best arranged by large-scale institutions. To move the interactional system towards more just arrangements, therefore, requires both bottom-up and top-down activism.

This, admittedly, does not give us a theory of justice, or a generalized solution to large problems. It gives us just more action and interaction. We can here agree with Dewey that "the level of action fixed by embodied intelligence is always the important thing" (2012, 166). Indeed, the solution to problems of unjust interactions is to start

---

[8]   Such might also qualify as a kind of justice in the wild, but one that is closer to what is called the "justice of the fish" (*matsyanyaya*—big fish eats little fish) in the Indian legal theorists discussed by Sen (2009, 20), or what in English is referred to as "dog eat dog."

[9]   As the *Magna Carta* suggests, we should not sell justice to the highest bidder. "*Nulli vendemus, nulli negabimus aut differemus, rectum aut justitiam*" (see Sen 1999, 73).

with what we have, to work to transform them, which can happen only by engaging in more interaction and communication, "so that genuine shared interest in the consequences of interdependent activities may inform desire and effort and thereby direct action" (ibid, 155). This is something to be done both in our own local actions and interactions, and in critical institutions that are able to leverage change where change is needed. As Dewey put it, the people who should be the ones to effect such transformations are "the people who constitute [such institutions], working as individuals – in collaboration with other individuals, each accepting his own responsibility" (Dewey 1973, 62f; see Manicas 1981, 290).

To summarize: realistically, in practice, justice is always imperfectly attained. Justice depends on alignments in actions, interactions, and (social-political) situations. In the case of individual action, basic activities have to be aligned to intentions (and D-intentions, P-intentions, M-intentions have to be reasonably aligned). An individual action is not just or unjust in itself, however—whether it is just or unjust is tied to (and affected by) its contribution to interaction. Since justice is primarily in interaction, it depends on intersubjective alignment. This alignment, and therefore justice in interaction, will depend on the arrangements of the social-political situation and the presence of limited, undistorted, relational autonomy. Justice consists in those arrangements that maximize compound, relational autonomy in our practices. In this regard justice is the same in its basic form of friendship and in the wider conceptions of social, economic, and political justice.

10.4 Reweaving the Fabric of Justice

Autonomy is relational, compound, and always contextualized. The *relata*—persons, and their circumstances of things, institutions, practices, affordances, and so on, are intertwined/entangled—as in an eco-system based on principles closer to biological organization, in contrast to instrumental or efficient distributions of objects or machines. The fact that these relational phenomena are arranged in a dynamical-holistic way means that they cannot be distributed on principles that treat them as *partes extra partes* without destroying/distorting what they are and changing relations with everything and everyone else. At the same time, on the one hand, we cannot ignore distributive arrangements entirely since such arrangements underpin (and either foster or undermine) social relations.[10] On the other hand, we shouldn't think that we can set up institutions or schemes of distribution that are once and for all just; human relations and cultural practices are constantly subject to material changes and to the evolution of practices, not to mention the constant changes in participating members.

---

[10] Nancy Fraser (1997; and in Fraser & Honneth 2003) defends a position that emphasizes the irreducibility and necessity of both recognition and (re)distribution in a two-dimensional concept of justice: "critical theorists should rebut the claim that we must make an either/or choice between the politics of redistribution and the politics of recognition. We should aim instead to identify the emancipatory dimensions of both problematics and to integrate them into a single, comprehensive framework" (1997, 4).

Thinking of distribution in broader terms that include both economic and extra-economic dimensions, we know that the arrangement of material things and access to information are not neutral since material engagement and the distribution of information can either support or undermine social interaction (Gallagher & Ransom 2016). Dynamical relations among intersubjective forces, normative and institutional practices, and the material conditions imposed by artifacts, tools, architectures, etc. play an important role in establishing a just or unjust arrangement. The material aspects of things (their shape and weight and substance) and their positions in local environments (which contribute to physical, social, and cultural affordances) matter for everyday interactions, including joint and collective actions. Joint action, for example, is not action in close proximity to others, accompanied by shared mental representations of goals and tasks. It is materially constrained or materially enabled in ways that redefine the affordance space and allow us to do things that we could not do on our own.

Material artifacts as well as architectural and informational spaces may afford the possibility for coordinating social action in ways that might not otherwise be possible, and in this regard there are cases where specific kinds of material engagement can disclose new social affordances. For example, it is often the case that in response to grass-roots political resistance movements, governments try to prevent or discourage people from gathering together in the same space. Despite such prohibitions, coordinated collective activity may take place, enabled and constrained by the detailed affordances of material and informational culture—the technology, the buildings, the places directly tied to cultural practices, and most recently through the use of social media—allowing for particular kinds of social-political action that would have been impossible in the absence of such materially constituted affordances. The same kinds of material and social affordances define the types of actions and sanctions (including bodily threats) that can be utilized by government agencies in response (Gallagher & Ransom 2016).

Public spaces are always landscaped with defined openings and closings—pathways for some and barriers for others. The critical theorist Nancy Fraser (1997, 88) rejects the idea of a public space where all voices are equal—because they aren't, even if they are treated "as if" they were equal. Specialized committees too often make decisions behind closed doors that close off debates and contestation.

Do walls make good neighbors? It depends on whether you listen to politicians or poets. Robert Frost addresses the question in his famous poem, *Mending Wall.* His neighbor wants the wall and claims: "Good fences make good neighbors." But Frost asks:

> *Why* do they make good neighbors? Isn't it
> Where there are cows? But here there are no cows.
> Before I built a wall I'd ask to know
> What I was walling in or walling out,
> And to whom I was like to give offense.

The presence or absence of cows is important. If my neighbor's wall is designed to keep his cows out of my field, then the wall may in fact serve a good purpose. Accordingly one cannot make judgments about walls in the abstract. Some barriers serve good purpose; others do not; and in some cases we get a mixed result or an uneasy tension. Walls are sometimes ambiguous. Are we on the inside or the outside of a wall? Does a wall keep things out, or keep things in? Can walls define a plurality of communities that may be in competition, in contrast to an all-encompassing "we," but still allow communication and broad-based debate—walls that keep the cows where they belong but allow neighbors to engage in friendly conversation?

Do laws make good neighbors? A law may stand in the way of friendship or education. It may promote the ownership of guns (Do guns make good neighbors?). It may impose limits on capitalist profits, or it may remove those limits. We can say of laws that they are just (or unjust) if they promote (or hinder) just (autonomy-producing) interactions. Accordingly, just legislation can readjust things and spaces that do not allow for such interactions.

In this respect, the distribution of things, information, regulations, etc. can certainly have an effect on justice relations. This kind of distribution, however, is not the same as parceling out of goods to individuals. In this respect Honneth is right to reject the notion of distribution in favor of relations of recognition (2012, 42). But we can also think of distribution differently; namely, as the arrangement or rearrangement of things, artifacts, informational systems, walls, and laws in ways that either interfere or do not interfere with justice within intersubjective interactions.

There is also the question of economic justice. Dewey suggests that there are three dimensions to consider.

(a) Factors pertaining to the organism: "efforts to satisfy the basic desires that are common to all men – the need for food and drink and protection from the elements." One can easily add healthcare.

(b) Factors pertaining to the environment: "the instrumentalities which men devise, the more effectively to meet their basic needs – machines, if you will, provided that you remember that the term 'machine' embraces such disparate things as a stick used as a lever and a great ocean liner." One can easily add institutions to this short list, including those institutions required to protect and make safe the natural and built environments we inhabit.

(c) Factors pertaining to goods and services: "the production and distribution of commodities which serve to meet human needs" (Dewey 1973, 100).

The third set of factors involves, according to Dewey, the division of labor and cooperation, and he gives familiar arguments to support their importance for individual survival and human flourishing. Writing before the rise of global corporations and the global economy, Dewey's examples are nineteenth-century (his lectures were in 1919–20) and some appear almost quaint today: blacksmiths, silversmiths, painters, and engineers—craft-oriented work arrangements dependent on social interactions that were already being disrupted by factory organization under classic capitalism. Borrowing from Hegel (see Dewey 1973, 139), Dewey's model is the organism: "the more complex society in which division of labor is the rule takes on an organic quality, with the activity of any one part necessarily affecting all the other parts in a way that is quite comparable to what happens in the individual organism" (1973, 102). Criticizing Herbert Spencer, however, Dewey rejects the extremes of this model; i.e., a blind faith in "enlightened selfishness" and the idea of shared gains from free trade when it is conducted without government regulation. Drawing from lessons learned in imperialist regimes of the nineteenth century, and then apparently forgotten, Dewey here anticipates the economic debate over unequal exchange that took place between Arghiri Emmanuel (1972) and Paul Samuelson (1976), and he acknowledges that such a model assumes equality of ability for all parties. Yet the "brute fact" is that this equality does not exist (Dewey 1973, 104). When cooperation is overshadowed by capitalist competition we do not get the kind of equal exchange that Marxists like Emmanuel or the labor unions argue for. When the organic processes of work are disrupted by the mechanistic division of tasks into meaningless segments, Dewey argues, the result is inequality and injustice. The individual in capitalist society who is pushed "to the wall" (105) is not equivalent to Keith Jensen's chimpanzee who is satisfied with a small amount of goods while others are getting more.

Perhaps realizing that there is no solution when issues are framed in the terms of these debates, or in terms of distribution *simpliciter*, Dewey declines to take sides but offers two suggestions. First, although cooperation and communication have the potential to bring positive effect—namely, the development of culture—the same phenomena that can unite one group can also bring the negative effect of conflict among groups. So the task is to arrange or rearrange things so as to reduce conflict and increase culture. It's unsurprising that Dewey sees education as a solution in this regard. Second, Dewey, citing the slogan of the French Revolution, "Liberty, Equality, Fraternity," recognizes, however, the real (historical) incommensurability between liberty and equality, and proposes that limitations be imposed on liberty in the service of creating more equality. Laws and regulations that apply to the workplace are his example. Dewey, endorsing one aspect of Hegel's theory, sees a greater role for government, over and above the slogan that "government is best that governs least." "[T]he responsibility of the state must not be limited to the protection of private property and the enforcement of contracts, but . . . it must also be responsible for the development of spiritual values" (1973, 139–40). Within the latter, perhaps, one might find friendship (something less gendered than fraternity), but these concepts are not explicitly addressed in Dewey's account.

We know today that it is quite easy to impose limitations on liberty and still not get equality. Moreover, we know the limitations of governments faced with global corporations, or what Fraser (1997, 3) calls "wall-to-wall capitalism," interested only in performativity and profits. Recent critical theorists see this development more than Dewey could. Rather than an improvement in the quality of labor, Honneth notes, "A growing portion of the population is struggling just to gain access to job opportunities that can secure a livelihood: others work under radically deregulated conditions that hardly enjoy any legal protection anymore; still others are forced to watch their previously secure careers become deprofessionalized and outsourced" (2012, 56). Much as Dewey scolded philosophers who ignored economic problems in their social analysis, Honneth decries the focus of the critical theory of society on culture rather than on conditions of production. The abandonment of focus on economic organization and the labor market, he contends, has been motivated by pessimism for any solution given the current circumstances of globalization. Honneth looks for a solution by means of what he calls an internal critique.

Rather than criticizing the arrangement of labor from an external and idealistic conception of an organismic design, or a lost world of craft, he proposes to look at such arrangements to see whether they deliver social integration. Once again, an appeal is made to Hegel and the idea that within the organization of labor there is a moral norm connected with welfare and mutual recognition—something that would ideally (rationally) be assured by the system itself to support its own continued existence, but practically may be monitored and enforced by corporations who would be invested in the welfare of their workers. "Thus Hegel has the corporations fulfill a task that constitutes a normative claim anchored within the conditions of existence of this new organizational form of societal labor" (2012, 65). In contemporary terms this Hegelian idea might include organizations that invest in the training and education of their workers and that do not want to lose that investment either because the worker falls ill, or decides to leave for a better position elsewhere. There is an intrinsic incentive to treat employees well, an internal logic that works only if the worker is sufficiently skilled so as to constitute an investment. Honneth attempts to update this idea, rejecting the opposing theory that there is no normative idea intrinsic to labor arrangements—that is, that the market economy is a strictly inhuman, profit-driven mechanism without moral restrictions.

There is still a problem with this, as Honneth acknowledges. If this internal normative logic truly prescribes the behavior of workplace relations, in practice these prescriptions are often violated. But, of course, that is the problem to be solved. What we have in this normative logic are the principles of the solution—principles that remains implicit in workplace practices, even if they are not yet actual. Following Durkheim, Honneth contends that "justice and fairness are not normative ideals externally imposed on the capitalist organization of labour, but constitute functionally necessary presuppositions within this economic framework" (2012, 69).

These presuppositions imply that there ought to be a transparency to these arrangements and practices that allow individual workers to understand the meaning of their work as it constitutes an interactive collaboration with others. Capitalist arrangements, if they are oriented to mere *system* integration (the efficient machine for the sake of profit), if they do not embody the normative principles of *social* integration, and if they practically fail to allow for this transparency, are self-contradictory (they violate their own intrinsic presuppositions) and will eventually self-destruct.

For Honneth the idea seems to be that if workers can see that they are working together towards some goal, and mutually recognize each other as co-workers, they will see meaning in their work and feel a kind of solidarity, social integration, and self-respect, which will be sufficient to establish relations of justice. Setting aside questions about whether we should expect this move towards a just arrangement to be effected by or forced on the corporation by its own inner logic[11] resulting in its

---

[11] Arendt, for one, questions whether there are these kinds of internal principles that Honneth suggests. She seemingly favors a set of walls. "The fences inclosing private property and insuring the limitations of each household, the territorial boundaries which protect and make possible the physical identity of a people, and the laws which protect and make possible its political existence, are of such great importance to the stability of human affairs precisely because no such limiting and protecting principles rise out of the activities going on in the realm of human affairs itself" (1958, 191).

long-term self-benefit, we can ask whether a worker's discovery of meaning in their work will be sufficient for establishing justice (an arrangement that maintains or increases their autonomy) in their employer–employee and/or co-worker relations? We can say, at least, that in many circumstances, this mutual recognition, and sense of collaborative goals, will not stand in the way of instantiating just arrangements. But even if we attain this transparency, as one might find in skillfully aligned teamwork, it is not clear that it would guarantee that other constraints would not impose themselves, including the typical work-related power plays, as well as racial prejudices, cultural differences, and so forth that could easily undermine relations of justice. This suggests that justice is not reducible to transparent work conditions, or more generally, that justice is not something accomplished purely in economic terms. Indeed, we are not just workers seeking transparency or meaning in our work.

10.5   A Sense of Justice

I want to pick up on some threads discussed in the last few chapters in order to show that what really pulls a set of justice relations together is the weave of affectivity involved in responsivity and *philia*. These are all ideas that concern social inter-actions and find their start in the enactivist rather than the Honneth/Winnicottian conception of primary intersubjectivity.

Across various levels, relations of justice are woven into (although not reducible to) a variety of affective dimensions, including emotional states that range from love to justified anger, but also the ambiguous feelings, perhaps in one's gut or in odd intersubjective tensions, that things are either right or not so right. In this respect, justice is neither a set of abstract relations nor a set of abstract rules externally imposed on our intersubjective or social relations. Rather, it is something that either emerges, or fails to emerge in the embodied affective dynamics of our social arrange-ments. These affective dimensions are not without reason; in many cases one can begin to explicate what is right or wrong about a situation affectively. As suggested in the previous section, a just arrangement is an arrangement that maximizes some-thing that is difficult to measure: the total amount of individual and interactional autonomy. It's difficult to measure since, given individual differences, what maxi-mizes my autonomy may be quite different from what maximizes your autonomy, and such differences may prevent the maximization of our interactional autonomy.

For example, there is no justice in the institution of slavery because there is extreme reification and no possibility of a caring, affective relation within the institutional arrangement that makes it a case of slavery. Similar circumstances can be found in other institutional arrangements and practices that distort or introduce pseudo-affective (and sometimes invisible) lines that can disrupt or undermine anything like authentic responsivity or recognition. Along these lines, and again not unrelated to problems connected to *procedural* and *substantive* accounts of autonomy (*Section 8.4*), Honneth points to several examples of public displays of recognition that maintain the existing relations of domination.

For example, the pride that "Uncle Tom" feels as a reaction to the constant praises of his submissive virtues make him into a compliant servant in a slave-owning society. The emotional appeals to the "good" mother and housewife made by churches, parliaments, or the mass media over the centuries caused women to remain trapped within a self-image that most effectively accommodates the gender-specific division of labour. (2012, 77)

Not only in the public sphere, but also in private lives, and lives of friendship, it takes a good amount of work, or the development of good habits, to practice justice. It can be difficult even in relations with someone you love, especially when pressure or stress is imposed by circumstances that are external to the relation. One reason for this is that actions are always part of a larger web of actions and interactions. The consequences of action, as Hannah Arendt suggested, "are boundless, because action, though it may proceed from nowhere, so to speak, acts into a medium where every reaction becomes a chain reaction and where every process is the cause of new processes" (1958, 190). Actions and interactions never exist in a closed circle, and can never be confined even to the intimacy of a dyadic relation. "Action, moreover, no matter what its specific content, always establishes relationships and therefore has an inherent tendency to force open all limitations and cut across all boundaries" (ibid). At the very least, normative contours permeate even the most basic of relationships. Mothers either treat their infants right or they don't. Lovers, as we know from a long tradition of poetry and music, either threat their partners right, or they do them wrong.

Granted the limitations of human nature and the imperfections of human relations, and bracketing complications related to pathologies such as sociopathy, and so forth (Gallagher 2014b), let's not pretend that we don't know injustice when we see it. As David Miller puts it, "[a]ll morally competent adults have a well-developed sense of justice that enables them to cope with the practical questions they confront from day to day" (1999, 21). In very large part this sense of justice comes from the affective domain, through our engagement in social interaction. For those who like to divide the cognitive realm by drawing neat lines, however, our intuitions along this line are (and ought to be) also strongly supported by reason(s). In this regard Sen acknowledges two points that echo Miller, both in response to Rawls.

It was the diagnosis of an intolerable injustice in slavery that made abolition an overwhelming priority, and this did not require the search for a consensus on what a perfectly just society would look like. (2009, 21)

Why should we regard hunger, starvation and medical neglect to be invariably less important than the violation of any kind of personal liberty? That question was first raised powerfully by Herbert Hart shortly after Rawls's *Theory of Justice* was published. (65)

There are, of course, serious complexities hiding behind these questions. It's true that we don't need to wait around for a perfect theory of justice, or an agreed upon definition of justice, to see the injustice in slavery; but if, to address the injustice, it takes a civil war that leads to hunger, starvation, and mass fatalities, because a significant minority is unable to see the injustice, we have a complication, to say the least. Indeed, how should we measure the restoration of personal liberty *vis-à-vis* war-related hunger, starvation, and death? As Miller goes on to suggest, just these types of questions motivate the search for a consensus theory of justice.

Acknowledging such complexities and motivations, however, does not mean that we need a theory of justice to say how we do in fact make judgments, form our intentions, and act in response to the injustices of slavery, hunger, starvation, medical neglect, or violent death, or on a smaller scale, how we cope with the minor injustices of everyday life. An appeal to *phronesis* (practical wisdom) as a virtuous judging case by case, has been a standard answer since Aristotle, although not one without problems of its own.

My intent in this chapter has not been to draw up a theory of justice; and here I won't try to solve all problems concerned with *phronesis* or the practice of judging. Rather I will try to motivate the idea that we should think of *phronesis* as an intentional attitude that integrates affect with practical reason. This conception of *phronesis* has not been the one promoted in recent analyses, but I think the roots of this view can be found in Aristotle.

Recent interpretations of *phronesis* confuse it with a kind of technical expertise or a quick imagination. Hubert Dreyfus, for example, takes *phronesis* to be a kind of "ethical expertise" which, rather than an intellectualization, is a matter of intuition that results from practice (Dreyfus & Dreyfus 1990, 2004). The *phronimos*, the person with *phronesis*, is an ethical expert for whom "Action becomes easier and less stressful [as the expert] simply sees what needs to be done rather than using a calculative procedure to select one of several possible alternatives" (Dreyfus 2002, 371). The expert not only sees what needs to be done, but also how to achieve it without deliberation, immediately—non-reflectively recognizing new situations as similar to previously encountered ones, and intuiting "what to do without recourse to rules." The expert, as a "virtuoso in living" (Dreyfus & Dreyfus 2004, 268), has the capacity to recognize important features as contextually sensitive.

Jean-Francois Lyotard offers a related conception of *phronesis*. Looking for a way to conceive of "sensitivity to differences" and the "ability to tolerate the incommen-surable" (1984, xxv), he explicitly turns to a theory of *phronesis* to develop his discussion of justice (Lyotard & Thebaud 1985). The concept of *phronesis* serves his purpose because, contrary to a Platonic conception of justice, it does not depend on theoretical criteria to inform judging. "This is, after all, what Aristotle calls [*phronesis*]. It consists in dispensing justice without models. It is not possible to produce a learned discourse upon what justice is" (1985, 26; also see p. 43). *Phronesis* involves a dialectic that requires judging "case by case," "because each situation is singular" and there are no external criteria to guide judgment (1985, 27). According to Lyotard the person with *phronesis* plays a good game—a just game—quickly without preparation, and only in the immediacy of the situation. Indeed, this is how he characterizes *phronesis*—a kind of speedy imagination, "the capacity to actualize the relevant data for solving a problem 'here and now,' and to organize that data into an efficient strategy" (1984, 51).

Characterizations of *phronesis* as a form of expertise or quick imagination, as we find in Dreyfus or Lyotard confuse it with what Aristotle calls cleverness, which he clearly distinguishes from *phronesis*.

There is a faculty called cleverness; and this is such as to be able to do the things that tend towards the mark we have set before ourselves, and to hit it. Now if the mark be noble, the cleverness is laudable, but if the mark be bad, the cleverness is mere smartness; hence we call even men of practical wisdom clever or smart. Practical wisdom is not this faculty, but it does not exist without this faculty.... practical wisdom is to cleverness—not the same, but like it.

(Aristotle 2009, 1144a22)

Even if a specialized expertise or quick imagination allows us to hit the mark we intend to hit, they lack something that would make them instances of *phronesis*. Indeed, Aristotle specifically denies that "quickness of mind" is sufficient for the excellence of deliberation, which is *phronesis* (1142b5–16). He explains why cleverness does not add up to *phronesis* by appealing to the notion of the good: "it is impossible to be practically wise without being good" (1144a22). Thus, you can be a clever criminal, an expert extortionist, or a terrorist quick of mind, but you would not have *phronesis*.

In defining the good as we know it in practical wisdom, however, Aristotle leads us back to intersubjectivity and the concept of friendship: one does not know the good, in the way that is required for *phronesis*, unless one learns it by hanging around with the right people. Although Aristotle does not put it this way, we can say that in moral development there is a deep connection between *philia* and *phronesis*. Interacting with others is clearly part of what Aristotle identified as the source of *phronesis*, not only being with and observing others, but also imitating and acting with them, receiving emotional confirmation or caution, and coming to know what actions are good and what are bad.[12]

Here, however, we find another problem—one we've already discussed several times under the heading of the diversity problem, and which is more generally discussed in terms of surrendering the idea of universalistic principles of justice (a criticism often levied against theories of recognition [see, e.g., Fraser & Honneth 2003, 15; Rorty 2005]). It concerns the notion of the good friend as a good person. Despite the fact that Aristotle takes the concept of *philia* or friendship to be a broad one, he also suggests that one has few friends of the sort that deserve the title of good friends. Indeed, friends of this sort constitute a relatively narrow "in-group," by definition, and this fosters the development of a very narrow virtue, lacking in flexibility and diversity. Aristotle and his good friends, after all, thought a certain type of slavery was perfectly acceptable.

On the one hand, there is reason to be cautious about any claim that to enrich our sensitivities to the diversity of situations and people we can simply appeal to narrative practices. As previously indicated (*Section 7.5*), there is no guarantee that a broad education in narratives will lead to greater empathy. On the other hand, it is not clear that there is any other way to foster a wider conception of *phronesis* than through an education in a broad variety of narratives, including critical narratives. *Phronesis*, which is neither theoretical knowledge nor technical knowledge, but includes a sensitivity to different situations, can anchor itself, not only in our close interactions with friends, as Aristotle suggests, but also in a rich narrative knowledge about the diversity of other people, their situations, and their cultures. A broad understanding

---

[12] Neither Dreyfus nor Lyotard acknowledge the importance of intersubjective interaction in regard to *phronesis*. A number of critics have engaged Dreyfus on this point, specifically in regard to his failure to mention the importance of social factors in gaining expertise (Collins 2004; Gallagher 2007b; Selinger & Crease 2002; Young 1990). Lyotard goes so far in this direction as to deny that *phronesis* depends upon education or the development of good habits that we might learn from others (see Lyotard & Thebaud 1985, 26).

of diverse situations can give us a basic sense of what to do, or how to respond, if in the face of injustice we have the ability to respond. It can also tell us how to join with others and to take action. Accordingly, *phronesis*, understood as a sense of justice, is a form of practical reason formed in our developed affective interactions with others, and informed by a diversity of narratives that are always about actions and interactions.

References

Aarts, H., Custers, R., and Wegner, D.M. 2005. On the inference of personal authorship: Enhancing experienced agency by priming effect information. *Consciousness and Cognition* 14(3): 439–58.

Abramova, E. and Slors, M. 2019. Mechanistic explanation for enactive sociality. *Phnomenology and the Cognitive Sciences* 18: 401–424.

Adams, F. 2001. Empathy, neural imaging and the theory versus simulation debate. *Mind & Language* 16(4): 368–92.

Adolphs, R., Tranel, D., and Damasio, A.R. 2003. Dissociable neural systems for recognizing emotions. *Brain and Cognition* 52 (1): 61–9.

Aggerholm, E, Jespersen, E., and Ronglan, L.T. 2011. Falling for the feint—An existential investigation of a creative performance in high-level football. *Sport, Ethics and Philosophy* 5(3): 343–58.

Albahari, M. 2016. *Analytical Buddhism: The Two-Tiered Illusion of Self.* Heidelberg: Springer.

Allen, J., Kautz, H., Pelavin, R., and Tenenberg, J. 2014. *Reasoning about Plans.* San Mateo, CA: Morgan Kaufmann.

Allison, T., Puce, Q., and McCarthy, G. 2000. Social perception from visual cues: role of the STS region. *Trends in Cognitive Science* 4(7): 267–78.

Anderson, M.L. 2010. Neural reuse: A fundamental reorganizing principle of the brain. *Behavioral and Brain Sciences* 33: 245–66.

Andrews, K. 2008. It's in your nature: A pluralistic folk psychology. *Synthese* 165(1): 13–29.

Anisfeld, M. 2005. No compelling evidence to dispute Piaget's timetable of the development of representational imitation in infancy. In G. Rizzolatti, S. Hurley, and N. Chater (eds.), *Perspectives on Imitation: From Neuroscience to Social Science* (107–31). Cambridge, MA: MIT Press.

Anscombe, G.E.M. 1957. *Intention.* Oxford: Blackwell Publishers.

Ansuini, C., Cavallo, A., Bertone, C., and Becchio, C. 2014. The visible face of intention: why kinematics matters. *Frontiers in Psychology* 5: 815. doi: 10.3389/fpsyg.2014.00815

Ansuini, C., Giosa, L., Turella, L., Altoè, G.M., and Castiello, U. 2008. An object for an action, the same object for other actions: effects on hand shaping. *Experimental Brain Research* 185: 111–19.

Ansuini, C., Santello, M., Massaccesi, S., and Castiello, U. 2006. Effects of end-goal on hand shaping. *J. Neurophysiology* 95: 2456–65.

Arendt, H. 1958. *The Human Condition.* Chicago, IL: University of Chicago Press.

Arendt, H. 1987. Labor, work, action. In J.W. Bernauer (ed.), *Amor Mundi* (29–42). Dordrecht, Netherlands: Martinus Nijhoff Publishers.

Aristotle. 2009. *Nicomachean Ethics* [350 BCE]. Trans. W.D. Ross. In R. McKeon (ed.), *The Basic Works of Aristotle.* New York, NY: Modern Library.

Aristotle. 2012. *Eudemian Ethics.* Trans. B. Inwood and R. Woolf. Cambridge: Cambridge University Press.

Ashliman, D.L. 1999–2018. Little Red Riding Hood. URL: http://www.pitt.edu/~dash/type0333.html. Accessed November 11, 2019.

Astington J. 1990. Narrative and the child's theory of mind. In B.K. Britton and D. Pellegrini (eds.), *Narrative Thought and Narrative Language* (151–71). Hillsdale, New Jersey: Erlbaum.

Ataria, Y. and Gallagher, S. 2015. Somatic apathy: Body disownership in the context of torture. *Journal of Phenomenological Psychology* 46(1): 105–22.

Atkinson, A.P., Tunstall, M.L., and Dittrich, W.H. 2007. Evidence for distinct contributions of form and motion information to the recognition of emotions from body gestures. *Cognition* 104(1): 59–72.

Austin, J.L. 1979. Other minds. In J.O. Urmson and G.J. Warnock (eds.), *Philosophical Papers* (76–116). Oxford: Oxford University Press.

Avenanti, A. and Aglioti, S.M. 2007. The sensorimotor side of empathy for pain. In M. Mancia (ed.), *Psychoanalysis and Neuroscience* (235–56). Milan: Springer Science & Business Media.

Babinski, J. 1899. De l'asynergie cérébelleuse. *Revue de Neurologie* 7: 806–16.

Baier, A. 1985. *Postures of the Mind: Essays on Mind and Morals*. Minneapolis, MN: University of Minnesota Press.

Bain, P., Park, J., Kwok, C., and Haslam, N. 2009. Attributing human uniqueness and human nature to cultural groups: Distinct forms of subtle dehumanization. *Group Process Intergroup* Relations 12: 789.

Baird, J.A. and Baldwin, D.A. 2001. Making sense of human behavior: Action parsing and intentional inference. In B.F. Malle, L.J. Moses, and D.A. Baldwin (eds.), *Intentions and Intentionality: Foundations of Social Cognition*. Cambridge, MA: MIT Press.

Baldwin, D.A. 1993. Infants' ability to consult the speaker for clues to word reference. *Journal of Child Language* 20(2): 395–418.

Baldwin, D.A. and Baird, J.A. 2001. Discerning intentions in dynamic human action. *Trends in Cognitive Science* 5(4): 171–8.

Barden, J., Maddux, W.W., Petty, R.E., and Brewer, M.B. 2004. Contextual moderation of racial bias: the impact of social roles on controlled and automatically activated attitudes. *J Pers Soc Psychol* 87: 5.

Bargh, J.A. 1999. The cognitive monster: The case against the controllability of automatic stereotype effects. In S. Chaiken and Y. Trope (eds.), *Dual-Process Theories in Social Psychology* (361–82). New York, NY: Guilford Press.

Barnier, A.J., Sutton, J., Harris, C.B., & Wilson, R.A. 2008. A conceptual and empirical framework for the social distribution of cognition: The case of memory. *Cognitive Systems Research* 9(1): 33–51.

Baron-Cohen, S. 1989. The autistic child's theory of mind: A case of specific developmental delay. *Journal of Child Psychology and Psychiatry* 30(2): 285–97.

Baron-Cohen, S. 1991. Precursors to a theory of mind: Understanding attention in others. In A. Whiten (ed.), *Natural Theories of Mind: Evolution, Development and Simulation of Everyday Mindreading*. (233–51). Cambridge, MA: Basil Blackwell.

Baron-Cohen, S. 1995. *Mindblindness: An Essay on Autism and Theory of Mind*. Cambridge, MA: MIT Press.

Barrett, L.F. and Bar, M. 2009. See it with feeling: affective predictions during object perception. *Philosophical Transactions of the Royal Society B: Biological Sciences* 364(1521): 1325–34.

Bartsch K. and Wellman H. 1995. *Children Talk About the Mind*. New York, NY: Oxford University Press.

Bastian, B. and Haslam, N. 2010. Excluded from humanity: the dehumanizing effects of social ostracism. *J Experimental Social Psychology* 46: 107–13.

Bayliss, A.P., Frischen, A., Fenske, M.J., and Tipper, S.P. 2007. Affective evaluations of objects are influenced by observed gaze direction and emotional expression. *Cognition* 104: 644–53.

Bayliss, A.P., Paul, M.A., Cannon, P.R., and Tipper, S.P. 2006. Gaze cuing and affective judgments of objects: I like what you look at. *Psychonomic Bulletin & Review* 13(6): 1061–6.

Becchio, C., Bertone, C., and Castiello, U. 2008. How the gaze of others influence object processing. *Trends in Cognitive Sciences* (12)7: 254–8.

Becchio C., Koul A., Ansuini C., Bertone C., and Cavallo A. 2017. Seeing mental states: An experimental strategy for measuring the observability of other minds. *Physics of Life Review* 24: 67–80. https://doi.org/10.1016/j.plrev.2017.10.002

Becchio, C., Manera V., Sartori L., Cavallo A., and Castiello U. 2012. Grasping intentions: from thought experiments to empirical evidence. *Frontiers in Human Neuroscience* 6: 117.

Bekoff, M. and Pierce, J. 2009. *Wild Justice: The Moral Lives of Animals.* Chicago, IL: University of Chicago Press.

Benhabib, S. 1986. *Critique, Norm, and Utopia: A Study of the Foundations of Critical Theory.* New York, IL: Columbia University Press.

Bennett, M.R. and Hacker, P.M.S. 2003. *Philosophical Foundations of Neuroscience.* Oxford: Blackwell Publishing

Benson, P. 1994. Free agency and self-worth. *Journal of Philosophy* 91: 650–68.

Bermúdez, J.L. 1996. The moral significance of birth. *Ethics* 106(2): 378–403.

Bermúdez, J.L. 2003. The domain of folk psychology. In A. O'Hear (ed.), *Minds and Persons* (25–48). Cambridge: Cambridge University Press.

Bermúdez, J.L. 2011. Bodily awareness and self-consciousness. In S. Gallagher (ed.), *The Oxford Handbook of the Self* (157–179). Oxford: Oxford University Press.

Bernier, P. 2002. From simulation to theory. In J. Dokic and J. Proust (eds.), *Simulation and Knowledge of Action* (33–48). Amsterdam: John Benjamins.

Berthoz, A. 2000. *The Brain's Sense of Movement.* Cambridge, MA: Harvard University Press.

Blair, I.V. 2002. The malleability of automatic stereotypes and prejudice. *Pers Soc Psychol Rev* 6: 242–61.

Bohl, V. and Gangopadhyay, N. 2013. Theory of mind and the unobservability of other minds. *Philosophical Explorations* 17(2): 203–22.

Boltanski, L. 1999. *Distant Suffering: Politics, Morality and the Media.* Cambridge: Cambridge University Press.

Bourdieu, P. 1990. *The Logic of Practice.* Stanford, CA: Stanford University Press.

Brandom, R.B. 2008. *Between Saying and Doing: Towards an Analytic Pragmatism.* Oxford: Oxford University Press.

Bratman, M.E. 1987. *Intention, Plans, and Practical Reason.* Cambridge, MA: Cambridge University Press.

Bratman, M.E. 1993. Shared intention. *Ethics* 104(1): 97–113.

Bratman, M.E. 2006. Dynamics of sociality. *Midwest Studies in Philosophy* 30(1): 1–15.

Braun, N., Debener, S., Spychala, N., Bongartz, E., Sorös, P., Müller, H. H.O., and Philipsen, A. 2018. The senses of agency and ownership: A review. *Frontiers in Psychology* 9: 535. doi: doi.org/10.3389/fpsyg.2018.00535

Bredekamp, H., Krois, J.M., Trempler, J., and Fingerhut, J. 2009. Bildakt und Verkörperung: Ein DFG-Projekt von Horst Bredekamp und John Michael Krois. *Humboldt-Spektrum* 16(2–3): 122–9.

Bregman, A.S. and Rudnicky, A.I. 1975. Auditory segregation: Stream or streams? *Journal of Experimental Psychology: Human Perception and Performance* 1: 263–7.

Brewer, M.B., Manzi, J.M., and Shaw, J.S. 1993. In-group identification as a function of depersonalization, distinctiveness, and status. *Psychological Science* 4(2): 88–92.

Brewer, M.B. and Silver, M.D. 2000. Group distinctiveness, social identification, and collective mobilization. In S. Stryker, T.J. Owens, and R.W. White (eds.), *Self, Identity, and Social Movements* (153–171). Minneapolis, MN: University of Minnesota Press.

Briegel, W. 2006. Neuropsychiatric findings of Moebius sequence—a review. *Clinical Genetics* 70(2): 91–7.

Brincker, M. and Torres, E.B. 2013. Noise from the periphery in autism. *Frontiers in Integrative Neuroscience* 7: 34.

Brouchon, M., Joanette, Y., and Samson, M. 1986. From movement to gesture: "Here" and "there" as determinants of visually guided pointing. In J.L. Nespoulos, A. Perron, and R. A. Lecours (eds.), *Biological Foundations of Gesture* (95–107). Hillsdale, NJ: Erlbaum.

Bruner, J.S. 1986. *Actual Minds, Possible Worlds*. Cambridge, MA: Harvard University Press.

Bruner, J.S. 1990. *Acts of Meaning*. Cambridge, MA: Harvard University Press.

Bruner, J.S. 1996. *The Culture of Education*. Cambridge, MA: Harvard University Press.

Bruner, J. and Kalmar, D.A. 1998. Narrative and metanarrative in the construction of self. In M. Ferrari and R.J. Sternberg (eds.), *Self-Awareness: Its Nature and Development* (308–31). New York, NY: Guilford Press.

Buckner, C., Shriver, A., Crowley, S., and Allen, C. 2009. How "weak" mindreaders inherited the earth. *Behavioral and Brain Sciences* 32: 140–1.

Butler, J. 2008. Taking another's view: ambivalent implications. In A. Honneth, *Reification. A New Look at an Old Idea* (97–119). Oxford: Oxford University Press.

Butterfill, S. A. and Apperly, I. A. 2013. How to construct a minimal theory of mind. *Mind & Language* 28 (5): 606–637.

Butterworth, G. and Hopkins, B. 1988. Hand-mouth coordination in the newborn baby. *British Journal of Developmental Psychology* 6: 303–14.

Butterworth, G., & Jarrett, N. 1991. What minds have in common is space: Spatial mechanisms serving joint visual attention in infancy. *British Journal of Developmental Psychology* 9(1): 55–72.

Caggiano, V., Fogassi, L., Rizzolatti, G., Pomper, J.K., Thier, P., Giese, M.A., et al. 2011. View-based encoding of actions in mirror neurons of area f5 in macaque premotor cortex. *Current Biology* 21(2): 144–8.

Caggiano, V., Fogassi, L., Rizzolatti, G., Thier, P., and Casile. A. 2009. Mirror neurons differentially encode the peripersonal and extrapersonal space of monkeys. *Science* 324: 403–6.

Caldara, R. 2017. Culture reveals a flexible system for face processing. *Current Directions in Psychological Science* 26(3): 249–55.

Calder, A.J., Keane, J., Manes, F., Antoun, N., and Young, A.W. 2000. Impaired recognition and experience of disgust following brain injury. *Nature Neuroscience* 3(11): 1077–8.

Calvo-Merino, B., Glaser, D.E., Grèzes, J., Passingham, R.E., and Haggard, P. 2005. Action observation and acquired motor skills: An fMRI with expert dancers. *Cerebral Cortex* 15: 1243–9. doi: 10.1093/cercor/bhi007

Calvo-Merino, B., Grèzes, J., Glaser, D.E., Passingham, R.E., and Haggard, P. 2006. Seeing or doing? Influence of visual and motor familiarity in action observation. *Current Biology* 16: 1905–10. doi: 10.1016/j.cub.2006.07.065

Campbell, J. 2005. Joint attention and common knowledge. In N. Eilan (ed.), *Joint Attention: Communication and Other Minds: Issues in Philosophy and* Psychology (287–97). Oxford: Oxford University Press.

Campbell, M.E. and Cunnington, R. 2017. More than an imitation game: Top-down modulation of the human mirror system. *Neuroscience & Biobehavioral Reviews* 75: 195–202.

Carpendale, J.I.M. and Lewis, C. 2004. Constructing an understanding of the mind: The development of children's social understanding within social interaction. *Behavioural and Brain Sciences* 27(1): 79–151.

Carpenter, M. 2009. Just how joint is joint action in infancy? *Topics in Cognitive Science* 1(2): 380–92.

Carr, D. 1986a. *Time, Narrative, and History*. Bloomington, IN: Indiana University Press.

Carr, D. 1986b. Narrative and the real world: An argument for continuity. History and Theory 25(2): 117–31.

Carruthers, P. 1996. Simulation and self-knowledge: A defence of the theory-theory. In P. Carruthers and P.K. Smith (eds.), *Theories of Theories of Mind* (22–38). Cambridge: Cambridge University Press.

Carruthers, P. 2002. The cognitive functions of language. *Behavioral and Brain Sciences* 25: 657–726.

Carruthers, P. 2009. How we know our own minds: the relationship between mindreading and metacognition. *Behavioral and Brain Sciences* 32(2): 121–82.

Carruthers, P. 2013. Mindreading in infancy. *Mind & Language* 28(2): 141–72.

Carruthers, P. 2015. Perceiving mental states. *Consciousness and Cognition* 36: 498–507.

Castiello, U., Becchio, C., Zoia, S., et al. 2010. Wired to be social: the ontogeny of human interaction. *PloS One* 5(10): e13199.

Castro, V. F. and Heras-Escribano, M. 2019. Social cognition: A normative approach. *Acta Analytica* doi.org/10.1007/s12136-019-00388-y

Catmur, C., Walsh, V., and Heyes, C. 2007. Sensorimotor learning configures the human mirror system. *Current Biology* 17(17): 1527–31.

Chaminade, T. and Decety, J. 2002. Leader or follower? Involvement of the inferior parietal lobule in agency. *Neuroreport* 13(15): 1975–8.

Chemero, A. and Turvey, M.T. 2007. Complexity, hypersets and the ecological approach to perception-action. *Biological Theory* 2: 1–14.

Chouliaraki, L. 2006. *The Spectatorship of Suffering*. London: Sage Publications.

Christman, J. 2004. Relational autonomy, liberal individualism, and the social constitution of selves. *Philosophical Studies* 117(1–2): 143–64.

Christman, J. 2009. *The Politics of Persons: Individual Autonomy and Socio-Historical Selves*. Cambridge: Cambridge University Press.

Chudnoff, E. 2016. Epistemic elitism and other minds. *Philosophy and Phenomenological Research* 96 (2): 276–98.

Clark, A. 1997. Economic reason: The interplay of individual learning and external structure. In J. Drobak and J. Nye (eds.), *The Frontiers of the New Institutional Economics*. San Diego, CA: Academic Press.

Clark, A. 2008. *Supersizing the Mind: Reflections on Embodiment, Action, and Cognitive Extension*. Oxford: Oxford University Press.

Clark, A. 2012. Dreaming the whole cat: Generative models, predictive processing, and the enactivist conception of perceptual experience. *Mind* 121(483): 753–71.

Clark, A. 2016. *Surfing Uncertainty: Prediction, Action, and the Embodied Mind*. Oxford: Oxford University Press.

Clark, A. and Chalmers, D. 1998. The extended mind. Analysis 58(1): 7–19.

Clark, V.P., Fan, S., and Hillyard, S.A. 1995. Identification of early visual cortex by crossmodal spatial attention. *Human Brain Mapping* 2: 170–87.

Code, L. 1991. *What Can She Know? Feminist Theory and the Construction of Knowledge*. Ithaca, NY: Cornell University Press.

Cole, E.J., Barraclough, N.E., and Enticott, P.G. 2018. Investigating mirror system (MS) activity in adults with ASD when inferring others' intentions using both TMS and EEG. *Journal of Autism and Developmental Disorders* 48(7): 2350–67.

Cole, J. 1995. *Pride and a Daily Marathon*. Cambridge, MA: MIT Press.

Cole, J. 1999. *About Face*. Cambridge, MA: MIT Press.

Cole, J., Gallagher, S., and McNeill, D. 2002. Gesture following deafferentation: A phenomenologically informed experimental study. *Phenomenology and the Cognitive Sciences* 1(1): 49–67.

Cole, J. and Montero, B. 2007. Affective proprioception. *Janus Head* 9(2): 299–317.

Cole, J. and Spalding, H. 2009. *The Invisible Smile: Living without Facial Expression*. Oxford: Oxford University Press.

Collins, H.M. 2004. Interactional expertise as a third kind of knowledge. *Phenomenology and the Cognitive Sciences* 3(2): 125–43.

Colombetti, G. 2014. *The Feeling Body: Affective Science meets the Enactive Mind*. Cambridge, MA: MIT Press.

Colzato, L.S., de Bruijn, E.R., and Hommel, B. 2012. Up to "me" or up to "us"? The impact of self-construal priming on cognitive self-other integration. *Frontiers in Psychology* 3: 341. doi: 10.3389/fpsyg.2012.00341

Colzato, L.S., Zech, H., Hommel, B., Verdonschot, R., van den Wildenberg, W.P., and Hsieh, S. 2012. Loving-kindness brings loving-kindness: The impact of Buddhism on cognitive self-other integration. *Psychonomic Bulletin & Review* 19(3): 541–5.

Coman, A., Momennejad, I., Drach, R.D., and Geana, A. 2016. Mnemonic convergence in social networks: The emergent properties of cognition at a collective level. *Proceedings of the National Academy of Sciences* 113(29): 8171–6.

Cook, J.L., Blakemore, S.J., and Press, C. 2013. Atypical basic movement kinematics in autism spectrum conditions. *Brain* 136: 2816–24.

Cook, R., Bird, G., Catmur, C., Press, C., and Heyes, C. 2014. Mirror neurons: from origin to function. *Behavioral and Brain Sciences* 37(2): 177–92. doi: 10.1017/S0140525X13000903

Corris, A. and Chemero, A. 2019. A second-order intervention. *Philosophical Studies*. https://doi.org/10.1007/s11098-018-01232-6

Couto, B., Sedeno, L., Sposato, L.A., Sigman, M., Riccio, P.M., Salles, A., Lopez, V., Schroeder, J., Manes, F., and Ibanez, A. 2013. Insular networks for emotional processing and social cognition: comparison of two case reports with either cortical or subcortical involvement. *Cortex* 49(5): 1420–34.

Craver, C.F. 2007. *Explaining the Brain: Mechanisms and the Mosaic Unity of Neuroscience*. Oxford: Oxford University Press.

Csibra, G. 2005. Mirror neurons and action observation. Is simulation involved? ESF Inter-disciplines. http://www.interdisciplines.org/mirror/papers/

Csibra, G. and Gergely, G. 2009. Natural pedagogy. *Trends in Cognitive Sciences* 13: 148–53.

Curd, C. 2016. Presocratic philosophy. *The Stanford Encyclopedia of Philosophy* (Winter 2016 Edition), Edward N. Zalta (ed.), <https://plato.stanford.edu/archives/win2016/entries/presocratics/>.

Curioni, A., Sebanz, N., and Knoblich, G. 2018. Can we identify others' intentions from seeing their movements? Comment on Becchio et al. *Physics of Life Reviews*. https://doi.org/10.1016/j.plrev.2017.10.002

Currie, G. 1995. *Image and Mind: Film, Philosophy and Cognitive Science*. Cambridge: Cambridge University Press.

Currie, G. 2007. Framing narratives. *Royal Institute of Philosophy Supplement* 60: 17–42.

Currie, G. 2008. Some ways of understanding people. *Philosophical Explorations* 11(3): 211–18.

Currie, G. and Ravenscroft, I. 2002. *Recreative Minds: Imagination in Philosophy and Psychology*. Oxford: Oxford University Press.

Currie, G. and Sterelny, K. 2000. How to think about the Modularity of Mind-Reading. *The Philosophical Quarterly* 50(199): 145–60.

Curzur, H.J. 2012. *Aristotle and the Virtues*. Oxford: Oxford University Press.

Damasio, A.R. and Maurer, R.G. 1978. A neurological model for childhood autism. *Archives of Neurology* 35(12): 777–86.

Danto, A.C. 1963. What we can do. *Journal of Philosophy* 60(15): 435–45.

Danto, A.C. 1965. Basic actions. *American Philosophical Quarterly* 2: 141–8.

Danto, A.C. 1969. Complex events. *Philosophy and Phenomenological Research* 30(1): 66–77.

Darwall, S. 2005. Fichte and the second-person standpoint. *Internationales Jahrbuch des deutschen Idealismus* 3: 91–113.

Davidson, D. 1967. The logical form of action sentences. In N. Rescher (ed.), *The Logic of Decision and Action* (81–95). Pittsburgh, PA: University of Pittsburgh Press.

Deans, C.E. 2019. Sense of agency: An interpersonally situated embodied approach. Ph.D. Dissertation. Macquarie University.

Deans, C. E., McIlwain, D. and Geeves, A. 2015. The interpersonal development of an embodied sense of agency. *Psychology of Consciousness: Theory, Research and Practice* 2 (3): 315–25.

Debruille, J.B., Brodeur, M.B., and Porras, C.F. 2012. N300 and social affordances: a study with a real person and a dummy as stimuli. *PloS One* 7(10): e47922.

De Bruin, L. and de Haan, S. 2012. Enactivism and social cognition: In search for the whole story. *Journal of Cognitive Semiotics* 4(1): 225–50.

DeCasper, A.J. and Fifer, W.P. 1980. Of human bonding: Newborns prefer their mothers' voices. *Science* 208(4448): 1174–6.

Decety, J. 2004. Empathie et mentalisation a la lumiere des neurosciences sociales. *Neuropsychiatrie: Tendances et Debats* 23: 25–35.

Decety, J. 2005. Une anatomie de l'empathie. *Psychiatrie, Sciences Humaines, Neurosciences* 3(11): 16–24.

Decety, J. 2011. Dissecting the neural mechanisms mediating empathy. *Emotion Review* 3(1): 92–108.

Decety, J. and Chaminade, T. 2003. Neural correlates of feeling sympathy. *Neuropsychologia* 41(2): 127–38.

Decety, J. and Cowell, J.M. 2015. Empathy, justice, and moral behavior. *AJOB Neuroscience* 6(3): 3–14.

Decety, J. and Grèzes, J. 2006. The power of simulation: Imagining one's own and other's behavior. *Brain Research* 1079: 4–14.

Decety, J. and Jackson, P.L. 2004. The functional architecture of human empathy. *Behavioral and Cognitive Neuroscience Reviews* 3(2): 71–100.

De Gelder, B. 2006. Towards the neurobiology of emotional body language. *Nature Reviews Neuroscience* 7(3): 242–9.

De Haan, S., Rietveld, E., Stokhof, M., and Denys, D. 2013. The phenomenology of deep brain stimulation-induced changes in OCD: an enactive affordance-based model. *Frontiers in Human Neuroscience* 7: 653.

Dehaene, S. 2005. Evolution of human cortical circuits for reading and arithmetic: The "neuronal recycling" hypothesis. In S. Dehaene, J.-R. Duhamel, M. D. Hauser, and G. Rizzolatti (eds.), *From Monkey Brain to Human Brain* (131–57). Cambridge, MA: MIT Press.

Dehaene, S., Le Clec, H.G., Poline, J.B., Le Bihan, D., and Cohen, L. 2002. The visual word form area: a prelexical representation of visual words in the fusiform gyrus. *Neuroreport* 13(3): 321–5.

De Jaegher, H. 2009. Social understanding through direct perception? Yes, by interacting. *Consciousness and Cognition* 18: 535–42.

De Jaegher, H., Di Paolo, E., and Gallagher, S. 2010. Does social interaction constitute social cognition? *Trends in Cognitive Sciences* 14(10): 441–7.

Delafield-Butt, J.T. and Trevarthen, C. 2015. The ontogenesis of narrative: from moving to meaning. *Frontiers in Psychology* 6: 1157. doi: 10.3389/fpsyg.2015.01157

Dennett, D.C. and Kinsbourne, M. 1992. Time and the observer: The where and when of consciousness in the brain. *Behavioral and Brain Sciences* 15(2): 183–201.

Denzau, A.T. and North, D.C. 1994. Shared mental models: ideologies and institutions. *Kyklos* 47(1): 3–31.

Deranty, J-P. 2005. The loss of nature in Axel Honneth's theory of recognition. *Critical Horizons* 6(1): 153–81.

Derrida, J. 1994. *Specters of Marx: The State of Debt, the Work of Mourning, and the New International.* New York, NY: Routledge.

Desmurget, M., Reilly, K.T., Richard, N., Szathmari, A., Mottolese, C., and Sirigu, A. 2009. Movement intention after parietal cortex stimulation in humans. *Science* 324(5928): 811–13.

De Vries, J.I.P., Visser, G.H.A., and Prechtl, H.F.R. 1984. Fetal motility in the first half of pregnancy. In H.F.R. Prechtl (ed.), *Continuity of Neural Functions from Prenatal to Postnatal Life* (46–64). Spastics International Medical Publications.

De Waal, H. 1996. *Good Natured: The Origins of Right and Wrong in Humans and Other Animals.* Cambridge, MA: Harvard University Press.

Dewey, J. 1895. The theory of emotion. *Psychological Review* 2(1): 13.

Dewey, J. 1896. The reflex arc concept in psychology. *Psychological Review* 3: 357–70 (online: http://psychclassics.yorku.ca/Dewey/reflex.htm).

Dewey, J. 1929. *Characters and Events: Popular Essays in Social and Political Philosophy* (two vols.). New York, NY: Henry Holt and Co.

Dewey, J. 1938. *The Theory of Inquiry.* New York, NY: Holt, Rinehart & Wiston.

Dewey, J. 1958. *Experience and Nature.* New York, NY: Dover.

Dewey, J. 1973. *Lectures in China.* Honolulu, HI: University Press of Hawaii.

Dewey, J. and Tufts, J.H. 1932. *Ethics.* New York, NY: H. Holt and Company.

Di Bono, M.G., Begliomini, C., Budisavljevic, S., Sartori, L., Miotto, D., Motta, R., et al. 2017. Decoding social intentions in human prehensile actions: Insights from a combined kinematics-fMRI study. *PLoS One* 12(8): e0184008. https://doi.org/10.1371/journal.pone.0184008

Dijksterhuis, A., Bos, M.W., Nordgren, L.F., and Van Baaren, R.B. 2006. On making the right choice: The deliberation-without-attention effect. *Science* 311(5763): 1005–7.

Dinstein, I., Thomas, C., Behrmann, M., and Heeger, D.J. 2008. A mirror up to nature. *Current Biology* 18(1): R13–18.

Di Paolo, E.A. 2009. The social and enactive mind. *Phenomenology and the Cognitive Sciences* 8(4).

Di Paolo, E.A. and De Jaegher, H. 2012. The interactive brain hypothesis. *Frontiers in Human Neuroscience* 6: 163. doi: 10.3389/fnhum.2012.00163

Di Paolo, E.A., Rohde, M., and Iizuka, H. 2008. Sensitivity to social contingency or stability of interaction? Modelling the dynamics of perceptual crossing. *New Ideas in Psychology* 26(2): 278–94.

Dittrich, W.H., Troscianko, T., Lea, S.E., and Morgan, D. 1996. Perception of emotion from dynamic point-light displays represented in dance. *Perception* 25(6): 727–38.

Dokic, J. and Proust, J. (eds.). 2002. *Simulation and Knowledge of Action.* Amsterdam: John Benjamins Publishing.

Dolk, T., Hommel, B., Colzato, L.S., Schütz-Bosbach, S., Prinz, W., and Liepelt, R. 2011. How "social" is the social Simon effect? *Frontiers in Psychology* 2: 84.

Dolk, T., Hommel, B., Colzato, L. S., Schütz-Bosbach, S., Prinz, W. and Liepelt, R. 2014. The joint Simon effect: a review and theoretical integration. *Frontiers in Psychology* 5: 974. doi: 10.3389/fpsyg.2014.00974

Dolk, T., Hommel, B., Prinz, W., and Liepelt, R. 2013. The (not so) social Simon effect: a referential coding account. *Journal of Experimental Psychology: Human Perception and Performance* 39(5): 1248.

Donald, M. 1991. *Origins of the Modern Mind.* Cambridge, MA: Harvard University Press.

Dretske, F. 1969. *Seeing and Knowing.* London: Routledge & K. Paul.

Dreyfus, H. 2002. Intelligence without representation: Merleau-Ponty's critique of mental representation. *Phenomenology and the Cognitive Sciences* 1(4): 367–83.

Dreyfus, H.L. 2007. The return of the myth of the mental. *Inquiry* 50(4): 352–65.

Dreyfus, H.L. and Dreyfus, S.E. 1990. What is morality? A phenomenological account of the development of ethical expertise. In D. Rasmussen (ed.), *Universalism vs. Communitarianism: Contemporary Debates in Ethic* (237–64). Cambridge, MA: MIT Press.

Dreyfus, H.L. and Dreyfus, S.E. 2004. The ethical implications of the five-stage skill-acquisition model. *Bulletin of Science, Technology and Society* 24(3): 251–64.

Du Bois, W. E. B. 2007. *The Souls of Black Folk* B. H. Edwards (ed.). New York: Oxford University Press.

Duranti, A. and Goodwin, C. 1992. *Rethinking Context: Language as an Interactive Phenomenon*. Cambridge: Cambridge University Press.

Düttmann, A.G. 2000. *Between Cultures: Tensions in the Struggle for Recognition*. Trans. K.B. Woodgate. London: Verso.

Dworkin, G. 1988. *The Theory and Practice of Autonomy*. Cambridge: Cambridge University Press.

Elfenbein, H.A. and Ambady, N. 2002a. On the universality and cultural specificity of emotion recognition: A meta-analysis. *Psychol Bull* 128: 203–35.

Elfenbein, H.A. and Ambady, N. 2002b. Is there an in-group advantage in emotion recognition? *Psychol Bull* 128: 243–9.

Elfenbein, H. A. and Ambady, N. 2003. When familiarity breeds accuracy: cultural exposure and facial emotion recognition. *J Pers Soc Psychol* 85: 276–90.

Elfenbein, H.A., Beaupré, M., Levesque, M., and Hess, U. 2007. Toward a dialect theory: cultural differences in the expression and recognition of posed facial expressions. *Emotion* 7: 131–46.

Emmanuel, A. 1972. *Unequal Exchange: A Study of the Imperialism of Trade*. New York, NY: Monthly Review Press.

Engbert, K., Wohlschläger, A., Thomas, R., and Haggard, P. 2007. Agency, subjective time, and other minds. *Journal of Experimental Psychology: Human Perception and Performance* 33(6): 1261.

Epley, N. and Waytz, A. 2010. Mind perception. In S.T. Fiske, D.T. Gilbert, and G. Lindzey (eds.), *Handbook of Social Psychology* (Vol. 2). Hoboken, NJ: John Wiley & Sons.

Erlenbusch-Anderson, V. 2015. Foucault und die Realitätsbedingungen leiblicher Erfahrung. In T. Bedorf and T. N. Klass (eds.), *Leib–Körper–Politik: Untersuchungen zur Leiblichkeit des Politischen* (43–60). Velbrück Wissenschaft.

Erlenbusch-Anderson, V. 2018. *Genealogies of Terrorism: Revolution, State Violence, Empire*. New York, NY: Columbia University Press.

Fagard, J., Esseily, R., Jacquey, L., O'Regan, K., and Somogyi, E. 2018. Fetal origin of sensorimotor behavior. *Frontiers in Neurorobotics* 12: 23.

Farrer, C., Franck, N., Georgieff, N., Frith, C.D., Decety, J., and Jeannerod, M. 2003. Modulating the experience of agency: a positron emission tomography study. *NeuroImage* 18(2): 324–33.

Farrer, C. and Frith, C.D. 2002. Experiencing oneself vs. another person as being the cause of an action: the neural correlates of the experience of agency. *NeuroImage* 15: 596–603.

Farrer, C., Valentin, G., and Hupé, J.M. 2013. The time windows of the sense of agency. *Consciousness and Cognition* 22(4): 1431–41.

Feldman, C.F., Bruner, J., Renderer, B., and Spitzer, S. 1990. Narrative comprehension. In B.K. Britton and A.D. Pellegrini (eds.), *Narrative Thought and Narrative Language* (1–78). Hillsdale, NJ: Lawrence Erlbaum Associates.

Ferrari, P.F. and Coudé, G. 2018. Mirror neurons, embodied emotions, and empathy. In K.Z. Meyza and E. Knapska (eds.), *Neuronal Correlates of Empathy: From Rodent to Human* (67–77). San Diego, CA: Elsevier Academic Press.

Fichte, J.G. 2000. *Foundations of Natural Right* [1796]. Cambridge: Cambridge University Press.

Fiebich, A. and Coltheart, M. 2015. Various ways to understand other minds. Towards a pluralistic approach to the explanation of social understanding. *Mind and Language* 30(3): 235–58.

Fiebich, A. and Gallagher, S. 2013. Joint attention in joint action. *Philosophical Psychology* 26(4): 571–87.

Fiebich, A., Gallagher, S., and Hutto, D. 2017. Pluralism, interaction and the ontogeny of social cognition (208–21). In J. Kiverstein (ed.), *Routledge Handbook of Philosophy of the Social Mind*. London: Routledge.

Firestone, C. and Scholl, B.J. 2015. Can you experience "top-down" effects on perception? The case of race categories and perceived lightness. *Psychonomic Bulletin & Review* 22(3): 694–700.

Firestone, C. and Scholl, B.J. 2016. Cognition does not affect perception: Evaluating the evidence for "top-down" effects. *Behavioral and Brain Sciences* 39. doi: 10.1017/S0140525X15000965, e229.

Fisher, J.C. 2006. Does simulation theory really involve simulation? *Philosophical Psychology* 19(4): 417–32.

Fiske, A.P. 1991. *Structures of Social Life: The Four Elementary Forms of Human Relations.* New York, NY: Free Press.

Fiske, A.P. 2004. Four modes of constituting relationships: Consubstantial assimilation; space, magnitude, time, and force; concrete procedures; abstract symbolism. In N. Haslam (ed.), *Relational Models Theory: A Contemporary Overview* (61–146). Mahwah, NJ: Lawrence Erlbaum Associates, Inc.

Fodor, J.A. and Pylyshyn, Z.W. 1981. How direct is visual perception? Some reflections on Gibson's "ecological approach." *Cognition* 9(2): 139–96.

Fogassi, L., Ferrari, P.F., Gesierich, B., Rozzi, S., Chersi, F., and Rizzolatti, G. 2005. Parietal lobe: from action organization to intention understanding. *Science* 308(5722): 662–7.

Foxx, J.J. and Simpson, G.V. 2002. Flow of activation from V1 to frontal cortex in humans: a framework for defining "early" visual processing, *Exp. Brain Res.* 142: 139–50.

Frankfurt, H. 1978. The problem of action. *American Philosophical Quarterly* 15: 157–62; reprinted in H. Frankfurt, 1988. *The Importance of What We Care About.* (69–79). Cambridge: Cambridge University Press.

Frankfurt, H.G. 1988. *The Importance of What We Care About: Philosophical Essays.* Cambridge: Cambridge University Press.

Franks, P. 2005. *All or Nothing: Systematicity, Transcendental Arguments, and Skepticism in German Idealism.* Cambridge, MA: Harvard University Press.

Fraser, N. 1997. *Justice Interruptus: Rethinking Key Concepts of a "Postsocialist" Age.* New York and London: Routledge.

Fraser, N. and Honneth, A. 2003. *Redistribution or Recognition? A Political-Philosophical Exchange.* London: Verso.

Freeman, J.B. and Johnson, K.L. 2016. More than meets the eye: Split-second social perception. *Trends in Cognitive Sciences* 20(5): 362–74.

Friston, K. 2011. What is optimal about motor control? *Neuron* 72(3): 488–98.

Friston, K. 2012. Prediction, perception and agency. *International Journal of Psychophysiology* 83(2): 248–52.

Friston, K. 2013. Life as we know it. *Journal of the Royal Society Interface* 10(86): 20130475. doi: 10.1098/rsif.2013.0475

Frith, C.D. 1992. *The Cognitive Neuropsychology of Schizophrenia*. Hillsdale, NJ: Lawrence Erlbaum Associates.

Frith, U. and Happé, F. 1999. Theory of mind and self-consciousness: What is it like to be autistic? *Mind & Language* 14(1): 82–9.

Froese, T. and Gallagher, S. 2012. Getting IT together: Integrating developmental, phenomenological, enactive and dynamical approaches to social interaction. *Interaction Studies* 13(3): 434–66.

Fuchs, T. and De Jaegher, H. 2009. Enactive intersubjectivity: Participatory sensemaking and mutual incorporation. *Phenomenology and the Cognitive Sciences* 8: 465–86.

Fusaroli, R., Perlman, M., Mislove, A., Paxton, A., Matlock, T., and Dale, R. 2015. Timescales of massive human entrainment. *PLoS One* 10(4): e0122742.

Gadamer, H.G. 1989. *Truth and Method*. Trans. J. Weinsheimer and D.G. Marshall. New York, NY: Continuum.

Gallagher, S. 1992. *Hermeneutics and Education*. Albany, NY: SUNY Press.

Gallagher, S. 1998. *The Inordinance of Time*. Evanston, IL: Northwestern University Press.

Gallagher, S. 2000a. Philosophical conceptions of the self: implications for cognitive science. *Trends in Cognitive Science* 4(1): 14–21.

Gallagher, S. 2000b. Self-reference and schizophrenia: A cognitive model of immunity to error through misidentification. In D. Zahavi (ed.), *Exploring the Self: Philosophical and Psychopathological Perspectives on Self-experience*. (203–39). Amsterdam & Philadelphia: John Benjamins.

Gallagher, S. 2001. The practice of mind: Theory, simulation or primary interaction? *Journal of Consciousness Studies* 8(5–6): 83–108.

Gallagher, S. 2004a. Understanding interpersonal problems in autism: Interaction theory as an alternative to theory of mind. *Philosophy, Psychiatry, and Psychology* 11(3): 199–217.

Gallagher, S. 2004b. Les conditions corporéité et d'intersubjectivité de la personne morale. *Theologiques* 12(1–2): 135–64.

Gallagher, S. 2005a. *How the Body Shapes the Mind*. Oxford: Oxford University Press.

Gallagher, S. 2005b. Phenomenological contributions to a theory of social cognition. *Husserl Studies* 21(2): 95–110.

Gallagher, S. 2007a. Simulation trouble. *Social Neuroscience* 2 (3–4): 353–65.

Gallagher, S. 2007b. Moral agency, self-consciousness, and practical wisdom. *Journal of Consciousness Studies* 14(5–6): 199–223.

Gallagher, S. 2008. Direct perception in the intersubjective context. *Consciousness and Cognition* 17(2): 535–43.

Gallagher, S. 2011. Narrative competency and the massive hermeneutical background. In P. Fairfield (ed.), *Education, Dialogue and Hermeneutics* (21–38). New York, NY: Continuum.

Gallagher, S. 2012. Time, emotion and depression. *Emotion Review* 4(2): 127–32. doi: 10.1177/1754073911430142

Gallagher, S. 2013. The socially extended mind. *Cognitive Systems Research* 25-6: 4–12.

Gallagher, S. 2014a. In your face: Transcendence in embodied interaction. *Frontiers in Human Neuroscience* 8: 495. doi.org/10.3389/fnhum.2014.00495

Gallagher, S. 2014b. *Phronesis* and psychopathy: The moral frame problem. *Philosophy, Psychology and Psychiatry* 20(4): 345–8.

Gallagher, S. 2015a. The new hybrids: Continuing debates on social cognition. *Consciousness and Cognition* 36: 452–65.

Gallagher, S. 2015b. The problem with 3-year olds. *Journal of Consciousness Studies* 22 (1–2): 160–82.

Gallagher, S. 2017a. *Enactivist Interventions: Rethinking the Mind*. Oxford: Oxford University Press.

Gallagher, S. 2017b. Deflationary accounts of the sense of ownership. In F. de Vignemont and A. Alsmith (eds.), *The Subject's Matter* (145–62). Cambridge, MA: MIT Press.

Gallagher, S. 2017c. Self-defense: Deflecting deflationary and eliminativist critiques of the sense of ownership. *Frontiers in Human Neuroscience* 8: 1612. https://doi.org/10.3389/fpsyg.2017.01612

Gallagher, S. 2017d. Embodied intersubjective understanding and communication in congenital deafblindness. *Journal of Deafblind Studies on Communication* 3: 46–58.

Gallagher, S. 2018a. New mechanisms and the enactivist concept of constitution. In M.P. Guta (ed.), *The Metaphysics of Consciousness*. London: Routlege.

Gallagher, S. 2018b. Seeing in context: Comment on Becchio et al. *Physics of Life Review*. http://www.sciencedirect.com/science/article/pii/S1571064517301495

Gallagher, S. 2018c. The therapeutic reconstruction of affordances. *Res Philosophica* 95(4): 719–36.

Gallagher, S. 2018d. The extended mind: State of the question. *Southern Journal of Philosophy* 56(4): 421–47.

Gallagher, S. and Aguda, B. 2020. Anchoring know-how: Action, affordance and anticipation. *Journal of Consciousness Studies* 27 (3–4): 3–37.

Gallagher, S. and Allen, M. 2018. Active inference, enactivism and the hermeneutics of social cognition. *Synthese* 195(6): 2627–48. doi: 10.1007/s11229-016-1269-8

Gallagher, S. and Bower, M. 2014. Making enactivism even more embodied. *AVANT/Trends in Interdisciplinary Studies* (Poland) 5(2): 232–47.

Gallagher, S. and Cole, J. 1995. Body schema and body image in a deafferented subject. *Journal of Mind and Behavior* 16: 369–90.

Gallagher, S. and Crisafi, A. 2009. Mental institutions. *Topoi* 28(1): 45–51.

Gallagher, S. and Fiebich, A. 2019. Being a pluralist about other minds. In A. Avramiedes and M. Parrott (eds.), *Other Minds*. (63–77) Oxford: Oxford University Press.

Gallagher, S. and Gallagher, J. 2019. Acting oneself as another: An actor's empathy for her character. *Topoi*. doi: 10.1007/s11245-018-9624-7

Gallagher, S. and Hutto, D. 2008. Understanding others through primary interaction and narrative practice. In J. Zlatev, T. Racine, C. Sinha, and E. Itkonen (eds.), *The Shared Mind: Perspectives on Intersubjectivity* (17–38). Amsterdam: John Benjamins.

Gallagher, S. and Hutto, D. 2019. Narrative in embodied therapeutic practice: Getting the story straight. In H. Payne, J. Tantia, S. Koch, and T. Fuchs (eds.), *The Routledge International Handbook of Embodied Perspectives in Psychotherapy* (28-39). London: Routledge.

Gallagher, S., Hutto, D., Slaby, J., and Cole, J. 2013. The brain as part of an enactive system (commentary). *Behavioral and Brain Sciences* 36(4): 421–2.

Gallagher, S. and Ilundáin-Agurruza, J. (2020). Self- and other-awareness in joint expert performance. In E. Fridland and C. Pavese (eds.), *Routledge Handbook on Skill and Expertise* (378-393). London: Routledge.

Gallagher, S. and Janz, B. 2018. Solitude, self and autonomy. *Discipline Filosofiche* 28(2): 159–75.

Gallagher, S. and Marcel, A. 1999. The self in contextualized action. *Journal of Consciousness Studies* 6(4): 4–30.

Gallagher, S., Mastrogiorgio, A., and Petracca, E. 2019. Economic reasoning in socially extended market institutions. *Frontiers in Psychology Frontiers in Psychology* 10: 1856. doi: 10.3389/fpsyg.2019.01856

Gallagher, S. and Meltzoff, A. 1996. The earliest sense of self and others: Merleau-Ponty and recent developmental studies. *Philosophical Psychology* 9(2): 213–36.

Gallagher, S. and Miyahara, K. 2012. Neo-pragmatism and enactive intentionality. In J. Schulkin (ed.), *Action, Perception and the Brain* (117–46). Basingstoke, UK: Palgrave-Macmillan.

Gallagher, S. and Povinelli, D. 2012. Enactive and behavioral abstraction accounts of social understanding in chimpanzees, infants, and adults. *Review of Philosophy and Psychology* 3(1): 145–69.

Gallagher, S. and Ransom, T. 2016. Artifacting minds: Material engagement theory and joint action. In C. Tewes (ed.), *Embodiment in Evolution and Culture* (337–51). Berlin: de Gruyter.

Gallagher, S. and Tollefsen, D. 2019. Advancing the "we" through narrative. *Topoi* 38(1): 211–19. doi: 10.1007/s11245-017-9452-1.

Gallagher, S. and Trigg, D. 2016. Agency and anxiety: Delusions of control and loss of control in schizophrenia and agoraphobia. *Frontiers in Neuroscience* 10:459. doi: 10.3389/fnhum.2016.00459

Gallagher, S. and Varela, F. 2003. Redrawing the map and resetting the time: Phenomenology and the cognitive sciences. *Canadian Journal of Philosophy* Supplementary Volume 29: 93–132.

Gallagher, S. and Varga, S. 2014. Social constraints on the direct perception of emotions and intentions. *Topoi* 33(1): 185–99.

Gallagher, S. and Varga, S. 2015. Conceptual issues in autism spectrum disorders. *Current Opinion in Psychiatry* 28(2): 127–32.

Gallagher, S. and Zahavi, D. 2012. *The Phenomenological Mind*. London: Routledge.

Gallagher, S. and Zahavi, D. 2014. Primal impression and enactive perception. In D. Lloyd and V. Arstila (eds.), *Subjective Time: The Philosophy, Psychology, and Neuroscience of Temporality* (83–99). Cambridge, MA: MIT Press.

Gallese, C. and Goldman, A. 1998. Mirror neurons and the simulation theory of mind-reading. *Trends in Cognitive Sciences* 12: 493–501.

Gallese, V. 2001. The "shared manifold" hypothesis: From mirror neurons to empathy. *Journal of Consciousness Studies* 8: 33–50.

Gallese, V. 2004. Intentional attunement: The mirror neuron system and its role in interpersonal relations. ESF Interdisciplines. Accessed on February 16, 2011 at http://www.inter disciplines.org/mirror/papers/1

Gallese, V. 2005. "Being like me": Self-other identity, mirror neurons and empathy. In S. Hurley and N. Chater (eds.), *Perspectives on Imitation* (101–18). Cambridge, MA: MIT Press.

Gallese, V. 2006. Intentional attunement: A neurophysiological perspective on social cognition and its disruption in autism. *Brain Research* 1079(1): 15–24.

Gallese, V. 2007. Before and below "theory of mind": embodied simulation and the neural correlates of social cognition. *Philosophical Transactions of the Royal Society, B-Biological Sciences* 362(1480): 659–69.

Gallese, V. 2010. Embodied simulation and its role in intersubjectivity. In T. Fuchs, H.C. Sattel, and P. Henningsen (eds.), *The Embodied Self: Dimensions, Coherence and Disorders* (78–92). Stuttgart: Schattauer.

Gallese, V. 2014. Bodily selves in relation: embodied simulation as second-person perspective on intersubjectivity. *Philosophical Transactions of the Royal Society B: Biological Sciences* 369(1644): 20130177.

Gallese, V. 2017. Neoteny and social cognition: A neuroscientific perspective on embodiment. In C. Durt, T. Fuchs, C. Tewes (eds.), *Embodiment, Enaction, and Culture: Investigating the Constitution of the Shared World* (309–32). Cambridge, MA: MIT Press.

Gallese, V., Eagle, M.N., and Migone, P. 2007. Intentional attunement: Mirror neurons and the neural underpinnings of interpersonal relations. *Journal of the American Psychoanalytic Association* 55(1): 131–75.

Gallese, V., Rochat, M., Cossu, G., and Sinigaglia, C. 2009. Motor cognition and its role in the phylogeny and ontogeny of action understanding. *Developmental Psychology* 45(1): 103–13.

Gallese, V. and Sinigaglia, C. 2011. What is so special about embodied simulation? *Trends in Cognitive Sciences* 15(11): 512–19.

Gangopadhyay, N. and Schilbach, L. 2012. Seeing minds: A neurophilosophical investigation of the role of perception-action coupling in social perception. *Social Neuroscience* 7(4): 410–23.

García-Pérez, R.M., Lee, A., and Hobson, R.P. 2007. On intersubjective engagement in autism: A controlled study of nonverbal aspects of conversation. *Journal of Autism and Developmental Disorders* 37(7): 1310–22.

Gauthier, I., Skudlarski, P., Gore, J.C., and Anderson, A.W. 2000. Expertise for cars and birds recruits brain areas involved in face recognition. *Nature Neuroscience* 3: 191–7.

Geangu, E., Ichikawa, H., Lao, J., Kanazawa, S., Yamaguchi, M.K., Caldara, R., and Turati, C. 2016. Culture shapes 7-month-olds' perceptual strategies in discriminating facial expressions of emotion. *Current Biology* 26(14): R663–4.

Gegenfurtner, K., Olkkonen, M., and Walter, S. 2006. Memory modulates color experience. *Nature Neuroscience* 9(11): 1367–8.

Genette, G. 1980. *Narrative Discourse: An Essay in Method*. Ithaca, NY: Cornell University Press.

Gentsch, A. and Synofzik, M. 2014. Affective coding: The emotional dimension of agency. *Frontiers in Human Neuroscience* 8: 608. doi: doi.org/10.3389/fnhum.2014.00608

Georgieff, N. and Jeannerod, M. 1998. Beyond consciousness of external reality: A "who" system for consciousness of action and self-consciousness. *Consciousness and Cognition* 7(3): 465–77.

Gergely, G. 2001. The obscure object of desire: "Nearly, but clearly not, like me": Contingency preference in normal children versus children with autism. *Bulletin of the Menninger Clinic* 65: 411–26.

Gerson, S.A., Bekkering, H., and Hunnius, S. 2015. Short-term motor training, but not observational training, alters neurocognitive mechanisms of action processing in infancy. *Journal of Cognitive Neuroscience* 27: 1207–14. doi: 10.1162/jocn_a_00774

Geuss, R. 2008. Philosophical anthropology and social criticism. In A. Honneth, *Reification. A New Look at an Old Idea* (120–30). Oxford: Oxford University Press.

Gibbon, J. and Malapani, C. 2001. Neural basis of timing and time perception. In L. Nadel (ed.), *Encyclopedia of Cognitive Science* (305–11). London: Wiley.

Gibbs, R.W. 2001. Intentions as emergent products of social interactions. In B.F. Malle, L.J. Moses, and D.A. Baldwin (eds.), *Intentions and Intentionality: Foundations of Social Cognition* (105–22). Cambridge, MA: MIT Press.

Gibson, J.J. 1977. The theory of affordances. In R. Shaw and J. Bransford. *Perceiving, Acting, and Knowing* (67–82). Hillsdale, NJ: Lawrence Erlbaum.

Gibson, J.J. 1979. *The Ecological Approach to Visual Perception*. Boston, MA: Houghton-Mifflin.

Gilbert, M.P. 2013. *Joint Commitment: How We Make the Social World*. New York, NY: Oxford University Press.

Gillett, C. 2013. Constitution, and multiple constitution, in the sciences: Using the neuron to construct a starting framework. *Minds & Machines* 23: 309–37.

Gode, D. and Sunder, S. 1993. Allocative efficiency of markets with zero-intelligence traders. *Journal of Political Economy* 101: 119–37.

Goffman, E. 1986. *Stigma: Notes on the Management of Spoiled Identity*. New York, NY: Simon & Schuster.

Goh, J.O. and Park, D.C. 2009. Culture sculpts the perceptual brain. *Progress in Brain Research* 178: 95–111.

Goldin-Medow, S. 1999. The role of gesture in communication and thinking. *Trends in Cognitive Sciences* 3: 419–29.

Goldin-Medow, S., Nusbaum, H., Kelly, S.D., and Wagner, S. 2001. Explaining math: Gesturing lightens the load. *Psychological Science* 12(6): 516–22.

Goldman, A. 2005. Mirror systems, social understanding and social cognition. *Interdisciplines*. (http://www.interdisciplines.org/mirror/papers/3).

Goldman, A. 2006. *Simulating Minds: The Philosophy, Psychology and Neuroscience of Mindreading*. Oxford: Oxford University Press.

Goldman, A. and Sripada, C.S. 2005. Simulationist models of face-based emotion recognition. *Cognition* 94(3): 193–213.

Goldman, A.I. 1970. *A Theory of Human Action*. New York, NY: Prentice Hall.

Goldman, A.I. 1989. Interpretation psychologized. *Mind and Language* 4: 161–85.

Goldman, A.I., 1995. Desire, intention and the simulation theory. In B.F. Malle, L.J. Moses, and D.A. Baldwin (eds.), *Intentions and Intentionality: Foundations of Social Cognition* (207–24). Cambridge, MA: MIT Press.

Goldman, A.I. 2002. Simulation theory and mental concepts. In J. Dokic and J. Proust (eds.), *Simulation and Knowledge of Action* (1–19). Amsterdam/Philadelphia: John Benjamins.

Goldman, A.I. 2005. Imitation, mind reading, and simulation. In S. Hurley and N. Chater (eds.), *Perspectives on Imitation II* (79–93). Cambridge, MA: MIT Press.

Goldman, A.I. 2008. Does one size fit all? Hurley on shared circuits. *Behavioral and Brain Sciences* 31(1): 27–8.

Goldman, A.I. 2009a. Mirroring, simulating and mindreading. *Mind & Language* 24(2): 235–52.

Goldman, A.I. 2009b. Replies to Perner and Brandl, Saxe, Vignemont, and Carruthers. *Philosophical Studies* 144(3): 477–91.

Goldman, A.I. 2011. Two routes to empathy. In A. Coplan and P. Goldie (eds.), *Empathy: Philosophical and Psychological Perspectives* (31–44). Oxford: Oxford University Press.

Goldstein, K. 1940. *Human Nature in the Light of Psychopathology*. Cambridge: Harvard University Press; reprinted by Shocken Books: 1963.

Goldstein, K. and M. Scheerer. 1964. *Abstract and Concrete Behavior. An Experimental Study with Special Tests*. Evanston, IL: Northwestern University. Reprint of *Psychological Monographs* 53(2): 1941.

Good, J.M.M. 1985. The perception of social actions from point light displays: an exploratory study. Presented at the Third International Conference on Event Perception and Action, Trieste, Italy.

Goodwin, C. 2000. Action and embodiment within situated human interaction. *Journal of Pragmatics* 32: 1489–522.

Goodwin, C. 2017. *Co-operative Action*. Cambridge: Cambridge University Press.

Gopnik, A. and Wellman, H.M. 1992. Why the child's theory of mind really is a theory. *Mind & Language* 7(1–2): 145–71.

Gopnik, A. and Meltzoff, A.N. 1997. *Words, Thoughts and Theories*. Cambridge, MA: MIT Press.

Gordon, R.M. 1986. Folk psychology as simulation. *Mind & Language* 1(2): 158–71.

Gordon, R.M. 1995. Simulation without introspection or inference from me to you. In M. Davies and T. Stone (eds.), *Mental Simulation*. London: Blackwell.

Gordon, R.M. 2004. Folk psychology as mental simulation. In N. Zalta (ed.), *The Stanford Encyclopedia of Philosophy*. (Retrieved January 12, 2007 from: http://plato.stanford.edu/archives/fall2004/entries/folkpsych-simulation/).

Gordon, R.M. 2005. Intentional agents like myself. In S. Hurley and N. Chater (eds.), *Perspectives on Imitation I* (95–106). Cambridge, MA: MIT Press.

Gordon, R. M. 2021. Simulation, predictive coding, and the shared world. In K. Ochsner and M. Gilead (eds.), *The Neural Basis of Mentalizing* (237-255). Berlin: Springer.

Gordon, R.M. and Barker, J.A. 1994. Autism and the "theory of mind" debate. In G. Graham and G.L. Stephens (eds.), *Philosophical Psychopathology* (163–81). Cambridge, MA: MIT Press.

Gorno-Tempini, M.L., Pradelli, S., Serafini, M., Pagnoni, G., Baraldi, P., Porro, C., Nicoletti, R., Umità, C., and Nichelli, P. 2001. Explicit and incidental facial expression processing: an fMRI study. *NeuroImage* 14(2): 465–73.

Graesser, A.C. 1978. How to catch a fish: The memory and representation of common procedures. *Discourse Processes* 1(1): 72–89.

Graham, G. and Stephens, G.L. 1994. Mind and mine. In G. Graham and G.L. Stephens (eds.), *Philosophical Psychopathology* (91–109). Cambridge, MA: MIT Press.

Graziano, M.S.A. and Botvinick, M. 2002. How the brain represents the body: Insights from neurophysiology and psychology. In W. Prinz and B. Homme (eds.), *Common Mechanisms in Perception and Action: Attention and Performance XIX* (136–57). Oxford: Oxford University Press.

Green, M. 2007. *Self-Expression*. Oxford: Oxford University Press.

Green, M. 2010. Perceiving emotions. *Aristot Soc Suppl* 84: 45–61.

Grossman, D. 1996. *On Killing: The Psychological Costs of Learning to Kill in War and Society*. New York, NY: Back Bay Books.

Grünbaum, T. 2010. Action and agency. In S. Gallagher and D. Schmicking (eds.), *Handbook of Phenomenology and Cognitive Science* (337–54). Dordrecht: Springer.

Grünbaum, T. 2015. The feeling of agency hypothesis: a critique. *Synthese* 192(10): 3313–37.

Guajardo, N.R. and Watson, A. 2002. Narrative discourse and theory of mind development. *The Journal of Genetic Psychology* 163(3): 305–25.

Gurwitsch, A. 1978. *Human Encounters in the Social World*. Pittsburgh, PA: Duquesne University Press.

Gut, A. and Mirski, R. 2016. In search of a theory: The interpretative challenge of empirical finding on cultural variance in mindreading. *Studies in Logic and Grammar and Rhetoric* 48(61): 201–30.

Gutsell, J.N. and Inzlicht, M. 2010. Empathy constrained: Prejudice predicts reduced mental simulation of actions during observation of outgroups. *Journal of Experimental Social Psychology* 46(5): 841–5.

Habermas, J. 1979. *Communication and the Evolution of Society*. Trans. T. McCarthy. Boston, MA: Beacon Press.

Habermas, J. 1980. The hermeneutic claim to universality. In J. Bleicher (ed.), *Contemporary Hermeneutics*. London: Routledge and Kegan Paul.

Habermas, J. 1984. *The Theory of Communicative Action. Vol. I: Reason and the Rationalization of Society*. Trans. T. McCarthy. Boston, MA: Beacon Press.

Habermas, J. 1987. *The Theory of Communicative Practice. Vol. 2*. Trans. T. McCarthy. Boston, MA: Beacon Press.

Habermas, J. 2007. The language game of responsible agency and the problem of free will. *Philosophical Explorations* 10(1): 13–50.

Habermas, J. and McCarthy, T. 1977. Hannah Arendt's communications concept of power. *Social Research* 44(1): 3–24.

Hacking, I. 1995. The looping effects of human kinds. In D. Sperber, D. Premack, and A.J. Premack (eds.), *Causal Cognition: A Multidisciplinary Approach* (351–83). New York, NY: Oxford University Press.

Hadders-Algra, M. 2018. Early human motor development: From variation to the ability to vary and adapt. *Neuroscience & Biobehavioral Reviews* 90: 411–27.

Haggard, P. 2003. Conscious awareness of intention and of action. In N. Eilan and J. Roessler (eds.), *Agency and Self-Awareness* (111–27). Oxford: Clarendon Press.

Haggard, P., Clark, S., and Kalogeras, J. 2002. Voluntary action and conscious awareness. *Nature Neuroscience* 5(4): 382–5.

Haith, M.M. 1993. Future-oriented processes in infancy: The case of visual expectations. In C. Granrud (ed.), *Carnegie-Mellon Symposium on Visual Perception and Cognition in Infancy* (235–64). Hillsdale, NJ: Lawrence Erlbaum Associates.

Halliday, M.A.K. 1978. Meaning and the construction of reality in early childhood. In J.H. Pick Jr. and E. Saltzman (eds.), *Psychological Modes of Perceiving and Processing Information* (67–98). Hillsdale, NJ: Erlbaum.

Hamlin, J.K., Mahajan, N., Liberman, Z., and Wynn, K. 2013. Not like me = bad: Infants prefer those who harm dissimilar others. *Psychological Science* 24(4): 589–94.

Harris, P.L., Johnson, C.N., Hutton, D., Andrews, G., and Cooke, T. 1989. Young children's theory of mind and emotion. *Cogn Emot* 3: 379–400.

Harrist, S. and Gelfand, S. 2005. Life story, dialogue and the ideal speech situation: Critical theory and hermeneutics. *Theory & Psychology* 15(2): 225–46.

Haslam, N. 2006. Dehumanization: an integrative review. *Pers Soc Psychol Rev* 10: 252–64.

Haslam, N. and Bain, P. 2007. Humanizing the self: Moderators of the attribution of lesser humanness to others. *Pers Soc Psychol Bull* 33: 57–68.

Haslam, N., Bain, P., Douge, L., Lee, M., and Bastian, B. 2005. More human than you: attributing humanness to self and others. *J Pers Soc Psychol* 89: 937–50.

Haslam, N., Kashima, Y., Loughnan, S., Shi, J., and Suitner, C. 2008a. Subhuman, inhuman, and superhuman: Contrasting humans with nonhumans in three cultures. *Social Cognition* 26: 248–58.

Haslam, N., Loughnan, S., Kashima, Y., and Bain, P. 2008b. Attributing and denying humanness to others. *European Review of Social Psychology* 19: 55–85.

Haslanger, S. 2012. *Resisting Reality: Social Construction and Social Critique.* Oxford: Oxford University Press.

Hatfield, G. 2002. Perception as unconscious inference. In D. Heyer (ed.), *Perception and the Physical World: Psychological and Philosophical Issues in Perception* (113–43). Chichester: John Wiley & Sons.

Hayes, A.E., Paul, M.A., Beuger, B., and Tipper, S.P. 2008. Self produced and observed actions influence emotion: the roles of action fluency and eye gaze. Psychological Research 72(4): 461–72.

Head, H. 1920. *Studies in Neurology.* Vol. 2. Oxford: Clarendon Press.

Heal, J. 1986. Replication and functionalism. In J. Butterfield (ed.), *Language, Mind, and Logic* (135–50). Cambridge: Cambridge University Press.

Heal, J. 1996. Simulation, theory, and content. In P. Carruthers and P.K. Smith (eds.), *Theories of Theories of Mind* (75–89). Cambridge: Cambridge University Press.

Heal, J. 1998. Co-cognition and off-line simulation: Two ways of understanding the simulation approach. *Mind & Language* 13(4): 477–98.

Hegel, G.W.F. 1952. *Hegel's Philosophy of Right.* Trans. T.M. Knox. Cambridge: Cambridge University Press.

Hegel, G.W.F. 1975. Jenaer Systementwürfe I: Das System der spekulativen Philosophie, K. Düsing and H. Kimmerle (eds.). In *Gesammelte Werke*, vol. 6. Hamburg: Meiner.

Hegel, G.W.F. 1997. *Phenomenology of Spirit.* Trans. A.V. Miller. Oxford: Oxford University Press.

Heidegger, M. 2015. Der Spruch des Anaximander [1946]. In *Holzwege* (321–74). Frankfurt: v. Klostermann.

Held, K. 1966. *Lebendige Gegenwart*. Den Haag: Martinus Nijhoff.

Held, V. 1993. *Feminist Morality: Transforming Culture, Society, and Politics*. Chicago, IL: University of Chicago Press.

Helmholtz, H. 1867. *Handbuch der Physiologishen Optik*. Leipzig: Leopold Voss; English translation: J. Southall. 2005. *Treatise on Physiological Optics*. Courier Corporation.

Heris, Y.A. 2017a. Why emotion recognition is not simulational. *Philosophical Psychology* 30(6): 711–30.

Heris, Y.A. 2017b. *Reading through mirror neurons?* Research Centre for Neurophilosophy and Ethics of Neuroscience. LMU. Munich: Doctoral dissertation.

Herschbach, M. 2007. The phenomenological critics of folk psychology: The case of false belief. Paper presented at the Berkeley-Stanford-Davis Graduate Student Conference, 14 April 2007. https://mechanism.ucsd.edu/~mitch/research/BSD-Critics_of_FP.pdf

Herschbach, M. 2008. Folk psychological and phenomenological accounts of social perception. *Philosophical Explorations* 11: 223–35.

Herschbach, M. 2012. On the role of social interaction in social cognition: a mechanistic alternative to enactivism. *Phenomenology and the Cognitive Sciences* 11(4): 467–86.

Heyes, C. 2010. Where do mirror neurons come from? *Neuroscience & Biobehavioral Reviews* 34(4): 575–83.

Hickok, G. 2009. Eight problems for the mirror neuron theory of action understanding in monkeys and humans. *Journal of Cognitive Neuroscience* 21(7): 1229–43.

Hirsch, J., Zhang, X., Noah, J.A., and Ono, Y. 2017. Frontal temporal and parietal systems synchronize within and across brains during live eye-to-eye. *Trends in Cognitive Sciences* 4(7): 267–78.

Hobson, J.A., Harris, R., García-Pérez, R., and Hobson, R.P. 2009. Anticipatory concern: A study in autism. *Developmental Science* 12(2): 249–63.

Hobson, P. 1993. The emotional origins of social understanding. *Philosophical Psychology* 6: 227–49.

Hobson, P. 2002. *The Cradle of Thought*. London: Macmillan.

Hobson, R.P. 2011. Autism and the self. In S. Gallagher (ed.), *Oxford Handbook of the Self*. Oxford: Oxford University Press.

Hobson, R.P. and Lee, A. 1999. Imitation and identification in autism. *The Journal of Child Psychology and Psychiatry and Allied Disciplines* 40(4): 649–59.

Hobson, R.P., Lee, A., and Hobson, J.A. 2007. Only connect? Communication, identification, and autism. *Social Neuroscience* 2(3–4): 320–35.

Hogan, R. 1969. Development of an empathy scale. *Journal of Consulting and Clinical Psychology* 33: 307–16.

Hohwy, J. 2013. *The Predictive Mind*. Oxford: Oxford University Press.

Hommel, B., Colzato, L.S., and Van Den Wildenberg, W.P. 2009. How social are task representations? *Psychological Science* 20(7): 794–8.

Honneth, A. 1995. *The Struggle for Recognition*. Cambridge: Polity Press.

Honneth, A. 1998. Philosophy in Germany, interview with S. Critchley. *Radical Philosophy* 89: 27–39.

Honneth, A. 2007. *Disrespect: The Normative Foundations of Critical Theory*. Cambridge: Polity Press.

Honneth, A. 2008a. *Reification: A New Look at an Old Idea*. Oxford: Oxford University Press.

Honneth, A. 2008b. Rejoinder. In Honneth (2008a), *A Reification: A New Look at an Old Idea* (147–59). Oxford: Oxford University Press.

Honneth A. 2012. *The I in the We: Studies in the Theory of Recognition*. Cambridge: Polity.

Hopkins, B. and Prechtl, H.F.R. 1984. A qualitative approach to the development of movements during early infancy. In H.F.R. Prechtl (ed.), *Continuity of Neural Functions from Prenatal to Postnatal Life*. Oxford: Blackwell.

Horgan, T. 2017. Injecting the phenomenology of agency into the free will debate. *Proceedings and Addresses of the American Philosophical Association* 91: 155–84.

Hornik, R., Risenhoover, N., and Gunnar, M. 1987. The effects of maternal positive, neutral, and negative affective communications on infant responses to new toys. *Child Development* 58(4): 937–44.

Hornsby, J. 2013. Basic activity. *Aristotelian Society Supplementary* 87(1): 1–18.

Hornsby, J. 2017. Agency, time and naturalism. *Proceedings and Addresses of the American Philosophical Association* 91: 137–53.

Howe, M.L. 2000. *The Fate of Early Memories: Developmental Science and the Retention of Childhood Experiences*. Washington, DC: American Psychological Association.

Hume, D. 1739. *A Treatise of Human Nature*. Clarendon Press (reprint 1975).

Hurley, S. 1998. *Consciousness in Action*. Cambridge, MA: Harvard University Press.

Hurley, S. 2008. The shared circuits model (SCM): How control, mirroring, and simulation can enable imitation, deliberation, and mindreading. *Behavioral and Brain Sciences* 31(1): 1–22.

Hurley, S.L. 2005. Active perception and perceiving action: The shared circuits model. In T. Gendler and J. Hawthorne (eds.), *Perceptual Experience* (205–59). New York, NY: Oxford University Press.

Husserl, E. 1960. *Cartesian Meditations: An Introduction to Phenomenology*. Trans. D. Cairns. The Hague: Martinus Nijhoff.

Husserl, E. 1973. *Ding und Raum. Vorlesungen 1907*. Husserliana 16. The Hague: Martinus Nijhoff, 1973. English translation: *Thing and Space: Lectures of 1907*. Trans. R. Rojcewicz. Dordrecht: Kluwer Academic, 1998.

Husserl, E. 1977. *Phenomenological Psychology*. Trans. J. Scanlan. The Hague: Martinus Nijhoff.

Husserl, E. 1989. *Ideas Pertaining to a Pure Phenomenology and to a Phenomenological Philosophy—Second Book: Studies in the Phenomenology of Constitution*. Trans. R. Rojcewicz and A. Schuwer. Dordrecht: Kluwer Academic.

Husserl, E. 1991. *On the Phenomenology of the Consciousness of Internal Time (1893–1917)*. Collected Works IV. Trans. J. Brough. Dordrecht: Kluwer Academic. Translation of (1966). *Zur Phänomenologie des inneren Zeitbewußtseins (1893–1917)*, Husserliana 10. Den Haag: Martinus Nijhoff.

Husserl, E. 2001. *Die Bernauer Manuskripte über das Zeitbewusstsein (1917–18)*, Husserliana 33. Dordrecht: Springer.

Hutchins, E. 1995. *Cognition in the Wild*. Cambridge, MA: MIT Press.

Hutto, D.D. 2006. Narrative practice and understanding reasons: Reply to Gallagher. In R. Menary (ed.), *Radical Enactivism* (231–47). Amsterdam: John Benjamins.

Hutto, D.D. 2007a. Folk psychology without theory or simulation. In D.D. Hutto and M. Ratcliffe (eds.), *Folk Psychology Reassessed* (115–35). Dordrecht: Springer.

Hutto, D.D. 2007b. The narrative practice hypothesis. In D.D. Hutto (ed.), *Narrative and Understanding Persons* (43–68). Royal Institute of Philosophy Supplement. Cambridge: Cambridge University Press.

Hutto, D.D. 2008. *Folk Psychological Narratives: The Sociocultural Basis of Understanding Reasons*. Cambridge, MA: MIT Press.

Hutto, D.D. 2011. Elementary mind minding, Enactivist-style. In A. Seeman (ed.), *Joint Attention: New Developments in Psychology, Philosophy of Mind, and Social Neuroscience* (307–47). Cambridge: MIT Press.

Hutto, D., Gallagher, S., Ilundáin-Agurruza, J., and Hipólito, I. 2020. Culture in mind—An enactivist account: Not cognitive penetration but cultural permeation. In L.J. Kirmayer, S. Kitayama, C.M. Worthman, R. Lemelson and C.A. Cummings (eds.), *Culture, Mind, and Brain: Emerging Concepts, Models, Applications* (163-187). New York: Cambridge University Press.

Hutto, D. and E. Myin 2013. *Radicalizing Enactivism: Basic Minds Without Content.* Cambridge, MA: MIT Press.

Iacoboni, M., Molnar-Szakacs, I., Gallese, V., Buccino, G., Mazziotta, J., and Rizzolatti, G. 2005. Grasping the intentions of others with one's own mirror neuron system. *PLoS Biology* 3(79): 1-7.

Iani, C., Anelli, F., Nicoletti, R., Arcuri, L., and Rubichi, S. 2011. The role of group membership on the modulation of joint action. *Experimental Brain Research* 211(3-4): 439-45.

Issartel, J., Marin, L., and Cadopi, M. 2007. Unintended interpersonal coordination: "Can we march to the beat of our own drum"? *Neuroscience Letters* 411: 174-9.

Izard, C.E. 1972. *Patterns of Emotions: A New Analysis of Anxiety and Depression.* New York, NY: Academic Press.

Izard, C.E., Ackerman, B.P., Schoff, K.M., and Fine, S.E. 2000. Self-organization of discrete emotions, emotion patterns, and emotion-cognition relations. In S.E. Lewis and I. Granic (eds.), *Emotion, Development, and Self-organization: Dynamic Systems Approaches to Emotional Development* (15-36). New York, NY: Cambridge University Press.

Jack, R.E., Blais, C., Scheepers, C., Schyns, P.G., and Caldara, R. 2009. Cultural confusions show that facial expressions are not universal. *Current Biology* 19(18): 1543-8.

Jacob, P. 2008. What do mirror neurons contribute to human social cognition? *Mind & Language* 23(2): 190-223.

Jacob, P. 2011. The direct perception model of empathy: A critique. *Review of Philosophy and Psychology* 2(3): 519-40.

James, W. 1890. *Principles of Psychology.* New York, NY: Dover, 1950.

Jay, M. 2008. Introduction. In A. Honneth (ed.), *Reification: A New Look at an Old Idea* (3-16). Oxford: Oxford University Press.

Jeannerod, M. (ed.). 1987. *Neurophysiological and Neuropsychological Aspects of Spatial Neglect* (Advances in Psychology, Vol. 45). Amsterdam: Elsevier.

Jeannerod, M. 2001. Neural simulation of action: A unifying mechanism for motor cognition. *NeuroImage* 14: S103-9.

Jeannerod, M. 2003. Self-generated actions. In S. Maasen, W. Prinz, and G. Roth (eds.), *Voluntary Action: Brains, Minds, and Sociality* (153-64). Oxford: Oxford University Press.

Jeannerod, M. and Pacherie, E. 2004. Agency, simulation, and self-identification. *Mind and Language* 19(2): 113-46.

Johnson, S., Slaughter, V., and Carey, S. 1998. Whose gaze will infants follow? The elicitation of gaze-following in 12-month-old infants. *Developmental Science* 1(2): 233-8.

Johnson, S.C. 2000. The recognition of mentalistic agents in infancy. *Trends in Cognitive Science* 4(1): 22-8.

Jones, S.S. 2006. Exploration or imitation? The effect of music on 4-week-old infants' tongue protrusions. *Infant Behavior and Development* 29(1): 126-30.

Jones, S.S. 2009. The development of imitation in infancy. *Philosophical Transactions of the Royal Society of London B: Biological Sciences* 364(1528): 2325-35.

Kalampratsidou, V. and Torres, E. 2018. Peripheral network connectivity analyses for the real-time tracking of coupled bodies in motion. *Sensors* 18(9): 3117.

Kaplan, J.T. and Iacoboni, M. 2007. Multimodal action representation in human left ventral premotor cortex. *Cognitive Processing* 8(2): 103-13.

Karmarkar, U.R. and Buonomano, D.V. 2007. Timing in the absence of clocks: Encoding time in neural network states. *Neuron* 53: 427–38.

Karmiloff-Smith, A. 1992. *Beyond Modularity: A Developmental Perspective on Cognitive Science*. Cambridge, MA: MIT Press.

Keller, E.F. 1985. *Reflection in Gender and Science* (158–76). New Haven, CT: Yale University Press.

Kelso, S. 1995. *Dynamic Patterns*. Cambridge, MA: MIT Press.

Kendon, A. 1990. *Conducting Interaction: Patterns of Behavior in Focused Encounters*. Cambridge: Cambridge University Press.

Kerby, P. 1993. *Narrative and the Self*. Bloomington, IN: Indiana University Press.

Keven, N. and Akins, K.A. 2017. Neonatal imitation in context: Sensory-motor development in the perinatal period. *Behavioral and Brain Sciences* 40(e381): 1–107.

Keysers, C. and Gazzola, V. 2006. Towards a unifying neural theory of social cognition. In S. Anders, G. Ende, M. Junghofer, and J. Kissler (eds.), *Understanding Emotions* (379–402). Amsterdam: Elsevier.

Kidd, D.C. and Castano, E. 2013. Reading literary fiction improves theory of mind. *Science* 342(6156): 377–80.

Kilner, J.M., Friston, K.J., and Frith, C.D. 2007. Predictive coding: an account of the mirror neuron system. *Cognitive Processing* 8(3): 159–66.

Kirchhoff, M.D. 2015. Extended cognition and the causal-constitutive fallacy: In search for a diachronic and dynamical conception of constitution. *Philosophy and Phenomenological Research* 9 (2): 320–60.

Kirchhoff, M. and Robertson, I. 2018. Enactivism and predictive processing: a non-representational view. *Philosophical Explorations* 21(2): 264–81.

Kitayama, S. and Park, J. 2010. Cultural neuroscience of the self: Understanding the social grounding of the brain. *Social Cognitive Affective Neuroscience* 5(2–3): 111–29.

Klinnert, M.D., Emde, R.N., Butterfield, P., and Campos, J.J. 1986. Social referencing: The infant's use of emotional signals from a friendly adult with mother present. *Developmental Psychology* 22(4): 427–32.

Knoblich, G. and Jordan, J. S. 2003. Action coordination in groups and individuals: Learning anticipatory control. *Journal of Experimental Psychology: Learning, Memory, and Cognition* 29 (5): 1006.

Konvalinka, I., Vuust, P., Roepstorff, A., and Frith, C. 2010. Follow you, follow me: Continuous mutual prediction and adaptation in joint tapping. *Q. J. Exp. Psychol.* 63: 2220–30.

Krueger, J. 2012. Seeing mind in action. *Phenomenology and the Cognitive Sciences* 11: 149–73.

Krueger, J. and Michael, J. 2012. Gestural coupling and social cognition: Möbius syndrome as a case study. *Frontiers in Human Neuroscience* 6: 81. doi: 10.3389/fnhum.2012.00081

Krueger, J. and Overgaard, S. 2012. Seeing subjectivity: Defending a perceptual account of other minds. *ProtoSociology: Consciousness and Subjectivity* 47: 239–62.

Kruskal, J.B. and Wish, M. 1978. *Multidimensional Scaling* (Vol. 11). Sage.

Lafargue, G., Paillard, J., Lamarre, Y., and Sirigu, A. 2003. Production and perception of grip force without proprioception: Is there a sense of effort in deafferented subjects? *European Journal of Neuroscience* 17(12): 2741–9.

Laine, M. and Martin, A. 2013. *Anomia: Theoretical and Clinical Aspects*. Psychology Press.

Lambie, J. 2020. The demanding world of emotion: A Gestalt approach to emotion experience. *New Ideas in Psychology* 56: 100751.

Lang, A. (ed.) 1889. *The Blue Fairy Book* (Vol. 1). London: Longmans, Green, and Company.

Langland-Hassan, P. 2008. Fractured phenomenologies: Thought insertion, inner speech, and the puzzle of extraneity. *Mind & Language* 23(4): 369–401.

Latham, A.J., Patston, L.L., and Tippett, L.J. 2013. The virtual brain: 30 years of video-game play and cognitive abilities. *Frontiers in Psychology* 4(629). doi. 10.3389/fpsyg.2013.00629

Latour, B. and Woolgar, S. 1979. *Laboratory Life: The Social Construction of Scientific Facts*. Beverly Hills, CA: Sage.

Lavelle, J.S. 2012. Theory-theory and the direct perception of mental states. *Review of Philosophy and Psychology* 3(2): 213–30.

Lavin, D. 2013. Must there be basic action? *Noûs* 47(2): 273–301.

Lear, J. 2008. The slippery middle. In A. Honneth, *Reification. A New Look at an Old Idea* (131–46). Oxford: Oxford University Press.

Legerstee, M. 1991. The role of person and object in eliciting early imitation. *Journal of Experimental Child Psychology* 51(3): 423–33.

Legerstee, M. 2005. *Infants' Sense of People: Precursors to a Theory of Mind*. Cambridge: Cambridge University Press.

Legrand, D. 2007. Pre-reflective self-consciousness: on being bodily in the world. *Janus Head* 9(2): 493–519.

Leontiev, A.N. and Zaporozhets, A.V. 1960. *Recovery of Hand Function*. Trans. B. Haigh. London: Pergamon. [Original Russian: 1945]

Leslie, A.M. 1987. Pretense and representation: The origins of "theory of mind." *Psychological Review* 94(4), 412–26. doi: 10.1037/0033-295X.94.4.412

Leslie, A.M. 1991. The theory of mind impairment in autism: Evidence for a modular mechanism of development? In A. Whiten (ed.), *Natural Theories of Mind: Evolution, Development and Simulation of Everyday Mindreading* (63–78). Cambridge, MA: Basil Blackwell.

Leslie, A.M. 2000. Theory of mind as a mechanism of selective attention. In M. Gazzaniga (ed.), *The New Cognitive Neurosciences* (1235–47). Cambridge, MA: MIT Press.

Leslie, A.M. and Frith, U. 1988. Autistic children's understanding of seeing, knowing and believing. *British Journal of Developmental Psychology* 6(4): 315–24.

Leudar, I. and Costall, A. 2004. On the persistence of the "problem of other minds" in psychology: Chomsky, Grice and "theory of mind." *Theory Psychol* 14: 601–21.

Levin, D.T. and Banaji, M.R. 2006. Distortions in the perceived lightness of faces: the role of race categories. *Journal of Experimental Psychology: General* 135(4): 501.

Levinas, E. 1969. *Totality and Infinity*. Trans. A. Lingis. Haag: Kluwer and Pittsburgh: Duquesne.

Levinas, E. 1991. *Entre nous: Essais sur le penser-à-'autre*. Paris: Le Livre de Poche.

Lew, A. and Butterworth, G.E. 1995. Hand-mouth contact in newborn babies before and after feeding. *Developmental Psychology* 31: 456–63.

Lew, A. and Butterworth, G.E. 1997. The development of hand-mouth coordination in 2- to 5-months old infants: Similarities with reaching and grasping. *Infant. Behav. Development* 20: 59–69.

Leyens, J-P., Yzerbyt, V., and Schadron G. 1994. *Stereotypes and Social Cognition*. London: Sage Publications.

Libet, B. 1985. Unconscious cerebral initiative and the role of conscious will in voluntary action. *Behavioral and Brain Sciences* 8: 529–66.

Lichtenstein, E.H. and Brewer, W.F. 1980. Memory for goal-directed events. *Cognitive Psychology* 12(3): 412–45.

Likowski, K.U., Mühlberger, A., Seibt, B., Pauli, P., and Weyers, P. 2008. Modulation of facial mimicry by attitudes. *J Experimental Social Psychology* 44: 1065–72.

Lillard, A. 1998. Ethnopsychologies: Cultural variations in theories of mind. *Psychological Bulletin* 123(1): 3–32.

Lindblom, J. 2007. Minding the body: Interacting socially through embodied action. Linköping Studies in Science and Technology. Dissertation No. 1112.

Lindblom, J. 2015. *Embodied Social Cognition*. Heidelberg: Springer.

Lindblom, J. and Ziemke, T. 2007. Embodiment and social interaction: A cognitive science perspective. In T. Ziemke, J. Zlatev, and R.M. Frank (eds.), *Body, Language, and Mind* Vol. 2 (129–62). Walter de Gruyter.

Lindblom, J. and Ziemke, T. 2008. Interacting socially through embodied action. In F. Morganti, A. Carassa, and G. Riva (eds.), *Enacting Intersubjectivity: A Cognitive and Social Perspective on the Study of Interactions* (49–64). Amsterdam: Ios Press.

Locke, J. 1690. *An Essay Concerning Human Understanding*. New York, NY: Dover, 1969.

Lymer, J.M. 2010. The phenomenology of the maternal-foetal bond. PhD Dissertation. University of Wollongong.

Lyotard, J-F. 1984. *The Postmodern Condition: A Report on Knowledge*. Trans. G. Bennington and B. Massumi. Minneapolis, MN: University of Minnesota Press.

Lyotard, J-F. and Thebaud, J.L. 1985. *Just Gaming*. Trans. W. Godzich. Minneapolis, MN: University of Minnesota Press.

MacIntyre, A. 1984. *After Virtue: A Study in Moral Theory*. Notre Dame, IN: University of Notre Dame Press.

MacKay, D. 1966. Cerebral organization and the conscious control of action. In J.C. Eccles (ed.), *Brain and Conscious Experience* (422–45). New York, NY: Springer.

Mackenzie C. 2007. Bare personhood? Velleman on selfhood. *Philosophical Explorations* 10(3): 263–81.

Mackenzie, C. and Stoljar, N. (eds.). 2000. *Relational Autonomy: Feminist Perspectives on Automony, Agency, and the Social Self*. Oxford: Oxford University Press.

Malafouris, L. 2013. *How Things Shape the Mind*. Cambridge, MA: MIT Press.

Malcolm, N. 1953. Direct perception. *The Philosophical Quarterly* 3(13): 301–16.

Manera, V., Becchio, C., Cavallo, A., Sartori L., and Castiello, U. 2011. Cooperation or competition? Discriminating between social intentions by observing prehensile movements. *Experimental Brain Research* 211: 547–56.

Manicas, P.T. 1981. John Dewey and the problem of justice. *Journal of Value Inquiry* 1(4): 279–91.

Marcel, A. 2003. The sense of agency: Awareness and ownership of action. In J. Roessler and N. Eilan (eds.), *Agency and Awarness* (48–93). Oxford: Oxford University Press.

Marcel, A.J. 1983. Conscious and unconscious perception: An approach to the relations between phenomenal experience and perceptual processes. *Cognitive Psychology* 15: 238–300.

Marcel, A.J. 1992. The personal level in cognitive rehabilitation. In N. von Steinbechel, E. Pöppel, and D. Cramon (eds.), *Neuropsychological Rehabilitation* (155–68). Berlin: Springer.

Marcelo, G. 2011. Paul Ricoeur and the utopia of mutual recognition. *Études Ricoeuriennes/ Ricoeur Studies* 2(1): 110–33.

Margolis, J. 2012. *Persons and Minds: The Prospects of Nonreductive Materialism* (Vol. 57). Springer Science & Business Media.

Marteniuk, R.G., MacKenzie, C.L., Jeannerod, M., Athenes, S., and Dugas, C. 1987. Constraints on human arm movement trajectories. *Canadian Journal of Psychology* 41: 365–78.

Matsumoto, D. 2002. Methodological requirements to test a possible in-group advantage in judging emotions across cultures. *Psychol Bull* 128: 236–42.

Maurer, D. and Barrera, M.E. 1981. Infants' perception of natural and distorted arrangements of a schematic face. *Child Development* 52(1): 196–202.

McDowell, J. 2011. Some remarks on intention in action. *The Amherst Lecture in Philosophy* 6: 1–18. <http://www.amherstlecture.org/mcdowell2011/>

McNeill, W. 2012. Embodiment and the perceptual hypothesis. *Philosophical Quarterly* 62(248): 569–91.

McTaggart, J.M.E. 1908. The unreality of time. *Mind* 17(New Series, no. 68): 457–74.

Mead, G.H. 1938. *The Philosophy of the Act.* Edited and with an introduction by C.W. Morris. Chicago, IL: University of Chicago Press.

Meehan, J. 2011. Recognition and the dynamics of intersubjectivity. In *Axel Honneth: Critical Essays* (89–124). Leiden: Brill.

Mele, A. and Moser, K. 1997. Intentional action. In A. Mele (ed.), *The Philosophy of Action* (223–55). Oxford: Oxford University Press.

Meltzoff, A. N. 1995. Understanding the intentions of others: re-enactment of intended acts by 18-month-old children. *Developmental Psychology* 31 (5): 838.

Meltzoff, A. N. and Brooks, R. 2001. "Like me" as a building block for understanding other minds: Bodily acts, attention, and intention. In B.F. Malle, L.J. Moses, and D.A. Baldwin, (Eds.). *Intentions and Intentionality: Foundations of Social Cognition* (171–191). Cambridge, MA: MIT Press.

Meltzoff, A.N. and Moore, M.K. 1977. Imitation of facial and manual gestures by human neonates. *Science* 198(4312): 75–8.

Meltzoff, A.N. and Moore, M.K. 1989. Imitation in newborn infants: Exploring the range of gestures imitated and the underlying mechanisms. *Developmental Psychology* 25(6): 954.

Meltzoff, A. and Moore, M.K. 1994. Imitation, memory, and the representation of persons. *Infant Behavior and Development* 17: 83–99.

Meltzoff, A.N., Ramírez, R.R., Saby, J.N., Larson, E., Taulu, S., and Marshall, P.J. 2018. Infant brain responses to felt and observed touch of hands and feet: An MEG study. *Developmental Science* 21(5): e12651.

Meltzoff, A.N., Saby, J.N., and Marshall, P.J. 2019. Neural representations of the body in 60-day-old human infants. *Developmental Science* 22(1): e12698.

Menary, R. 2008. Embodied narratives. *Journal of Consciousness Studies* 15(6): 63–84.

Mendoça, D. 2012. Pattern of sentiment: Following a Deweyan suggestion. *Trans. C. S. Peirce Soc.* 48: 209–27. doi: 10.2979/trancharpeirsoc.48.2.209

Merleau-Ponty, M. 1964a. *The Primacy of Perception.* Evanston, IL: Northwestern University Press.

Merleau-Ponty, M. 1964b. *Sense and Non-Sense.* Trans. H. Dreyfus and P.A. Dreyfus. Evanston, IL: Northwestern University Press.

Merleau-Ponty, M. 1964c. *Signs.* Evanston, IL: Northwestern University Press.

Merleau-Ponty, M. 1968. *The Visible and the Invisible.* Trans. A. Lingis. Evanston, IL: Northwestern University Press.

Merleau-Ponty, M. 1973. *Consciousness and the Acquisition of Language.* Trans. H.J. Silverman. Evanston, IL: Northwestern University Press.

Merleau-Ponty, M. 1983. *The Structure of Behavior.* Trans. A. Fischer. Pittsburgh, PN: Duquesne University Press.

Merleau-Ponty, M. 2012. *Phenomenology of Perception.* Trans. D.A. Landes. London: Routledge.

Messinger, D. and Fogel, A. 2007. The interactive development of social smiling. *Advances in Child Development and Behavior* 35: 328–66.

Metzinger, T. 2004. *Being No One: The Self-Model Theory of Subjectivity.* Cambridge, MA: MIT Press.

Michael, J., Christensen, W., and Overgaard, S. 2014. Mindreading as social expertise. *Synthese* 191(5): 817–40.

Michael, J. and Overgaard, S. 2012. Interaction and social cognition: A comment on Auvray et al.'s perceptual crossing paradigm. *New Ideas in Psychology* 30(3): 296–9.

Miller, D. 1999. *Principles of Social Justice.* Cambridge, MA: Harvard University Press.

Miller, M., Kiverstein, J. and Rietveld, E. 2020. Embodying addiction: A predictive processing account. *Brain and Cognition* 138: 105495.

Mills, C. 2005. "Ideal theory" as ideology. *Hypatia* 20(3): 165–83.

Milton, A. and Pleydell-Pearce, C.W. 2016. The phase of pre-stimulus alpha oscillations influences the visual perception of stimulus timing. *NeuroImage* 133: 53–61. doi: 10.1016/j.neuroimage.2016.02.065 pmid:26924284

Minio-Paluello, I., Avenanti, A., and Aglioti, S.M. 2006. Left hemisphere dominance in reading the sensory qualities of others' pain? *Social Neuroscience* 1(3–4): 320–33.

Mink, L.O. 1970. History and fiction as modes of comprehension. *New Literary History* 1: 541–58.

Mirowski, P. and Nik-Khah, E. 2017. *The Knowledge We Have Lost in Information: The History of Information in Modern Economics.* New York, NY: Oxford University Press.

Mirski, R. and Gut, A. 2018. Action-based versus cognitivist perspectives on socio-cognitive development: Culture, language and social experience within the two paradigms. *Synthese*, 1–27. https://link.springer.com/article/10.1007/s11229-018-01976-y

Mitchell, J.P. 2008. Contributions of functional neuroimaging to the study of social cognition. *Current Directions in Psychological Science* 17(2): 142–6.

Molnar-Szakacs, I., Wu, A.D., Robles F.J., and Iacoboni, M. 2007. Do you see what I mean? Corticospinal excitability during observation of culture-specific gestures. *PLoS One* 2: e626.

Morales, M., Mundy, P., Crowson, M., et al. 2005. Individual differences in infant attention skills, joint attention, and emotion regulation behavior. *International Journal of Behavioral Development* 29(3): 259–63.

Morton, A. 1996. Folk psychology is not a predictive device. *Mind* 105: 119–37.

Moses, L.J., Baldwin, D.A., Rosicky, J.G., and Tidball, G. 2001. Evidence for referential understanding in the emotions domain at twelve and eighteen months. *Child Development* 72: 718–35.

Muir, D.W. 2002. Adult communications with infants through touch: The forgotten sense. *Human Development* 45: 95–9.

Müller B.C.N., Brass M., Kühn S., Tsai C.C., Nieuwboer W., Dijksterhuis A., et al. 2011. When Pinocchio acts like a human, a wooden hand becomes embodied: Action co-representation for non-biological agents. *Neuropsychologia* 49(5), 1373–7.

Murray, L. and Trevarthen, C. 1985. Emotional regulations of interactions between two-month-olds and their mothers. In T.M. Field and N.A. Fox (eds.), *Social Perception in Infants* (177–97). Norwood, NJ: Ablex Publishing.

Myowa-Yamakoshi M. and Takeshita H. 2006. Do human fetuses anticipate self-oriented actions? A study by four-dimensional (4D) ultrasonography. *Infancy* 10(3): 289–301.

Nadel, J., Carchon, I., Kervella, C., Marcelli, D., and Réserbat-Plantey, D. 1999. Expectancies for social contingency in 2-month-olds. *Developmental Science* 2: 164–73.

Nagel, T. 1970. *The Possibility of Altruism.* Oxford: Clarendon.

Nagy, E., Pal, A., and Orvos, H. 2014. Learning to imitate individual finger movements by the human neonate. *Developmental Science* 17: 841–57.

Nagy, E., Pilling, K., Orvos, H., and Molnar, P. 2013. Imitation of tongue protrusion in human neonates: Specificity of the response in a large sample. *Developmental Psychology* 49(9): 1628.

Nalepka, P., Riehm, C., Mansour, C.B., Chemero, A., and Richardson, M.J. 2015. Investigating strategy discovery and coordination in a novel virtual sheep herding game among dyads. In *Proceedings of the 37th Annual Meeting of the Cognitive Science Society* (1703–8). Cognitive Science Society.

Nance, M. 2015. Recognition, freedom, and the self in Fichte's *Foundations of Natural Right*. *European Journal of Philosophy* 23(3): 608–32.

Nance, M. 2016. Freedom, coercion and the relation of right. In G. Gottlieb (ed.), *Fichte's Foundations of Natural Right: A Critical Guide* (196–217). Cambridge: Cambridge University Press.

Nelson, K. 1992. Emergence of autobiographical memory at age 4. *Human Development* 35: 172–7.

Nelson K. 2003a. Narrative and the emergence of a consciousness of self. In G.D. Fireman, T.E. J. McVay, and O. Flanagan (eds.), *Narrative and Consciousness* (17–36), Oxford: Oxford University Press.

Nelson, K. 2003b. Self and social functions: Individual autobiographical memory and collective narrative. *Memory* 11(2): 125–36.

Nelson, K. 2009. Narrative practices and folk psychology: A perspective from developmental psychology. *Journal of Consciousness Studies* 16(6–8): 69–93.

Neumann, A., Sodian, B., and Thoermer, C. 2009. Belief-based action anticipation in 18-month-old infants. Paper presented at the Biennial Meeting of the Society for Research in Child Development, Denver, CO; April 2009.

Newen, A., Welpinghus, A., and Jukel, G. 2015. Emotion recognition as pattern recognition: The relevance of perception. *Mind and Language* 30(2): 187–208.

Newman-Norlund, R.D., Noordzij, M.L., Meulenbroek, R.G.J., and Bekkering, H. 2007. Exploring the brain basis of joint attention: Co-ordination of actions, goals and intentions. *Social Neuroscience* 2(1): 48–65.

Nguyen, L. and Frye, D. 1999. Children's theory of mind: Understanding of desire, belief and emotion with social referents. *Social Development* 8(1): 70–92.

Nichols, S. and Stich, S.P. 2003. *Mindreading: An Integrated Account of Pretence, Self-Awareness, and Understanding Other Minds*. Oxford: Clarendon Press/Oxford University Press.

Noë, A. 2004. *Action in Perception*. Cambridge, MA: MIT Press.

Nussbaum, M.C. 1997. *Cultivating Humanity: A Classical Defense of Reform in Liberal Education*. Cambridge, MA: Harvard University Press.

Oatley, K. 2016. Fiction: Simulation of social worlds. *Trends in Cognitive Sciences* 20(8): 618–28.

Oberman, L.M. and Ramachandran, V.S. 2007. The simulating social mind: The role of the mirror neuron system and simulation in the social and communicative deficits of autism spectrum disorders. *Psychological Bulletin* 133(2): 310–27.

Oller, D.K., Caskey, M., Yoo, H., Bene, E.R., Jhang, Y., Lee, C-C., Dale, D., Bowman, D.D., Long, H.L., Buder, E.H., and Vohr, B. 2019. Preterm and full term infant vocalization and the origin of language. *Scientific Reports* 9: 14734.

Onishi, K.H. and Baillargeon, R. 2005. Do 15-month-old infants understand false beliefs? *Science* 308(5719): 255–8.

Oppermann, J.P. 2003. Anaximander's rhythm and the question of justice. *Law and Critique* 14(1): 45–69.

Orlandi, N. 2012. Embedded seeing-as: Multi-stable visual perception without interpretation. *Philosophical Psychology* 25(4): 555–73.

Orlandi, N. 2014. *The Innocent Eye: Why Vision is not a Cognitive Process*. Oxford: Oxford University Press.

Oshana, M.A. 1998. Personal autonomy and society. *Journal of Social Philosophy* 29(1): 81–102.

Overgaard, S. 2005. Rethinking other minds: Wittgenstein and Levinas on expression. *Inquiry* 48(3): 249–74.

Overgaard, S. 2017. Other minds embodied. *Continental Philosophy Review* 50(1): 65–80.

Overgaard, S. 2019. Embodiment and social perception. In A. Avramiedes and M. Parrott (eds.), *Other Minds* (127–47). Oxford: Oxford University Press.

Overgaard, S. and Michael, J. 2015. The interactive turn in social cognition research: A critique. *Philosophical Psychology* 28(2): 160–83.

Pacherie, E. 2005. Perceiving intentions. In João Sàágua (ed.), *A Explicação da Interpretação Humana* (401–14). Lisbon: Edições Colibri.

Pacherie, E. 2006. Towards a dynamic theory of intentions. In S. Pockett, W.P. Banks, and S. Gallagher (eds.), *Does Consciousness Cause Behavior? An Investigation of the Nature of Volition* (145–67). Cambridge, MA: MIT Press.

Pacherie, E., 2007. The sense of control and the sense of agency. *Psyche* 13(1): 1–30.

Pacherie, E. 2012. The phenomenology of joint action: Self-agency vs. joint-agency. In A. Seemann (ed.), *Joint Attention: New Developments* (343–89). Cambridge, MA: MIT Press.

Palmer, S.E. 1999. *Vision Science: Photons to Phenomenology.* Cambridge, MA: MIT Press.

Palumbo, L. and Jellema, T. 2013. Beyond face value: Does involuntary emotional anticipation shape the perception of dynamic facial expressions? *PloS One* 8(2): e56003.

Park, J. and Kitayama, S. 2012. Interdependent selves show face-induced facilitation of error processing: Cultural neuroscience of self-threat. *Social Cognitive & Affective Neuroscience* 9(2): 201–8.

Patterson K., Purell C., and Morton J. 1983. The faciliation of word retrieval in aphasia. In C. Code and D. Muller (eds.), *Aphasia Therapy.* London: Edward Arnold.

Perner, J. 1991. *Understanding the Representational Mind.* Cambridge, MA: MIT Press.

Perner, J. 1992. Grasping the concept of representation: Its impact on 4-year olds' theory of mind and beyond. *Human Development* 35: 146–55.

Perner, J. and Ruffman, T. 2005. Infants' insight into the mind: How deep? *Science* 308(5719): 214–16.

Perrault, C. 1697. *Histoires ou contes du temps passé, avec des moralités: Contes de ma mère l'Oye.* Paris.

Pettit, P. 2015. *The Robust Demands of the Good: Ethics with Attachment, Virtue, and Respect.* New York, NY: Oxford University Press.

Phillips, W., Baron-Cohen, S., and Rutter, M. 1992. The role of eye-contact in the detection of goals: Evidence from normal toddlers, and children with autism or mental handicap. *Development and Psychopathology* 4(3): 375–83.

Pinker, S. 2011. *The Better Angels of Our Nature: Why Violence Has Declined.* New York, NY: Viking.

Poizner, H., Klima, E.S., and Bellugi, U. 1987. *What the Hands Reveal About the Brain.* Cambridge, MA: MIT Press/Bradford Books.

Pöppel, E. 1994. Temporal mechanisms in perception. *International Review of Neurobiology* 37: 185–202.

Prechtl, H.F.R. and Hopkins, B. 1986. Developmental transformations of spontaneous movements in early infancy. *Early Human Development* 14: 233–83.

Premack, D. and G. Woodruff. 1978. Does the chimpanzee have a theory of mind? *Behavioral and Brain Sciences* 1: 515–26.

Preston, B. 2013. *A Philosophy of Material Culture: Action, Function, and Mind.* London: Routledge.

Prinz, J. 2004. *Gut Reactions: A Perceptual Theory of Emotion.* New York, NY: Oxford University Press.

Protevi, J. 2008. Affect, agency and responsibility: The act of killing in the age of cyborgs. *Phenomenology and the Cognitive Sciences* 7: 405–13.

Pylyshyn, Z. 1999. Is vision continuous with cognition? The case for cognitive impenetrability of visual perception. *Behavioral and Brain Sciences* 22(3): 341–65.

Quintard, V., Jouffre, S., Croizet, J.C., and Bouquet, C.A. 2018. The influence of passionate love on self-other discrimination during joint action. *Psychological Research*. https://doi.org/10.1007/s00426-018-0981-z

Ramstead, M.J.D., Kirchhoff, M.D., Constant, A., and Friston, K.J. 2019. Multiscale integration: Beyond internalism and externalism. *Synthese*. Published online: doi: doi.org/10.1007/s11229-019-02115-x

Ramstead, M.J.D., Veissière, S.P., and Kirmayer, L.J. 2016. Cultural affordances: scaffolding local worlds through shared intentionality and regimes of attention. *Frontiers in Psychology* 7. doi: 10.3389/fpsyg.2016.01090

Ray, E. and Heyes, C. 2011. Imitation in infancy: The wealth of the stimulus. *Developmental Science* 14(1): 92–105.

Ratcliffe, M. 2007. *Rethinking Commonsense Psychology: A Critique of Folk Psychology, Theory of Mind and Simulation*. Basingstoke: Palgrave Macmillan.

Reddy, V. 1991. Playing with others' expectations: teasing and mucking about in the first year. In A. Whiten (ed.), *Natural Theories of Mind* (143–58). Oxford: Blackwell.

Reddy, V. 2008. *How Infants Know Minds*. Cambridge, MA: Harvard University Press.

Reddy, V. 2012. Moving others matters. In A. Foolen, U.M. Lüdtke, T.P. Racine, and J. Zlatev (eds.), *Moving Ourselves, Moving Others: Motion and Emotion in Intersubjectivity, Consciousness and Language* (139–63). Amsterdam: John Benjamins.

Reddy, V. 2015. Joining intentions in infancy. *Journal of Consciousness Studies* 22(1–2): 24–44.

Reissland, N., Francis, B., Aydin, E., Mason, J., and Schaal, B. 2014. The development of anticipation in the fetus: A longitudinal account of human fetal mouth movements in reaction to and anticipation of touch. *Developmental Psychobiolology* 56(5): 955–63.

Repacholi, B., Olsen, B.R., and Meltzoff, A.N. 2006. How infants integrate attentional and emotional cues in order to regulate their imitative responses. Paper presented at the annual meeting of the XVth Biennial International Conference on Infant Studies, Westin Miyako, Kyoto, Japan.

Repacholi, B.M. and Meltzoff, A.N. 2007. Emotional eavesdropping: Infants selectively respond to indirect emotional signals. *Child Development* 78(2): 503–21.

Repacholi, B.M., Meltzoff, A.N., and Olsen, B. 2008. Infants' understanding of the link between visual perception and emotion: "If she can't see me doing it, she won't get angry." *Developmental Psychology* 44: 561–74.

Richardson, M.J., Marsh, K.L., Isenhower, R.W., Goodman, J.R., and Schmidt, R.C. 2007. Rocking together: Dynamics of intentional and unintentional interpersonal coordination. *Human Movement Science* 26(6): 867–91.

Richner, E.S. and Nicolopoulou, A. 2001. The narrative construction of differing conceptions of the person in the development of young children's social understanding. *Early Education and Development* 12(3): 393–432.

Ricoeur, P. 1984 *Time and Narrative*, Vol. 1, trans. K. Blamey and D. Pellauer. Chicago, IL: University of Chicago Press.

Ricoeur, P. 1988. *Time and Narrative*, Vol. 3, trans. K. Blamey and D. Pellauer. Chicago, IL: University of Chicago Press.

Ricoeur, P. 1992. *Oneself as Another*. Chicago, IL: University of Chicago Press.

Ricoeur P. 2005. *The Course of Recognition*. Cambridge, MA: Harvard University Press.

Rietveld, E. 2012. Bodily intentionality and social affordances in context. In F. Paglieri (ed.), *Consciousness in Interaction. The Role of the Natural and Social Context in Shaping Consciousness* (207–26). Amsterdam: John Benjamins.

Rietveld, E. and Kiverstein, J. 2014. A rich landscape of affordances. *Ecological Psychology* 26(4): 325–52.

Rizzolatti, G. Fadiga, L., Matelli, M., Bettinardi, V., Paulesu, E., Perani, D., and Fazio, F. 1996. Localization of grasp representations in humans by PET: I. Observation versus execution. *Experimental Brain Research* 111: 246–52.

Rizzolatti, G., Fogassi, L., and Gallese, V. 2001. Neurophysiological mechanisms underlying the understanding and imitation of action. *Nature Reviews Neuroscience* 2: 661–70.

Robinson, T.E. and Berridge, K.C. 1993. The neural basis of drug craving: an incentive-sensitization theory of addiction. *Brain Research Reviews* 18(3): 247–91.

Robinson, T.E. and Berridge, K.C. 2000. The psychology and neurobiology of addiction: An incentive–sensitization view. *Addiction* 95(8s2): 91–117.

Rochat, P. and Hespos, S.J. 1997. Differential rooting response by neonates: Evidence for an early sense of self. *Early Development and Parenting* 6(34): 105–12.

Roepstorff, A. and Frith, C. 2004. What's at the top in the top-down control of action? Script-sharing and "top-top" control of action in cognitive experiments. *Psychological Research* 68(2–3): 189–98.

Roessler, J. 2005. Joint attention and the problem of other minds. In N. Eilan (ed.), *Joint Attention: Communication and Other Minds: Issues in Philosophy and* Psychology (230–59). Oxford: Oxford University Press.

Ronconi, L. and Melcher, D. 2017. The role of oscillatory phase in determining the temporal organization of perception: evidence from sensory entrainment. *Journal of Neuroscience* 37(44): 10636–44.

Rorty, R. 1989. *Contingency, Irony, and Solidarity*. Cambridge: Cambridge University Press.

Rorty, R. 2005. Is "cultural recognition" a useful notion for left politics. In N. Fraser and K. Olson (eds.), *Adding Insult to Injury: Social Justice and the Politics of Recognition*. London: Verso.

Rothwell, C.D., Shalin, V.L., and Romigh, G.D. 2017. Quantitative models of human-human conversational grounding processes. *Proceedings of the Cognitive Science Society* 198: 1016–21.

Rowlands, M. 2002. *Animals Like Us*. London: Verso.

Ruby, P. and Decety, J. 2001. Effect of subjective perspective taking during simulation of action: a PET investigation of agency. *Nature Neuroscience* 4(5): 546–50.

Runeson, S. and Frykholm, G. 1983. Kinematic specification of dynamics as an informational basis for person-and-action perception: Expectation, gender recognition, and deceptive intention. *Journal of Experimental Psychology: General* 112(4): 585–615.

Ryle, G. 1949. *The Concept of Mind*. London: Routledge.

Sacks, O. 1995. *An Anthropologist on Mars: Seven Paradoxical tales*. New York, NY: Vintage.

Salice, A. 2015. There are no primitive we-intentions. *Review of Philosophy and Psychology*. 6(4): 695–715.

Samuelson, P. 1976. Illogic of neo-Marxist doctrine of unequal exchange. In Belsley et al. (eds.), *Inflation, Trade, and Taxes*. Columbus, OH: Ohio State University Press.

Sandis, C. 2010. Basic actions and individuation. In T. O'Connor and C. Sandis (eds.), *A Companion to the Philosophy of Action* (10–17). London: Wiley-Blackwell.

Sartori, L., Becchio, C., and Castiello, U. 2011a. Cues to intention: The role of movement information. *Cognition* 119: 242–52.

Sartori, L., Straulino, E., and Castiello, U. 2011b. How objects are grasped: The interplay between affordances and end-goals. *PLoS One* 6(9): e25203. doi: 10.1371/journal.pone.002520

Sartre, J-P. 1956. *Being and Nothingness*. Trans. H. Barnes. New York, NY: Philosophical Press.

Sartre, J-P. 1976. *Critique of Dialectical Reason*. Trans. A. Sheridan-Smith. London: NLB.

Sass, L. and Pienkos, E. 2015. Faces of intersubjectivity. *Journal of Phenomenological Psychology* 46(1): 1–32.

Schechtman, M. 1996. *The Constitution of Selves*. Ithaca, NY: Cornell University Press.

Schechtman, M. 2011. The narrative self. In S. Gallagher (ed.), *The Oxford Handbook of the Self*. (394–416) Oxford: Oxford University Press.

Scheler, M. 1954. *The Nature of Sympathy*. Trans. P. Heath. London: Routledge and Kegan Paul. Original: *Wesen und Formen der Sympathie*. Bonn: Verlag Friedrich Cohen, 1923.

Schienle, A., Schäfer, A., Hermann, A., Walter, B., Stark, R., and Vaitl, D., 2006. fMRI responses to pictures of mutilation and contamination. *Neuroscience Letters* 393(2): 174–8.

Schienle, A., Schfer, A., Stark, R., Walter, B., and Vaitl, D. 2005. Relationship between disgust sensitivity, trait anxiety and brain activity during disgust induction. *Neuropsychobiology* 51(2): 86–92.

Schienle, A., Stark, R., Walter, B., Blecker, C., Ott, U., Kirsch, P., Sammer, G., and Vaitl, D. 2002. The insula is not specifically involved in disgust processing: An fMRI study. *Neuroreport* 13(16): 2023–26.

Schilbach, L., Timmermans, B., Reddy, V., Costall, A., Bente, G., Schlicht, T., and Vogeley, K. 2013. A second-person neuroscience in interaction. *Behavioral and Brain Sciences* 36(4): 441–62.

Schlegel, A., Alexander, P., Sinnott-Armstrong, W., Roskies, A., Peter, U.T., and Wheatley, T. 2013. Barking up the wrong free: Readiness potentials reflect processes independent of conscious will. *Experimental Brain Research* 229(3): 329–35.

Schneller, C. 1867. "Das Rothhütchen." In *Märchen und Sagen aus Wälschtirol: Ein Beitrag zur deutschen Sagenkunde* (no. 6, 9–10). Innsbruck: Verlag der Wagner'schen Universitäts-Buchhandlung.

Scholl, B.J. and Leslie, A.M. 1999. Modularity, development and "theory of mind." *Mind & Language* 14(1): 131–53.

Scholl, B.J. and Tremoulet, P.D. 2000. Perceptual causality and animacy. *Trends in Cognitive Sciences* 4(8): 299–309.

Schurger, A., Sitt, J.D., and Dehaene, S. 2012. An accumulator model for spontaneous neural activity prior to self-initiated movement. *Proceedings of the National Academy of Sciences* 109(42): E2904–13.

Searle, J. 2002. Collective intentions and actions. In J. Searle. *Consciousness and Language*. (90–105). Cambridge: Cambridge University Press.

Searle, J. 1992. *The Rediscovery of the Mind*. Cambridge, MA: MIT Press.

Searle, J.R. 1978. Literal meaning. *Erkenntnis* 13(1): 207–24.

Searle, J.R. 1983. *Intentionality: An Essay in the Philosophy of Mind*. Cambridge: Cambridge University Press.

Sebanz, N., Knoblich, G., and Prinz, W. 2003. Representing others' actions: Just like one's own? *Cognition* 88: B11–21.

Sebanz, N., Knoblich, G., Prinz, W., and Wascher, E. 2006. Twin peaks: An ERP study of action planning and control in coacting individuals. *Journal of Cognitive Neuroscience* 18(5): 859–70.

Segal, G. 1996. The modularity of theory of mind. In P. Carruthers and P. Smith (eds.), *Theories of Theories of Mind* (141–57). Cambridge: Cambridge University Press.

Selinger, E.M. and Crease, R.P. 2002. Dreyfus on expertise: The limits of phenomenological analysis. *Continental Philosophy Review* 35: 245–79.

Sellars, W. 1956. *Science, Perception, and Reality*. London: Routledge and Kegan Paul.

Sen, A. 1999. *Commodities and Capabilities*. Oxford: Oxford University Press.

Sen, A. 2009. *The Idea of Justice*. Cambridge, MA: Harvard University Press.

Senju, A., Johnson, M.H., and Csibra, G. 2006. The development and neural basis of referential gaze perception. *Social Neuroscience* 1(3–4): 220–34.

Setiya, K. 2004. Explaining action. *Philosophical Review* 112: 339–93.

Setiya, K. 2007. *Reasons without Rationalism*. Princeton, NJ: Princeton University Press.

Shanahan, M. 2016. The frame problem. In E.N. Zalta (ed.), *The Stanford Encyclopedia of Philosophy*. (https://plato.stanford.edu/archives/spr2016/entries/frame-problem/).

Sharrock, W. and Coulter, J. 2009. "Theory of Mind": a critical commentary continued. In I. Leudar and A. Costall (eds.), *Against Theory of Mind* (56–88). London: Palgrave Macmillan.

Shaver, P.R., Murdaya, U., and Fraley, R.C. 2001. Structure of the Indonesian emotion lexicon. *Asian Journal of Social Psychology* 4(3): 201–24.

Shuler, M.G. and Bear, M.F. 2006. Reward timing in the primary visual cortex. *Science* 311(5767): 1606–9.

Siegel, S. 2011. Cognitive penetrability and perceptual justification. *Noûs* 46(2): 201–22.

Siep, L. 1979. *Anerkennung als Prinzip der praktischen Philosophie*. Freiburg: Karl Albert.

Sigman, M.D., Kasari, C., Kwon, J.H., et al. 1992. Responses to the negative emotions of others by autistic, mentally retarded, and normal children. *Child Development* 63: 796–807.

Simon, J.R. 1969. Reactions towards the source of stimulation. *Journal of Experimental Psychology* 81: 174–6.

Singer, T., Wolpert, D., and Frith, C. 2004. Introduction: the study of social interactions. In *The Neuroscience of Social Interaction: Decoding, Imitating, and Influencing the Actions of Others* (xiii–xxvii). Oxford: Oxford University Press.

Slaby, J. and Gallagher, S. 2015. Critical neuroscience and the socially extended mind. *Theory, Culture & Society* 32(1): 33–59.

Slors, M. 2019. Symbiotic cognition as an alternative for socially extended cognition. *Philosophical Psychology*. 32(8): 1179–1203 doi.org/10.1080/09515089.2019.1679591

Slovic, P. 2007. If I look at the mass I will never act: Psychic numbing and genocide. *Judgment and Decision Making* 2: 79–95.

Small, D.A., Loewenstein, G., and Slovic, P. 2007. Sympathy and callousness: Affect and deliberations in donation decisions. *Organizational Behavior and Human Decision Processes* 102: 143–53.

Smith, J. 2010. Seeing other people. *Philosophy and Phenomenological Research* 81(3): 731–48.

Sneddon, A. 2006. *Action and Responsibility*. Berlin: Springer Science & Business Media.

Soliman, T.M. and Glenberg, A.M. 2014. The embodiment of culture. In L. Shapiro (ed.), *The Routledge Handbook of Embodied Cognition* (207–20). London: Routledge.

Song, H.J., Onishi, K.H., Baillargeon, R., and Fisher, C. 2008. Can an agent's false belief be corrected by an appropriate communication? Psychological reasoning in 18-month-old infants. *Cognition* 109(3): 295–315.

Southgate, V., Chevallier, C., and Csibra, G. 2010. Seventeen-month-olds appeal to false beliefs to interpret others' referential communication. *Developmental Science* 13(6): 907–12.

Southgate, V., Senju, A., and Csibra, G. 2007. Action anticipation through attribution of false belief by 2-year-olds. *Psychological Science* 18(7): 587–92.

Spaulding, S. 2012. Introduction to debates on embodied social cognition. *Phenomenology and the Cognitive Sciences* 11(4): 431–48.

Spaulding, S. 2017a. How we think and act together. *Philosophical Psychology* 30(3): 302–18.

Spaulding, S. 2017b. On whether we can see intentions. *Pacific Philosophical Quarterly* 98(2): 150–70.

Spaulding, S. 2018. *How We Understand Others: Philosophy and Social Cognition*. New York, NY: Routledge.

Stanley, J. 2011. *Know How*. Oxford: Oxford University Press.

Stark, R., Schienle, A., Walter, B., Kirsch, P., Sammer, G., Ott, U., Blecker, C., and Vaitl, D. 2003. Hemodynamic responses to fear and disgust-inducing pictures: An fMRI study. *International Journal of Psychophysiology* 50(3): 225–34.

Stenzel, A., Dolk, T., Colzato, L.S., Sellaro, R., Hommel, B., and Liepelt, R. 2014. The joint Simon effect depends on perceived agency, but not intentionality, of the alternative action. *Frontiers in Human Neuroscience* 8: 595. doi: 10.3389/fnhum.2014.00595

Stephens, G.L. and Graham, G. 2000. *When Self-Consciousness Breaks: Alien Voices and Inserted Thoughts*. Cambridge, MA: MIT Press.

Stern, D.N., 2010. *Forms of Vitality: Exploring Dynamic Experience in Psychology, the Arts, Psychotherapy, and Development*. Oxford: Oxford University Press.

Steward, H. 2012. Actions as processes. *Philosophical Perspectives* 26: 373–88.

Stich, S. and Nichols, S. 1992. Folk psychology: Simulation or tacit theory? *Mind & Language* 7(1–2): 35–71.

Stormark, K.M. and Braarud, H.C. 2004. Infants' sensitivity to social contingency: A "double video" study of face-to-face communication between 2- and 4-month-olds and their mothers. *Infant Behavior and Development* 27: 195–203.

Stoutland, F. 1968. Basic actions and causality. *Journal of Philosophy* 65(16): 467–75.

Straube, T., Weisbrod, A., Schmidt, S., Raschdorf, C., Preul, C., Mentzel, H.-J., and Miltner, W.H.R. 2010. No impairment of recognition and experience of disgust in a patient with a right-hemispheric lesion of the insula and basal ganglia. *Neuropsychologia* 48(6): 1735–41.

Straus, E. 1966. *Philosophical Psychology*. New York, NY: Basic Books.

Strawson, G. 1997. The self. *Journal of Consciousness Studies* 4: 405–28.

Strawson, G. 2009. *Selves: An Essay in Revisionary Metaphysics*. Oxford: Oxford University Press.

Striblen, C. 2013. Collective responsibility and the narrative self. *Social Theory and Practice* 39(1): 147–65.

Strijbos, D.W. and De Bruin, L.C. 2013. Universal belief-desire psychology?: A dilemma for theory and simulation theory. *Philosophical Psychology* 26(5): 744–64.

Stueber, K.R. 2006. *Rediscovering Empathy: Agency, Folk-Psychology and the Human Sciences*. Cambridge, MA: MIT Press.

Stueber, K.R. 2008. Reasons, generalizations, empathy, and narratives: The epistemic structure of action explanation. *History and Theory* 47: 31–43.

Stueber, K.R. 2012. Varieties of empathy, neuroscience and the narrativist challenge to the contemporary theory of mind debate. *Emotion Review* 4(1): 55–63.

Surian, L., Caldi, S., and Sperber, D. 2007. Attribution of beliefs by 13-month-old infants. *Psychological Science* 18(7): 580–6.

Sutton, J., Harris, C.B., Keil, P.G., and Barnier, A.J. 2010. The psychology of memory, extended cognition, and socially distributed remembering. *Phenomenology and the Cognitive Sciences* 9(4): 521–60.

Synofzik, M., Vosgerau, G., and Newen, A. 2008. Beyond the comparator model: A multifactorial two-step account of agency. *Consciousness and Cognition* 17(1): 219–39.

Tager-Flusberg, H. 2005. How language facilitates the acquisition of false-belief understanding in children with autism. In J.W. Astington and J.A. Baird (eds.), *Why Language Matters for Theory of Mind* (298–318). Oxford: Oxford University Press.

Tajfel, H., Billig, M.G., Bundy, R.P., and Flament, C. 1971. Social categorization and intergroup behaviour. *Eur J Soc Psychol* 1(2): 149–78.

Takahama, S., Kumada, T., and Saiki, J. 2005. Perception of other's action influences performance in Simon task. *Journal of Vision* 5(8): 396. 5(8): 396A. doi: 10.1167/5.8.396

Tamietto, M. 2013. Attentional and sensory unawareness for emotions: Neurofunctional and neuroanatomical systems. Conference presentation. The Scope and Limits of Direct Perception. University of Copenhagen. December 13, 2013.

Taminiaux, J. 1985. Hegel and Hobbes. In J. Decker and R. Crease. *Dialectic and Difference* (1–37). London: Palgrave Macmillan.

Taminiaux, J. 1997. *The Thracian Maid and the Professional Thinker: Arendt and Heidegger.* Albany, NY: SUNY Press.

Taylor, C. 1989. *Sources of the Self: The Making of the Modern Identity.* Cambridge, MA: Harvard University Press.

Teitelbaum, P.O., Teitelbaum, J., Nye, J., et al. 1998. Movement analysis in infancy may be useful for early diagnosis of autism. *Proc Natl Acad Sci USA* 95: 13982–7.

Testo, I. 2012. How does recognition emerge from nature? The genesis of consciousness in Hegel's Jena writings. *Critical Horizons* 13(2): 176–96.

Teufel, C., Fletcher, P.C., and Davis, G. 2010. Seeing other minds: Attributed mental states influence perception. *Trends in Cognitive Sciences* 14: 376–382.

Thompson, E. 2007. *Mind in Life: Biology, Phenomenology, and the Sciences of Mind.* Cambridge, MA: Harvard University Press.

Thompson, E. and Stapleton, M. 2009. Making sense of sense-making: Reflections on enactive and extended mind theories. *Topoi* 28(1): 23–30.

Thompson, M. 2008. *Life and Action.* Cambridge, MA: Harvard University Press.

Tollefsen, D. 2015. *Groups as Agents.* New York, NY: Polity Press.

Tollefsen, D. and Gallagher, S. 2017. We-narratives and the stability and depth of shared agency. *Philosophy of the Social Sciences* 47(2): 95–110.

Tollefsen, D.P., Dale, R., and Paxton, A. 2013. Alignment, transactive memory, and collective cognitive systems. *Review of Philosophy and Psychology* 4(1): 49–64.

Tomasello, M. 1995. Joint attention as social cognition. In C. Moore (ed.), *Joint Attention: Its Origins and Role in Development* (103–30). Psychology Press.

Tomasello, M., Carpenter, M., Call, J., Behne, T., and Moll, H. 2005. In search of the uniquely human. *Behavioral and Brain Sciences* 28(5): 721–7.

Torres, E.B. 2013. Atypical signatures of motor variability found in an individual with ASD. *Neurocase* 19: 150–65.

Torres, E.B, Brincker M., Isenhower R.W., et al. 2013. Autism: The micro-movement perspective. *Frontiers in Integrative Neuroscience* 7: 32. doi: 10.3389/fnint.2013.00032.

Trevarthen, C. 1979. Communication and cooperation in early infancy: A description of primary intersubjectivity. In M. Bullowa (ed.), *Before Speech: The Beginning of Interpersonal Communication.* Cambridge: Cambridge University Press.

Trevarthen, C. 1999. Musicality and the intrinsic motive pulse: evidence from human psychobiology and infant communication. *Musicae Scientiae* 3(1 suppl): 155–215.

Trevarthen, C. 2008. Why theories will differ. In J. Zlatev, T.P. Racine, C. Sinha, and E. Itkonen (eds.), *The Shared Mind: Perspectives on Intersubjectivity* (vii–xiii). Amsterdam: John Benjamins Publishing.

Trevarthen, C. 2011. What is it like to be a person who knows nothing? Defining the active intersubjective mind of a newborn human being. *Infant and Child Development* 20(1): 119–35.

Trevarthen, C. 2013. Born for art, and the joyful companionship of fiction. In D. Narvaez, J. Panksepp, A. Schore, and T. Gleason (eds.), *Evolution, Early Experience and Human Development: From Research to Practice and Policy* (202–18). New York, NY: Oxford University Press.

Trevarthen, C., Aitken, K., Papoudi, D., and Robarts, J. 1998. *Children with Autism: Diagnosis and Intervention to Meet their Needs,* 2nd edn. London: Jessica Kingsley Publishers.

Trevarthen, C. and Aitken, K.J. 2001. Infant intersubjectivity: Research, theory, and clinical applications. *Journal of Child Psychology and Psychiatry* 42(1): 3–48.

Trevarthen, C., Aitken, K.J., Nagy, E., Delafield-Butt, J.T., and Vandekerckhove, M. 2006. Collaborative regulations of vitality in early childhood: Stress in intimate relationships and postnatal psychopathology. In D. Cicchetti and D.J. Cohen (eds.), *Developmental Psychopathology* (65–126). New York, NY: John Wiley and Sons.

Trevarthen, C. and Hubley, P. 1978. Secondary intersubjectivity: Confidence, confiding and acts of meaning in the first year. In A. Lock (ed.), *Action, Gesture and Symbol: The Emergence of Language* (183–229). London: Academic Press.

Tronick, E. 2007. Interactive mismatch and repair: Challenges to the coping infant in the neurobehavioral and social-emotional development of infants and children (155–164). New York: WW Norton & Company.

Tronick, E., Als, H., Adamson, L., Wise, S., and Brazelton, T.B. 1978. The infant's response to entrapment between contradictory messages in face-to-face interaction. *Journal of the American Academy of Child Psychiatry* 17(1): 1–13.

Tsakiris, M. and Haggard, P. 2003. Awareness of somatic events associated with a voluntary action. *Experimental Brain Research* 149: 439–46.

Tsakiris, M. and Haggard, P. 2005. Experimenting with the acting self. *Cognitive Neuropsychology* 22(3/4): 387–407.

Tsakiris, M., Longo, M.R., and Haggard, P. 2010. Having a body versus moving your body: Neural signatures of agency and body-ownership. *Neuropsychologia* 48(9): 2740–9.

Turvey, M.T. 2007. Action and perception at the level of synergies. *Human Movement Science* 26: 657–97.

Vallacher, R.R. and Wegner, D.M. 2014. *A Theory of Action Identification*. Psychology Press.

Vallacher, R.R., Wegner, D.M., Bordieri, J., and Wenzlaff, R. 1981. Models of act identity structures. *Unpublished research data*.

Van Gelder, T. 1996. Wooden iron? Husserlian phenomenology meets cognitive science. *Electronic Journal of Analytic Philosophy* 4; reprinted in J. Petitot, F.J. Varela, B. Pachoud, and J-M. Roy (eds.) (1999), *Naturalizing Phenomenology: Issues in Contemporary Phenomenology and Cognitive Science* (245–265). Stanford, CA: Stanford University Press.

Van Orden, G., Hollis, G., and Wallot, S. 2012. The blue-collar brain. *Frontiers in Physiology* 3: 207.

Varela, F.J. 1995. Resonant cell assemblies: A new approach to cognitive functioning and neuronal synchrony. *Biological Research* 28: 81–95.

Varela, F.J. 1999. The specious present: A neurophenomenology of time consciousness. In J. Petitot, F.J. Varela, B. Pachoud, and J.-M. Roy (eds.), *Naturalizing Phenomenology: Issues in Contemporary Phenomenology and Cognitive Science* (266–314). Stanford, CA: Stanford University Press.

Varela, F., Lachaux, J.P., Rodriguez, E., and Martinerie, J. 2001. The brainweb: Phase-synchronization and long-range integration. *Nature Reviews Neuroscience* 2: 229–39.

Varela, F.J., Thompson, E., and Rosch, E. 1991. *The Embodied Mind: Cognitive Science and Human Experience*. Cambridge, MA: MIT Press.

Varela, F.J., Toro, A., John, E.R., and Schwartz, E.L. 1981. Perceptual framing and cortical alpha rhythm. *Neuropsychologia* 19: 675–86.

Varga, S. 2010. Critical theory and the two-level account of recognition: Towards a new foundation? *Critical Horizons* 11(1): 19–33.

Varga, S. and Gallagher, S. 2012. Critical social philosophy, Honneth, and the role of primary intersubjectivity. *European Journal of Social Theory* 15(2): 243–60.

Vaughan, H.G. and Arezzo, J.C. 1988. The neural basis of event-related potentials. In T.W. Picton (ed.), *Human Event-related Potentials. Handbook of Electroencephalography and Clinical Neurophysiology*. Revised Series, Vol. 3 (45–96). Amsterdam: Elsevier.

Vaughan, H.G., Ritter, W., and Simson, R. 1980. Topographic analysis of auditory event-related potentials, *Progress in Brain Research* 54: 279–85.

Velleman, J.D. 2000. *The Possibility of Practical Reason*. Oxford: Oxford University Press

Velleman, J.D. 2005. Self as narrator. In J. Christman and J. Anderson (eds.), *Autonomy and the Challenges to Liberalism: New Essays* (56–76). New York, NY: Cambridge University Press.

Velleman, J.D. 2006. *Self to Self: Selected Essays*. New York, NY: Cambridge University Press.

Vignemont, de F. 2004. The co-consciousness hypothesis. *Phenomenology and the Cognitive Sciences* 3(1): 97–114.

Vignemont, de F. and Jacob, P. 2012. What is it like to feel another's pain? *Philosophy of Science* 79(2): 295–316.

Vignemont, de F. and Singer, T. 2006. The empathic brain: how, when and why? *Trends in Cognitive Sciences* 10(10): 435–41.

Vincini, S. and Jhang, Y. 2018. Association but not recognition: An alternative model for differential imitation from 0 to 2 months. *Review of Philosophy and Psychology* 9(2): 395–427.

Vincini, S., Jhang, Y., Buder, E.H., and Gallagher, S. 2017a. An unsettled debate: Key empirical and theoretical questions are still open (Commentary on Keven and Akins). *Behavioral and Brain Sciences* 40: e401.

Vincini, S., Jhang, Y., Buder, E.H., and Gallagher, S. 2017b. Neonatal imitation: Theory, experimental design and significance for the field of social cognition. *Frontiers in Psychology—Cognitive Science*. 8: 1323. doi: 10.3389/fpsyg.2017.01323

Vinson, D.W., Abney, D.H., Amso, D., Chemero, A., Cutting, J.E., Dale, R., Freeman, J.B., Feldman, L.B., Friston, K.J., Gallagher, S., Jordan, J.S., et al. 2016. Perception, as you make it. *Behavioral and Brain Sciences* 39. doi: 10.1017/S0140525X15002678, e260.

Vulkan, N., Roth, A.E., and Neeman, Z. (eds.). 2013. *The Handbook of Market Design*. New York, NY: Oxford University Press

Vygotsky, L.S. 1986. *Thought and Language*. Cambridge, MA: MIT Press.

Walden, T.A. and Ogan, T.A. 1988. The development of social referencing. *Child Development* 59: 1230–40.

Walker, A.S. 1982. Intermodal perception of expressive behaviors by human infants. *Journal of Experimental Child Psychology* 33(3): 514–35.

Weigl, E. 1961. The phenomenon of temporary deblocking in aphasia. *STUF-Language Typology and Universals* 14(1–4): 337–64.

Wellman, H. 1993. Early understanding of mind: The normal case. In S. Baron-Cohen, H. Tager-Flusberg, and D.J. Cohen (eds.), *Understanding Other Minds: Perspectives from Autism*. Oxford: Oxford University Press.

Wellman, H. and Banerjee, M. 1991. Mind and emotion: children's understanding of the emotional consequences of beliefs and desires. *British Journal of Developmental Psychology* 9: 191–214.

Wellman, H., Cross, D., and Watson, J. 2001. Meta-Analysis of theory-of-mind development: The truth about false belief. *Child Development* 72: 655–84.

Wellman, H. and Phillips, A. 2001. Developing intentional understandings. In B. Malle, L.J. Moses, and D.A. Baldwin (eds.), *Intentions and Intentionality* (125–48) Cambridge, MA: MIT Press.

Wellmer, A. 1971. *Critical Theory of Society*. Trans. J. Cumming. New York, NY: Herder and Herder.

Wells, S. 1996. *Sweet Reason: Rhetoric and the Discourses of Modernity*. Chicago, IL: University of Chicago Press.

Wertsch, J.V. 2008a. Collective memory and narrative templates. *Social Research: An International Quarterly* 75(1): 133–56.

Wertsch, J.V. 2008b. The narrative organization of collective memory. *Ethos* 36(1): 120–35.

Wheeler, M. 2014. The revolution will not be optimised: Enactivism, embodiment and relationality. In *Proceedings of the 50th Anniversary Convention of the AISB*. Online at: https://www.doc.gold.ac.uk/aisb50/AISB50-S25/AISB50-S25-Wheeler-extabs.pdf (accessed November 18, 2019).

Wicker, B., Keysers, C., Plailly, J., Royet, J.P., Gallese, V., and Rizzolatti, G. 2003. Both of us disgusted in my insula: the common neural basis of seeing and feeling disgust. *Neuron* 40(3): 655–64.

Williams, R.R. 1992. *Recognition: Fichte and Hegel on the Other*. Albany, NY: SUNY Press.

Williams, R.R. 2008. Ricoeur on recognition. *European Journal of Philosophy* 16(3): 467–73.

Wilson, M. and Knoblich, G. 2005. The case for motor involvement in perceiving conspecifics. *Psychological Bulletin* 131(3): 460–73.

Wiltshire, T.J., Lobato, E.J.C., McConnell, D.S., and Fiore, S.M. 2015. Prospects for direct social perception: A multi-theoretical integration to further the science of social cognition. *Frontiers in Human Neuroscience* 8: 1007. doi: 10.3389/fnhum.2014.01007

Wimmer, H. and Perner, J. 1983. Beliefs about beliefs: Representation and constraining function of wrong beliefs in young children's understanding of deception. *Cognition* 13(1): 103–28.

Winnicott, D. 1989. *Playing and Reality*. London: Routledge.

Winston, J.S., O'Doherty, J., and Dolan, R.J. 2003. Common and distinct neural responses during direct and incidental processing of multiple facial emotions. *NeuroImage* 20(1): 84–97.

Witt, J.K. Sugovic, M., Tenhundfeld, N.L., and Kinga, Z.R. 2016. An action-specific effect on perception that avoids all pitfalls. Behavioral and Brain Sciences 39. doi: 10.1017/S0140525X15002563, e261.

Wittgenstein, L. 1980. *Remarks on the Philosophy of Psychology*, Vol. II. G.H. von Wright and H. Nyman (eds.); C.G. Luckhardt and M.A.E. Aue (trans.). Oxford: Blackwell.

Wohlschläger, A., Engbert, K., and Haggard, P. 2003. Intentionality as a constituting condition for the own self—and other selves. *Consciousness and Cognition* 12(4): 708–16.

Wohlschläger, A., Haggard, P., Gesierich, B., and Prinz, W. 2003. The perceived onset time of self-and other-generated actions. *Psychological Science* 14(6): 586–91.

Wolf, S. 1990. *Freedom within Reason*. New York, NY: Oxford University Press,

Wolpert, D.M. and Flanagan, J.R. 2001. Motor prediction. *Current Biology* 11(18): R729–R732.

Wolpert, D.M., Ghahramani, Z., and Jordan, M.I. 1995. An internal model for sensorimotor integration. *Science* 269: 1880–2.

Woodward, A.L. and Sommerville, J.A. 2000. Twelve-month-old infants interpret action in context. *Psychological Science* 11: 73–7.

Wutz, A., Weisz, N., Braun, C., and Melcher, D. 2014. Temporal windows in visual processing: "Prestimulus brain state" and "poststimulus phase reset" segregate visual transients on different temporal scales. *Journal of Neuroscience* 34: 1554–65.

Xu, Y. 2005. Revisiting the role of the fusiform face area in visual expertise. *Cerebral Cortex* 15(8): 1234–42.

Xu, Y., Zuo, X., Wang, X., and Han, S. 2009. Do you feel my pain? Racial group membership modulates empathic neural responses. *Journal of Neuroscience* 29(26): 8525–9.

Yarbus, A.L. 1967. *Eye Movements and Vision*. Boston, MA: Springer.

Yott, J. and Poulin-Dubois, D. 2012. Breaking the rules: Do infants have a true understanding of false belief? *British Journal of Developmental Psychology* 30(1): 156–71.

Young, I.M. 1980. Throwing like a girl: A phenomenology of feminine body comportment motility and spatiality. *Human Studies* 3(1): 137–56.

Young, I.M. 1990. *Justice and the Politics of Difference*. Princeton, NJ: Princeton University Press.

Zahavi, D. 1994. Husserl's phenomenology of the body. *Études Phénoménologiques* 19: 63–84.

Zahavi, D. and Overgaard, S. 2012. Empathy without isomorphism: A phenomenological account. In Decety, J. (ed.), *Empathy: From Bench to Bedside* (3–20). MIT Press.

Zahavi, D. and Parnas, J. 2003. Conceptual problems in infantile autism research: Why cognitive science needs phenomenology. *Journal of consciousness studies* 10(9–10): 53–71.

Zapata-Fonseca, L., Dotov, D.G., Fossion, R.Y.M., Froese, T., Schilbach, L., Vogeley, K., and Timmermans, B. 2019. Multi-scalar coordination of distinctive movement patterns during embodied interaction between adults with high-functioning autism and neurotypicals. *Frontiers in Psychology* 9: 2760. https://doi.org/10.3389/fpsyg.2018.02760

Zeki, S. 2003. The disunity of consciousness. *Trends in Cognitive Sciences* 7(5): 214–18.

Index

For the benefit of digital users, indexed terms that span two pages (e.g., 52–53) may, on occasion, appear on only one of those pages.

theory of mind (ToM) 2, 69ff, 82ff, 94, 99,
    100ff, 111, 115–116, 118ff, 128–129, 134ff,
    144, 148, 152, 155, 164, 166n5, 169,
    170, 228
theory theory (TT) 69ff, 72, 74, 76ff, 81ff,
    93–94, 97, 108, 111, 116, 122, 136–137,
    139, 143, 146, 170
Thompson, E. 30n4, 36n9
Thompson, M. 21ff
timescales 29ff, 32, 39, 58, 60, 159; elementary
    29ff, 41, 58, 82, 174ff; integration 29ff,
    41, 82, 175ff; narrative (see *narrative
    timescale*)
Tollefsen, D. 160, 218, 221–222
Torres, E. 134–135
transcendence (in the face-to-face) 205ff
Trevarthen, C. 39, 100ff, 104, 161–162, 187,
    190ff, 195, 197, 239–240
Tsakiris, M. 44–45

unobservability principle 71, 73, 78, 99,
    118–119, 137, 141

Vallacher, R. R. 17, 21
Varela, F. 29ff
Varga, S. 201n10
Velleman, D. 218
Vygotsky, L. S. 161

Wegner, D. M. 17, 21
Wells, S. 230
we-narrative 218ff
Wittgenstein, L. 122, 171
Winnicott, D. 190, 192ff, 202, 254

Young, I. M. 226, 247n6

Zahavi, D. 34, 176n8, 179
Zlatev, J. 165n4